Systems That Learn

LD
&CC

Learning, Development, and Conceptual Change

Lila Gleitman, Susan Carey, Elissa Newport, and Elizabeth Spelke, editors

Names for Things: A Study in Human Learning, John Macnamara, 1982

Conceptual Change in Childhood, Susan Carey, 1985

"Gavagai!" or the Future History of the Animal Language Controversy, David Premack, 1986

Systems That Learn: An Introduction to Learning Theory for Cognitive and Computer Scientists, Daniel N. Osherson, Michael Stob, and Scott Weinstein, 1986

From Simple Input to Complex Grammar, James L. Morgan, 1986

Concepts, Kinds, and Cognitive Development, Frank C. Keil, 1989

Learnability and Cognition: The Acquisition of Argument Structure, Steven Pinker, 1989

Mind Bugs: The Origins of Procedural Misconception, Kurt VanLehn, 1990

Categorization and Naming in Children: Problems of Induction, Ellen M. Markman, 1990

The Child's Theory of Mind, Henry W. Wellman, 1990

The Organization of Learning, Charles R. Gallistel, 1990

Understanding the Representational Mind, Josef Perner, 1991

An Odyssey in Learning and Perception, Eleanor J. Gibson, 1991

Beyond Modularity: A Developmental Perspective on Cognitive Science, Annette Karmiloff-Smith, 1992

Mindblindness: An Essay on Autism and "Theory of Mind," Simon Baron-Cohen, 1995

Speech: A Special Code, Alvin M. Liberman, 1995

Theory and Evidence: The Development of Scientific Reasoning, Barbara Koslowski, 1995

Race in the Making: Cognition, Culture, and the Child's Construction of Human Kinds, Lawrence A. Hirschfeld, 1996

Words, Thoughts, and Theories, Alison Gopnik and Andrew N. Meltzoff, 1996

The Cradle of Knowledge: Development of Perception in Infancy, Philip J. Kellman and Martha E. Arterberry, 1998

Language Creation and Change: Creolization, Diachrony, and Development, edited by Michel DeGraff, 1998

Systems That Learn: An Introduction to Learning Theory, Second Edition, Sanjay Jain, Daniel M. Osherson, James S. Royer, and Arun Sharma, 1999

Systems That Learn

An Introduction to Learning Theory

Second Edition

Sanjay Jain

Daniel Osherson

James S. Royer

Arun Sharma

A Bradford Book

The MIT Press
Cambridge, Massachusetts
London, England

This book was set in Computer Modern by the authors and was printed and bound in the United States of America.

Libary of Congress Cataloging-in-Publication Data

Systems that learn : an introduction to learning theory / Sanjay Jain
    ... [et al.] — 2nd ed.
        p.   cm. — (Learning, development, and conceptual change)
    "A Bradford book."
    Includes bibliographical references and index.
    ISBN 0–262–10077–0 (hardcover: alk. paper)
    1. Learning—Mathematical aspects. 2. Learning. Psychology of.
3. Human information processing—Mathematical models. I. Jain,
Sanjay, 1965 Feb. 22–   II. Series.
    BF318.083   1999
    153.1′5′015113—dc21   98–34861
                                                            CIP

Contents

Series Foreword

This series in learning, development, and conceptual change includes state-of-the-art reference works, seminal book-length monographs, and texts on the development of concepts and mental structures. It spans learning in all domains of knowledge, from syntax to geometry to the social world, and is concerned with all phases of development, from infancy through adulthood.

This series intends to engage such fundamental questions as:

The nature and limits of learning and maturation: the influence of the environment, of initial structures, and of maturational changes in the nervous system on human development; learnability theory; the problem of induction; domain-specific constraints on development.

The nature of conceptual change: conceptual organization and conceptual change in child development, in the acquisition of expertise, and in the history of science.

Lila Gleitman
Susan Carey
Elissa Newport
Elizabeth Spelke

Preface

The book in your hands offers an introduction to *Formal Learning Theory* and a review of its principal results. The theory is one of several mathematical approaches to the issues centering on intelligent adaptation to the environment. Other perspectives (not discussed here) include Bayesian probability theory, PAC ("probably, approximately correct") learning, and artificial life. The analysis developed in the present book conceives learners number theoretically and deploys the tools of recursive-function theory to understand how they can stabilize to an accurate view of reality. This line of inquiry was initiated in the 1960s by Hilary Putnam, R. J. Solomonoff, and E. Mark Gold. Since then it has developed prodigiously, to the point that a single work cannot encompass its many theorems.

The book is self-contained, inasmuch as necessary material from the theory of computation is explained in Chapter 2. In addition, exercises throughout the text provide experience in using computational arguments to prove facts about learning.

The present edition is built upon the first, but has aimed for wider coverage of the field. We are grateful to Scott Weinstein and Michael Stob for permission to rework and integrate the original text. The magnitude of our intellectual debt to them will be obvious to anyone who compares the two editions.

We would like to express our gratitude to John Case and Mark Fulk. John introduced three of us to formal learning theory and helped shape our early understanding of the field. Mark was an invaluable friend. In his brief career he produced some beautiful results that have enriched the present work. Other profound intellectual debts are to the works of E. Mark Gold and Noam Chomsky. Gold [80] established the formal framework within which learning theory has developed. Chomsky's writings have revealed the intimate connection between the projection problem and human intelligence. In addition, we have been greatly influenced by the research of Blum and Blum [18], Angluin [6], Case and Smith [35], and Wexler and Cullicover [194].

It is also our pleasure to thank Andris Ambainis, Robert Daley, Rusins Freivalds, William Gasarch, Klaus Jantke, Bala Kalyanasundaram, Shyam Kapur, Efim Kinber, Stuart Kurtz, Martin Kummer, Steffen Lange, Eric Martin, Franco Montagna, Matthias Ott, Carl Smith, Frank Stephan, Mahe Velauthapillai, Rolf Wiehagen, and Thomas Zeugmann for countless discussions about learning. Many of their discoveries have been recounted in the pages to follow. For what is missing or mistold we alone are responsible.

We thank the following institutions for support in preparing the second edition of this book.

- The Australian Research Council (contract numbers A49530274 and A49600456 to A. Sharma)
- The Department of Electrical Engineering and Computer Science, Syracuse University
- The Department of Information Systems and Computer Science, National University of Singapore
- The Istituto San Raffaele (Milan, Italy)
- The National Science Foundation (grants CCR-89011154 and CCR-9522987 to J. Royer)
- The Office of Naval Research (contract number N00014-89-J-1725 to D. Osherson and S. Weinstein)
- The Psychology Department, Rice University
- The School of Computer Science and Engineering, The University of New South Wales

We would also like to acknowledge the support of Prof. S. N. Maheshwari of the Department of Computer Science and Engineering at IIT Delhi for making the facilities of his department available to one of us during the early stages of this project.

Finally, special thanks to Elaine Weinman for her careful reading of the manuscript and to Neil Jones for the timely loan of some LaTeX macros.

We would be pleased to hear from our readership, for better or for worse. To contact us, try: sanjay@iscs.nus.edu.sg, osherson@rice.edu, royer@top.cis.syr.edu, or arun@cse.unsw.edu.au. An errata list for the book will be maintained at the address http://www.cis.syr.edu/~royer/stl2e/.

Part I

Fundamentals of Learning Theory

1 Introduction

The present chapter introduces the subject matter of this book, namely, formal models of empirical inquiry. We begin by indicating the issues that motivate our study. Next come illustrations of models, followed by discussion of their principal features.

§1.1 Empirical inquiry

Many people who have reflected about human understanding and its origins have noticed an apparent disparity. Bertrand Russell [164] (cited in Chomsky [40]) put the matter this way:

> How comes it that human beings, whose contacts with the world are brief and personal and limited, are nevertheless able to know as much as they do know?

Focusing attention on intellectual development, the disparity is between the information available to children about their environment, and the understanding they ultimately achieve about that environment. The former has a sparse and fleeting character whereas the latter is rich and systematic.

To better understand the issue, consider the acquisition of a first language.[1] A few years of casual contact with the ambient language suffices for the infant to master a grammatical system so complex that it still defies description by linguists. Within broad limits, the particular sample of language to which the infant is exposed does not seem to affect the grammatical principles induced, since children raised in different households within the same linguistic community are able to communicate effectively. Moreover, the child's learning mechanism is apparently built to acquire any human language, for children of different racial or ethnic backgrounds are able to acquire the same languages with the same facility. Evidently, some mental process (perhaps largely unconscious) allows children to convert the fragmentary information available about the ambient language into systematic principles that describe it generally.

The same kind of process underlies other tasks of childhood. By an early age the child is expected to master the moral code of his household and community, to assimilate its artistic conventions and its humor, and at the same time to begin to understand the physical principles that shape the material environment. In each case the child is

---

[1] For an overview and guide to the literature, see Pinker [148].

required to convert data of a happenstance character into the understanding (implicit or explicit) that renders his world predictable and intelligible.

It is not surprising that so little is known about the mental processes responsible for children's remarkable intellectual achievements. Even elementary questions remain the subject of controversy and inconclusive findings. For example, there is little agreement about whether children use a general-purpose system to induce the varied principles bearing on language, social structure, etc., or whether different domains engage special-purpose mechanisms in the mind.[2]

The disparity just noted for intellectual development has also been observed in the acquisition of scientific knowledge by adults. Like the child, scientists typically have limited access to data about the environment, yet are sometimes able to convert this data into theories of astonishing generality and veracity. At an abstract level, the inquiries undertaken by child and adult may be conceived as a process of theory elaboration and test. From this perspective, both agents react to available data by formulating hypotheses, evaluating and revising old hypotheses as new data arrive. In the favorable case, the succession of hypotheses stabilizes to an accurate theory that reveals the nature of the surrounding environment. We shall use the term "empirical inquiry" to denote any enterprise that possesses roughly these features.

It is evident that both forms of empirical inquiry — achieved spontaneously in the early years of life, or more methodically later on — are central to human existence and cultural evolution. It is thus no accident that they have been the subject of speculation and inquiry for millenia.[3] The present book describes a set of conceptual and mathematical tools for analyzing empirical inquiry. Their purpose is to shed light on both intellectual development and scientific discovery. They may also be of use in guiding the development and evaluation of artificial systems of empirical inquiry (such as those described in Langley, Simon, Bradshaw, and Zytkow [123]).

Since the pioneering studies of Putnam [155], Solomonoff [184, 185], Gold [80], and the Blums [18] a large technical literature has been devoted to the development and use of the tools at issue here. Papers within this tradition are spread over journals and books in mathematics, computer science, linguistics, psychology, and philosophy. Our topic has variously been called "The Theory of Scientific Discovery," "Formal Learning Theory," "The Theory of Machine Inductive Inference," "Computational Learning Theory," and "The Theory of Empirical Inquiry." We shall use all these terms to describe the collection of definitions, examples, and theorems that emerge from the literature. Our goal is to

---

[2] For discussion, see Chomsky [40], Pinker [148], and Osherson and Wasow [142].

[3] See Russell [163] for an historical overview.

organize part of this material, and to render it accessible to students and researchers interested in empirical inquiry. Along the way we shall provide pointers to areas given little coverage in these pages.

§1.2 Paradigms

The material to be presented facilitates the definition and investigation of precise models of empirical inquiry. Such models are often referred to as "paradigms." A paradigm offers formal reconstruction of the following concepts, each central to empirical inquiry.

1.1   (a) *a theoretically possible reality*

       (b) *intelligible hypotheses*

       (c) *the data available about any given reality, were it actual*

       (d) *a scientist*

       (e) *successful behavior by a scientist working in a given, possible reality*

The concepts figure in the following picture of scientific inquiry, conceived as a game between Nature and a scientist. First, a class of "possible worlds," or possible realities, is specified in advance; the class is known to both players of the game. Nature is conceived as choosing one member from the class, to be the actual world; her choice is initially unknown to the scientist. Nature then provides a series of clues about the actual reality. These clues constitute the data upon which the scientist will base his hypotheses. Each time Nature provides a new clue, the scientist may produce a new hypothesis. The scientist wins the game if his hypotheses ultimately become stable and accurate. Whether the scientist can win the game depends on the breadth of the set of possible worlds. The more constrained Nature's choice of actual world, the more likely the scientist is to discover it.

Different paradigms formalize this picture in different ways, resulting in different games. To fix our ideas, let us now examine some simple paradigms, without concern for rigor at this point.

§1.3 Some simple paradigms

Call a set of positive integers "describable" just in case it can be uniquely described using an English expression. For example, the set $\{2, 4, 6, 8, \ldots\}$ is one such set since it is uniquely described by the expression "all positive, even integers." The describable sets are the theoretically possible realities of the current paradigm (in the sense of 1.1a).

To play the game, it will help to focus on a proper subset of all these realities, namely, the subcollection $\mathcal{C}$ defined as follows. $\mathcal{C}$ contains all sets that consist of every positive integer with a sole exception. Plainly, every set in $\mathcal{C}$ is describable; the set $\{1, 3, 4, 5, 6, \ldots\}$, for example, is uniquely described by "all positive integers except for 2."

In what follows, we shall play the role of Nature; you play the role of scientist. In our role as Nature, we select one member of $\mathcal{C}$, and you (in your role as scientist) must discover the set that we have in mind. Clues about our choice will be provided in the following way. First, we shall order all the elements of the set in the form of a list; then the list will be presented one element at a time. There is no constraint on the list made from the chosen set, except that it must contain all the elements of the set, and only these. For example, one list of the set $\{2, 3, 4, 5, 6, 7, 8, 9, \ldots\}$ is: $3, 2, 5, 4, 7, 6, 9, 8, \ldots$. Aside from seeing the list's members presented one by one, you are provided no further information about it. A list of our set corresponds to 1.1c, the data made available about the possible reality chosen to be actual.

Each time a number is presented, you may announce a conjecture about the set chosen from $\mathcal{C}$ at the beginning of the game (guesses about how we listed the chosen set are not required). Your guesses must take the form of English expressions that uniquely describe a set of positive integers. It is these expressions that constitute the intelligible hypotheses of our paradigm (see 1.1b). Your conjectures at any given moment will be based exclusively on the data available to you, so for purposes of this game you may be construed as a system that translates data into hypotheses. Indeed, any such system is considered to be a "scientist" within the current paradigm, in the sense of 1.1d.

All of items 1.1a-d have now been specified. As for 1.1e, we stipulate that you win the game just in case you make only a finite number of conjectures, and the last one is correct.

Let's play. We have selected a set and ordered it. Here is the first member of the list: 1. Guess, if you like. Next member: 3. Guess again, if you like. To abbreviate, here are the next ten members of the list: $4, 5, 6, 7, 8, 9, 10, 11, 12, 13$. Perhaps your latest conjecture is "all positive integers except for 2." That is a reasonable conjecture. However, it is wrong since according to our list the next number is 2. So go ahead and guess again. Here are the subsequent ten members: $15, 16, 17, 18, 19, 20, 21, 22, 23, 24$. Perhaps now your latest conjecture is "all positive integers except for 14."

The game goes on forever, so we interrupt it at this point to consider the paradigm in more general terms. Let us say that a "guessing rule" is a set of instructions for converting the clues received up to a given point into a conjecture about the chosen set. Your own guesses may well have been chosen according to some guessing rule, and you might take a moment to attempt to articulate it.

Now consider the following guessing rule:

1.2   Guessing rule: Suppose that S is the set of numbers that have been presented so far. Let m be the least positive integer that is not a member of S. (S must be finite, so such a number certainly exists.) Emit the conjecture "all positive integers except for m" unless this was your last conjecture (in which case make no conjecture at all).

To illustrate, if the numbers presented so far were $\{4, 5, 8, 1\}$, then rule 1.2 would direct you to conjecture "all positive integers except for 2" (unless you had just made this conjecture, in which case you would not do it again). You should be able to convince yourself of the following fact:

1.3   Fact: No matter which set was chosen from $\mathcal{C}$ at the start of the game, and no matter what list was made from that set, consistent application of guessing rule 1.2 is a winning strategy; that is, if you use rule 1.2, then you win in all cases.

Now let us modify the game by adding the set of all positive integers (without exception) to the initial collection $\mathcal{C}$. So our choice of set as "actual reality" is expanded to include one new possibility, namely, $\{1, 2, 3, 4, 5, \ldots\}$. This changes matters quite a bit. For example, guessing rule 1.2 is no longer guaranteed to succeed at the game. Indeed, it is clear that, faced with any listing for the new set $\{1, 2, 3, 4, 5, \ldots\}$, the rule changes its guess infinitely often, and hence never produces a last, accurate conjecture. A more significant fact is the following.

1.4   Fact: No guessing rule is guaranteed to win the new game. That is, for every guessing rule R there is a set in the (expanded) collection $\mathcal{C}$ and some way to list the set such that R fails to produce a last, correct conjecture on the list.

The techniques needed to prove Fact 1.4 will be presented in Chapter 3. You can grasp the matter intuitively, however, by playing the new game with a friend. This time you play the role of Nature, and try to defeat your opponent with the following tactic. Begin with the list $2, 3, 4, 5, 6, 7, \ldots$, extending it until your friend announces the hypothesis "all positive integers except 1." Suppose that your list must be extended to 33 for this to happen. Then continue your list with $1, 35, 36, 37, 38, 39, 40, \ldots$ until you have extracted the hypothesis "all positive integers except 34." Suppose that the list has reached 61 at this point. Then continue with $34, 63, 64, 65, 66, 67, \ldots$ until you hear "all positive integers except 62." If you continue in this devious way, one of two things will happen. Either:

(a) your friend will go for the bait each time, and thereby change her hypothesis infinitely often, or

(b) she will at some point refuse to adopt the conjecture that you intended for her.

In both cases your friend will fail to make a last, correct conjecture about the list you have made. Moreover, in both cases the list you make belongs to the game. To see this, consider the two cases. In case (a), you will end up listing every positive integer. Since this set is a member of the initial collection $\mathcal{C}$, your list represents a legitimate choice for Nature at the start of the game. In case (b), you will end up listing some set consisting of every positive integer with a sole exception. This set is also in $\mathcal{C}$. Thus, in both cases your friend's guessing rule fails on some list for a set that might have been Nature's initial choice. Hence her guessing rule is not guaranteed to win the new game, which proves 1.4. (A more rigorous version of the proof is given in Chapter 3.)

Let's play the last game again (with the extended collection $\mathcal{C}$), but this time within a slightly different paradigm. Instead of being able to arbitrarily order the chosen set, Nature is now required to present the set in increasing order. So there is just one possible listing of any given set in $\mathcal{C}$. For this paradigm, it is easy to formulate a guessing rule that wins in all cases (try stating such a rule).

The foregoing variations point to a basic question about any, well-defined paradigm. The question is: For what collections of realities can winning guessing rules be formulated? This question is a dominant theme of our book.

§1.4 Discussion of the paradigms

We now comment on various aspects of the paradigms just introduced. In fact, our remarks are relevant to almost all of the paradigms discussed in this book.

§1.4.1 Possible realities as sets of numbers

Limiting the possible realities to sets of positive integers is not as austere as it might seem at first. This is because integers may be conceived as codes for objects and events found in scientific or developmental contexts. For example, the sentences to which children are exposed in the course of language acquisition (like all sentences of human language) are complex structures involving phonetic, syntactic, and semantic levels of representation. Their complexity notwithstanding, it may nonetheless be possible to enumerate all possible sentences in a kind of alphabetical order in something like the way pairs, triples, or quadruples of integers can be enumerated.[4] If the enumeration can be carried out by a computable process, then it yields a useful correspondence between sentences and integers, and the latter can be used as codes for the former. In this case, a set of integers corresponds to a language, namely, the language whose sentences are coded by the integers in the set.[5]

Notice that a correspondence of this kind requires that the set of coded entities be denumerable, i.e., have the same cardinality as the integers serving as codes. It might be thought that the restriction to denumerable domains excludes scientific contexts bearing on physical quantities whose values are arbitrary real numbers. However, the rational numbers provide sufficient precision in scientific practice, and the rationals are a denumerable set. So integers can also be used to code many situations involving physical quantities.

For mathematical simplicity, the possible realities figuring in this book are taken to be sets of numbers, or else functions from numbers to numbers. We limit ourselves thereby to studying scientific or developmental contexts in which the relevant objects of inquiry (like sentences) can be coded as integers. It is our belief that much insight into empirical investigation can be achieved within this limitation, a claim that the reader will ultimately have to evaluate for him- or herself.[6]

There is an additional, noteworthy property of the sets and functions that play the role of possible realities in most of what follows. They are "computable" in the sense of being manipulable and recognizable by computer programs (this will be made precise in the next chapter). It is important to recognize that most sets of numbers and most numerical functions are not computable. In fact, from the point of view of their respective cardinalities, the computable functions stand in the same relation to the class of all numerical functions as do the integers to the real line. It follows that by limiting attention to possible realities of a computable nature our theory does not embrace every conceivable scientific situation (we return to this point in Chapter 3). Once again, we believe that this restriction leaves a large and important class of scientific contexts within the purview

---

[4]For exposition of this kind of enumeration, see Boolos and Jeffery [21, Chapter 1].

[5]For more extended discussion see Weihrauch [192, Chapter 3.3].

[6]Paradigms involving more expressive scientific languages are discussed in Martin and Osherson [127, 128].

of the theory, although we admit to having no proof of this claim.

Another concession to mathematical simplicity can be noted here. Starting in the next chapter, the natural numbers $\{0, 1, 2, 3, \ldots\}$ will be used to construct possible realities, rather than the positive integers $\{1, 2, 3, 4, \ldots\}$. This choice facilitates the use of techniques and results from the theory of recursive functions.

§1.4.2 Intelligible hypotheses

We take hypotheses to be symbolic representations of a real or fictitious world. For example, most hypotheses announced in scientific journals are written in the symbols of the Roman alphabet, supplemented with mathematical notation. Alternatively, the alphabet might be drawn from some system of neural notation used by the brain to represent the structure of the ambient language.

To be intelligible, a symbolic system must provide finite representations of the reality it is designed to depict, even if that reality is infinite in size. For example, the English expressions like "all positive integers except 5" is a finite string of letters that uniquely describes an infinite set. Computer programs can also be conceived as finite descriptions of sets of numbers. Specifically, program P can be taken as specifying the set of all numbers n such that P given input n eventually stops running. This is the approach described in the next chapter and used throughout the sequel. The emphasis on computer programs as hypotheses stems in part from the desire for technological applications. Moreover, it is felt that programs stand in a particularly intimate relation to the sets they describe, inasmuch as they provide a means for recognizing the members of the set. In contrast, the English description "all positive integers that Gauss ever wrote down" uniquely describes a set of numbers, but gives little access to its members.

§1.4.3 Scientists

In our sample paradigm above, scientists were conceived as systems that convert finite sequences of numbers into hypotheses. The scientist may thus be pictured as traveling down an infinite list of numbers, examining the finite amount of data available at any point in the voyage, and emitting hypotheses from time to time about the contents of the entire list, including the infinite, unseen portion. For most of the book, it will be assumed that scientists are *mechanical*, that is, simulable by a computer. Indeed, we shall usually equate scientists with computer programs. It will sometimes prove helpful, however, to remove the assumption of computability from our conception of scientists, in which case they will be conceived as arbitrary functions mapping finite data-sets into conjectures. This liberal attitude will allow us to separate information-theoretic from computability-theoretic aspects of scientific discovery, as will become clearer in Chapter 3.

On the other hand, much of our attention will also be devoted to scientists drawn from narrow subsets of the class of computable processes. That is, we shall consider scientists who operate under various constraints concerning the time devoted to processing data, available memory, selection of hypotheses, ability to change hypotheses, etc. Study of such restrictions will shed light on several issues, including:

(a) the impact of various design features on the performance of computers as scientists, for example, the feature that prevents a computer from abandoning an hypothesis that is consistent with all available data;

(b) the prospects for success by scientists who possess human characteristics, such as time and memory limitations; and

(c) the wisdom of conforming to "rational policies" such as never producing an hypothesis falsified by current data, or never producing an hypothesis that describes a theoretical possibility ruled out in advance.

It will be seen that exploration of such issues sometimes leads to unexpected conclusions.

§1.4.4 Success versus confidence about success

To be successful on a list of numbers, the scientist must produce a final, correct conjecture about the contents of the entire list. She is not required, however, to "know" that any specific conjecture is final. To see what is at issue, consider the first paradigm introduced above in which $\mathcal{C}$ contains just the sets of positive integers with a sole exception. Upon seeing $2, 3, 4, \ldots, 1000$, a scientist might be confident that the list contains the set of positive integers except for 1. But her confidence does not prevent the list from continuing this way: $1, 1002, 1003, 1004 \ldots, 2000$. Confidence at 2000 that the list holds all positive integers except for 1001 is equally unfounded, since the list may continue: $1001, 2002, 2003, 2004, \ldots$. Thus, the scientist is never justified in feeling certain that her latest conjecture will be her last.

On the other hand, Fact 1.3 does warrant a different kind of confidence, namely, that systematic application of guessing rule 1.2 will eventually lead to an accurate, last conjecture on any list generated from a member of $\mathcal{C}$. The relevant distinction may be put this way: If we know that the actual world is drawn from $\mathcal{C}$, then we can be certain that our inquiry will ultimately succeed (if the right guessing rule is applied). But we cannot be certain at any given stage of our inquiry that success has finally arrived.

This asymmetry is a fundamental characteristic of empirical inquiry. In the usual case, scientists can never feel completely confident that their current theory will remain uncontradicted by tomorrow's data. They can only hope that the mental system by which they select hypotheses is adapted to the reality they face. Distinguishing these two issues allows us to focus on scientific success itself, rather than on the secondary question of warranted belief that success has been obtained. Thus, our question will typically be:

> What kind of scientist reliably succeeds on a given class of problems?

rather than:

> What kind of scientist "knows" when she is successful on a given class of problems?

Clarity about this distinction was one of the central insights that led to the mathematical study of empirical discovery (see Gold [80, pp. 465-6]).

§1.4.5 Criteria of success

Compare guessing rule 1.2 to the following, revised version.

1.5   **Guessing rule:** Suppose that S is the set of numbers that have been presented so far. Let m be the least positive integer that is not a member of S. If 2^m is not a member of S, make no conjecture. Otherwise, emit the conjecture "all positive integers except for m" unless this was your last conjecture (in which case make no conjecture at all).

Thus, 1.5 is just like 1.2 except that it imposes a possible delay in producing the conjecture "all positive integers except for m." Although the delay is pointless, it is easy to see that systematic use of 1.5, as with use of 1.2, guarantees success in the first paradigm introduced above.

Rule 1.5 highlights the liberal attitude embodied in our current definition of scientific success. We require that the scientist produce a final conjecture that is correct, but there is no requirement that this final conjecture come as quickly as possible. Let us admit, however, that scientists who examine extravagant amounts of data before making a final, correct conjecture might be considered as useless as scientists who never guess correctly at all. So we might be led to formulate more stringent criteria of scientific success that impose standards of efficiency. Indeed, this is the topic of Chapter 12, below.

Although liberal with respect to efficiency, our present success criterion is stringent about accuracy. To succeed on a given list, the scientist must produce an English description for exactly the numbers in the list, with no omissions or additions. Such accuracy is required in order to make our games interesting, since the sets in play differ by only a few numbers. But what if the initial collection $\mathcal{C}$ were such that every pair of members was infinitely different? In this case, a small error in the scientist's final conjecture might be tolerable. Success in this approximate sense is the topic of Chapters 6 and 7.

More generally, we shall investigate success criteria that are liberal and stringent in a wide variety of ways. In addition to efficiency and accuracy, we shall be concerned with tolerance for noisy data, with different senses of "last conjecture on a list," with behavior on lists outside of a given scientist's competence, and so forth. Of two, distinct criteria we often ask: What kinds of scientific problems can be solved under one criterion that cannot be solved under the other? In this way we hope to shed light on the limits of empirical inquiry that emerge from different kinds of scientific ambition.[7]

Beyond what has been mentioned so far, many additional topics will occupy the chapters of the present book. But enough preliminaries! To get started in a serious way, it is now necessary to review a body of notation and conventions drawn from the theory of computation. This is the topic of the next chapter. Subsequently, in the remaining two chapters of Part I, we formally define and investigate some elementary paradigms.

Summary

The Theory of Machine Inductive Inference (or "Computational Learning Theory," etc.) attempts to clarify the process by which a child or adult discovers systematic generalizations about her environment. The clarification is achieved through the analysis of formal models — called *paradigms* — of scientific inquiry. Each paradigm specifies five concepts central to empirical inquiry, namely:

(a) *a theoretically possible reality*

(b) *intelligible hypotheses*

(c) *the data available about any given reality, were it actual*

---

[7] As mentioned in the preface, however, the book is far from exhaustive in treating paradigms with claim to illuminating aspects of scientific discovery. In particular, we do not discuss PAC models of learning (see Kearns and Vazirani [105] for an excellent overview).

(d) *a scientist*

(e) *successful behavior by a scientist working in a given, possible reality*

One important question about a given paradigm is this: For what classes of possible realities do there exist scientists who are guaranteed to succeed within any reality drawn from the class?

In order to apply the resources of computational theory to the problem of inductive inference, possible realities are often conceived as sets of integers. In turn, the integers can be conceived as codes for complex objects such as sentences or experimental data. Hypotheses within our theory are usually taken to be computer programs operating over integer inputs. A scientist is any system that converts the finite data sets generated by an environment into hypotheses about the totality of that environment. We shall mainly be concerned with scientists whose behavior is simulable by computer. Much of our inquiry will be devoted to scientists who possess special properties, such as efficiency, ability to cope with noisy data, etc.

Through a simple game, we illustrated one criterion of successful scientific behavior; subsequent chapters will investigate a variety of alternatives. It was noted that our theory distinguishes scientific success from the confidence that a scientist might feel about such success. Only the former will be at issue here.

2 Formalities

We now review the standard notations and definitions to be used in the sequel. This material is designed to be more of a reference than part of our main story. So we advise the reader to skim the present chapter, consulting it later as needed.

What we assume of the reader. We assume that the reader has some background in the theory of computation. In particular, we assume the reader is acquainted with the Church-Turing Thesis, the existence of universal Turing machines, the unsolvability of the halting problem, the partial recursive functions, the (total) recursive functions, and the recursively enumerable sets. Almost any text on the theory of computation covers these topics. See, for example, any of Rogers [158], Hopcroft and Ullman [82], Cutland [45], and Lewis and Papadimitriou [126].

The natural numbers. N denotes the set of natural numbers $\{\,0,\,1,\,2,\,\ldots\,\}$ and N^+ denotes the set of positive integers; '#' and '∗' are special constants that are not elements of N. For two natural numbers m and n,

$$m \dotminus n \;=\; \begin{cases} m - n, & \text{if } m \geq n; \\ 0, & \text{otherwise.} \end{cases}$$

Ranges of variables. If a symbol is said to be a variable that ranges over a particular domain, then by convention decorated versions of the symbol (e.g., superscripted and subscripted versions of the symbol) are also variables over the same domain. Generally, e, i, j, k, l, m, n, $\ldots$, x, y, z range over N; a, b, c, d range over $(N \cup \{*\})$; f, g, h, p, q, and r range over total functions from N to N; and η, ν, θ, and ξ range over (possibly) partial functions from N to N. Uppercase roman letters are generally used as variables over subsets of N and sometimes N^k for some $k > 1$. Upper case script letters, $\mathcal{A}$, $\mathcal{B}$, $\mathcal{C}$, $\ldots$, are generally used as variables ranging over classes of sets or functions.

Sets. The symbols $\subset$, $\supset$, $\subseteq$, and $\supseteq$ denote proper subset, proper superset, subset (possibly proper) and superset (possibly proper), respectively. $\in$ denotes 'element of.' $\emptyset$ denotes the empty set. $card(A)$ denotes the cardinality of A. $\aleph_0$ denotes $card(N)$ and $2^{\aleph_0}$ denotes the cardinality of the power-set of N. $min(A)$ denotes the minimum element of A, where $min(\emptyset) = \infty$. $max(A)$ denotes the maximum element of A, where $max(A) = \infty$

if A is infinite and $max(\emptyset) = 0$. By convention, $min(x_1, \ldots, x_k) = min(\{x_1, \ldots, x_k\})$ and $max(x_1, \ldots, x_k) = max(\{x_1, \ldots, x_k\})$. For each $n \in N$, $A[n]$ denotes $\{x \in A \mid x < n\}$. $A - B$ denotes the set $\{x \mid x \in A \text{ and } x \notin B\}$. For $A \subseteq N$, $\overline{A}$ denotes the complement of A, that is, $N - A$. $A \bigtriangleup B$ denotes the symmetric difference of A and B, that is, $(A - B) \cup (B - A)$. $A \oplus B$ denotes the disjoint union of A and B, that is, $\{2x \mid x \in A\} \cup \{2x + 1 \mid x \in B\}$. For each $n \in N$, $A =^n B$ means that $card(A \bigtriangleup B) \leq n$; A and B are called *n-variants*. $A =^* B$ means that $card(A \bigtriangleup B)$ is finite; A and B are called *finite variants*.

For each finite set A, we define the *canonical index* of A to be the natural number $\sum_{x \in A} 2^x$. (The canonical index of $\emptyset$ is thus 0.) The canonical indexing provides a one-to-one correspondence between finite sets and the natural numbers. D_x denotes the finite set whose canonical index is x (see Rogers [158]).

For natural numbers x and z, let:

$$[x, z] = \{y \in N \mid x \leq y \leq z\}. \qquad (x, z) = \{y \in N \mid x < y < z\}.$$
$$[x, z) = \{y \in N \mid x \leq y < z\}. \qquad (x, z] = \{y \in N \mid x < y \leq z\}.$$

Let $\mathbf{R}$ denote the set of real numbers. For each a and $c \in \mathbf{R}$, let:

$$[\![a, c]\!] = \{b \in \mathbf{R} \mid a \leq b \leq c\}. \qquad (\!(a, c)\!) = \{b \in \mathbf{R} \mid a < b < c\}.$$
$$[\![a, c)\!) = \{b \in \mathbf{R} \mid a \leq b < c\}. \qquad (\!(a, c]\!] = \{b \in \mathbf{R} \mid a < b \leq c\}.$$

Logical symbols.   As usual, $\forall$ and $\exists$ are used for universal and existential quantifiers. $\overset{\infty}{\forall}$, $\overset{\infty}{\exists}$, and $\exists!$ denote 'for all but finitely many,' 'there exist infinitely many,' and 'there exists a unique.' That is:

$$(\overset{\infty}{\forall} x)P(x, \vec{y}) \quad \equiv \quad \{x \mid \neg P(x, \vec{y})\} \text{ is finite.}$$
$$(\overset{\infty}{\exists} x)P(x, \vec{y}) \quad \equiv \quad \{x \mid P(x, \vec{y})\} \text{ is infinite.}$$
$$(\exists! x)P(x, \vec{y}) \quad \equiv \quad \{x \mid P(x, \vec{y})\} \text{ is a singleton.}$$

The symbols $\neg$, $\vee$, and $\wedge$, respectively, denote logical *negation, or* and *and*. Fix an $I \subseteq N$, and, for each $i \in I$, let $P_i(\vec{x})$ be a predicate. Then, $\bigwedge_{i \in I} P_i(\vec{x})$ denotes $(\forall i \in I)[P_i(\vec{x})]$ and $\bigvee_{i \in I} P_i(\vec{x})$ denotes $(\exists i \in I)[P_i(\vec{x})]$.

Functions.   Let A and B be arbitrary sets (that is, not necessarily subsets of N). Then $A \rightharpoonup B$ (respectively, $A \to B$) denotes the collection of all partial (respectively, total) functions from A to B. Unless otherwise specified, when we say ψ is a partial function we will mean that $\psi: N \rightharpoonup N$ and when we say f is a total function, we will mean that $f\colon N \to N$. The domain and range of ψ are denoted by $domain(\psi)$ and $range(\psi)$, respectively. $\mathcal{F}$ denotes the class $N \to N$. $\mathcal{R}$ denotes the class of all total recursive functions. $\mathcal{P}$ denotes the class of all partial recursive functions. $\mathcal{R}^+$ denotes the class of recursive functions with range in N^+. $\mathcal{C}$, $\mathcal{S}$, and occasionally other script capital letters range over classes of recursive functions.

We often identify a (partial) function, η, with its set of ordered pairs (that is $\{\,(x, \eta(x)) \mid x \in domain(\eta)\,\}$). Thus $\emptyset$ is used to denote the everywhere undefined function. $\eta(x)\!\downarrow$ means that η is defined on x, and $\eta(x)\!\downarrow = y$ means that η is defined on x and $\eta(x) = y$; $\eta(x)\!\uparrow$ and $\eta(x) = \uparrow$ both mean that η is not defined on x. Thus $domain(\eta) = \{\, x \mid \eta(x)\!\downarrow \,\}$ and $range(\eta) = \{\, \eta(x) \mid \eta(x)\!\downarrow \,\}$. $\eta(x) = \theta(x)$ means that either $\eta(x)\!\downarrow = \theta(x)\!\downarrow$ or else both $\eta(x)\!\uparrow$ and $\theta(x)\!\uparrow$. $\eta \subseteq \theta$ means that the graph of η is contained in the graph of θ or, equivalently, for all $x \in domain(\eta)$, $\eta(x) = \theta(x)$. $\eta \circ \theta$ denotes the composition of η and θ, that is, for each x,

$$(\eta \circ \theta)(x) \;=\; \begin{cases} \eta(\theta(x)), & \text{if } \theta(x)\!\downarrow; \\ \uparrow, & \text{otherwise.} \end{cases}$$

$\eta[n]$ denotes the partial function such that, for each x,

$$\eta[n](x) \;=\; \begin{cases} \eta(x), & \text{if } x < n; \\ \uparrow, & \text{if } x \geq n. \end{cases}$$

For each $A \subseteq N$ and partial function η, $\eta(A) = \{\, \eta(x) \mid x \in A \text{ and } \eta(x)\!\downarrow \,\}$. For each $n \in N$, $\eta =^n \theta$ means that $card(\{\, x \mid \eta(x) \neq \theta(x)\,\}) \leq n$; η and θ are called *n-variants*. Also $\eta =^* \theta$ means that $card(\{\, x \mid \eta(x) \neq \theta(x)\,\})$ is finite; η and θ are called *finite variants*. The *characteristic function* of a set A is denoted by χ_A, that is, for all x,

$$\chi_A(x) \;=\; \begin{cases} 1, & \text{if } x \in A; \\ 0, & \text{otherwise.} \end{cases}$$

Suppose Q is an n-ary predicate. Then,

$$\mu x_1.Q(x_1, \ldots, x_n) \;=\; \begin{cases} x, & \text{if } x \text{ is the least integer such that} \\ & \quad Q(x, x_2, \ldots, x_n) \text{ holds, provided} \\ & \quad \text{such an } x \text{ exists;} \\ \uparrow, & \text{if no such } x \text{ exists.} \end{cases}$$

Suppose that $\mathsf{E}(x_1, \ldots, x_n)$ is an expression with $x_1, \ldots, x_n$ as its only free variables. Then $\lambda x_1, \ldots, x_n.\mathsf{E}(x_1, \ldots, x_n)$ denotes the function that maps $(x_1, \ldots, x_n)$ to the value $\mathsf{E}(x_1, \ldots, x_n)$. For example, $\lambda x.x + 1$ denotes the function that maps x to $x + 1$, and $\lambda x, y.x + y$ denotes the function that maps (x, y) to $x + y$.

Pairing functions.   A *pairing function* is a recursive one–one correspondence between $N \times N$ (pairs of natural numbers) and N (the natural numbers themselves). We use the following pairing function. For each x and y, define $\langle x, y \rangle$ to be the number whose binary representation is an interleaving of the binary representations of x and y where we alternate x's and y's digits and start on the right with the least most significant y digit. For example, $\langle 15, 2 \rangle = 94$, since $15 = 1111$ (binary), $2 = \mathbf{10}$ (binary) $= \mathbf{0010}$ (binary), and $94 = \mathbf{10101110}$ (binary). Define π_1 and π_2 to be the functions such that, for all x and y, $\pi_1(\langle x, y \rangle) = x$ and $\pi_2(\langle x, y \rangle) = y$; π_1 and π_2 are, respectively, called the *first* and *second projection functions* for $\langle \cdot, \cdot \rangle$. This particular pairing function and its projection functions are computable (on deterministic multi-tape Turing Machines) in simultaneous linear time and constant space. (See Royer and Case [161] for details.) By convention, for all x, $\langle x \rangle = x$ and, for all $x_1, \ldots, x_{n+1}$, $\langle x_1, \ldots, x_{n+1} \rangle = \langle x_1, \langle x_2, \ldots, x_{n+1} \rangle \rangle$, where $n \geq 2$. The function $\lambda x_1, \ldots, x_n . \langle x_1, \ldots, x_n \rangle$ is a one-one correspondence between N^n and N. Following the usual conventions of computability theory we will freely identify a partial function $\psi \colon N^k \rightharpoonup N$ with the partial function $\psi' \colon N \rightharpoonup N$ such that, for all $x_1, \ldots, x_k$,

$$\psi(x_1, \ldots, x_k) \;=\; \psi'(\langle x_1, \ldots, x_k \rangle).$$

For each $A, B \subseteq N$, we define $A \otimes B = \{\, \langle a, b \rangle \mid a \in A \text{ and } b \in B \,\}$.

Languages.   Henceforth we use the term *language* as a synonym for "recursively enumerable subset of natural numbers," and we often let L serve as a variable for languages. $\mathcal{REC}$ denotes the class of all recursive languages. $\mathcal{E}$ denotes the class of all recursively enumerable languages. Observe that the empty set is recursively enumerable, so $\emptyset \in \mathcal{E}$. $\mathcal{L}$ ranges over collections of recursively enumerable languages.

A language L is sometimes said to represent the set $\{\, (x, y) \mid \langle x, y \rangle \in L \,\}$. We say L is a *single-valued* language if and only if, for each x, there is at most one y such that $\langle x, y \rangle \in L$ (hence, L represents a partial recursive function). We say that L is a *single-valued total* language if and only if, for each x, there is exactly one y such that $\langle x, y \rangle \in L$ (hence, L represents a total recursive function).

For each $A \subseteq N$ and for each $x \in N$, it is useful to define the following:

$$\begin{aligned}
\mathrm{row}_x(A) &= \{\, y \mid \langle y, x \rangle \in A \,\}. \\
\mathrm{col}_x(A) &= \{\, y \mid \langle x, y \rangle \in A \,\}.
\end{aligned}$$

Functionals and operators.   In this book a *functional* is a (possibly partial) mapping from either $(N \rightharpoonup N)^k \times N^\ell$ or $(N \to N)^k \times N^\ell$ to N, and an *operator* is a total mapping from either $(N \rightharpoonup N)^k \times N^\ell$ or $(N \to N)^k \times N^\ell$ to $N \rightharpoonup N$.

Let $\langle \sigma_i \rangle_{i \in N}$ be a canonical indexing of finite functions.[1] $F \colon (N \rightharpoonup N) \times N \rightharpoonup N$ is a *recursive functional* (or, more accurately, an *effective continuous functional*) if and only if there is an r.e. set A such that, for all $\alpha \colon N \rightharpoonup N$ and all $x, z \in N$, $F(\alpha, x){\downarrow} = z$ $\Longleftrightarrow$ $(\exists i)[\sigma_i \subseteq \alpha$ and $\langle i, x, z \rangle \in A]$. (For all k and ℓ, recursive functionals of type $(N \rightharpoonup N)^k \times N^\ell \rightharpoonup N$ can be defined similarly.) A recursive functional F has the following two topological properties for all $\alpha \colon N \rightharpoonup N$ and $x \in N$.

> *Monotonicity:* $F(\alpha, x){\downarrow} \Rightarrow (\forall \beta \supseteq \alpha)[\, F(\beta, x){\downarrow} = F(\alpha, x)\,]$.

> *Compactness:* $F(\alpha, x){\downarrow} \Rightarrow (\exists \sigma \subseteq \alpha)[\, \sigma$ is finite and $F(\sigma, x){\downarrow} = F(\alpha, x)\,]$.

We say that such an F is a *total recursive functional* if and only if, for all $f \colon N \to N$ and $x \in N$, $F(f, x){\downarrow}$.

We say $\Theta \colon (N \rightharpoonup N)^k \times N^\ell \to (N \to N)$ is a *recursive operator* if and only if there is a recursive functional $F \colon (N \rightharpoonup N)^k \times N^{\ell+1}$ such that, for all $\alpha_1, \dots, \alpha_k, x_1, \dots, x_\ell$,

$$\Theta(\alpha_1, \dots, \alpha_k, x_1, \dots, x_\ell) \;=\; \lambda y. F(\alpha_1, \dots, \alpha_k, x_1, \dots, x_\ell, y).$$

In the setting of recursive operators, the analog of both the monotonicity and compactness properties is the following property that holds for all $\alpha \colon N \rightharpoonup N$.

> *Continuity:* $\Theta(\alpha) = \bigcup_{\sigma \subseteq \alpha} \Theta(\sigma)$, where σ ranges over finite functions.

We say Θ is a *total recursive operator* if and only if Θ is a recursive operator such that, whenever $\alpha_1, \dots, \alpha_k$ are all total, so is $\Theta(\alpha_1, \dots, \alpha_k, x_1, \dots, x_\ell)$.

Programming systems.   A *programming system* for a class of partial recursive functions $\mathcal{C}$ is a partial recursive function ν such that $\{\, \lambda x. \nu(p, x) \mid p \in N \,\} = \mathcal{C}$. By convention, if we do not specify a $\mathcal{C}$, then $\mathcal{C} = \mathcal{P}$ is assumed. Intuitively, ν, a programming system for $\mathcal{P}$, corresponds to an interpreter for some programming language capable of expressing all the partial recursive functions; $\nu(p, x)$ is the result, if any, of running ν-program p on datum x. We typically write $\nu_p(x)$ in place of $\nu(p, x)$. Thus, ν_p is the partial recursive function computed by ν-program p and $\langle \nu_p \rangle_{p \in N}$ is an effective

---

[1] The details of this indexing do not matter. All that we care about is that every finite function has an index and that there is a recursive function r such that, for all i, $r(i) = \langle k, \langle x_0, y_0 \rangle, \dots, \langle x_{k-1}, y_{k-1} \rangle \rangle$ and $\{\, (x_i, y_i) \mid i < k \,\}$ is the graph of σ_i.

indexing of the partial recursive functions. We often refer to p as the ν-*index* of the function ν_p and typically drop the "ν-" prefix when ν is understood.

Fix a programming system ν. For each i, define $W_i^\nu = domain(\nu_i)$. Recall that a set is recursively enumerable if and only if the set is the domain of some partial recursive function. Thus it follows that $\langle W_i^\nu \rangle_{i \in N}$ is an indexing of the recursively enumerable sets. We sometimes say that i is the ν-*grammar* for W_i^ν.

An *acceptable programming system* ν is a programming system with the additional property that: for all other programming systems ψ, there is a recursive function t, such that, for all p,

$$\nu_{t(p)} \;=\; \psi_p.$$

One can think of t as an effective translator of ψ-programs into equivalent ν-programs (i.e., a compiler). Thus, 'ν is acceptable' means that ν has the maximality property that, given any other programming system ψ, there is an effective way of re-expressing ψ-programs as ν-programs. Almost any reasonable formalism for the partial recursive functions (e.g., Turing machines, Algol 60, Fortran, ML, etc.) corresponds to an acceptable programming system, although it is not hard to construct nonacceptable programming systems. We fix one particular acceptable programming system as our standard and let φ denote it. For ease of notation, we often drop φ from W_i^φ.

All acceptable programming systems satisfy the following theorem (stated for φ) due to Kleene.

2.1 Theorem (The S-m-n Theorem) *For each m and $n > 0$, there is a recursive function $s_m^n \colon N^{m+1} \to N$ such that, for all p, $x_1, \ldots, x_m$, and $y_1, \ldots, y_n$ in N,*

$$\varphi_{s_m^n(p, x_1, \ldots, x_m)}(y_1, \ldots, y_n) \;=\; \varphi_p(x_1, \ldots, x_m, y_1, \ldots, y_n).$$

Moreover, one can take each s_m^n function to be one-one and monotone increasing in each of its arguments.

To help see the import of this theorem, consider the $m = n = 1$ case and think of p as a program with its only input statement as:

```
input(a,b)
```

Then, intuitively, the program $s(p, x)$ is the modification of p produced by replacing the input statement by:

```
a ← x; input(b)
```

Thus, x is treated as a datum which s stores in the "text" of the program p. This may seem a very innocuous property, but is in fact extremely powerful. For example, one can characterize the acceptable programming systems as exactly those programming systems for which the s-m-n theorem holds. The s-m-n theorem will be a key tool in the technical work of this book. Here is a simple application that establishes another property of acceptable programming systems.

2.2 Lemma *There is a one-one, strictly increasing, recursive function* $pad(()\cdot,\cdot)$ *such that, for all p and x,*

$$\varphi_{\mathrm{pad}(p,x)} \;=\; \varphi_p.$$

Thus, p, $\mathrm{pad}(p,0)$, $\mathrm{pad}(p,1),\ldots$ is an infinite, strictly increasing sequence of programs for φ_p.

Proof: Suppose i is a φ-program such that, for all p, x, and y, $\varphi_i(p,x,y) = \varphi_p(y)$. (Since $\lambda p,y\,.\,\varphi_p(y)$ is partial recursive, such an i must exist.) Define $\mathrm{pad} = \lambda p,x\,.\,s_2^1(i,p,x)$. By Theorem 2.1 pad is one-one, strictly increasing, and, for all p, x, and y,

$$\varphi_{\mathrm{pad}(p,x)}(y) \;=\; \varphi_{s_2^1(i,p,x)}(y) \;=\; \varphi_i(p,x,y) \;=\; \varphi_p(y).$$

Thus, $\mathrm{pad}(\cdot,\cdot)$ is as required. ∎

Recursion theorems. Another important property satisfied by acceptable programming systems is Kleene's recursion theorem. This theorem provides us with the means to construct programs that self-referentially refer to their own program text. Here is the theorem's formal statement.

2.3 Theorem (Kleene's Recursion Theorem) *For each partial recursive ψ, there is a φ-index e such that, for all x,*

$$\varphi_e(x) \;=\; \psi(e,x). \tag{2.1}$$

Moreover, one can uniformly, effectively find such an e. That is, there is a recursive function r such that, for each p, $\varphi_{r(p)} = \lambda x\,.\,\varphi_p(r(p),x)$.

Consider the φ-program e in (2.1). Intuitively, this program, on input x, creates a (quiescent) copy of its own "program text" and then uses that "text" together with x as input on which to emulate p. In effect, e *creates* a self–model which it uses together with *its* input as input to an emulation of p; e can be thought of as "having" (or more properly, creating) self-knowledge which it employs in a computation of ψ; ψ represents the use to which e puts its self-knowledge.

Proof (of Theorem 2.3): Let d be a φ-index be such that, for all x and y, $\varphi_d(x, y) = \psi(s_1^1(x, x), y)$. Hence,

$$\varphi_{s_1^1(d,x)}(y) \;=\; \varphi_d(x, y) \;=\; \psi(s_1^1(x, x), y).$$

Let $e = s_1^1(d, d)$. Note that

$$\varphi_e(y) \;=\; \varphi_{s_1^1(d,d)}(y) \;=\; \varphi_d(d, y) \;=\; \psi(s_1^1(d, d), y) \;=\; \psi(e, y).$$

Therefore, e is as required. See Exercise 2-1 for the proof of the moreover clause. ∎

The recursion theorem is among our most important technical tools. Here is a simple application of Theorem 2.3 that we will have occasion to use later.

2.4 Lemma *There exists a φ-index e such that, for all y, $\varphi_e(y) = e$, i.e., for all inputs, e outputs its own program.*

Proof: Let $\psi = \lambda x, y.x$. Clearly, ψ is recursive. Hence, by the recursion theorem there is an e such that, for all y, $\varphi_e(y) = \psi(e, y) = e$. ∎

On occasion we will have recourse to use two strengthenings of the recursion theorem: the *k-ary recursion theorem* $(k > 0)$ and the *operator recursion theorem*. The k-ary recursion theorem permits us to construct sets of k distinct programs, each of which may refer to its own and any of its $k - 1$ many sibling's program text. The operator recursion theorem is, intuitively, an infinitary version of the k-ary theorem. The formal statements of these theorems are given just below. The proof of Theorem 2.5 is left to Exercise 2-7.

2.5 Theorem (The k-ary Recursion Theorem, Smullyan [181]) *For each $k \geq 1$, $m \geq 0$ and $n \geq 1$, there are recursive functions $r_1, \ldots, r_k$ such that, for all $p_1, \ldots, p_k$ $(= \vec{p})$, $x_1, \ldots, x_m$ $(= \vec{x})$, and $y_1, \ldots, y_n$ $(= \vec{y})$, we have:*

$$\varphi_{r_1(\vec{p}, \vec{x})}(\vec{y}) \;=\; \varphi_{p_1}(r_1(\vec{p}, \vec{x}), \ldots, r_k(\vec{p}, \vec{x}), \vec{x}, \vec{y}).$$

$$\vdots$$

$$\varphi_{r_k(\vec{p}, \vec{x})}(\vec{y}) \;=\; \varphi_{p_k}(r_1(\vec{p}, \vec{x}), \ldots, r_k(\vec{p}, \vec{x}), \vec{x}, \vec{y}).$$

2.6 Theorem (The Operator Recursion Theorem, Case [24]) *Suppose Θ is a recursive operator; then there is a recursive, monotone increasing h such that, for all n and x,*

$$\varphi_{h(n)}(x) \quad = \quad \Theta(h)(\langle n, x \rangle).$$

Proof: Let f be a recursive function such that, for all i, $\Theta(\varphi_i) = \varphi_{f(i)}$. By the s-m-n theorem, there is a recursive, monotone increasing s such that, for all p, x, y, and z,

$$\varphi_{s(p,x,y)}(z) \quad = \quad \varphi_p(x, y, z).$$

Consider $\Theta\left(\lambda m.s(x, x, m)\right)(\langle n, y \rangle)$. There is a recursive g such that, for all x, $\varphi_{g(x)} = \lambda m.s(x, x, m)$. Thus,

$$\Theta\left(\lambda m.s(x, x, m)\right)(\langle n, y \rangle) \quad = \quad \varphi_{f(g(x))}(\langle n, y \rangle).$$

Let d be such that $\varphi_d = \lambda x, n, y.\varphi_{f(g(x))}(\langle n, y \rangle)$. Then

$$\varphi_{s(d,x,n)}(y) \quad = \quad \varphi_d(x, n, y) \quad = \quad \Theta\left(\lambda m.s(x, x, m)\right)(\langle n, y \rangle).$$

Taking $x = d$ we have

$$\varphi_{s(d,d,n)}(y) \quad = \quad \Theta\left(\lambda m.s(d, d, m)\right)(\langle n, y \rangle).$$

Let $h = \lambda n.s(d, d, n)$ and we are done. ∎

Here is a sample application of Theorem 2.6. See Exercise 2-5 for the proof.

2.7 Lemma *There are distinct numbers a_0, a_1, ...such that, for all i, $W_{a_i} = \{a_{i+1}\}$.*

Program size complexity. One typically thinks of the "size" of a program as something like the number of characters in the program text, the number of lines in the program (where there is an *a priori* bound on line lengths), or the number of bytes in the compiled version of the program. In theoretical settings (where programs are identified with elements of N or $\{0,1\}^*$), one often uses $|p|$ or just p itself as the size of program p. Blum observed [20] that all the natural examples have in common that, given size m, one can effectively construct a finite table of all of the programs of size m. We state Blum's "axiom" for program size in the following equivalent form for an arbitrary programming system ν.

2.8 Definition A recursive function s is a *program size measure for ν* if and only if there exists a recursive function *bound* such that, for all ν-programs p and all $m \in N$, if $s(p) \leq m$, then $p \leq bound(m)$.

Clearly, $\lambda p.|p|$ and $\lambda p.p$ are examples of program size measures. Blum [20] showed that all program size measures are equivalent in the following sense.

2.9 Theorem *Suppose s and s' are both program size measures for ν. Then there is a recursive function h such that, for all p,*

$$s(p) \leq h(s'(p)) \quad and \quad s'(p) \leq h(s(p)).$$

Thus, for recursively invariant results concerning program size (which is all that we will be concerned with in this book), the choice of program size measure does not matter. Therefore, for simplicity we take the size of ν-program p to be just p itself. For each partial recursive function α, we define $MinProg^{\nu}(\alpha)$ to be the least number p such that $\nu_p = \alpha$. Also, for each language L, we define $MinGram^{\nu}(L)$ to be the least number i such that $W_i^{\nu} = L$.

Dynamic program complexity. A two-place partial recursive function Φ is a *complexity measure* (Blum [19]) *for φ* if and only if Φ satisfies the two Blum axioms:
   (i) For all p, $domain(\varphi_p) = domain(\lambda x.\Phi(p,x))$.
   (ii) The predicate $\lambda p, x, t.[\Phi(p,x) \leq t]$ is recursively decidable.
By convention, for all p, Φ_p denotes $\lambda x.\Phi(p,x)$. Intuitively, $\Phi_p(x)$ is the amount of some dynamic resource used by φ-program p in computing $\varphi_p(x)$. Here is an example. Suppose φ is an acceptable programming system based on deterministic multi-tape Turing Machines, and suppose $\Phi(p,x)$ is the number of instructions the Turing Machine coded by p executes on input x, where $\Phi(p,x)$ is undefined if the Turing Machine fails to halt on input x. Then Φ satisfies the Blum axioms. Blum showed that complexity measures are all equivalent in the following sense.

2.10 Theorem *Suppose Φ and Φ' are complexity measures for φ. Then, there is a recursive function h such that, for all p and all but finitely many x,*

$$\Phi_p(x) \leq h(x, \Phi'_p(x)) \quad and \quad \Phi'_p(x) \leq h(x, \Phi_p(x)).$$

Thus, for recursively invariant results concerning computational complexity (which is all that we will be concerned with in this book), the choice of complexity measure does not matter. Thus, Φ will denote a fixed, arbitrary complexity measure.

We use Φ to introduce clipped versions of φ and the indexing $\langle W_i \rangle_{i \in N}$. For each i and s, define:

$$\varphi_{i,s} = \lambda x. \begin{cases} \varphi_i(x), & \text{if } max(x, \Phi_i(x)\downarrow) < s; \\ \uparrow, & \text{otherwise.} \end{cases}$$

$$W_{i,s} = domain(\varphi_{i,s}) = \{ x \mid max(x, \Phi_i(x)\downarrow) < s \}.$$

Note that there are recursive functions f and g such that, for all i and s, $D_{f(i,s)} = \{ \langle x, \varphi_i(x) \rangle \mid x \in domain(\varphi_{i,s}) \}$ and $D_{g(i,s)} = W_{i,s}$.

Computation relative to an oracle. Informally, we say that a function α is computable relative to a set A if and only if α can be computed by an algorithm that, along with all the usual things algorithms are permitted to do, is allowed to use χ_A as a "built-in" subroutine. Formally, we say that α *is computable relative to A* if and only if there is a recursive functional F such that $\alpha = \lambda x. F(\chi_A, x)$. For example, let K denote the diagonal halting problem set, that is, $K = \{ x \mid x \in W_x \}$. ($K$ is a recursively enumerable, nonrecursive set.) Then, $\lambda x. max(\{ \Phi_i(x) \mid i \leq x \ \& \ \varphi_i(x)\downarrow \})$ is computable relative to K. (See Exercise 2-8.)

Limiting computability. Suppose $\langle a_i \rangle_{i \in N}$ is an infinite sequence of integers. We write $\lim_{i \to \infty} a_i = b$ if and only if, for all but finitely many i, $a_i = b$. If, for infinitely many i, $a_i \neq a_{i+1}$, we write $\lim_{i \to \infty} a_i \uparrow$. We say that α is *limiting partial recursive* if and only if there is a (total) recursive function g such that, for all x, $\alpha(x) = \lim_{y \to \infty} g(x, y)$. So, $\alpha(x)$ is defined if and only if the limit exists. We say that α is *limiting recursive* if and only if α is total and limiting partial recursive. The following lemma is essentially due to Post.

2.11 Lemma *A function α is limiting partial recursive if and only if α is partial recursive in the halting problem.*

Thus, the limiting partial recursive functions form a strictly larger class than $\mathcal{P}$. A set A is *limiting recursive* if and only if χ_A is limiting recursive. A functional $\mathbf{F}: (N \to N) \times N \to N$ is limiting recursive if and only if there is a total recursive functional $F: (N \to N) \times N^2 \to N$ such that, for all f and x, $\mathbf{F}(f, x) = \lim_{y \to \infty} F(f, x, y)$.

Exercises

2-1 Suppose d is such that, for all p, x, and y, $\varphi_d(x, p, y) = \varphi_p(s_1^2(x, x, p), y)$. Show that $r = \lambda p.s_1^2(d, d, p)$ is as required for the moreover clause of Theorem 2.3.

2-2 Use the recursion theorem to show that, for each partial recursive function ψ, there is another partial recursive function ψ' such that

(i) $\varphi_{\psi'(0)} = \psi'$ and

(ii) for all $x > 0$, $\psi'(x) = \psi(x)$.

See page 16 for definition of finite variant of a function.

2-3 (Wiehagen [196]) Use the recursion theorem to show that, for each r.e. set L, there is another r.e. set L' such that

(i) L and L' are finite variants and

(ii) $L' = W_x$ where x is the smallest element in L'.

See page 16 for definition of finite variant of a set.

2-4 Use the 2-ary recursion theorem to show the existence of distinct φ-programs e_1 and e_2 such that, for all x, $\varphi_{e_1}(x) = e_2$ and $\varphi_{e_2}(x) = e_1$.

2-5 Use the operator recursion theorem to show that there is a recursive function h such that, for all x, $W_{h(x)} = \{ h(x+1) \}$. Taking, $a_i = h(i)$, $i \in N$, it follows that the a_i's are as required in Lemma 2.7.

2-6 Show that there is a limiting recursive function h such that for all recursive f, for all but finitely many x, $f(x) < h(x)$.

2-7

(a) Prove Theorem 2.5 from Theorem 2.6.

(b) Prove Theorem 2.5 directly from Theorem 2.1.

2-8 Show that $\lambda x. max(\{ \Phi_i(x) \mid i \leq x \ \& \ \varphi_i(x)\downarrow \})$ is computable relative to K.

3 Identification

In Chapter 1 we introduced the idea of a paradigm for scientific discovery and enumerated the concepts that must be specified before a paradigm takes on mathematical meaning. A set of tools for building the needed concepts was described in Chapter 2. In the present chapter we deploy some of this apparatus in the investigation of two fundamental paradigms and some variants thereof. They are called:

- identification of languages; and
- identification of functions.

These paradigms are the barest and simplest to be encountered in this book, yet their underlying structure will show up in all of our ensuing work.

Pursuant to the analysis in Section 1.2, the paradigms are presented by specifying their component concepts, namely:

3.1 (a) *a theoretically possible reality*

  (b) *intelligible hypotheses*

  (c) *the data available about any given reality, were it actual*

  (d) *a scientist*

  (e) *successful behavior by a scientist working in a given, possible reality*

We shall devote considerable discussion to 3.1a-e in the context of language identification. Our discussion of function identification — and of subsequent paradigms in later chapters — can then be briefer, since many of the same considerations carry over to the new settings. The ideas discussed in this chapter derive from seminal papers by Gold [80] and Blum and Blum [18].

The theoretically possible realities proper to our first paradigm are languages, in the technical sense of Chapter 2, so we begin with their intended interpretation within the paradigm of language identification.

§3.1 Languages as theoretically possible realities

Languages can arise as objects of inquiry within either a scientific or a developmental context. We consider these two contexts in turn.

§3.1.1 Languages as scientific possibilities

Consider a scientist studying periodicity in the arrangement of atoms packed into the microstructure of a certain class of alloys. She poses the question: For what natural numbers n are there alloys from the class that exhibit periodicity n? Let us call this latter set *periods*. The results of her observations can be summarized by statements like:

3.2 $3 \in periods, 41 \in periods, 17 \in periods, 53 \in periods, 75 \in periods, \ldots$

or more compactly by:

3.3 $3, 41, 17, 53, 75, \ldots$

The scientist's goal is to transform these data into an accurate and stable conjecture about *periods*. A language L in this setting corresponds to one possible reality, namely, the reality in which $periods = L$.

In what follows we shall assume the set *periods* to be recursively enumerable. It is possible that Nature is not so kind as to guarantee the machine acceptability of sets of integers that correspond to physical processes. However, to keep our topic manageable, we shall limit attention to situations in which the recursive enumerability of the underlying reality is a reasonable assumption; let us take it to be so in the *periods* example.

In the simplified metaphysics that governs our analysis of science, we always assume that Nature selects exactly one underlying reality to be actual. However, not every logically possible reality need be assumed a genuine alternative. Rather, attention may be focused on some proper subset $\mathcal{L}$ of the class of all languages. Such a focus amounts to stipulating that the theoretically possible alternatives are limited to $\mathcal{L}$, other languages being mere logical possibilities ruled out on scientific grounds. Stipulations of this kind allow us to frame questions such as the following: "Suppose that it is known in advance that *periods* falls in $\mathcal{L}$. What kinds of scientists (if any) are sure to discover which member of $\mathcal{L}$ is equal to *periods*?"

A scientist might obtain assurance that *periods* is limited to a subclass of languages in two ways. On the one hand, prior research carried out by other scientists (e.g., her professors) might allow certain languages to be ruled out of the class of genuine alternatives. On the other hand, it is possible that human genetic endowment imposes certain true beliefs about Nature's choice of language, making languages discrepant with these beliefs seem highly implausible.

§3.1.2 Human languages and comparative grammar

Turning to the developmental context, languages in our technical sense may be conceived as representing human languages like Chinese or German that must be mastered by children in the course of their development. Within this perspective, human languages are conceived in a manner familiar from the theory of formal grammar (see Hopcroft and Ullman [82, Chapter 1]) where a sentence is taken to be a finite string of symbols drawn from some fixed, finite alphabet, and a language is construed as a subset of all possible sentences. This definition embraces rich conceptions of sentences, for which derivational histories, meanings, and even bits of context are parts of sentences. Since finite derivations of almost any nature can be collapsed into strings of symbols drawn from a suitably extended vocabulary, it is sufficiently general to construe a language as the set of such strings. By coding strings numerically (see Section 1.4.1), a human language may then be conceived as a subset of the natural numbers N. However, not just any subset of N can play this role. Since human languages are generally considered to have grammars, and since grammars are intertranslatable with Turing Machines, we restrict attention to the recursively enumerable subsets of N — that is, to "languages" in our technical sense.

Now it seems evident to many linguists (notably, Chomsky [40, 43]) that children are not genetically prepared to acquire any arbitrary language on the basis of the kind of casual linguistic exposure typically afforded the young. Instead, a relatively small class $\mathcal{H}$ of languages may be singled out as "humanly possible" on the basis of their amenability to acquisition by children, and it falls to the science of linguistics to propose a nontrivial description of $\mathcal{H}$. Specifically, the branch of linguistics known as "comparative grammar" is the attempt to characterize the class of (biologically possible) natural languages through formal specification of their grammars; and a *theory* of comparative grammar is such a specification of some definite collection. Contemporary theories of comparative grammar begin with Chomsky (e.g., [38, 39]), but there are several different proposals currently under investigation (see Wasow [190] and Lasnik [124]).

Theories of linguistic development stand in an intimate relation to theories of comparative grammar. For if anything is certain about natural language, it is this: children can master any natural language in a few years' time on the basis of rather casual and unsystematic exposure to it. This fundamental property of natural language can be formulated as a necessary condition on theories of comparative grammar: such a theory is true only if it embraces a collection of languages that is learnable by children. For this necessary condition to be useful, however, it must be possible to determine whether given collections of languages are learnable by children. How can this information be acquired? Direct experimental approaches are ruled out for obvious reasons. Investigation of existing languages is indispensable, since such languages have already been shown to be learnable by children; as revealed by recent studies (e.g., van Riemskijk and Williams [189] and Werker [193]), much knowledge can be gained by examining even a modest number of languages. We might hope for additional information about learnable languages from the study of children acquiring a first language. Indeed, many relevant findings have emerged from child language research. For example a child's linguistic environment appears to be devoid of explicit information about the nonsentences of her language (see Section 3.2, below). As another example, the rules in a child's immature grammar are not simply a subset of the rules of the adult grammar but appear instead to incorporate distinctive rules that will be abandoned later (see Pinker [148]).

However, such findings do not directly condition theories of comparative grammar. They do not by themselves reveal whether some particular class of languages is accessible to children or whether it lies beyond the limits of their learning. The theory of empirical discovery described in this book may be conceived, in part, as an attempt to provide the inferential link between the results of acquisitional studies and theories of comparative grammar. It undertakes to translate empirical findings about language acquisition into information about the kinds of languages accessible to young children. Such information can in turn be used to evaluate theories of comparative grammar.

To fulfill its inferential role, the theory of empirical discovery offers a range of models of language acquisition. This is achieved by providing precise construal of concepts generally left informal in studies of child language, namely, the five concepts listed in Section 1.2. The interesting paradigms from the point of view of comparative grammar are those that best represent the circumstances of actual linguistic development in children. The deductive consequences of such models yield information about the class of possible natural languages. Of course, the paradigm to be presented in this chapter is only a crude representation of language acquisition by children. Many of the models to be discussed later are attempts to improve its fidelity.

More extensive discussion of the role of paradigms in comparative grammar is available in Wexler and Culicover [194], in Osherson, Stob, and Weinstein [138], in Osherson and Weinstein [144], and in Osherson, Weinstein, de Jongh, and Martin [145]. We shall return frequently to both language acquisition and scientific discovery in order to motivate our theory.

§3.2 Language identification: Hypotheses, data

Let us now complete the definition of the language identification paradigm. It has already been said that the theoretically possible realities — item 3.1a in our list of concepts — are the members of $\mathcal{E}$, the collection of all languages. It is thus natural to conceive of "intelligible hypotheses" as computer programs or "grammars" for accepting languages. More precisely, it will prove simpler to assimilate hypotheses to the *indexes* associated with programs, as explained in Chapter 2. To aid intuition, however, we shall often revert to the terminology of grammars and programs. Items 3.1a,b are thereby specified.

Turning to 3.1c, we consider the data that Nature makes available about any given language, L. The totality of all such data is conceived as a listing of L in some arbitrary order. To allow such a list to contain pauses in the presentation of data (corresponding to moments in which there is no linguistic input), we adjoin a nonnumerical element $\#$ to N. Our conception of 3.1c may then be rendered as follows.

3.4 Definition (Gold [80])

(a) A *text* is any mapping of N into $N \cup \{\#\}$. A text may be visualized as an infinite sequence $x_0, x_1, x_2, \ldots$ of members of $N \cup \{\#\}$. (The typical variable for texts is T.)

(b) The set of numbers appearing in a text T is denoted by *content*(T). (Thus, the content of a text never includes $\#$.)

(c) Let $S \subseteq N$ and text T be given. T is *for S* just in case *content*$(T) = S$.

For example, consider the following text T:

3.5 $0, 0, \#, \#, 2, 2, \#, \#, 4, 4, \#, \#, 6, 6, \ldots$

content$(T) = \{0, 2, 4, 6, \ldots\}$, so T is "for" the set of even numbers. We note that there are uncountably many texts for any nonempty language. On the other hand, there is only one text for $\emptyset$, namely: $\#, \#, \#, \ldots$.

From the point of view of language acquisition, texts may be understood as follows. We imagine that the sentences of a language are presented to the child in an arbitrary order, repetitions allowed, with no ungrammatical intrusions. Negative information is withheld — that is, ungrammatical strings, so marked, are not presented. Each sentence of the language eventually appears in the available corpus, but no restriction is placed on the order of their arrival. In the event that the language in question is infinite, different sentences continually arise, even though there may also be repetitions of previously presented sentences. If the language is finite, it is possible for the text to finish with an infinite string of #'s; alternatively (if the language is nonempty), it must present at least one sentence infinitely often.

The foregoing picture of the child's linguistic environment is motivated by studies of language acquisition. Several investigations (for example, Brown and Hanlon [22], Hirsh-Pasek, Treiman, and Schneiderman [81], and Demetras, Post, and Snow [55]) give reason to believe that negative information is not systematically available to the learner. Other studies (e.g., Newport, Gleitman, and Gleitman [136] and Schieffelin and Eisenberg [168]) underline the relative insensitivity of the acquisition process to variations in the order in which language is addressed to children. And Lenneberg [125] describes clinical cases revealing that a child's own linguistic productions are not essential to his or her mastery of an incoming language. For further discussion, see Pinker [148].

§3.3 Language identification: Scientists

We turn to 3.1d, the concept of scientist in the present model. The following notation will be used here and later.

3.6 Definition

(a) Let text T and $n \in N$ be given. The nth member of T is denoted by $T(n)$. The initial finite sequence of T of length n is denoted $T[n]$.

(b) The set $\{T[n] \mid T$ a text and $n \in N\}$ is denoted by SEQ; σ, τ, γ are variables over SEQ.

(c) Let $\sigma \in$ SEQ be given. The length of σ is denoted by $|\sigma|$. The unique $\sigma \in$ SEQ with $|\sigma| = 0$ is denoted $\emptyset$. The set of numbers appearing in σ is denoted by *content*(σ). For $n < |\sigma|$, the nth member of σ is denoted by $\sigma(n)$, and the initial sequence of length n in σ is denoted by $\sigma[n]$.

For example, if T is the text of 3.5, then $T(2) = \#$, $T[5] = 0, 0, \#, \#, 2$, and *content*$(T[5]) = \{0, 2\}$. We note the following facts about this notation.

3.7 Lemma *Let text T and $\sigma \in$ SEQ be given.*

(a) *The "first" member of T is $T(0)$; $T(1)$ is the second member.*

(b) *$T[n]$ does not extend to $T(n)$, so content$(T[n])$ does not in general include $T(n)$.* *(For example, if T is 3.5, then $2 \notin$ content$(T[4])$.)*

(c) T *begins with* σ *if and only if* $T[|\sigma|] = \sigma$.

(d) $T(0) \in N \cup \{\#\}$, *but* $T[0] = \emptyset$, *the empty sequence*.

(e) SEQ *is just the collection of all finite sequences over* $N \cup \{\#\}$. *This collection is countably infinite*.

Consider again our scientist studying periodicity, and suppose that her research gives rise to the text T of 3.3 (representing 3.2). $T(n)$ may be conceived as the data generated at the nth moment of investigation, so $T[n]$ is all the evidence available to the scientist about *periods* up to the nth moment, the so-called "evidential state" of the scientist at that time. More generally, any $\sigma \in$ SEQ constitutes a logically possible evidential state at the $|\sigma|$ moment. Now within the present paradigm, empirical inquiry is conceived as the process of converting evidence into theories. Since the set of all possible evidential states is represented by SEQ and the set of all intelligible hypotheses is represented by N, it is natural to take a scientist to be any system that maps the former into the latter. Officially, then, a *scientist* within the language identification paradigm is any function — partial or total, computable or noncomputable — from SEQ to N. We use $\mathbf{F}$ as a variable for scientists, especially when it is not specified whether the scientist in question is computable.

Let text T and $n \in N$ be such that $\mathbf{F}(T[n])\downarrow$. Then $W_{\mathbf{F}(T[n])}$ denotes the language corresponding to the grammar that $\mathbf{F}$ produces upon examining the finite sequence of length n in T. We often say that this language is "conjectured by $\mathbf{F}$ on $T[n]$." If $\mathbf{F}(T[n])\uparrow$, then $W_{\mathbf{F}(T[n])}$ is not defined.

Intuitively, it is helpful to picture a scientist as traveling down a text from left to right, examining the entries in turn. At each step, the scientist is confronted with a new member of SEQ — that is, a new evidential situation σ. The scientist may respond to σ with either a new or previously-emitted hypothesis (in which case, she is defined on σ); alternatively, she may produce no hypothesis at all (in which case she is undefined on σ).

To illustrate, the scientist in our *periods* example might implement the function $\mathbf{F}_{periods}$: SEQ $\rightarrow N$ defined as follows. Let P and O be the sets of prime numbers and odd numbers, respectively. Let n, o, and p be indexes for N, O, and P.

3.8   For all $\sigma \in$ SEQ :

$$
\mathbf{F}_{periods}(\sigma) \;=\; \begin{cases} p, & \text{if } content(\sigma) \subset P; \\ o, & \text{if } content(\sigma) \subset O \text{ but } content(\sigma) \not\subset P; \\ n, & \text{otherwise.} \end{cases}
$$

So, if T is 3.3 then $\mathbf{F}_{periods}(T[i]) = p$ for $i \leq 4$, and $\mathbf{F}_{periods}(T[5]) = o$.

Two other examples of scientists can be entered here.

3.9   For all $\sigma \in \mathrm{SEQ}$:

  (a) $\mathbf{F}_{finite}(\sigma) = $ the least index for the language $content(\sigma)$;

  (b) $\mathbf{F}_{five}(\sigma) = 5$.

Scientist $\mathbf{F}_{finite}$ behaves as if its current evidential state includes all the numbers it will ever see. Consequently, it conjectures a grammar for the finite language made up of just the elements seen to date. Being parsimonious, $\mathbf{F}_{finite}$ selects the smallest possible grammar. Scientist $\mathbf{F}_{five}$ has fixed ideas about the incoming language; indeed, its behavior does not even depend on the data presented. We shall have occasion to refer to these two functions later.

Our conception of scientist is broad in some respects. The everywhere undefined function $\emptyset$ is a scientist, as are functions that seem to make non-optimal use of data. For example, if our scientist keeps poor records of past experiments, her hypotheses might depend only on the last datum examined, i.e., only on $T(n)$ rather than on $T[n+1]$. Or she might change her conjecture upon encountering #, even though # provides no information about the underlying language. Such scientists might be termed "subrational," and will be central to paradigms that attempt to model children (for example, in Section 3.8 below). In addition, as Chapter 5 will reveal, our intuitions about scientific rationality are not always trustworthy in the context of precise models of empirical inquiry. So it is wise at this stage not to eliminate any potential scientists from consideration.

Our conception is broad, as well, in allowing both computable and noncomputable functions to be scientists. For those convinced that human intellectual capacities are computer simulable, noncomputable scientists might seem of scant interest. Indeed, most of the paradigms to be discussed in this book restrict attention to the computable case. Nonetheless, our encounter with noncomputable scientists is useful for two reasons. First, despite considerable speculation it is still unclear whether noncomputable processes exist in nature (for discussion see Webb [191] and Suppes [187]). In particular, it is simply not known whether the human brain is suitably modeled as a computational agent. Worse yet, the answers to such questions depend on apparently arbitrary conventions about what to count as inputs and outputs to naturally occurring processes (see Osherson [137]). A second reason to study noncomputable scientists is that many results in the theory of inductive inference do not depend upon computability assumptions; rather, they are *information theoretic* in character (examples arise in Section 3.6 below). Consideration of noncomputable scientists thereby facilitates the analysis of proofs, making it clearer which assumptions carry the burden. This issue will be revisited in Chapter 11.

On the other hand, Chapters 9 and 10 will discuss senses in which our present conception of scientist is too narrow. Note, for example, that scientists as defined here cannot make decisions on a random basis by including the outcome of a coin-toss as an additional input.

§3.4 Language identification: Scientific success

Languages, hypotheses, texts, and scientists are the *dramatis personae* of the identification paradigm. To develop its story-line we turn now to the criterion of successful inquiry, 3.1e, which is defined in three steps.

§3.4.1 Identifying texts

3.10 Definition Let scientist $\mathbf{F}$, text T, and $i \in N$ be given.

(a) $\mathbf{F}$ *converges to i* on T (written: $\mathbf{F}(T)\!\downarrow = i$) just in case for all but finitely many $n \in N$, $\mathbf{F}(T[n]) = i$. If there exists an i such that $\mathbf{F}(T)\!\downarrow = i$, then we say $\mathbf{F}(T)\!\downarrow$; otherwise we say $\mathbf{F}(T)$ diverges (written: $\mathbf{F}(T)\!\uparrow$).

(b) $\mathbf{F}$ *identifies* T just in case there is $j \in N$ such that $\mathbf{F}$ converges to j on T, and $W_j = content(T)$.

So, to identify T, $\mathbf{F}$'s conjectures must eventually stabilize to a single grammar for $content(T)$. This is impossible, of course, if T is for a non-r.e. set. In the case of interest, however, T is for some language $L \in \mathcal{E}$, hence there are infinitely many grammars for $content(T)$.

Suppose that $\mathbf{F}$ identifies T. Definition 3.10 places no finite bound on the number of times that $\mathbf{F}$ "changes its mind" on T. In other words, the set $\{n \in N \mid \mathbf{F}(T[n]) \neq \mathbf{F}(T[n+1])\}$ may be any finite size; it may not, however, be infinite. Similarly, the smallest $m \in N$ such that $W_{\mathbf{F}(T[m])} = content(T)$ may be any finite number, so $\mathbf{F}$'s first correct guess may occur arbitrarily late in T. It is also permitted that for some $n \in N$, $W_{\mathbf{F}(T[n])} = content(T)$, but $W_{\mathbf{F}(T[n+1])} \neq content(T)$. That is, $\mathbf{F}$ may abandon correct conjectures, provided that $\mathbf{F}$ eventually sticks with some correct conjecture. Observe that to identify a text, a scientist can be undefined on at most a finite number of its initial sequences.

If the text T indicated in 3.3 continues by listing all the odd numbers, then $\mathbf{F}_{periods}$ of 3.8 identifies T. In contrast, if T is for any set other than P, O, or N, then $\mathbf{F}_{periods}$ does not identify T. For other examples, let $\mathbf{F}_{finite}$ and $\mathbf{F}_{five}$ be as specified in 3.9. $\mathbf{F}_{finite}$ identifies any text for a finite language and no text for an infinite one. $\mathbf{F}_{five}$ identifies a given text T if and only if $content(\mathrm{T}) = W_5$.

§3.4.2 Identifying languages

Children are able to learn a language on the basis of many orderings of its sentences. Since Definition 3.10 pertains to individual texts, it does not represent this feature of language acquisition. Similarly, our scientist studying *periods* might converge to a correct grammar for the set, regardless of the way Nature lists it for her. The next definition incorporates this feature of empirical inquiry.

3.11 Definition (Gold [80]) Let scientist $\mathbf{F}$ and $L \in \mathcal{E}$ be given. $\mathbf{F}$ *identifies* L just in case $\mathbf{F}$ identifies every text for L.

It is easy to verify that $\mathbf{F}_{periods}$ identifies P, O, and N. $\mathbf{F}_{finite}$ identifies every finite language but no infinite one. $\mathbf{F}_{five}$ identifies W_5 and nothing else.

Suppose that scientist $\mathbf{F}$ identifies language L, and let T and T' be different texts for L. It is consistent with Definition 3.11 that $\mathbf{F}$ converge on T and T' to different grammars for L. Likewise, $\mathbf{F}$ might require more inputs from T than from T' before emitting a grammar for L.

§3.4.3 Identification of a collection of languages

Children are able to learn any arbitrarily selected language drawn from a large class; that is, their acquisition mechanism is not prewired for just a single language. Similarly, there might be a wide subcollection $\mathcal{L}$ of $\mathcal{E}$ such that our scientist studying *periods* would succeed on any text for any member of $\mathcal{L}$. Our definition of identification is now extended accordingly.

3.12 Definition (Gold [80]) Let scientist $\mathbf{F}$ and $\mathcal{L} \subseteq \mathcal{E}$ be given. $\mathbf{F}$ *identifies* $\mathcal{L}$ just in case $\mathbf{F}$ identifies each $L \in \mathcal{L}$. $\mathcal{L}$ is said to be *identifiable* just in case some scientist identifies it; it is said to be *unidentifiable* otherwise.

We use $\mathcal{L}$ to represent collections of languages. The following reformulation of Definition 3.12 is worth recording.

3.13 Lemma *Scientist* **F** *identifies* $\mathcal{L} \subseteq \mathcal{E}$ *if and only if* **F** *identifies every text for each* $L \in \mathcal{L}$.

Definition 3.12 implies that $\mathbf{F}_{periods}$ identifies $\{P, O, N\}$, and that $\mathbf{F}_{finite}$ identifies the collection of all finite languages. This latter collection will arise frequently in our discussion, so it is well to have a name for it.

3.14 Definition The collection $\{D \subseteq N \mid D \text{ finite}\}$ of all finite languages is denoted by $\mathcal{FIN}$.

We thus have:

3.15 Proposition $\mathbf{F}_{finite}$ *identifies* $\mathcal{FIN}$ *(so* $\mathcal{FIN}$ *is identifiable).*

$\mathbf{F}_{five}$ identifies $\{W_5\}$ and no more. Indeed, every singleton collection $\{L\}$ of languages is identifiable by a suitable, constant scientist. In contrast, questions about the identifiability of collections of more than one language are often nontrivial, since many such questions receive negative answers (as will be seen in Section 3.6). Such is the consequence of requiring a single scientist to determine which of several languages is inscribed in a given text.

Constant scientists serve to highlight the liberal attitude that we have adopted about empirical discovery. The function $f \colon \text{SEQ} \to \{m\}$ identifies $\{W_m\}$ but exhibits not the slightest "intelligence" thereby (like the man who announces an imminent earthquake every morning). Within the identification paradigm it may thus be seen that successful inquiry presupposes neither rationality nor warranted belief, but merely stable and true conjectures in the sense provided by the last three definitions. Does this liberality render identification irrelevant to human learning? The answer depends on both the domain in question and the specific criterion of rationality to hand. To take a pertinent example, normal linguistic development seems not to culminate in warranted belief in any interesting sense, since natural languages exhibit a variety of syntactic regularities that are profoundly underdetermined by the linguistic evidence available to the child (see Chomsky [42, 41]). Indeed, one might extend this argument (as does Chomsky [42]) to every nontrivial example of human learning, that is, to every situation involving a rich set of deductively interconnected beliefs to be discovered by (and not simply told to) the learner. In any such case of empirical discovery, hypothesis selection is subject to drastic underdetermination by available data, and thus selected hypotheses, however true, have little warrant. It must be admitted, however, that all of this is controversial (for an opposing point of view, see Putnam [156] and Pullum [154]). In any case we shall later consider paradigms that incorporate rationality requirements in one or another sense (see Chapter 5).

Definition 3.12 is slightly different from the criterion of successful performance that we introduced informally in Section 1.3. Our earlier criterion required the learner to produce a last, correct guess, and to cease guessing thereafter. It thus corresponds to the following version of identification, here labeled "identification*."

3.16 Definition Scientist $\mathbf{F}$ *identifies** $\mathcal{L} \subseteq \mathcal{E}$ just in case for every text T for any $L \in \mathcal{L}$, $X_T = \{n \in N \mid \mathbf{F}(T[n])\downarrow\}$ is finite and nonempty, and $content(T) = W_{\mathbf{F}(T[n])}$ for the greatest $n \in X_T$. In this case $\mathcal{L}$ is *identifiable**.

The reader can easily verify that the two criteria of success are equivalent in the sense of the next proposition.

3.17 Proposition $\mathcal{L} \subseteq \mathcal{E}$ *is identifiable if and only if $\mathcal{L}$ is identifiable*.*

Identification* is one of many criteria that are transparently equivalent to identification; another is presented in Exercise 3-4. (Criteria that are not equivalent to identification arise in Chapter 6.)

To close this section we record the identifiability of a collection of languages that recalls the discussion of Section 1.3.

3.18 Proposition *Let $\mathcal{L} = \{N - \{x\} \mid x \in N\}$. Then $\mathcal{L}$ is identifiable.*

Proof: Given any $\sigma \in \mathrm{SEQ}$, let x_σ be the least $x \in N$ such that $x \notin content(\sigma)$. Let scientist $\mathbf{F}$ be defined by the condition that for all $\sigma \in \mathrm{SEQ}$, $\mathbf{F}(\sigma) =$ the least index for $N - \{x_\sigma\}$. It is clear that $\mathbf{F}$ identifies $\mathcal{L}$. ∎

§3.5 Identification as a limiting process

Let scientist $\mathbf{F}$ identify text T, and let $n \in N$ be given. We say that $\mathbf{F}$ "begins to identify T at moment n" just in case n is the least integer such that:

(a) $W_{\mathbf{F}(T[n])} = content(T)$, and
(b) for all $m > n$, $\mathbf{F}(T[m]) = \mathbf{F}(T[n])$.

Now suppose that scientist $\mathbf{F}_{finite}$ of 3.9 is working on text T for $L \in \mathcal{FIN}$. By Proposition 3.15 $\mathbf{F}_{finite}$ identifies T. However, no finite initial segment of T provides sufficient information to determine the moment at which $\mathbf{F}_{finite}$ begins to identify T. This is because no $T[n]$ in T excludes the possibility that the next element of T (namely, $T(n)$) lies outside of *content*$(T[n])$, thus falsifying $\mathbf{F}_{finite}$'s present conjecture.

More generally, identification is a limiting process in the sense that it concerns the behavior of a learning function on an infinite subset of its domain.[1] Because of the limiting nature of identification, the behavior of a scientist $\mathbf{F}$ on a text T cannot in general be predicted from $\mathbf{F}$'s behavior on any finite portion of T. The unpredictability is not connected to our external viewpoint, requiring us to observe scientists from the outside. To make this clear, let us briefly consider scientists that announce their own convergence, and may thus be considered to observe their own operation.

3.19 Definition (after Freivalds and Wiehagen [67]) A scientist $\mathbf{F}$ is *self-monitoring* just in case for all texts T, if $\mathbf{F}$ identifies T, then

(a) there is a unique $n \in N$ with $\mathbf{F}(T[n]) = 0$, and

(b) for this n, $\mathbf{F}(T[i]) = \mathbf{F}(T[n+1])$ for all $i > n$.

Intuitively, a scientist is self-monitoring just in case she signals her own convergence, where 0 serves as the signal. The following proposition is suggested by our earlier remarks.

3.20 Proposition *No self-monitoring scientist identifies $\mathcal{FIN}$.*

Proof: See Exercise 3-5.   ∎

Propositions 3.20 and 3.15 show that identifiability does not entail identifiability by a self-monitoring scientist. Informally, a scientist can identify a text without it being possible for her to ever know that she has done so. (Compare Section 1.4.4, above.)

The limiting nature of identification implies that the behavior of a scientist on short members of SEQ is irrelevant to the class of languages it identifies. To say this more clearly, call a scientist *n-mute* just in case it is undefined on all $\sigma \in$ SEQ with $|\sigma| \leq n$. Then, it is easy to verify that for all $n \in N$, $\mathcal{L} \subseteq \mathcal{E}$ is identifiable if and only if some n-mute scientist identifies $\mathcal{L}$. This fact invites the thought that some scientists make more efficient use of data than others, and that a more realistic model of empirical discovery would integrate concern for the resources consumed by inquiry. Such concerns will in

---

[1] For this reason Gold [80] refers to identification as "identification in the limit."

fact be addressed in Chapter 12. Let us here consider a related issue, bearing on the infinitary nature of scientific success as we have defined it.

Texts are infinitely long, and convergence takes forever. These features of identification will be preserved in most of the paradigms discussed in this book. However, language acquisition is a finite affair, so our theory might seem from the outset to have little bearing on linguistic development. Similar remarks apply to scientific discovery.

We offer two replies to the foregoing objection. First, although convergence is an infinite process, the onset of convergence occurs only finitely far into an identified text. What is termed "language acquisition" may be taken to be the acquisition of a grammar that is accurate and stable in the face of new inputs from the linguistic environment; such a state is reached at the onset of convergence, not the end.

This first reply notwithstanding, convergence involves grammatical stability over infinitely many inputs, and such ideal behavior may seem removed from the reality of linguistic development. We therefore reply, secondly, that our theory is best interpreted as relevant to the design of a language acquisition system, not to the resources (either spatial or temporal) made available to the system that implements that design. Analogously, a computer implementing a standard multiplication algorithm is limited to a finite class of calculations, whereas the algorithm itself is designed to determine products of arbitrary size. In this light, consider the language acquisition mechanism $\mathcal{A}$ built into the three-year-old child. However mortal the child, $\mathcal{A}$ is timeless and eternal, forever three years old in design. Various questions can be raised about $\mathcal{A}$, for example: What class of languages does $\mathcal{A}$ identify? If comparative grammar is cast as the study of the design of the human language faculty — as abstracted from various features of its implementation — then such questions are central to linguistic theory, just as analogous questions are central to the study of scientific competence. (For more discussion, see Matthews and Demopoulos [129].)

§3.6 Characterization of identifiable $\mathcal{L} \subseteq \mathcal{E}$

The present section provides a necessary and sufficient condition for the identifiability of a collection of languages. Its proof rests on a preliminary result that will appear often in our work.

§3.6.1 Locking sequences

First, we introduce some important notation.

3.21 Definition Let $\sigma, \tau \in \mathrm{SEQ}$ be given.

(a) The result of concatenating τ onto the end of σ is denoted by $\sigma \diamond \tau$. Sometimes we abuse notation slightly and write $\sigma \diamond x$ (where $x \in N \cup \{\#\}$) to denote the sequence formed by adding x at the end of σ.

(b) We write "$\sigma \subseteq \tau$" if σ is an initial segment of τ, and "$\sigma \subset \tau$" if σ is a proper initial segment of τ.

(c) Likewise, we write $\sigma \subset T$ if σ is an initial finite sequence of text T.

(d) Let finite sequences $\sigma^0, \sigma^1, \sigma^2 \ldots$ be given such that $\sigma^0 \subseteq \sigma^1 \subseteq \sigma^2 \subseteq \ldots$ and $\lim_{i \to \infty} |\sigma^i| = \infty$. Then there is unique text T such that for all $n \in N$, $\sigma^n = T[|\sigma^n|]$. This text is denoted $\bigcup_n \sigma^n$.

3.22 Theorem (Blum and Blum[18]) *Suppose that scientist* $\mathbf{F}$ *identifies* $L \in \mathcal{E}$. *Then there is* $\sigma \in \mathrm{SEQ}$ *such that:*

(a) $content(\sigma) \subseteq L$;

(b) $W_{\mathbf{F}(\sigma)} = L$; *and*

(c) *for all* $\tau \in \mathrm{SEQ}$, *if* $content(\tau) \subseteq L$, *then* $\mathbf{F}(\sigma \diamond \tau) = \mathbf{F}(\sigma)$.

Proof (following Blum and Blum): Let scientist $\mathbf{F}$ and $L \in \mathcal{E}$ be given. Without loss of generality, we assume that $\mathbf{F}$ is defined for all σ. Assume that there is no $\sigma \in \mathrm{SEQ}$ meeting conditions (a)–(c) of the proposition. This implies the following.

3.23   For each $\sigma \in \mathrm{SEQ}$ such that $content(\sigma) \subseteq L$ and $W_{\mathbf{F}(\sigma)} = L$, there is some $\tau \in \mathrm{SEQ}$ such that $content(\tau) \subseteq L$ and $\mathbf{F}(\sigma \diamond \tau) \neq \mathbf{F}(\sigma)$.

We show that 3.23 implies the existence of a text T for L which $\mathbf{F}$ does not identify. This proves the contrapositive of the theorem.

Let $U = u(0), u(1), u(2), \ldots$ be an arbitrary text for L. We construct the promised text T in stages. At each stage n we specify a sequence σ^n such that $\sigma^n \subset T$.

Construction of T

Stage 0: $\sigma^0 = \emptyset$. Note that $content(\sigma^0) \subseteq L$.

Stage n+1: Suppose that σ^n has been defined and that $content(\sigma^n) \subseteq L$. There are two cases.

   Case 1: $W_{\mathbf{F}(\sigma^n)} \neq L$. Then $\sigma^{n+1} = \sigma^n \diamond u(n)$.

Case 2: $W_{\mathbf{F}(\sigma^n)} = L$. Then by 3.23 and the fact that $content(\sigma^n) \subseteq L$, choose $\tau \in$ SEQ such that $content(\tau) \subseteq L$ and $\mathbf{F}(\sigma^n \diamond \tau) \neq \mathbf{F}(\sigma^n)$; let $\sigma^{n+1} = \sigma^n \diamond \tau \diamond u(n)$.

Observe that $\sigma^i \subset \sigma^{i+1}$ for all $i \in N$. Let $T = \bigcup_n \sigma^n$. T is a text for L, since $u(n)$ is added to T at stage n (so $L \subseteq content(T)$) and no nonmembers of L are ever added to T (so $content(T) \subseteq L$). Finally, $\mathbf{F}$ does not converge on T to an index for L, since for each $n + 1 \in N$ either $W_{\mathbf{F}(\sigma^n)} \neq L$ or, for some $\tau \in$ SEG with $\sigma^n \diamond \tau \subseteq \sigma^{n+1}$, $\mathbf{F}(\sigma^n \diamond \tau) \neq \mathbf{F}(\sigma^n)$. Thus, there are infinitely many numbers $m_0, m_1, m_2, \ldots$ such that either $\mathbf{F}(T[m_i])$ is an incorrect index or $\mathbf{F}(T[m_i]) \neq \mathbf{F}(T[m_{i+1}])$. $\blacksquare$

Intuitively, if $\mathbf{F}$ identifies T, then Theorem 3.22 guarantees the existence of $\sigma \in$ SEQ that "locks" $\mathbf{F}$ onto a conjecture for L in the following sense: no presentation from L can dislodge $\mathbf{F}$ from $\mathbf{F}(\sigma)$. This suggests the following definition.

3.24 Definition (Blum and Blum [18]) Let $L \in \mathcal{E}$, scientist $\mathbf{F}$ and $\sigma \in$ SEQ be given. σ is a *locking sequence for* $\mathbf{F}$ *on* L just in case:

(a) $content(\sigma) \subseteq L$;

(b) $W_{\mathbf{F}(\sigma)} = L$;

(c) for all $\tau \in$ SEQ, if $content(\tau) \subseteq L$, then $\mathbf{F}(\sigma \diamond \tau) = \mathbf{F}(\sigma)$.

So Theorem 3.22 can be put this way:

3.25 Corollary (Blum and Blum [18]) *If scientist* $\mathbf{F}$ *identifies* $L \in \mathcal{E}$, *then there is a locking sequence for* $\mathbf{F}$ *on* L.

Note that Theorem 3.22 does not characterize $\mathbf{F}$'s behavior on elements drawn from $\overline{L}$. In particular, if $\tau \in$ SEQ is such that $content(\tau) \not\subseteq L$, then even if σ is a locking sequence for $\mathbf{F}$ on L, $\mathbf{F}(\sigma \diamond \tau)$ may well differ from $\mathbf{F}(\sigma)$.

§3.6.2 Characterization

We now state and prove a characterization of the collections of identifiable languages.

3.26 Theorem (Based on Angluin [6]) $\mathcal{L} \subseteq \mathcal{E}$ *is identifiable if and only if for all* $L \in \mathcal{L}$ *there is finite* $D_L \subseteq L$ *such that for all* $L' \in \mathcal{L}$, *if* $D_L \subseteq L'$ *then* $L' \not\subset L$.

Proof: Let $\mathcal{L} \subseteq \mathcal{E}$ be given. For the left-to-right direction, suppose that scientist **F** identifies $\mathcal{L}$. By Corollary 3.25, for each $L \in \mathcal{L}$ choose a locking sequence σ_L for **F** on L. Since $content(\sigma_L)$ is a finite subset of L, it suffices to prove that for all $L' \in \mathcal{L}$, if $content(\sigma_L) \subseteq L'$, then $L' \not\subset L$. For a contradiction, suppose that for some $L, L' \in \mathcal{L}$, $content(\sigma_L) \subseteq L'$ and $L' \subset L$. Let T be a text for L' such that $T[|\sigma_L|] = \sigma_L$. Such a text exists because $content(\sigma_L) \subseteq L'$. Because σ_L is a locking sequence for **F** on L, and because $content(T) = L' \subset L$, **F** converges on T to an index for L. But $L \neq L'$, so **F** fails to identify T, hence fails to identify L'. This contradicts our choice of **F**.

For the right-to-left direction, suppose the hypothesis of the theorem, namely:

3.27   For all $L \in \mathcal{L}$ there is finite $D_L \subseteq L$ such that for all $L' \in \mathcal{L}$, $D_L \subseteq L'$ implies $L' \not\subset L$.

To show that $\mathcal{L}$ is identifiable, we define a scientist **F**′ as follows. For all $\sigma \in$ SEQ, $\mathbf{F}'(\sigma) =$ the least i such that for some $L \in \mathcal{L}$:

(a) i is an index for L; and

(b) $D_L \subseteq content(\sigma) \subseteq L$.

$\mathbf{F}'(\sigma)$ is undefined if no such i exists.

To see that **F**′ identifies $\mathcal{L}$, fix $L' \in \mathcal{L}$, and let T be a text for L'. Then for some $n_0 \in N$, $D_{L'} \subseteq content(T[n_0]) \subseteq L'$. Let i_0 be the least index for L'. Hence, to prove that **F**′ converges on T to i_0 (and thus identifies T), it suffices to show that for all $j < i_0$ and $m \in N$, if j is for some $L \in \mathcal{L}$ and $D_L \subseteq content(T[m])$, then for all sufficiently large $n \in N$, $content(T[n]) \not\subseteq L$. So let $j < i_0$ and $m \in N$ be given such that j is for some $L \in \mathcal{L}$ and $D_L \subseteq content(T[m])$. Then $L \neq L'$ and $D_L \subseteq content(T) = L'$. Hence by 3.27 there is $x_0 \in L' - L$. Since T is for L', let $n \in N$ be large enough so that $x_0 \in content(T[n])$. Then $content(T[n]) \not\subseteq L$.   ■

Theorem 3.26 allows us to prove that certain collections of languages are not identifiable. We give two examples.

3.28 Corollary (Gold [80]) *Let* $L \in \mathcal{E}$ *be infinite. Then* $\{L\} \cup \mathcal{FIN}$ *is not identifiable.*

Proof: Let $\mathcal{L} = \{L\} \cup \mathcal{FIN}$. The condition expressed by 3.26 fails for the infinite language $L \in \mathcal{L}$. This is because for each finite $D \subseteq L$ there is $L' \in \mathcal{L}$ (namely, D itself!) such that $D \subseteq L'$ and $L' \subset L$.   ■

3.29 Corollary $\{N\} \cup \{N - \{x\} \mid x \in N\}$ *is not identifiable.*

Proof: Let $\mathcal{L} = \{N\} \cup \{N - \{x\} \mid x \in N\}$. The condition expressed by 3.26 fails for N, because for each finite $D \subseteq N$, there is $L' \in \mathcal{L}$ such that $D \subseteq L'$ and $L' \subset L$. This L' has the form $N - \{x\}$ for some $x \notin D$. ∎

To gain insight into the phenomenon of nonidentifiability, consider a scientist $\mathbf{F}$ that identifies N, and let us see why $\mathbf{F}$ does not identify $\mathcal{FIN}$. By Corollary 3.25 let σ be a locking sequence for $\mathbf{F}$ on N. Let T be the text: $\sigma \diamond \# \# \# \dots$. Then $\mathbf{F}$ converges on T to an index for N, whereas T is for $content(\sigma) \in \mathcal{FIN}$. Since no index for N is an index for a finite set, $\mathbf{F}$ does not identify T and hence does not identify the finite set $content(\sigma)$.

Corollary 3.28 yields some lattice-theoretic properties of the class of identifiable subsets of $\mathcal{E}$.

3.30 Corollary

(a) Although $\mathcal{FIN}$ is identifiable, none of its proper extensions are identifiable.

(b) Although both $\mathcal{FIN}$ and $\{N\}$ are identifiable, their union is not identifiable.

Corollary 3.30b may be expressed this way: the class of identifiable subsets of $\mathcal{E}$ is not closed under finite union. This aspect of identifiability is exploited in Chapter 9.

§3.7 Some alternative paradigms

If normal linguistic development is correctly construed as a species of identification, then Corollaries 3.28 and 3.29 yield nonvacuous constraints on theories of comparative grammar. No such theory, for example, could admit as natural some infinite and all finite languages. The force of such constraints is attenuated, however, by the fact that identification is far from adequate as a representation of normal linguistic development. Children's linguistic environments, for example, are probably not arbitrary texts for the target language: on the one hand, texts do not allow for the grammatical omissions and ungrammatical intrusions that likely characterize real environments; on the other hand, many texts constitute bizarre orderings of sentences, orderings that are unlikely to participate in normal language acquisition. In addition, the identification paradigm provides no information about the special character of the child's system for language acquisition. To claim that this system implements some function from SEQ to the set of (indexes for) programs is to say essentially nothing at all. Even the criterion of successful learning is open to question, because linguistic development does not always culminate in the perfectly accurate, perfectly stable grammar envisioned in the definition of identification.

The defects in the identification paradigm can be remedied only in light of detailed information about children's linguistic development. For the most part, the needed information seems not to be currently available. Consequently, we shall not in this book defend the empirical adequacy of any specific model of language acquisition. Rather, the chapters that follow survey a variety of paradigms of varying relevance to intellectual development and to scientific inquiry. The survey, it may be hoped, will suggest questions about linguistic development whose answers can be converted into useful constraints on theories of comparative grammar. It may also suggest new ways of thinking about scientific discovery, both from the normative point of view, and from the point of view of machine implementation.

The present section provides a glimpse of the vast array of paradigms that can be defined (more comprehensive treatment begins in Chapter 5). We shall modify the identification paradigm by narrowing, in turn, its interpretations of "scientist" and "data."

§3.8 Memory-limited scientists

It seems evident that children have limited memory for the sentences presented to them. Once processed, sentences are likely to be quickly erased from the child's memory. Here we shall consider scientists that undergo similar information loss. The following notation is used.

3.31 Definition Let $\sigma \in \text{SEQ}$ be given.

(a) The result of removing the last member of σ is denoted by σ^-; if $|\sigma| = 0$, then $\sigma^- = \sigma$ $(= \emptyset)$.

(b) $\sigma(|\sigma| - 1)$ — i.e., the last member of σ — is denoted by σ_{last} ; if $|\sigma| = 0$, then $\sigma_{last} = \#$.

The following definition says that a scientist is memory-limited if her current conjecture depends on no more than her last conjecture and the current datum.

3.32 Definition (Wexler and Culicover [194]) Scientist $\mathbf{F}$ is *memory limited* just in case for all $\sigma, \tau \in \text{SEQ}$, if $\mathbf{F}(\sigma^-) = \mathbf{F}(\tau^-)$ and $\sigma_{last} = \tau_{last}$, then $\mathbf{F}(\sigma) = \mathbf{F}(\tau)$.

Intuitively, a child is memory-limited if her conjectures arise from the interaction of the current input sentence with the latest grammar that she has formulated and stored. This grammar, of course, may provide information about all the sentences seen to date.

To illustrate, $\mathbf{F}_{finite}$ — defined in 3.9a — is memory-limited. To see this, suppose that $\mathbf{F}_{finite}(\sigma^-) = \mathbf{F}_{finite}(\tau^-)$ and $\sigma_{last} = \tau_{last}$. These equalities imply that $content(\sigma) = content(\tau)$ so $\mathbf{F}_{finite}(\sigma) = \mathbf{F}_{finite}(\tau)$. In view of Proposition 3.15, this proves:

3.33 Proposition $\mathbf{F}_{finite}$ *is memory-limited, and hence some memory limited scientist identifies* $\mathcal{FIN}$.

The foregoing example shows that memory limitation is not uniformly fatal, even for nontrivial problems. Nonetheless, memory limitation places genuine restrictions on the identifiable collections of languages, as shown by the next proposition.

3.34 Proposition *There is an identifiable collection of languages that is not identified by any memory-limited scientist.*

Proof: As a witness to the proposition, let $\mathcal{L} \subset \mathcal{E}$ consist of the language $L = \{\langle 0, x \rangle \mid x \in N\}$ along with, for each $j \in N$, both the languages:

$$L_j = L \cup \{\langle 1, j \rangle\} \text{ and } L'_j = L_j - \{\langle 0, j \rangle\}.$$

It is easy to verify that $\mathcal{L}$ is identifiable. On the other hand, suppose that memory-limited scientist $\mathbf{F}$ identifies L. We will show that $\mathbf{F}$ does not identify $\{L_j, L'_j \mid j \in N\}$. By Corollary 3.25, let σ be a locking sequence for $\mathbf{F}$ on L. Choose $j_0 \in N$ such that $\langle 0, j_0 \rangle \notin content(\sigma)$. Because $\langle 0, j_0 \rangle \in L$, we have:

3.35 $\mathbf{F}(\sigma) = \mathbf{F}(\sigma \diamond \langle 0, j_0 \rangle)$.

Let:

$$\tau = \sigma \diamond \langle 1, j_0 \rangle.$$
$$\gamma = \sigma \diamond \langle 0, j_0 \rangle \diamond \langle 1, j_0 \rangle.$$

Then $\mathbf{F}(\tau^-) = \mathbf{F}(\gamma^-)$ by 3.35, and $\tau_{last} = \gamma_{last}$. So, since $\mathbf{F}$ is memory-limited, $\mathbf{F}(\tau) = \mathbf{F}(\gamma)$. Now let S be a text obtained by omitting all instances of $\langle 0, j_0 \rangle$ from a given text for L. Define:

$$T = \gamma \diamond S, \text{ a text for } L_{j_0}.$$
$$T' = \tau \diamond S, \text{ a text for } L'_{j_0}.$$

Because of memory limitation, it is easy to see that $\mathbf{F}$ converges on T and T' to the same index. Hence, since these two texts are for different members of $\{L_j, L'_j \mid j \in N\}$, $\mathbf{F}$ does not identify $\{L_j, L'_j \mid j \in N\}$ and hence does not identify $\mathcal{L}$.   ∎

Proposition 3.34 shows that, compared to the original paradigm, the memory limited model of linguistic development makes a stronger claim about comparative grammar. This is because the latter model imposes a more stringent condition on the class of human languages: it must not only be identifiable, but identifiable by a memory-limited learner. Of course, this greater stringency represents progress only if children are in fact memory-limited in something like the fashion envisioned by Definition 3.32.

§3.8.1 Fat text

It may be that in the long run every sentence of a given human language will be uttered indefinitely often. What effect would this have on learning?

3.36 Definition

(a) A text T is *fat* just in case for all $i \in content(T)$, $\{n \mid T(n) = i\}$ is infinite.

(b) Let scientist $\mathbf{F}$ and $\mathcal{L} \subseteq \mathcal{E}$ be given. $\mathbf{F}$ *identifies* $\mathcal{L}$ *on fat text* just in case for every fat text T for any $L \in \mathcal{L}$, $\mathbf{F}$ identifies T. In this case, $\mathcal{L}$ is *identifiable on fat text.*

Thus, every number appearing in a fat text appears infinitely often. Since each fat text for a language L is also a text for L, it is obvious that every identifiable collection of languages is identifiable on fat text. The converse proposition is Exercise 3-15.

Fat text is more interesting in the context of memory limitation. The next proposition shows that the former entirely compensates for the latter. We leave its proof as an advanced exercise.

3.37 Proposition *Suppose that $\mathcal{L} \subseteq \mathcal{E}$ is identifiable. Then some memory-limited scientist identifies $\mathcal{L}$ on fat text.*

This concludes our discussion of language identification in the present chapter. Later paradigms bearing on $\mathcal{E}$ will be variations of this first one, and the reader should interpret terminology and notation in the sense defined here unless there is indication to the contrary. The same may be said of our next paradigm, function identification, to which we now turn.

§3.9 Second paradigm: Identification of functions

The theoretically possible realities proper to our second paradigm are total recursive functions, introduced in Chapter 2. Many of the paradigms defined later in the book bear likewise on functions, so it is appropriate to begin our discussion by considering their intended interpretation.

§3.9.1 Recursive functions as possible realities

Scientists often investigate physical systems that implement functions on a suitably chosen domain. The volume of a gas, for example, varies functionally with its temperature and pressure, and the electrical response of a photoreceptor depends functionally on the incident light. Such functions can be approximated with arbitrary precision using rational numbers, which may in turn be coded as natural numbers. In this way, scientific inquiry may often be represented as an attempt to discover which numerical function is actually implemented by Nature. To simplify our discussion we assume that the functions in question are total recursive mappings from N to N. Recall that the class of all such functions is denoted by $\mathcal{R}$. As with the earlier limitation to recursively enumerable sets (see Section 3.1.1 above), restricting attention to $\mathcal{R}$ represents the nontrivial assumption that many natural phenomena can be construed as computational processes. Such will be our supposition.

The class $\mathcal{R}$ may also be considered from the point of view of automatic program synthesis. In this case, the role of Nature is played by a person P who has knowledge of some functional relation $f: N \to N$ but cannot easily write a program to compute f (perhaps for lack of expertise, or simply time). We assume that P's knowledge of f amounts to P being able to respond to any argument $n \in N$ with the value $f(n)$. We seek a computerized system that discovers a program for f on the basis of the pairs fed to it. Once again we assume that P is "mechanical" in an appropriate sense, so that P's knowledge of f guarantees f's computability. (For more discussion of program synthesis in the context of the theory of empirical discovery, see Shapiro [172] and Jantke [98].)

There is also a linguistic interpretation of $\mathcal{R}$. Some theories of language take a sentence to be an ordered pair of representations, one superficial, the other located at a deeper linguistic level. The latter representation stands in close relation to the meaning of the sentence, the former to its phonological realization. It is further assumed that the relation between underlying and superficial representations is a species of functional dependence, different languages implementing different functions of this kind. Competence in a language thus consists in knowing the function that maps one representation onto the other. Under suitable encoding, this competence amounts to knowing which member of $\mathcal{R}$ effects the mapping embodied by the language. The class of human languages corresponds to only a proper subset of $\mathcal{R}$, possibly quite narrow. (Variants of this basic framework are possible; see Wexler and Culicover [194] for discussion.)

Within this perspective, language acquisition proceeds as follows. Nature (in the guise of parents) selects some function f from the human subset of $\mathcal{R}$ and presents the child with the sentences corresponding to f. Contextual clues give the child access to the underlying representation of these sentences, whereas their superficial representations are made available acoustically. She thus receives, in effect, an enumeration of the graph of f. In response she produces a series of conjectures about f, hoping to stabilize on an accurate program for it.

$\mathcal{R}$ thus corresponds to 3.1a, in our list of concepts to be specified by any paradigm of empirical inquiry. We proceed now to specify the others.

§3.9.2 Function identification: Hypotheses, data

Since theoretical possibilities are members of $\mathcal{R}$, we conceive of "intelligible hypotheses" as programs for computing functions. As usual, it is simpler to assimilate such hypotheses to the indexes associated with programs (see Chapter 2). Item 3.1b thus reduces to N though we shall continue to use "program" as an informal synonym for "index" in the context of function identification. Note the following detail. Whereas only total functions are possible realities, many programs compute properly partial functions. Such programs are legitimate conjectures, but within the present paradigm they are necessarily inaccurate. (Their existence will be crucial to more refined models of empirical inquiry, treated later, e.g., in Chapters 5 and 6.)

We turn now to 3.1c, the data that Nature makes available about any given function, f. The totality of all such data is conceived as a list of the graph of f in some arbitrary order. For simplicity, we do not allow pauses in the presentation of data, so # does not appear. Officially:[2]

3.38 Definition

(a) We extend the concept of "text" (see Definition 3.4) to include any single-valued infinite sequence over $N \times N$, i.e., any infinite list of pairs of numbers such that, for each

---

[2] In what follows it will be helpful to recall the modern interpretation of a function, which identifies it with its "graph." See Chapter 2.

x, there is at most one y such that (x, y) occurs in the sequence. We use G as a typical variable for texts over $N \times N$.

(b) Similarly to before, the set of pairs appearing in a text G is denoted by *content*(G).

(c) Let total function $f\colon N \to N$, and text G be given. G is *for* f just in case *content*$(G) = f$.

Thus, the following sequence represents a text for the squaring function.

3.39 $(1, 1)$ $(0, 0)$ $(3, 9)$ $(2, 4)$ $(5, 25)$ $(4, 16) \ldots$

Notation for texts introduced for languages in 3.6 carries over to functions. Thus, let text G and $n \in N$ be given. The nth pair in G is denoted by $G(n)$. The initial finite sequence of G of length n is denoted $G[n]$.

Texts for functions have a property not shared by texts for languages. Let G be a text for a total function, and let T be a text for a language. For any $(n, m) \in N \times N$, examination of some initial segment of G suffices to verify the presence or absence of (n, m) in G once and for all. In particular, if (n, m') is found in G, where $m' \neq m$, then $(n, m) \notin content(G)$. In contrast, no finite examination of T can definitively verify the absence of a number from T. This asymmetry renders function discovery easier than language discovery, as will be seen shortly.

§3.9.3 Function identification: Scientists

In order to specify the concept of "scientist" in the current paradigm, we remind the reader that a subset X of $N \times N$ is a (graph of a) function just in case X contains no two elements of the form $(x, y), (x, z)$ with $y \neq z$. Also, we record the fact:

3.40 Lemma *Every finite function over $N \times N$ is a subset of some member of $\mathcal{R}$.*

3.41 Definition The set $\{G[n] \mid G$ a text for some total function and $n \in N\}$ is denoted by SEG; σ, τ, γ are variables over SEG. (It will be clear from context whether such variables are supposed to range over SEQ or SEG.)

Notation for members of SEQ carries over to SEG. Thus, let $\sigma \in$ SEG be given. The length of σ is denoted $|\sigma|$. The set of pairs appearing in σ is denoted *content*(σ). For $n < |\sigma|$, the nth pair appearing in σ is denoted $\sigma(n)$, and the initial sequence of length n in σ is denoted $\sigma[n]$. For example, if G is the text of 3.39, then $G(3) = (2, 4)$, $G[2] = (1, 1)$ $(0, 0)$, and *content*$(G[3]) = \{(1, 1), (0, 0), (3, 9)\}$. Note that SEG is countably infinite. $\sigma \diamond \tau$ denotes the concatenation of σ and τ. We also use $\sigma \diamond (x, y)$ to denote the addition of the pair (x, y) at the end of σ. We introduce one special piece of notation for SEG; we let $\hat{\sigma}$ be the finite function from N to N whose graph is *content*(σ). Thus $\hat{\sigma}(x) = y$ provided (x, y) occurs in σ.

As in the language context, a scientist examining a text G may be conceived as entering "evidential state" $G[n]$ at moment n. So it is natural to take a scientist to be any system that maps the class of all possible evidential states — namely, SEG — into the set of all hypotheses, namely, N. Officially, a *scientist* within the function identification paradigm is any mapping — partial or total, computable or noncomputable — from SEG to N. As before, we use $\mathbf{F}$ as a variable for scientists, allowing context to determine whether $\mathbf{F}$ stands for scientists over SEQ or SEG.

Let text G and $n \in N$ be such that $\mathbf{F}(G[n]) \downarrow$. Then $\varphi_{\mathbf{F}(G[n])}$ denotes the function corresponding to the program that $\mathbf{F}$ emits upon examining the finite sequence of length n in G. We often say that this function is "conjectured by $\mathbf{F}$ on $G[n]$." If $\mathbf{F}(G[n]) \uparrow$, then $\varphi_{\mathbf{F}(G[n])}$ is not defined. Note that $\varphi_{\mathbf{F}(G[n])}$ need not be total.

§3.9.4 Function identification: Scientific success

The criterion of success associated with our second paradigm is a straightforward adaptation of the criterion for language identification given in Section 3.4 above.

3.42 Definition (Gold [80]) Let scientist $\mathbf{F}$, text G, $f \in \mathcal{R}$, and $\mathcal{C} \subseteq \mathcal{R}$ be given.

(a) $\mathbf{F}$ *converges on* G *to* $i \in N$ (written: $\mathbf{F}(G) \downarrow = i$) just in case for all but finitely many $n \in N$, $\mathbf{F}(G[n]) = i$. If there exists an i such that $\mathbf{F}(G) \downarrow = i$, then we say that $\mathbf{F}(G) \downarrow$; otherwise we say that $\mathbf{F}(G)$ *diverges* (written: $\mathbf{F}(G) \uparrow$).

(b) $\mathbf{F}$ *identifies* G just in case there is $j \in N$ such that $\mathbf{F}$ converges to j on G, and $\varphi_j = content(G)$.

(c) $\mathbf{F}$ *identifies* f just in case $\mathbf{F}$ identifies every text for f.

(d) $\mathbf{F}$ *identifies* $\mathcal{C}$ just in case $\mathbf{F}$ identifies every $f \in \mathcal{C}$. $\mathcal{C}$ is said to be *identifiable* just in case some scientist identifies it; it is said to be *unidentifiable* otherwise.

§3.10 Characterization of identifiable $\mathcal{C} \subseteq \mathcal{R}$

Identifiability in the current paradigm turns out to be a trivial matter, inasmuch as every subset of $\mathcal{R}$ is identifiable. This is the content of the next theorem.

3.43 Theorem $\mathcal{R}$ *is identifiable.*

Proof: The key property of $\mathcal{R}$ is this. Suppose that $f, g \in \mathcal{R}$ and $f \neq g$. Then there are $x, y, z \in N$ such that $(x, y) \in f$, $(x, z) \in g$ and $y \neq z$. It follows that if G is a text for f, there is $n \in N$ such that the information in $G[n]$ shows that G is not for g.

Now define scientist $\mathbf{F}$ as follows. For all $\sigma \in \mathrm{SEG}$, let $\mathbf{F}(\sigma)$ be the least $i \in N$ such that:

(a) φ_i is total; and

(b) $content(\sigma) \subset \varphi_i$.

By Lemma 3.40, $\mathbf{F}$ is well defined.

Thus, $\mathbf{F}$ guesses the first member of $\mathcal{R}$ that is consistent with σ. Our preceding remarks show that, given a text G for $f \in \mathcal{R}$, $\mathbf{F}$ will eventually conjecture and stay with the least index for f, having verified that G is not a text for any function with smaller index. ∎

Although some scientist identifies $\mathcal{R}$, there is no guarantee that a scientist with various special properties can do so as well. In particular, we shall see in the next chapter that no computable scientist has this ability. Memory limitation also prevents identification of $\mathcal{R}$, even by scientists representing noncomputable mappings of SEG to N. We examine this matter now; it is the last topic to be discussed in the present chapter.

§3.10.1 Memory limitation for function identification

The following definitions parallel those given in Section 3.8 for the language case.

3.44 Definition Let $\sigma \in \mathrm{SEG}$ be given.

(a) The result of removing the last pair in σ is denoted by σ^-; if $|\sigma| = 0$, then $\sigma^- = \sigma$ $(= \emptyset)$.

(b) $\sigma(|\sigma| - 1)$ — i.e., the last pair in σ — is denoted by σ_{last}; if $|\sigma| = 0$, then σ_{last} is undefined.

3.45 Definition Scientist $\mathbf{F}$ is *memory limited* just in case for all $\sigma, \tau \in \mathrm{SEG}$ of positive length, if $\mathbf{F}(\sigma^-) = \mathbf{F}(\tau^-)$ and $\sigma_{last} = \tau_{last}$, then $\mathbf{F}(\sigma) = \mathbf{F}(\tau)$.

We shall now define a simple collection of functions that is identified by no memory-limited scientist. For this purpose, the following standard terminology is helpful. Recall from Chapter 2 that $f \colon N \to \{\, 0, 1 \,\}$ is the *characteristic function* of $X \subseteq N$ just in case, for all $x \in N$, $f(x) = 1$ if and only if $x \in X$. Let $\mathcal{C}_0$ be the collection of all $f \colon N \to \{\, 0, 1 \,\}$ such that f is the characteristic function of a finite set, or f is the characteristic function of N. Of course, $\mathcal{C}_0 \subseteq \mathcal{R}$.

3.46 Proposition *No memory-limited scientist identifies* $\mathcal{C}_0$.

Hence, no memory-limited scientist identifies $\mathcal{R}$.

Our demonstration of Proposition 3.46 rests on the following version of Exercise 3-6. Its proof is a simple adaptation of the argument used to establish Theorem 3.22, and is left for the reader.

3.47 Theorem *Suppose that scientist* $\mathbf{F}$ *identifies* $f \in \mathcal{R}$, *and let* $\gamma \in \mathrm{SEG}$ *be such that* $\gamma \subset f$. *Then there is nonempty* $\sigma \in \mathrm{SEG}$ *such that:*

(a) *content*$(\gamma \diamond \sigma) \subseteq f$;

(b) $\varphi_{\mathbf{F}(\gamma \diamond \sigma)} = f$; *and*

(c) *for all* $\tau \in \mathrm{SEG}$, *if content*$(\tau) \subset f$, *then* $\mathbf{F}(\gamma \diamond \sigma \diamond \tau) = \mathbf{F}(\gamma \diamond \sigma)$.

Proof (of Proposition 3.46): Let f be the characteristic function of N, and suppose that memory-limited $\mathbf{F}$ identifies f. It will be shown that $\mathbf{F}$ fails to identify the characteristic function of some finite set.

By choosing $\gamma = \emptyset$ in Theorem 3.47, we may choose nonempty $\sigma \in \mathrm{SEG}$ such that:

3.48   (a) *content*$(\sigma) \subseteq f$;

(b) $\varphi_{\mathbf{F}(\sigma)} = f$; *and*

(c) for all $\tau \in \mathrm{SEG}$, if *content*$(\tau) \subset f$, then $\mathbf{F}(\sigma \diamond \tau) = \mathbf{F}(\sigma)$.

Let $D = \{x \mid (x, 1) \in content(\sigma)\}$, and let g be the characteristic function of D. Thus, $g \in \mathcal{C}_0$ because D is finite. Suppose that $\mathbf{F}$ identifies g (otherwise, $\mathbf{F}$ fails to identify the characteristic function of some finite set, and the proof is finished). Letting γ in 3.47 be σ, choose σ' such that:

3.49   (a) *content*$(\sigma \diamond \sigma') \subseteq g$;

(b) $\varphi_{\mathbf{F}(\sigma \diamond \sigma')} = g$; *and*

(c) for all $\tau \in \mathrm{SEG}$, if *content*$(\tau) \subset g$, then $\mathbf{F}(\sigma \diamond \sigma' \diamond \tau) = \mathbf{F}(\sigma \diamond \sigma')$.

Finally, choose an $n \in N$ be such that neither $(n, 0)$ nor $(n, 1)$ is in $content(\sigma \diamond \sigma')$, and let $g' \in \mathcal{C}_0$ be the characteristic function for $D \cup \{n\}$. We will show that $\mathbf{F}$ fails to identify some text for g'.

By 3.48(c) and the fact that $(n, 1) \in f$, we have:

3.50 $\mathbf{F}(\sigma \diamond (n, 1)) = \mathbf{F}(\sigma)$.

From 3.50 and the memory-limitation of $\mathbf{F}$, we have:

3.51 $\mathbf{F}(\sigma \diamond (n, 1) \diamond \sigma') = \mathbf{F}(\sigma \diamond \sigma')$.

By the choice of σ', 3.49 and 3.51 imply:

3.52 $\mathbf{F}(\sigma \diamond (n, 1) \diamond \sigma')$ is an index for g.

On the other hand, by 3.51 and memory-limitation, we have:

3.53   For all $\tau \in \mathrm{SEG}$, if $content(\tau) \subset g$, then $\mathbf{F}(\sigma \diamond (n, 1) \diamond \sigma' \diamond \tau) = \mathbf{F}(\sigma \diamond \sigma' \diamond \tau)$.

We deduce from 3.49, 3.52, and 3.53:

3.54   For all $\tau \in \mathrm{SEG}$, if $content(\tau) \subseteq g$, then $\mathbf{F}(\sigma \diamond (n, 1) \diamond \sigma' \diamond \tau)$ is an index for g.

Let G' be an enumeration of all the pairs of g' except for $(n, 1)$ (hence $G'[m] \subset g$, for all $m \in N$). Let G be the text that begins with $\sigma \diamond (n, 1) \diamond \sigma'$ and finishes with G'. Then it is easy to verify that G is a text for g'. However, by 3.54, $\mathbf{F}$ converges on G to an index for $g \neq g'$, hence fails to identify g'.   ∎

It is easy to verify that every singleton collection of functions is identifiable by a memory-limited scientist, and that the collection of characteristic functions for finite sets is similarly identifiable. So Proposition 3.46 implies that the family of subsets of $\mathcal{R}$ that are identifiable by a memory-limited scientist is not closed under finite union.

§3.11 Summary

The present chapter defined and investigated two paradigms of scientific discovery that are fundamental to our work. The paradigms introduced in later chapters may be conceived as elaborations or revisions of these two.

The first paradigm takes languages (that is, r.e. sets of numbers) as possible realities, and grammars as scientific hypotheses. The data generated by a language is represented by a text, which is essentially an enumeration of the numbers in the language. Each finite, initial segment of a text is an "evidential position," summarizing all the information available to a scientist up to a given moment of her inquiry. In particular, the initial segment $T[n]$ of text T is the evidential position at moment n of a scientist working on T. A scientist is any function — partial or total, computable or noncomputable — from the set of all such evidential positions to the set N of (indexes for) grammars. For a scientist $\mathbf{F}$ to *identify* a collection $\mathcal{L}$ of languages, it must be the case that for every text T for any language $L \in \mathcal{L}$, there is grammar i for L such that $\mathbf{F}(T[n]) = i$ for all but finitely many $n \in N$.

Identification in the foregoing sense is a nontrivial concept inasmuch as there exist rich, identifiable collections of languages as well as rich unidentifiable ones. A necessary and sufficient condition for identifiability is given in Theorem 3.26.

There are several respects in which the foregoing paradigm is inadequate as a model of language acquisition by children. To take just one example, children are unlikely to remember the entire record of sentences ever addressed to them. We are thus led to define formal scientists who operate under memory restrictions. It was shown in Section 3.7 that such scientists have less scientific competence than their memory-unlimited counterparts. Later chapters will consider other modifications to the language identification paradigm.

The second major paradigm introduced in this chapter takes total recursive functions as the class of possible realities. Hypotheses are construed as (indexes for) programs to compute these functions. The information made available to scientists about a given function f is conceived as an enumeration of the graph of f. The criterion of successful inquiry is a straightforward adaptation of that defined for language identification.

Function identification has a trivial aspect in the sense that there is a single scientist that can identify the entire class of recursive functions. We shall see in the next chapter, however, that this scientist cannot itself be computable.

Similarly to language identification, scientists working under memory limitation suffer from a reduced ability to identify collections of recursive functions.

§3.12 Exercises

3-1 Let $L \in \mathcal{E}$ be given. Show that $\{L \cup D \mid D \text{ finite}\}$ is identifiable.

3-2 Let $\{S_i \mid i \in N\}$ be any collection of nonempty, pairwise disjoint, recursive subsets of N. Show that $\{N - S_i \mid i \in N\}$ is identifiable.

3-3 Prove the following facts.

(a) Every subset of an identifiable collection of languages is identifiable.

(b) No superset of an unidentifiable collection of languages is identifiable.

3-4 Given $p \in [0, 100]$, scientist $\mathbf{F}$, and $\mathcal{L} \subseteq \mathcal{E}$, $\mathbf{F}$ is said to "p percent identify" $\mathcal{L}$ just in case for each $L \in \mathcal{L}$ and each text T for L, there is $i \in N$ such that:

(a) $W_i = L$; and

(b) for all but finitely many $m \in N$, $\mathbf{F}(T[j]) = i$ for p percent of $\{j \mid m \leq j \leq m + 99\}$.

In this case, $\mathcal{L}$ is "p percent identifiable." Prove that if $p > 50$, then $\mathcal{L} \subseteq \mathcal{E}$ is identifiable if and only if $\mathcal{L}$ is p percent identifiable.

3-5 Call $\mathcal{L} \subseteq \mathcal{E}$ *easily distinguishable* just in case for all $L \in \mathcal{L}$ there exists finite $D \subseteq L$ such that for all $L' \in \mathcal{L}$, if $L' \neq L$ then $D \not\subseteq L'$.

(a) Specify an identifiable collection of languages that is not easily distinguishable.

(b) Let $\mathcal{L} \subseteq \mathcal{E}$ be given. Prove the following. Some self-monitoring scientist identifies $\mathcal{L}$ if and only if $\mathcal{L}$ is easily distinguishable.

3-6 Suppose that $\mathbf{F}$ identifies $L \in \mathcal{E}$. Let $\sigma \in \mathrm{SEQ}$ be such that $content(\sigma) \subseteq L$. Prove that there is a $\tau \in \mathrm{SEQ}$ such that $\sigma \diamond \tau$ is a locking sequence for $\mathbf{F}$ on L.

3-7 Let σ be a locking sequence for $\mathbf{F}$ on $L \in \mathcal{E}$. Let $\tau \in \mathrm{SEQ}$ be such that $content(\tau) \subseteq L$. Show that $\sigma \diamond \tau$ is a locking sequence for $\mathbf{F}$ on L.

3-8 Refute the converse to Corollary 3.25. In other words, exhibit scientist $\mathbf{F}$, $L \in \mathcal{E}$, and $\sigma \in \mathrm{SEQ}$ such that σ is a locking sequence for $\mathbf{F}$ on L, but $\mathbf{F}$ does not identify L.

3-9 Suppose that scientist $\mathbf{F}$ identifies $L \in \mathcal{E}$. Let T be a text for L. T is called a "locking text for $\mathbf{F}$ on L" just in case there exists $n \in N$ such that $T[n]$ is a locking sequence for $\mathbf{F}$ on L. Provide a counterexample to the following conjecture: If $\mathbf{F}$ identifies $L \in \mathcal{E}$, then every text for L is a locking text for $\mathbf{F}$ on L.

3-10 Show that some unidentifiable $\mathcal{L} \subseteq \mathcal{E}$ is 49 percent identifiable (see Exercise 3-4).

3-11 Let $\{X_i \subseteq N \mid i \in N\}$ be any indexed collection of subsets of N. Suppose that the X_i are used as languages in place of the indexed collection W_i of r.e. sets. How much of the discussion in Section 3.6 carries over to the X_i setting?

3-12 For each $i \in N$ and each $X \subseteq N$, define $L_{i,X} = \{\langle i, x \rangle \mid x \in X\}$. For each $Q \subseteq N$ define a collection of languages $\mathcal{L}_Q$ by:

$$\mathcal{L}_Q = \{L_{i,N} \mid i \in Q\} \cup \{L_{i,D} \mid i \notin Q \text{ and } D \text{ finite}\}.$$

Show that for every $Q \subseteq N$, $\mathcal{L}_Q$ is identifiable.

3-13 We define a generalization of the concept of memory limitation.

3.55 Definition Let $n \in N$ be given.

(a) The result of removing the last n members of σ is denoted by $\sigma^- n$; if $|\sigma| < n$, then $\sigma^- n = \emptyset$.

(b) The finite sequence consisting of the last n members of $\sigma \in \text{SEQ}$ is denoted by $\sigma_{last\ n}$; if $|\sigma| < n$ then $\sigma_{last\ n} = \sigma$.

(c) Scientist $\mathbf{F}$ is *n-memory limited* just in case for all $\sigma, \tau \in \text{SEQ}$, if $\mathbf{F}(\sigma^- n) = \mathbf{F}(\tau^- n)$ and $\sigma_{last\ n} = \tau_{last\ n}$, then $\mathbf{F}(\sigma) = \mathbf{F}(\tau)$.

Thus, memory limitation corresponds to 1-memory limitation. Show that for all $n \geq 1$ and $\mathcal{L} \subseteq \mathcal{E}$, some n-memory-limited scientist identifies $\mathcal{L}$ if and only if some 1-memory-limited scientist identifies $\mathcal{L}$. *Hint:* Use the "padding function" described in Chapter 2.

3-14 The present exercise concerns another generalization of memory-limitation.

3.56 Definition A scientist $\mathbf{F} \colon \text{SEQ} \to N$ is called *weakly memory limited* just in case there is a function $g \colon \text{SEQ} \to N$ with the following properties. For all $\sigma, \tau \in \text{SEQ}$,

(a) $g(\sigma) \in content(\sigma)$;

(b) if $g(\sigma) \neq g(\sigma^-)$, then $g(\sigma) = \sigma_{last}$; and

(c) if $g(\sigma^-) = g(\tau^-)$, $\sigma_{last} = \tau_{last}$, and $\mathbf{F}(\sigma^-) = \mathbf{F}(\tau^-)$ then $\mathbf{F}(\sigma) = \mathbf{F}(\tau)$.

Intuitively, $\mathbf{F}$ can remember any single previous datum of her choice. Clause (b) means that $\mathbf{F}$ can change the contents of her memory only by storing the datum currently in view. $\mathbf{F}$ is memory-limited in the sense that a given conjecture depends only on (a) the one datum she remembers, (b) the datum currently under examination, and (c) her latest conjecture.

(a) Exhibit $\mathcal{L} \subseteq \mathcal{E}$ such that:

   (i) $\mathcal{L}$ is identifiable; but

   (ii) no weakly memory-limited scientist identifies $\mathcal{L}$.

(b) Exhibit $\mathcal{L} \subseteq \mathcal{E}$ such that:

   (i) some weakly memory-limited scientist identifies $\mathcal{L}$; but

   (ii) no memory-limited scientist identifies $\mathcal{L}$.

3-15   Prove that $\mathcal{L} \subseteq \mathcal{E}$ is identifiable if and only if $\mathcal{L}$ is identifiable on fat texts.

3-16   A text is called "lean" just in case it never repeats a number. Prove that $\mathcal{L} \subseteq \mathcal{E}$ is identifiable if and only if $\mathcal{L}$ is identifiable on lean text.

3-17   (***Advanced***)   Prove Proposition 3.37.

3-18   Text T is called "ascending" just in case for all $n, m \in N$, if $T(n) \neq \#$ and $T(m) \neq \#$ and $n \leq m$, then $T(n) \leq T(m)$. $\mathcal{L} \subseteq \mathcal{E}$ is *identifiable on ascending text* just in case some scientist **F** identifies every ascending text for every $L \in \mathcal{L}$. Prove:

(a) There is $\mathcal{L} \subseteq \mathcal{E}$ such that:

   (i) $\mathcal{L}$ is not identifiable, but

   (ii) $\mathcal{L}$ is identifiable on ascending text.

(b) There is $\mathcal{L} \subseteq \mathcal{E}$ such that $\mathcal{L}$ is not identifiable on ascending text.

3-19   Text T is called "strictly ascending" just in case $\#$ does not occur in T, and for all $n, m \in N$, if $n < m$, then $T(n) < T(m)$. Show that $\{L \in \mathcal{E} \mid L \text{ infinite}\}$ is identifiable on strictly ascending text.

3-20   Let us see what happens if we tighten our success criterion by requiring that scientists never converge to an incorrect index.

> **3.57 Definition (Minicozzi [132])**   Let scientist **F** and $\mathcal{L} \subseteq \mathcal{E}$ be given. **F** *identifies $\mathcal{L}$ reliably* just in case:
>
> (a) **F** identifies $\mathcal{L}$;
>
> (b) for all texts T, if **F** converges on T to $i \in N$, then $content(T) = W_i$.
>
> In this case, $\mathcal{L}$ is *reliably identifiable*.

For example, it is easy to see that $\mathbf{F}_{finite}$ reliably identifies $\mathcal{FIN}$.

Reliability is a useful property of scientists, since a reliable scientist never fails to signal the inaccuracy of a previous false conjecture. The signal is given by eventually changing the previous conjecture, or by producing no conjecture at all on a later input. Show, however, that reliability is an excessively strong success criterion by proving the following.

Suppose that $\mathcal{L} \subseteq \mathcal{E}$ is reliably identifiable. Then $\mathcal{L} \subseteq \mathcal{FIN}$.

3-21 $\mathbf{F}$ identifies $\mathcal{L} \subseteq \mathcal{E}$ *confidently* just in case $\mathbf{F}$ identifies $\mathcal{L}$ and $\mathbf{F}$ converges (to some number or other) on every text for a language in the complement of $\mathcal{L}$. Show that there is identifiable $\mathcal{L} \in \mathcal{E}$ such that no scientist identifies $\mathcal{L}$ confidently.

3-22 One strategy for generating conjectures is to choose the first index in some list of indexes that is consistent with the data seen so far. This strategy is known as "induction by enumeration," and is employed by the scientist in Proposition 3.43 concerning function identification. Let us now see how well induction by enumeration works in the paradigm of language identification.

> **3.58 Definition (Gold [80])** A scientist $\mathbf{F}\colon \mathrm{SEQ} \to N$ is an *enumerator* just in case there is total $f\colon N \to N$ such that for all $\sigma \in \mathrm{SEQ}$, $\mathbf{F}(\sigma) = f(i)$, where i is the least number such that $content(\sigma) \subseteq W_{f(i)}$ (f need not be computable).

(a) Show that

   (i) some enumerator identifies $\mathcal{FIN}$.

   (ii) some enumerator identifies $\{N - \{x\} \mid x \in N\}$.

(b) Given $n \in N$, define $L_n = \{x \mid x \geq n\}$ and $\mathcal{L} = \{L_n \mid n \in N\}$. Show that $\mathcal{L}$ is identifiable, but not by any enumerator.

3-23 Let $\mathcal{J}$ be the collection of all $f\colon N \to N$ such that f is the characteristic function of a finite set. Let $\mathcal{K}$ be the collection of all $f\colon N \to N$ such that f is the characteristic function of a cofinite set. Show:

(a) Some memory-limited scientist identifies $\mathcal{J}$.

(b) Some memory-limited scientist identifies $\mathcal{K}$.

(c) No memory-limited scientist identifies $\mathcal{J} \cup \mathcal{K}$.

4   Identification by Computable Scientists

The focus of our book is the inductive competence of scientists whose behavior can be simulated by computer. The technological interest of this topic is evident, since it lies at the heart of attempts to develop artificial systems of empirical inquiry (see Carbonell [23] and Langley, Simon, Bradshaw, and Zytkow [123]). An additional reason for our focus comes from Cognitive Science. The computer simulability of human ratiocination is one of the most popular hypotheses in that discipline, so it is natural to speculate that children's learning functions are algorithmic processes. By studying the consequences of this hypothesis, it may be possible to provide further constraints on the theory of comparative grammar (see Section 3.1.2).

The present chapter considers the simplest paradigms in which computable scientists appear. Much of the material in later chapters will depend on the results and definitions to be presented here. As before, we discuss language identification prior to function identification. As a preliminary, we introduce a system of notation that will occur throughout the rest of our study.

§4.1 Preliminaries

§4.1.1 An indexing for the computable scientists

Computer simulable scientists can be conceived from either an extensional or an intensional point of view. Extensionally, a computable scientist — like any scientist — is a function from SEQ or SEG to N; it is computable in virtue of there being a procedure that recognizes its pairs. Intensionally, a computer scientist *is* such a procedure, i.e., a computer program that accepts members of SEQ or SEG and returns (if defined) members of N. Our official viewpoint is extensional, so that by "computable scientist" we mean a certain kind of function. As an aid to intuition, however, we sometimes take the intensional point of view, referring to a scientist as a program or Turing Machine.

There are thus three kinds of computable functions now in play within our theory. They may be distinguished by their domains. First, there are the recursive functions (partial and total) with domain N. Next, there are computable scientists within the paradigm of language identification; these functions have domain SEQ. Finally, there are computable scientists within the paradigm of function identification; they have domain

SEG. To implement these functions we could conceive of three types of Turing Machine, each with its own domain. The following strategy is simpler, however. We now fix two recursive isomorphisms, one between SEQ and N, the other between SEG and N. The countability of SEQ and SEG (and their simple structure) guarantees the existence of these isomorphisms, whose details will not concern us. The isomorphisms allow the members of SEQ and SEG to be coded as natural numbers, and using these codes the same Turing Machine TM may be conceived alternately as computing any of the three kinds of functions distinguished above. Thus, to implement a scientist for languages the arguments of TM are construed as members of SEQ, thought of as codes for N. Now recall that an acceptable programming system φ_i was fixed, once and for all, in Chapter 2 (see page 2). The foregoing conventions about SEQ and SEG allow us to interpret the indexes i of this system as also referring to functions with domain SEQ or SEG. In particular, when discussing language identification we often let φ_i refer to scientists with domain SEQ. And when discussing function identification, we often let φ_i refer to scientists with domain SEG. The first enumeration can be conceived as listing all the computable scientists in the language domain. The second lists all the computable scientists in the function domain. We use M, with or without decorations, to denote a computable scientist whose domain (either SEQ or SEG) is determined by context.

§4.1.2 Names for paradigms

In the chapters to follow, many models of empirical inquiry will be defined and analyzed. For the sake of concision, each paradigm will be associated with a symbolic name that abbreviates its main features. Such names can be illustrated with the paradigms of Chapter 3.

4.1 Definition

(a) The class of all identifiable collections of languages (in the sense of Section 3.4) is denoted by **Lang**.

(b) The class of all identifiable collections of functions (in the sense of Section 3.9.4) is denoted by **Func**.

   Thus, **Lang** $= \{\mathcal{L} \subseteq \mathcal{E} \mid \mathcal{L}$ is identifiable$\}$.[1] To illustrate the use of this notation, Exercise 3-3 and Corollary 3.28 imply that $\mathcal{E} \notin$ **Lang**. For another illustration, Proposition 3.43 implies that **Func** is the power set of $\mathcal{R}$. It will be convenient to use this kind

---

[1] So **Lang** is a set of sets of sets of numbers.

of notation in slightly ambiguous fashion. Officially, a symbol like **Lang** denotes a class of collections of languages. However, we also use it unofficially to denote the associated paradigm, that is, an ensemble of definitions concerning possible realities, scientists, and so forth. This allows us to make reference to "the paradigm" **Lang**. We take the same liberty with **Func** and the other names to be introduced.

§4.2 Language identification by computable scientist

§4.2.1 The paradigm TxtEx

We now introduce the paradigm **TxtEx**. The symbol **Txt** signifies that the paradigm concerns the identification of languages on texts. **Ex** signifies that the success criterion is the one specified in Section 3.4, namely, convergence to a single index for the language of the incoming text (**Ex** stands for **Ex**plains). Notice that no part of the name **TxtEx** refers explicitly to the computable nature of scientists. This is because the restriction to the computable case will henceforth be a feature of all the paradigms to be introduced.[2] The only difference between **TxtEx** and **Lang** is this: "scientist" now means a *computable* function — either partial or total — from SEQ to N. All other aspects of the paradigm are the same as before, including the criterion of success given in Definitions 3.10-3.12. Here is the official definition:

4.2 Definition (Gold [80])

(a) Let **M** be a computable scientist and let $L \in \mathcal{E}$. **M** **TxtEx**-*identifies* L (written: $L \in$ **TxtEx(M)**) just in case **M** identifies L.

(b) **TxtEx** = $\{ \mathcal{L} \subseteq \mathcal{E} \mid (\exists \text{ computable } \mathbf{M})[\mathcal{L} \subseteq \mathbf{TxtEx(M)}] \}$.

So, **TxtEx(M)** in the above definition denotes the collection of all languages identified by **M**. Considered as classes of collections of languages, what is the relation between **Lang** and **TxtEx**? Since the computable scientists are a subset of the class of all scientists, it follows that **TxtEx** $\subseteq$ **Lang**. Now we consider whether the inclusion is strict.

---

[2] **TxtEx** has other names in the literature, e.g., **INT** and **Lim**. The terminology **TxtEx** is due to Case and Lynes [33].

§4.2.2 Lang compared to TxtEx

We cannot conclude from the mere fact that there are uncomputable scientists that **TxtEx** is a proper subset of **Lang**, for there are proper subsets of the class of all scientists such that every identifiable collection of languages is identified by some member of the subset (see Exercise 4-3, below). However, **TxtEx** $\subset$ **Lang** does follow from the fact that the computable scientists form a countable subset of the uncountable class of all scientists.[3] This is explained by the following proposition.

4.3 Proposition *Let* Ψ *be any countable collection of functions from* SEQ *to* N, *and let* $\mathbf{L}_\Psi = \{\mathcal{L} \subseteq \mathcal{E} \mid \text{some } \mathbf{F} \in \Psi \text{ identifies } \mathcal{L}\}$. *Then* $\mathbf{L}_\Psi \subset \mathbf{Lang}$.

Proof: For each $i \in N$ and each $X \subseteq N$, define $L_{i,X} = \{\langle i, x \rangle \mid x \in X\}$. For each $Q \subseteq N$ define a collection of languages $\mathcal{L}_Q$ by:

$$\mathcal{L}_Q = \{L_{i,N} \mid i \in Q\} \cup \{L_{i,D} \mid i \notin Q \text{ and } D \text{ finite}\}.$$

Exercise 3-12 shows that for every $Q \subseteq N$, $\mathcal{L}_Q \in \mathbf{Lang}$. We now demonstrate:

4.4   No scientist identifies both $\mathcal{L}_Q$ and $\mathcal{L}_{Q'}$ for $Q \neq Q'$.

To prove 4.4, let $Q \subseteq N$ and $Q' \subseteq N$ be given, with $i \in Q - Q'$. Suppose that scientist **F** identifies $\mathcal{L}_Q$. Then, **F** identifies $L_{i,N} \in \mathcal{L}_Q$. By Corollary 3.25, let σ be a locking sequence for **F** on $L_{i,N}$. Choose finite $D \subseteq N$ such that $content(\sigma) \subseteq L_{i,D}$. Observe that $L_{i,D} \in \mathcal{L}_{Q'}$. Extend σ to a text T for $L_{i,D}$. Then, since $L_{i,D} \subseteq L_{i,N}$, **F** converges on T to an index for $L_{i,N}$. Thus, **F** does not identify $L_{i,D}$ and hence does not identify $\mathcal{L}_{Q'}$. This proves 4.4.

It is easy to see that 4.4 implies 4.3 since there are uncountably many $Q \subseteq N$ and each $\mathbf{F} \in \Psi$ identifies at most one of the classes $\mathcal{L}_Q$. ∎

4.5 Corollary TxtEx $\subset$ Lang.

It will facilitate later developments to exhibit a specific collection of languages that falls in **Lang** $-$ **TxtEx**.

4.6 Definition Let K be the r.e., nonrecursive set defined on page 25. The collection of languages $\{K \cup \{x\} \mid x \in N\}$ is denoted $\mathcal{K}^*$.

---

[3]The computable scientists are countable because the collection of machines that compute them is countable. In contrast, it is easy to see that the collection of all scientists — i.e., functions from SEQ to N — has the power of the continuum.

4.7 Proposition $\mathcal{K}^* \in \textbf{Lang} - \textbf{TxtEx}$.

Proof: By Exercise 3-1, $\mathcal{K}^* \in \textbf{Lang}$. To show $\mathcal{K}^* \notin \textbf{TxtEx}$, suppose by way of contradiction that a computable scientist **M** identifies $\mathcal{K}^*$. Note that $K \in \mathcal{K}^*$ since $K = K \cup \{x\}$ for any $x \in K$. Therefore, by Corollary 3.25, there is a locking sequence σ_0 for **M** on K. Suppose that $\mathbf{M}(\sigma_0) = i_0$, an index for K. Using **M** and σ_0 we will exhibit $\overline{K}$ as recursively enumerable, contradicting the nonrecursivity of K.

Let $k_0, k_1, k_2, \ldots$ be some fixed, recursive enumeration of K. For every $x \in N$, let T^x be the text $\sigma_0 \diamond x \diamond k_0 \diamond k_1 \diamond k_2 \diamond \cdots$. Note that:

4.8   (a) For all $x \in K$, T^x is a text for K.

    (b) For all $x \in \overline{K}$, T^x is a text for $K \cup \{x\} \neq K$, and $K \cup \{x\} \in \mathcal{K}^*$.

By 4.8a and the choice of σ_0, we have:

4.9   Suppose that $x \in K$. Then $\mathbf{F}(T^x[n]) = i_0$ for all $n > |\sigma_0|$.

On the other hand, from 4.8b, the fact that i_0 is an index for no set of the form $K \cup \{x\}$ with $x \in \overline{K}$, and the choice of **M**, we may infer:

4.10   Suppose that $x \in \overline{K}$. Then $\mathbf{M}(T^x[n]) \neq i_0$ for some $n > |\sigma_0|$.

Thus, 4.9 and 4.10 imply:

4.11   For all $x \in N$, $x \in \overline{K}$ if and only if there is an $n > |\sigma_0|$ such that $\mathbf{M}(T^x[n]) \neq i_0$.

Now define the function $\chi : N \to N$ by the condition that for all $x \in N$,

$$\chi(x) = \text{ the least } n > |\sigma_0| \text{ such that } \mathbf{M}(T^x[n]) \neq i_0.$$

Since $k_0, k_1, k_2, \ldots$ is a recursive enumeration, it is easy to see that χ is partial recursive. However, the domain of χ is $\overline{K}$, which implies that $\overline{K}$ is recursively enumerable.   ∎

We mentioned in Section 3.3 that consideration of noncomputable scientists can clarify the respective roles of computational and information-theoretic factors in our theory. This is illustrated by comparing the collections $\mathcal{K}^*$ and $\{N\} \cup \mathcal{FIN}$. By Propositions 4.7 and 3.28, no computable scientist identifies either collection. However, the reasons for the nonidentifiability differ in the two cases. $\mathcal{K}^*$ presents a computable scientist with an insurmountable computational problem, whereas the computational structure of $\{N\} \cup \mathcal{FIN}$ is trivial. In contrast, $\{N\} \cup \mathcal{FIN}$ presents the scientist with an insurmountable informational problem, namely, that no $\sigma \in$ SEQ allows the finite and infinite cases to be distinguished. No such informational problem exists for $\mathcal{K}^*$. The available information simply cannot be put to use by a recursive learning function.

§4.2.3 A comprehensive, identifiable collection of languages

The languages comprising $\{N\} \cup \mathcal{FIN}$ and $\{N\} \cup \{N - \{x\} \mid x \in N\}$ are computationally transparent, yet Corollaries 3.28 and 3.29 show that neither is identifiable. In conjunction with Proposition 4.7, these facts might encourage the belief that **TxtEx** contains only computationally impoverished subsets of $\mathcal{E}$. The purpose of the present section is to show that this belief is mistaken. In particular, it will be seen that there is a computable scientist of simple design that identifies "nearly all" of $\mathcal{E}$. This idea is made precise by the following definition. First, recall from Chapter 2 that two languages L and L' are *finite variants* just in case both $L - L'$ and $L' - L$ are finite.

4.12 Definition Let $\mathcal{L} \subseteq \mathcal{E}$ be given. $\mathcal{L}$ *covers* $\mathcal{E}$ just in case for every $L \in \mathcal{E}$ there is $L' \in \mathcal{L}$ such that L and L' are finite variants.

   Languages that are finite variants have similar computational properties. For example, if one is recursive, then so is the other, and similarly for being decidable in polynomial time, etc. Hence, if $\mathcal{L}$ covers $\mathcal{E}$, then even the most computationally complex sets in $\mathcal{E}$ have equally complex counterparts in $\mathcal{L}'$. Nonetheless:

4.13 Proposition (Wiehagen [196]) *There is* $\mathcal{L} \in$ **TxtEx** *such that* $\mathcal{L}$ *covers* $\mathcal{E}$.

Proof: By Exercise 2-3, one can construct, for each $L \in \mathcal{E}$, an $L' \in \mathcal{E}$ such that:

(a) L and L' are finite variants; and

(b) $L' = W_x$ where x is the smallest member of L'.

It follows that $\mathcal{L} = \{ L' \mid L \in \mathcal{E} \}$ covers $\mathcal{E}$. Now define scientist **M** by the condition that for all $\sigma \in$ SEQ, $\mathbf{M}(\sigma) = $ the least $x \in content(\sigma)$. It is evident that **M** is computable and identifies $\mathcal{L}$.   ∎

§4.2.4 Computability in the context of other constraints

In Section 3.7 we noted that a model of language acquisition places greater constraint on theories of comparative grammar to the extent that it succeeds in locating the language acquisition mechanism of children in a narrow subset of the class of all scientists. One such subset was discussed, namely, memory-limited scientists, and it was shown that there are identifiable collections of languages that are not identified by any memory-limited scientist. The computable scientists constitute another subset of the same nature, as shown by Corollary 4.5.

Let us now consider how such hypotheses interact with each other. Consider two subsets A and B of scientists. Exercise 4-3 shows that it is possible for a collection $\mathcal{L}$ of languages to be identified by some member of A and by some member of B without being identified by any member of $A \cap B$. Thus, the constraint on comparative grammar offered by two hypotheses about children's learning mechanisms cannot be conceived as the intersection of the classes of collections of languages that each permits. This point is illustrated by memory limitation and computability.

4.14 Proposition *There is $\mathcal{L} \subseteq \mathcal{E}$ such that:*

(a) *$\mathcal{L} \in \textbf{TxtEx}$;*

(b) *some memory limited scientist identifies $\mathcal{L}$; and*

(c) *no computable, memory limited scientist identifies $\mathcal{L}$.*

Proof: Let $A \subseteq N$ be a fixed, nonrecursive r.e. set, let $L = \{\langle 0, x \rangle \mid x \in A\}$, and define for all $n \in N$, $L_n = L \cup \{\langle 1, n \rangle\}$, $L'_n = L \cup \{\langle 0, n \rangle, \langle 1, n \rangle\}$. The collection $\mathcal{L} = \{L\} \cup \{L_n, L'_n \mid n \in N\}$ will witness the proposition.

We give informal proofs of parts (a) and (b) of the proposition. A computable scientist $\textbf{M}$ that identifies $\mathcal{L}$ works as follows. On incoming text T, $\textbf{M}$ conjectures L until some pair $\langle 1, n \rangle$ appears in T; then $\textbf{M}$ conjectures L_n forever unless $\langle 0, n \rangle$ appears or has already appeared in T, in which case $\textbf{M}$ conjectures L'_n forever. Note that $\textbf{M}$ is computable but not memory limited. A memory limited scientist $\textbf{F}'$ that identifies $\mathcal{L}$ does the following on T. $\textbf{F}'$ conjectures L until either $\langle 1, n \rangle$ appears in T for any $n \in N$, or $\langle 0, n \rangle$ appears in T for $n \notin A$. In the former case, $\textbf{F}'$ conjectures L_n forever unless $\langle 0, n \rangle$ appears in T, in which case $\textbf{F}'$ conjectures L'_n forever. In the latter case, $\textbf{F}'$ conjectures L'_n forever. It can be seen that $\textbf{F}'$ is memory limited but not computable (since $\textbf{F}'$ determines whether $n \in A$ for nonrecursive A).

To prove part (c) of the proposition, suppose for a contradiction that some computable, memory limited scientist $\textbf{M}$ identifies $\mathcal{L}$. Let σ be a locking sequence for $\textbf{M}$ on L. This implies that for every $n \in A$, $\textbf{M}(\sigma \diamond \langle 0, n \rangle) = \textbf{M}(\sigma)$. It follows that for some $m \in \overline{A}$, $\textbf{M}(\sigma \diamond \langle 0, m \rangle) = \textbf{M}(\sigma)$, for if this were not the case it would be easy to show (since $\textbf{M}$ is computable) that $\overline{A}$ is r.e., and this would contradict the choice of A. Fix such an m, and let S be any enumeration of L. We define two texts, T and T' thus.

$$
\begin{aligned}
T &= \sigma \diamond \langle 1, m \rangle \diamond S. \\
T' &= \sigma \diamond \langle 0, m \rangle \diamond \langle 1, m \rangle \diamond S.
\end{aligned}
$$

By $\mathbf{M}$'s memory limitation and the choice of m, $\mathbf{M}(\sigma \diamond \langle 0, m \rangle \diamond \langle 1, m \rangle) = \mathbf{M}(\sigma \diamond \langle 1, m \rangle)$. So, again by $\mathbf{M}$'s memory limitation, $\mathbf{M}(T'[n+1]) = \mathbf{M}(T[n])$ for all $n > |\sigma| + 1$, that is, $\mathbf{M}$ converges on T' and T to the same index. But T' is a text for L'_n, T is a text for L_n, and $L'_n \neq L_n$. Therefore $\mathbf{M}$ does not identify at least one of L'_n and L_n, contradicting our choice of $\mathbf{M}$. ∎

We shall see similar interactions with computability in later chapters.

§4.2.5 Identifiability by total scientists

The definitions of Section 3.4 do not require a scientist that identifies text T to be defined on every initial segment $T[n]$ of T. However, there is little effect limiting attention to such scientists. Indeed, we can go further, and limit attention to scientists representing total functions from SEQ to N (hence defined on every initial segment of any environment). Scientists with this property are called "total," and suffice to identify any identifiable collection." This is shown by the following.

4.15 Proposition *Let* $\mathbf{M}^0, \mathbf{M}^1, \ldots$ *be an enumeration of all (possibly partial) computable scientists. There is total recursive* $f: N \to N$ *such that for all* $i \in N$:

(a) $\mathbf{M}^{f(i)}$ *is total; and*

(b) *For all* $L \in \mathcal{E}$, *if* $\mathbf{M}^i$ *identifies* L *then* $\mathbf{M}^{f(i)}$ *identifies* L.

Proof: Given $i \in N$, we want $\mathbf{M}^{f(i)}$ to simulate $\mathbf{M}^i$ on $\sigma \in$ SEQ but not wait forever if $\mathbf{M}^i(\sigma)\uparrow$. Therefore, we will allow $\mathbf{M}^{f(i)}$ to wait only $|\sigma|$ steps for $\mathbf{M}^i(\sigma)\downarrow$. Define: $\mathbf{M}^{f(i)}(\sigma) = \mathbf{M}^i(\tilde{\sigma})$ where $\tilde{\sigma}$ is the longest initial segment of σ such that $\mathbf{M}^i(\tilde{\sigma})\downarrow$ in $|\sigma|$ steps, if such exists; $= 0$ otherwise.

$\mathbf{M}^{f(i)}$ is computable because the condition defining $\tilde{\sigma}$ can be checked recursively (since the waiting time is bounded by $|\sigma|$). To see that $\mathbf{M}^{f(i)}$ identifies every language L that $\mathbf{M}^i$ does, let T be a text for such an L. Then there is $n \in N$ and index j for L such that for all $m \geq n$, $\mathbf{M}^i(T[m]) = j$. Let $s \in N$ be the running time of $\mathbf{M}^i(T[n])$. By the definition of $\mathbf{M}^{f(i)}$, if m exceeds both s and n, then $\mathbf{M}^{f(i)}(T[m]) = \mathbf{M}^i(T[k])$ for some $k \geq n$. Thus $\mathbf{M}^{f(i)}$ converges on T to j. ∎

The foregoing proof uses two techniques that appear frequently within our theory. First, the scientist $\mathbf{M}^{f(i)}$ whose existence must be proved relies upon an internal simulation of the given scientist $\mathbf{M}^i$. $\mathbf{M}^{f(i)}$ feeds $\mathbf{M}^i$ some version of the incoming data and then uses $\mathbf{M}^i$'s output for its own conjectures. Such proofs may be called "internal simulation" arguments. Second, at moment n, $\mathbf{M}^{f(i)}$ does not use $\mathbf{M}^i$'s response to the entire sequence $T[n]$ of incoming text T. Rather, $\mathbf{M}^{f(i)}$ uses $\mathbf{M}^i$'s response to some possibly proper initial segment $T[j]$ of $T[n]$. Although the gap between the available and used segments of T may increase with time, $\mathbf{M}^{f(i)}$ eventually produces $\mathbf{M}^i$'s response to larger and larger initial segments of T on which $\mathbf{M}^i$ is defined. This feature of the proof may be called "falling back on the text."

Proposition 4.15 gives us something more.

4.16 Corollary *There exists a recursively enumerable sequence of total computable scientists* $\mathbf{M}_0, \mathbf{M}_1, \ldots$, *such that* $(\forall \mathcal{L} \in \mathbf{TxtEx})(\exists i)[\mathcal{L} \subseteq \mathbf{TxtEx}(\mathbf{M}_i)]$.

We can take $\mathbf{M}^{f(0)}, \mathbf{M}^{f(1)}, \ldots$ to be one such enumeration. A counterpart of the above corollary holds for many of the paradigms considered in this book (with identical proofs). This fact can often be exploited to make diagonalization arguments simpler.

§4.3 Function identification by computable scientist

§4.3.1 The paradigm Ex

We now introduce the paradigm **Ex**. As in the language case, the letters "Ex" are short for "explains" and signify that the success criterion is convergence to a single index for the target function. Scientists in the **Ex** model are computable functions — either partial or total — from SEG to N. All other aspects of the **Ex** paradigm are the same as for **Func**. We define:

4.17 Definition (Gold [80])

(a) Let $\mathbf{M}$ be a computable scientist and let $f \in \mathcal{R}$. $\mathbf{M}$ **Ex**-*identifies* f (written: $f \in \mathbf{Ex}(\mathbf{M})$) just in case $\mathbf{M}$ identifies f.

(b) $\mathbf{Ex} = \{\, \mathcal{C} \subseteq \mathcal{R} \mid (\exists \text{ computable } \mathbf{M})[\mathcal{C} \subseteq \mathbf{Ex}(\mathbf{M})] \,\}$.

Analysis of **Ex** is facilitated by limiting attention to texts of a special kind.

4.18 Definition Let G be a text for total function f. G is *canonical* just in case for all $n \in N$, $G(n) = (n, f(n))$ (that is, the pair $(n, f(n))$ occurs in the $(n+1)^{st}$ position of G). Similarly, $\sigma \in \text{SEG}$ is in *canonical order* just in case $\sigma = (0, x_0), (1, x_1), \ldots, (n, x_n)$ for $n = |\sigma| - 1$ and $x_0, \ldots, x_n \in N$. Let INIT be the collection of all $\sigma \in \text{SEG}$ that are in canonical order.

Although the canonical text for $f \in \mathcal{R}$ constitutes only one among uncountably many orderings of f, there is an algorithm A that progressively converts any incoming text G into a canonical text G' for the same function. Informally, A works on G by reading and storing the members of G until some pair of the form $(0, x)$ appears. (If G is for some $f \in \mathcal{R}$, then exactly one such pair must eventually occur.) A writes this pair as the first member of G'. Next, A searches its memory for some pair of the form $(1, x)$; if no such pair is found in memory, A reads and stores more of G until such a pair is found. This pair is written onto G', and A then searches for a pair of the form $(2, x) \ldots$. This process continues indefinitely. Although A may be required to store ever larger initial segments of G, its storage requirements are finite at any given time. It is clear that A gradually produces a canonical text for *content*(G). Formally, we let $F_A : \mathrm{SEG} \to \mathrm{INIT}$ be defined as follows.

4.19 Definition For all $\sigma \in \mathrm{SEG}$, $F_A(\sigma)$ is the longest $\tau \in \mathrm{INIT}$ such that *content*$(\tau) \subseteq$ *content*(σ).

F_A is computable, and applying it to ever longer initial segments of a text produces ever longer initial segments of the corresponding, canonical text. That is:

4.20 Lemma *If G is an arbitrary text for $f \in \mathcal{R}$, then $\bigcup_{m \in N} F_A(G[m])$ is the canonical text for f.*

The ability to algorithmically transform any text into canonical order simplifies the **Ex** paradigm. This is shown by the following proposition.

4.21 Proposition *Let $\mathcal{C} \subseteq \mathcal{R}$ be given. $\mathcal{C} \in$ **Ex** if and only if there is a computable scientist that identifies the canonical text for any member of $\mathcal{C}$.*

Proof: The left-to-right direction is immediate. For the other direction, we use an internal simulation argument. Suppose that computable scientist $\mathbf{F}$ identifies the canonical text for any member of $\mathcal{C} \subseteq \mathcal{R}$. Define scientist $\mathbf{F}^*$ as follows. For all $\sigma \in \mathrm{SEG}$, $\mathbf{F}^*(\sigma) = \mathbf{F}(F_A(\sigma))$. $\mathbf{F}^*$ is computable because it is the composition of computable functions. Moreover, $\mathbf{F}^*$ converges to $i \in N$ on text G for $f \in \mathcal{R}$ if $\mathbf{F}$ converges to i on the corresponding canonical text. Since $\mathbf{F}$ identifies the latter, $\mathbf{F}^*$ identifies the former and thus identifies $\mathcal{C}$. ∎

To prove claims of the form $\mathcal{C} \in$ **Ex** or $\mathcal{C} \notin$ **Ex** we shall henceforth rely implicitly on Proposition 4.21, and consider only canonical texts. The following slight abuse of terminology will also be employed. We often identify a function f with its canonical text (and vice versa). Thus $f \in \mathcal{R}$ will denote both the function f as well as the canonical text for f. Moreover, $f[n]$ will denote both the partial function $\{\,(x, f(x)) \mid x < n\,\}$ and the initial segment of length n of the canonical text for f. Context will determine which one is intended. The obvious analogue to Proposition 4.15 may also be recorded here (in which the $\mathbf{M}^i$'s represent machines with domain SEG).

4.22 Proposition *Let* $\mathbf{M}^0, \mathbf{M}^1, \ldots$ *be an enumeration of all (possibly partial) computable scientists. There is a total recursive* $f \colon N \to N$ *such that for all* $i \in N$:

(a) $\mathbf{M}^{f(i)}$ *is total;*

(b) *For all* $g \in \mathcal{R}$, *if* $\mathbf{M}^i$ *identifies* g *then* $\mathbf{M}^{f(i)}$ *identifies* g.

4.23 Corollary *There exists a recursively enumerable sequence of total computable scientists* $\mathbf{M}_0, \mathbf{M}_1, \ldots$, *such that* $(\forall \mathcal{S} \in \mathbf{Ex})(\exists i)[\mathcal{S} \subseteq \mathbf{Ex}(\mathbf{M}_i)]$.

§4.3.2 Identifiability in Ex

Proposition 3.43 shows that the identifiability problem has a trivial solution in the **Func** paradigm: every set of total recursive functions is identifiable. In contrast, identifiability within **Ex** is not such a simple affair, as we shall now see. Define two subsets of $\mathcal{R}$ as follows.

4.24 Definition

(a) $\mathcal{SD}$ is the set of all $f \in \mathcal{R}$ such that $\varphi_{f(0)} = f$.

(b) $\mathcal{AEZ}$ is the set of all $f \in \mathcal{R}$ such that for all but finitely many $x \in N$, $f(x) = 0$.

The symbol $\mathcal{SD}$ may be read as "self-describing." The symbol $\mathcal{AEZ}$ may be read as "almost everywhere zero." Lemma 2.4 shows that $\mathcal{SD} \neq \emptyset$.

4.25 Theorem (The Nonunion Theorem, Blum and Blum [18]) $\mathcal{SD} \in \mathbf{Ex}$ *and* $\mathcal{AEZ} \in \mathbf{Ex}$, *but* $\mathcal{SD} \cup \mathcal{AEZ} \notin \mathbf{Ex}$.

Proof: Exercise 4-10 shows that both $\mathcal{SD}$ and $\mathcal{AEZ}$ are in **Ex**. It remains to prove that $\mathcal{SD} \cup \mathcal{AEZ} \notin \mathbf{Ex}$. So, suppose that computable scientist $\mathbf{M}$ identifies $\mathcal{AEZ}$. By Proposition 4.22 we may assume without loss of generality that $\mathbf{M}$ is total. It suffices to exhibit an element of $\mathcal{SD}$ that $\mathbf{M}$ fails to identify. By use of the recursion theorem, we shall exhibit an index e such that:

4.26   (a) $\varphi_e \in \mathcal{R}$. (b) $\mathbf{M}$ fails to identify φ_e. (c) $\varphi_e(0) = e$.

Given such an e, φ_e is the required element of $\mathcal{SD}$.

We construct φ_e in stages. For each s, σ^s will denote the finite initial segment of the graph of φ_e defined as of the end of stage s. We will have $\sigma^s \subseteq \sigma^{s+1}$, and we let $\varphi_e = \{\, (x, y) \mid (\exists s)[(x, y) \in content(\sigma^s)]\,\}$.

By the recursion theorem we can choose e such that $\varphi_e(0) = e$, and we set $\sigma^0 = \varphi_e[1]$ (that is $\sigma^0 = (0, e)$). For remaining stages of the construction we rely on the following claim.

4.27 Claim *Given a $\sigma \in$ INIT, one can effectively find a $\tau \in$ INIT such that $\sigma \subseteq \tau$ and $\mathbf{M}(\sigma) \neq \mathbf{M}(\tau)$.*

Proof: (of Claim 4.27) Note that if there exists a $\tau \supseteq \sigma$ such that $\mathbf{M}(\sigma) \neq \mathbf{M}(\tau)$ one can effectively find such a τ by exhaustive search. Therefore it suffices to show that for each σ there is such a τ. Suppose for a contradiction that for all canonical $\tau \supseteq \sigma$, $\mathbf{M}(\sigma) = \mathbf{M}(\tau)$. But then $\mathbf{M}$ can **Ex**-identify at most one function whose canonical text begins with σ. Since there are infinitely many functions in $\mathcal{AEZ}$ whose canonical text begins with σ, we have a contradiction to $\mathbf{M}$ **Ex**-identifying each function in $\mathcal{AEZ}$. $\square$

Here then is the construction.

The Construction of φ_e:

Stage 0: $\sigma^0 = (0, e)$.

Stage s+1: Suppose that σ^s has been defined. Find a canonical $\tau \supseteq \sigma^s$ such that $\mathbf{M}(\sigma^s) \neq \mathbf{M}(\tau)$. (By Claim 4.27 such a τ can be found effectively from σ^s.) Set $\sigma^{s+1} = \tau$.

It is easy to verify that φ_e satisfies 4.26 as promised.   ∎

Theorem 4.25 shows that **Ex** is not closed under union. As another corollary we have:

4.28 Theorem (Gold [80]) $\mathcal{R} \notin \mathbf{Ex}$.

§4.3.3 Finding unidentified functions

For this subsection, let $\mathbf{M}_0$, $\mathbf{M}_1$, ... be an indexing of total computable scientists as in Corollary 4.23. Now, Theorem 4.28 states that for every computable scientist $\mathbf{M}$, there is $f \in \mathcal{R}$ such that $\mathbf{M}$ does not identify f. But can an index for such an f be found effectively from an index for $\mathbf{M}$? An affirmative answer to this question would imply the existence of a total recursive $h : N \to N$ such that:

4.29   (a) for all $i \in N$, $\varphi_{h(i)} \in \mathcal{R}$, and

   (b) $\mathbf{M}_i$ does not identify $\varphi_{h(i)}$.

However, we now show:

4.30 Proposition *There is no total recursive $h : N \to N$ that satisfies the conditions in 4.29.*

Proof: Suppose by way of contradiction that there is such an h. Then by the recursion theorem there is an e such that for all σ, $\mathbf{M}_e(\sigma) = h(e)$. Clearly, $\mathbf{M}_e$ identifies $\varphi_{h(e)}$, a contradiction. ∎

Proposition 4.30 shows that no evil demon of a mechanical nature can examine the internal program of a given scientist and then select a function that the scientist fails to identify. On the other hand, the demon can map an arbitrary scientist's program into a different conundrum, described by the following proposition.

4.31 Proposition *There is a total recursive function $h : N \to N$ such that for all $i \in N$:*

(a) $W_{h(i)}$ contains exactly one index for a total function, say, j ($W_{h(i)}$ may or may not contain indexes for partial functions);

(b) $\mathbf{M}_i$ does not identify φ_j; and

(c) $\varphi_j(0) = i$.

Clause (c) means that φ_j "names" the scientist $\mathbf{M}_i$ for which $W_{h(i)}$ has been constructed (this property of h will be used later).

Proof: Let $i \in N$ be given. We describe, in stages, a procedure that uses $\mathbf{M}_i$ to enumerate the graphs of functions (in canonical order). Although many graphs will be initiated, only one will be extended indefinitely; the others will terminate after some finite initial segment. $\mathbf{M}_i$ will fail to identify the unique total function to be enumerated. Our construction will be uniformly effective in i and thus constitutes the witness h to the proposition. The following terminology is needed. First, we fix a standard method (uniform in i) for enumerating the set:

$$\mathbf{G} \;=\; \{\,(\sigma, x, y) \mid \sigma \in \mathrm{SEG},\; x, y \in N,\; \text{and}\; \varphi_{\mathbf{M}_i(\sigma)}(x) = y\,\}.$$

Next, given $x, y \in N$ and $\sigma \in \mathrm{SEG}$, we say that $\mathbf{M}_i$ "predicts (x, y) on σ" just in case:

(a) $\varphi_{\mathbf{M}_i(\sigma)}(x) = y$ and

(b) no pair of the form (x, z) occurs in *content*(σ) for any $z \in N$.

Finally, given text G and $x, y, j, m \in N$, we say that $\mathbf{M}_i$ "is seen within m steps to predict (x, y) in G at point j" just in case $\mathbf{M}_i$ predicts (x, y) on $G[j + 1]$, and $(G[j + 1], x, y)$ emerges from our standard enumeration of $\mathbf{G}$ within m steps of computation.

We now give a procedure for enumerating the graph of a (possibly partial) function f as well as (possibly partial) functions $g_0, g_1, \ldots$. (There may be finitely or infinitely many g_i.) Exactly one of these functions will be total and each of the other functions will be defined on some finite initial segment of N. (Which of these functions will be total depends on the behavior of $\mathbf{M}_i$.) The enumeration of a function's graph proceeds by specifying its canonical text. In particular, G_f will denote the canonical text that enumerates f. Initially, $G_f = (0, i)$.

Procedure for enumerating the graphs of f and the g_i's

Stage n: Suppose that p is the current length of G_f. Let $G = G_f[p] \diamond (p, 0) \diamond (p + 1, 0) \ldots$. Search for the least number $\langle x, j, m \rangle$ such that $p \le j < x, m$ and $\mathbf{M}_i$ is seen in m steps to predict $(x, 0)$ in G at point j. If such a $\langle x, j, m \rangle$ exists, then set $g_n = G_f[p] \diamond (p, 0) \diamond (p + 1, 0) \diamond \ldots \diamond (m, 0)$ and also set

$$G_f[x + 1] \;=\; G_f[p] \diamond (p, 0) \diamond (p + 1, 0) \diamond \ldots \diamond (j, 0) \diamond \ldots \diamond (x, 1).$$

If no such $\langle x, j, m \rangle$ exists, then let g_n be the function whose graph is enumerated by G and extend G_f no further. Proceed to the next stage only if $\langle x, j, m \rangle$ exists; in this case, no more pairs will be enumerated into g_n, which is thus finite. (Observe that if $\langle x, j, m \rangle$ exists then no matter how f is extended subsequently, $\mathbf{M}_i$ has made a new, incorrect guess about f on $G_f[j + 1]$. On the other hand, if no such $\langle x, j, m \rangle$ exists, then f is finite, g_n is total, $\mathbf{M}_i$ fails to identify g_n's canonical text, and no other functions are created.)

It is easy to verify that if the construction proceeds through only n many stages, then:

(a) only $n + 2$ functions $f, g_0, g_1, \ldots, g_n$ are specified;

(b) only g_n is total; and

(c) $\mathbf{M}_i$ fails to identify g_n's canonical text.

On the other hand, if the construction proceeds through infinitely many stages, then:

(a) infinitely many functions $f, g_0, g_1, \ldots$ are specified;

(b) only f is total; and

(c) $\mathbf{M}_i$ fails to identify f's canonical text.

So in either case, $\mathbf{M}_i$ fails to identify the one, total function specified. Finally, observe that for all of the functions h specified in the construction (whether partial or total), $h(0) = i$. ∎

§4.4 Parameterized scientists

Real scientists are sensitive not only to evidence from their laboratories but also to general information about the character of the scientific problem they confront. In particular, the hypothesis produced by scientists in response to given data depends in part on the background knowledge they obtain from teachers and colleagues. Such knowledge rules out certain logically possible realities and embraces others. In the paradigms discussed so far, it is not possible to communicate with scientists in this sense. They thus have "one-track minds," being adapted to a single class of possibilities but no others. This feature of scientists is appropriate for modeling language acquisition — since parents have no means of informing infants about the class of human languages — but limits the fidelity of our results to adult, scientific discovery. The present section introduces a model in which scientists are given a description of a class of theoretical possibilities and must then adapt their conjectures accordingly. The ideas in this section are due to Jantke [98], and explored further by Osherson, Stob, and Weinstein [141].

§4.4.1 Communicating with scientists

Numbers will be used to inform scientists of the class of theoretical possibilities they face. The following definition shows how numbers are used for this purpose.

4.32 Definition

(a) Any mapping of N into the power set of $\mathcal{E}$ is a *descriptor for languages*.

(b) Any mapping of N into the power set of $\mathcal{R}$ is a *descriptor for functions*.

Thus, a descriptor for languages maps each natural number into a collection of languages, and similarly for descriptors for functions. In the context of descriptor **DL**, we call $i \in N$ a "description" of **DL**(i). Description i may be conceived as an inductive inference problem posed to a scientist, namely, the problem of identifying **DL**(i). A well-rounded, generally intelligent scientist should respond to i by adapting her scientific strategy in such a way that she identifies the described collection **DL**(i). Here are two examples of descriptors that will occupy us in the sequel.

4.33 Definition

(a) $[\cdot]$ denotes the descriptor for languages defined as follows. For all $i \in N$, $[i] = \{W_j \mid j \in W_i\}$.

(b) $[\cdot]_f$ denotes the descriptor for functions defined as follows. For all $i \in N$, $[i]_f = \{\varphi_j \in \mathcal{R} \mid j \in W_i\}$.

Thus, $[\cdot]$ interprets i as the collection of all languages with indexes in W_i. $[\cdot]_f$ interprets i as the collection of all total recursive functions with indexes in W_i. Note that W_i may well contain indexes j such that φ_j is only partial, hence not a member of $\mathcal{R}$. Such partial functions φ_j are not described by $[i]_f$ and hence do not figure in the scientific problem posed by i. Indexes in $[i]_f$ for nontotal functions should thus be considered as "noise" in the description. No such noise occurs for $[\cdot]$. In this sense, $[\cdot]$ is more transparent than $[\cdot]_f$.

Given $i \in N$, W_i may contain equivalent indexes, that is, multiple indexes for the same language. It is thus possible for W_i to have more members than $[i]$. The same is true of $[\cdot]_f$. This is a sense in which neither descriptor is perfectly transparent.

Scientists that accept descriptions of problems have an additional, numerical argument. They are thus called "parameterized."

4.34 Definition

(a) A *parameterized scientist for languages* is any computable mapping (partial or total) from $N \times$ SEQ into N.

(b) A *parameterized scientist for functions* is any computable mapping (partial or total) from $N \times$ SEG into N.

By "parameterized scientist" is meant either parameterized scientist for languages or for functions; context determines which kind is at issue. As a variable for parameterized scientists, we use Γ.

If the first argument, i, of a parameterized scientist Γ is fixed, the resulting function is just a scientist in the usual sense. This scientist can be denoted by $\lambda\sigma.\Gamma(i,\sigma)$. The $\lambda\sigma$ signifies that Γ is to be considered as a function only of its second argument, the first argument having been fixed at i. Thus, if Γ is a parameterized scientist for languages, then for every $i \in N$, $\lambda\sigma.\Gamma(i,\sigma)$ is a computable function from SEQ to N.

In general, a parameterized scientist can identify some of the collections described to it but not others; and it may succeed if the description is described in one way but not another. To characterize the competence of a parameterized scientist we rely on the following definition.

4.35 Definition Let $X \subseteq N$, parameterized scientist Γ, and descriptor **DL** (either for languages or functions) be given. Γ *performs* X *on* **DL** just in case for all $i \in X$, $\lambda\sigma.\Gamma(i,\sigma)$ identifies **DL**(i). X is *performable on* **DL** just in case some parameterized scientist performs X on **DL**.

Thus, to perform $X \subseteq N$ on **DL**, Γ must convert any description $i \in X$ into a scientist $\lambda\sigma.\Gamma(i,\sigma)$ that identifies **DL**(i). In this sense a parameterized scientist may be conceived as a device that synthesizes ordinary scientists on the basis of input problem descriptions. The synthesizer provides trustworthy responses only to the set of descriptions that it performs.

§4.4.2 Performability on [·]

Suppose that $i_0 \in N$ is such that W_{i_0} contains an index for N and also an index for each finite set. Then by Corollary 3.28, no $X \subseteq N$ for which $i_0 \in X$ is performable on [·]. Is unidentifiability the only reason for nonperformability? That is, if $[i] \in$ **TxtEx** for all $i \in X$, does it follow that X is performable on [·]? We shall now see that the answer is negative inasmuch as every finite collection of languages is identifiable (Exercise 4-1), yet $\{\, i \in N \mid W_i \text{ finite } \}$ is not performable on [·]. Indeed, the next proposition makes an even stronger claim.

4.36 Proposition $\{i \in N \mid card(W_i) = 2\}$ *is not performable on* [·].

Proof: Fix a parameterized scientist Γ. Let p be an index for N and let h be a recursive function such that for all j, $W_{h(j)} = \{\, p, j \,\}$. By an application of the recursion theorem we shall construct an e such that $\lambda\sigma.\Gamma(h(e),\sigma)$ fails to identify $\{\, W_j \mid j \in W_{h(e)} \,\} = \{\, W_p, W_e \,\}$. The existence of such an e implies the proposition.

We will construct W_e in stages $s = -1, 0, 1, 2, \ldots$. By the recursion theorem we allow the construction to have access to the desired index e. The construction of W_e may complete all the stages, or else reach only finitely many of them. In each stage s that is entered we define a number $m_s \in N$, and a text T^s, and also indicate what new elements are enumerated into W_e. It will be the case that at the end of every completed, odd-numbered stage s, T^s is a text for N, and for every completed, even-numbered stage s, T^s is a text for the finite part of W_e enumerated by the end of stage s.

Stage −1: Set $m_{-1} = 0$ and $T^{-1} = 0, 1, 2, \ldots$. Leave W_e empty.

Stage 2n, for $n \geq 0$: Suppose that m_{2n-1} and text T^{2n-1} for N have been defined. Search for $m_{2n} > m_{2n-1}$ such that

$$content(T^{2n-1}[m_{2n}]) \subset W_x, \quad \text{where } x = \Gamma(h(e), T^{2n-1}[m_{2n}]).$$

If the search for m_{2n} fails to terminate, then the enumeration of W_e ceases at this stage. In this case, W_e is finite, and $\lambda\sigma.\Gamma(h(e), \sigma)$ fails to identify the text T^{2n-1} for N, because for each $m > m_{2n-1}$, $\Gamma(h(e), T^{2n-1}[m])$ is an index for a language that does not properly include $content(T^{2n-1}[m])$. If the search for m_{2n} is successful, then enumerate the contents of $T^{2n-1}[m_{2n}]$ into W_e and set text

$$T^{2n} = T^{2n-1}[m_{2n}] \diamond \# \diamond \# \ldots.$$

Note that T^{2n} is a text for the finite set of numbers enumerated into W_e up to this stage.

Stage 2n+1, for $n \geq 0$: Suppose that text T^{2n} and m_{2n} have been defined. Search for $m_{2n+1} > m_{2n}$ such that

$$\Gamma(h(e), T^{2n}[m_{2n}]) \neq \Gamma(h(e), T^{2n}[m_{2n+1}]).$$

If the search for m_{2n+1} fails to terminate, then the enumeration of W_e ceases at this stage. In this case, T^{2n} is a text for the finite language W_e, and $\lambda\sigma.\Gamma(h(e), \sigma)$ fails to identify T^{2n} because it converges on T^{2n} to an index for a superset of $content(T^{2n}) = W_e$. If the search for m_{2n+1} is successful, then enumerate $content(T^{2n}[m_{2n+1}]) \cup \{n\}$ into W_e and set text

$$T^{2n+1} = T^{2n}[m_{2n+1}] \diamond n \diamond 0, 1, 2, \ldots.$$

Note that T^{2n+1} is a text for N.

If the enumeration of W_e fails to progress past some even stage of the foregoing construction, then W_e is finite and $\lambda\sigma.\Gamma(h(e), \sigma)$ fails to identify some text for N.

If the enumeration of W_e fails to progress past some odd stage, then W_e is finite and $\lambda\sigma.\Gamma(h(e),\sigma)$ fails to identify some text for W_e.

If the construction progresses past all stages, then $W_e = N$ and $\lambda\sigma.\Gamma(h(e),\sigma)$ fails to converge on some text for W_e and so fails to identify W_e (in this case e and p are equivalent indexes, both for N).

Thus, in all cases $\lambda\sigma.\Gamma(h(e),\sigma)$ fails to identify $\{W_p, W_e\} = [h(e)]$. ∎

In conjunction with Exercise 4-1, Proposition 4.36 implies:

4.37 Corollary $\{i \in N \mid [i] \text{ is identifiable}\}$ *is not performable on* $[\cdot]$.

Thus, no parameterized scientist can adapt herself to the identification of an arbitrary, identifiable $\mathcal{L} \subseteq \mathcal{E}$ on the basis of an $[\cdot]$ description of $\mathcal{L}$. In this sense there is no universal learning machine for $[\cdot]$ and **TxtEx**.

The proof of Proposition 4.36 rests on the possible presence of equivalent indexes in the description of a class of languages. Disallowing such equivalences in fact makes performability easier. The next definition helps to make this claim precise.

4.38 Definition $\mathcal{NE} = \{i \in N \mid \text{for all } j,k \in W_i, j \neq k \text{ implies } W_j \neq W_k\}$.

So, if $i \in \mathcal{NE}$ then W_i contains no two equivalent indices. (The symbol "$\mathcal{NE}$" may be read as "no equivalences.")

4.39 Proposition $\{i \in \mathcal{NE} \mid card(W_i) \text{ is finite}\}$ *is performable on* $[\cdot]$.

Proof: Exercise 4-15.

Is the finiteness qualification in Proposition 4.39 essential? The next proposition shows that it is.

4.40 Proposition $\{i \in \mathcal{NE} \mid [i] \text{ is identifiable}\}$ *is not performable on* $[\cdot]$.

Thus, no parameterized scientist can adapt itself to the identification of an arbitrary, identifiable $\mathcal{L} \subseteq \mathcal{E}$ even on the basis of an $[\cdot]$ description of $\mathcal{L}$ that is purged of equivalent indices. A proof of 4.40 is given in Osherson, Stob, and Weinstein [141, Proposition 3C] and omitted here.

§4.4.3 Performability on $[\cdot]_f$

If n is an index for N, then Theorem 4.28 shows that no superset of $\{n\}$ is performable on $[\cdot]_f$. However, nonperformability also infects much simpler sets of indexes, as the following proposition reveals.

4.41 Proposition (Jantke [98]) *Let $I \subseteq N$ be the set of all indexes x with the following property: there is exactly one $j \in W_x$ such that φ_j is total. Then I is not performable on $[\cdot]_f$.*

So, no parameterized scientist can take an arbitrary $i \in I$ and adapt itself to identify the sole $f \in \mathcal{R}$ with an index in W_i.

Proof:[4] Let total recursive h be the function guaranteed by Proposition 4.31. Then:

4.42   For all $i \in N$, $h(i) \in I$.

Given $i \in N$, let g_i be the sole member of $\mathcal{R}$ with an index in $W_{h(i)}$. It follows immediately from 4.31 that:

4.43 $\{g_i \mid i \in N\}$ is not identifiable.

Now for a contradiction, suppose that parameterized scientist Γ performs I on $[\cdot]_f$. Then:

4.44   For all $i \in N$, $\lambda\sigma.\Gamma(h(i), \sigma)$ identifies g_i.

Define (unparameterized) scientist **M** as follows. For all $\sigma \in \text{SEG}$, if $content(\sigma)$ does not contain exactly one occurrence of a pair of the form $(0, i)$, then **M** is undefined. Otherwise, if $(0, i) \in content(\sigma)$ then $\mathbf{M}(\sigma) = \Gamma(h(i), \sigma)$. It follows from 4.44 that **M** identifies $\{g_i \mid i \in N\}$, contradicting 4.43.   ∎

4.45 Corollary $\{i \in N \mid [i]_f \text{ is identifiable}\}$ *is not performable on $[\cdot]_f$.*

It is the presence of indexes for nontotal functions in the descriptions delivered by $[\cdot]_f$ that causes nonperformability. To see this, we first define the set of descriptions free of this problem.

4.46 Definition $\mathcal{AT} = \{i \in N \mid \text{ for all } j \in W_i, \varphi_j \in \mathcal{R}\}$.

The symbol "$\mathcal{AT}$" may be read as "all total." We leave the following proposition as an exercise.

---

[4] A different proof is given in [98].

4.47 Proposition $\mathcal{AT}$ *is performable on* $[\cdot]_f$.

Further discussion of parameterized scientists may be found in Jantke [98].

§4.5 Exact identification

In this final section of the chapter, we advance a paradigm designed to refine the constraints on comparative grammar provided by considerations of learnability (see Section 3.1.2, above). Only the identification of languages is at issue.

§4.5.1 Exact learning and comparative grammar

The converse of the dictum that natural languages are learnable by children (via casual exposure) is that nonnatural languages are not learnable. Put differently, the natural languages are generally taken to be the *largest* collection of child-learnable languages. We are thus led to consider paradigms in which learners are required to respond successfully to all languages in a given collection and to respond unsuccessfully to all other languages. One such paradigm relies on a modification of the identification concept that is defined as follows.

4.48 Definition

(a) Let scientist $\mathbf{F}\colon \mathrm{SEQ} \to N$ and $\mathcal{L} \subseteq \mathcal{E}$ be given. $\mathbf{F}$ *identifies* $\mathcal{L}$ *exactly* just in case for all texts T, $\mathbf{F}$ identifies T if and only if T is for some $L \in \mathcal{L}$. In this case $\mathcal{L}$ is *exactly identifiable*.

(b) The class of all $\mathcal{L} \subseteq \mathcal{E}$ such that some computable $\mathbf{M}\colon \mathrm{SEQ} \to N$ identifies $\mathcal{L}$ exactly is denoted by **TxtExExact**.

For example, the scientist defined in the proof of Proposition 3.18 identifies $\{N - \{x\} \mid x \in N\}$ exactly. Similarly, let g be some recursive function such that $W_{g(\sigma)} = content(\sigma)$ for each $\sigma \in \mathrm{SEQ}$ and consider a scientist $\mathbf{F}$ that on $\sigma \in \mathrm{SEQ}$ emits $g(\sigma)$. Clearly, this $\mathbf{F}$ identifies $\mathcal{FIN}$ exactly. Hence $\mathcal{FIN} \in \mathbf{TxtExExact}$.

Two points should be borne in mind about Definition 4.48. First, if $\mathbf{F}$ identifies $\mathcal{L} \subseteq \mathcal{E}$, then $\mathbf{F}$ identifies every subset of $\mathcal{L}$ and may identify some proper supersets of $\mathcal{L}$ as well (see Exercise 3-3). In contrast, if $\mathbf{F}$ identifies $\mathcal{L}$ exactly, then $\mathbf{F}$ exactly identifies no collection $\mathcal{L}' \neq \mathcal{L}$. Second, if $\mathbf{F}$ identifies $\mathcal{L} \subseteq \mathcal{E}$ exactly, then there is a strong sense in which $\mathbf{F}$ fails to identify $L \notin \mathcal{L}$; namely, $\mathbf{F}$ fails to identify *any* text for such an L, not simply one text. A weaker version of the exact identification paradigm is discussed in Exercise 4-21.

Since each scientist exactly identifies only one collection of languages, **TxtExExact** can contain no more collections than there are computable scientists to exactly identify them. Hence, the cardinality of **TxtExExact** is at most countably infinite. On the other hand, every singleton collection $\{W_i\}$ of languages is exactly identifiable. So **TxtExExact** is countably infinite. In contrast, **TxtEx** is uncountable. This is because **TxtEx** contains collections with infinitely many members ($\mathcal{FIN}$, for example) and each of the uncountably many subsets of such a collection is also in **TxtEx**. We conclude:

4.49 Proposition (**TxtEx** − **TxtExExact**) *is uncountable.*

Proposition 4.49 shows that the criterion of exact identification places more constraint on theories of human language than does identification *tout court*. Should we require of such a theory that it embrace an exactly identifiable collection? Although the remarks at the beginning of this section suggest an affirmative response, the matter is clouded by the following consideration.

Human languages are not only learnable, they are also highly *expressive* in the sense that many thoughts can be communicated within any one of them. Let us therefore stipulate that a language be counted as human just in case it is both learnable and highly expressive. Now consider the impoverished language consisting of the single expression "Go!" with its usual meaning. The Go-language may well be learnable by children through casual exposure. If so, then not every learnable language is human, and hence the human languages are a proper subset of the class of learnable languages. This entails that a theory of human language can be legitimately evaluated against the standard of identifiability, but not against the standard of exact identifiability.

It may be possible to disarm the foregoing objection to exact learning. There is evidence that children exposed to inexpressive languages (e.g., pidgins) as well as children denied access to any ambient language (e.g., deaf children in certain circumstances) invent linguistic devices of considerable complexity and communicative potential (see Feldman, Goldin-Meadow, and Gleitman [57], Sankoff and Brown [166], Bickerton [17], and Gleitman and Newport [79]). These findings suggest that children may not be capable of learning profoundly inexpressive languages. If this is true, then the human languages coincide exactly with the learnable languages, and exact identifiability is the appropriate standard for the evaluation of theories of comparative grammar.

Finally, suppose that certain inexpressive languages turn out to be learnable after all. In this case it is possible that comparative grammar can be investigated more successfully if such languages are admitted as human, perhaps as special cases. Exact identification would then, once again, be the appropriate standard of learnability.

§4.6 Summary

Computable scientists occupy center stage in our theory of scientific inquiry. To study them we extend our conception of Turing Machines so that they also represent functions from SEQ to N and from SEG to N. The choice of domain depends on whether we consider natural numbers as codes for SEQ or for SEG. In either case, the class of computable scientists is indexed as $\mathbf{M}_i$.

A wide variety of paradigms are defined and analyzed in the chapters to follow. For concision, each is associated with a symbolic name that refers to the family of collections of languages or functions that can be identified within them. For example, **Lang** is the family of all collections of languages that can be identified in the sense of Section 3.4, and **Func** is the family of all identifiable collections of functions in the sense of Section 3.9.4. Restricting attention to computable scientists, these paradigms become **TxtEx** and **Ex**, respectively.

Introducing the computability constraint on scientists limits the collections that can be identified. In particular, it was shown that both **Lang** − **TxtEx** and **Func** − **Ex** are nonempty. When computability is considered in conjunction with other characteristics of scientists, the impact on identifiability is not straightforwardly deducible from the impact of each characteristic considered separately. This was illustrated by considering the kinds of collections of languages that can be identified by scientists who are either computable, memory-limited, or both.

Real scientists have flexibility that is not represented by functions from SEQ or SEG to N. In particular, scientists can often take account of background knowledge communicated to them from an external source such as colleagues or professors. To incorporate this feature of empirical inquiry into our theory we consider "parameterized scientists" who receive an additional, numerical input. The input is conceived as a code for a class of languages or functions that delimit the possible realities that the scientist must envision. Given a set of such codes, we ask whether there exists a computable, parameterized scientist that can identify the class associated with any code in the set. Two kinds of codes were considered, one for communicating classes of languages to scientists, the other for communicating classes of functions.

Finally, we returned to the study of comparative grammar and observed that the class of human languages is generally defined as including *all and only* the languages that children can acquire in normal fashion. This reflection leads to a new criterion of successful performance called "exact identification." To identify exactly a collection $\mathcal{L}$ of languages the learner must identify $\mathcal{L}$ and fail to identify any text for any language outside of $\mathcal{L}$.

§4.7 Exercises

4-1   Suppose that $\mathcal{L} \subset \mathcal{E}$ contain only finitely many languages. Show that $\mathcal{L} \in \textbf{TxtEx}$.

4-2   Let K be the r.e., nonrecursive set defined on page 25. Define

$$\mathcal{K}^0 \ = \ \{\, K \cup \{x\} \mid x \in \overline{K}\,\}.$$

Show that $\mathcal{K}^0 \in \textbf{TxtEx}$.

4-3   Given a class $\mathcal{M}$ of scientists, denote by $\|\mathcal{M}\|$ the class of $\mathcal{L} \subseteq \mathcal{E}$ such that some $\mathbf{M} \in \mathcal{M}$ identifies $\mathcal{L}$.

(a) Show that if $\mathcal{M} \subset \mathcal{M}'$, then $\|\mathcal{M}\| \subseteq \|\mathcal{M}'\|$ but $\|\mathcal{M}\| = \|\mathcal{M}'\|$ is possible.

(b) Evaluate the validity of the following claims.

    (i) $\|\mathcal{M} \cup \mathcal{M}'\| = \|\mathcal{M}\| \cup \|\mathcal{M}'\|$.

    (ii) $\|\mathcal{M} \cap \mathcal{M}'\| \subseteq \|\mathcal{M}\| \cap \|\mathcal{M}'\|$.

    (iii) $\|\mathcal{M} \cap \mathcal{M}'\| \supseteq \|\mathcal{M}\| \cap \|\mathcal{M}'\|$.

    (iv) $\|\{\,\varphi_i \mid i \in N\,\} - \mathcal{M}\| = \|\{\,\varphi_i \mid i \in N\,\}\| - \|\mathcal{M}\|$.

4-4   Given $i \in N$, let $L_i = \{0, 1, \ldots, i\}$. Let $\mathcal{L} = \{L_i \mid i \in N\}$. Suppose that $\mathcal{L}' \in \textbf{TxtEx}$. Show that $\mathcal{L} \cup \mathcal{L}' \in \textbf{TxtEx}$ if and only if $N \notin \mathcal{L}'$.

4-5   Show that $\textbf{TxtEx}$ is not closed under finite union.

4-6   Show that there is $\mathcal{L} \subseteq \mathcal{E}$ with the following properties.

(a) $\mathcal{L} \in \textbf{TxtEx}$.

(b) Some scientist (not necessarily computable) identifies $\mathcal{L}$ confidently (see Exercise 3-21).

(c) No computable scientist identifies $\mathcal{L}$ confidently.

4-7 (Angluin [6]) Most practical classes of languages are uniformly decidable. A sequence of nonempty languages $L_0, L_1, \ldots$ is an *indexed family* just in case there exists a computable function f such that for each $i \in N$ and for each $x \in N$,

$$f(i, x) \quad = \quad \begin{cases} 1 & \text{if } x \in L_i, \\ 0 & \text{otherwise.} \end{cases}$$

In other words, there is a uniform decision procedure for languages in the class. The purpose of this and the next two exercises is to explore the identifiability of indexed families of computable languages. In this exercise we establish Angluin's characterization (described in Theorem 3.26) for an indexed family of computable languages. To this end, we define a finite tell-tale set.

Let $\mathcal{L} = \{ L_i \mid i \in N \}$ be an indexed family of computable languages. A is a *finite tell-tale* of L_i just in case A is a finite subset of L_i and there is no j such that $A \subseteq L_j \subset L_i$.

Show that an indexed family of computable languages $\mathcal{L} = \{ L_i \mid i \in N \}$ belongs to **TxtEx** just in case there is a procedure, effective in i, that enumerates all elements in a finite tell-tale of L_i.

There has been considerable work on identification of several natural indexed families of computable languages, e.g., subclasses of elementary formal systems, of logic programming languages, and of formal languages in the Chomsky hierarchy. For results on elementary formal systems, we refer the reader to the papers of Arikawa, Miyano, Ayumi Shinohara, Takeshi Shinohara, and Yamamoto [9, 8, 175]. Sample results about identification of logic programming languages can be found in Arimura and Shinohara [10] and Krishna Rao [112]. Yokomori [205] contains results about identification of languages accepted by a class of deterministic automata. See Sakakibara [165] for a survey of related results about grammatical inference.

4-8 (Angluin [5]) A collection of languages $\mathcal{L}$ has *finite thickness* just in case for each $n \in N$, $card(\{ L \in \mathcal{L} \mid n \in L \})$ is finite.

Show that if an indexed family of computable languages $\mathcal{L}$ has finite thickness, then $\mathcal{L} \in$ **TxtEx**.

4-9 (Wright [204], see also Motoki, Shinohara, and Wright [133]) A collection of languages $\mathcal{L}$ has *infinite elasticity* just in case there exists an infinite sequence of pairwise distinct numbers, $\{ w_i \in N \mid i \in N \}$, and an infinite sequence of pairwise distinct languages, $\{\, A_i \in \mathcal{L} \mid i \in N \,\}$, such that for each $k \in N$, $\{\, w_i \mid i < k \,\} \subseteq A_k$, but $w_k \notin A_k$. $\mathcal{L}$ is said to have *finite elasticity* just in case $\mathcal{L}$ does not have infinite elasticity.

1. If a class of languages has finite thickness, then show that it has finite elasticity.

2. Show that if an indexed family of computable languages $\mathcal{L}$ has finite elasticity, then $\mathcal{L} \in \textbf{TxtEx}$.

4-10   Show that both $\mathcal{SD}$ and $\mathcal{AEZ}$ are members of **Ex**.

4-11   Does the analogue to Proposition 4.30 hold for language identification?

4-12   Let $\mathcal{C} \in \textbf{Ex}$ be given. Show that there is $\mathcal{C}' \supset \mathcal{C}$ such that $\mathcal{C}' \in \textbf{Ex}$.

4-13   Consider the scientist **F** defined in the proof of Theorem 3.43. It follows from Theorem 4.28 that **F** is not computable. Describe the aspect of **F** that renders it uncomputable.

4-14   Show that Proposition 3.46 can be strengthened to the following: There is $\mathcal{L} \in \textbf{Ex}$ such that no memory limited scientist (computable or not) identifies $\mathcal{L}$.

4-15   Prove Proposition 4.39.

4-16   Prove Proposition 4.47.

4-17   Let $J \subseteq N$ be the set of all indexes x such that $card(W_x)$ is finite. Show that J is performable on $[\cdot]_f$.

4-18   Let $\mathcal{K}^0$ be as defined in Exercise 4-2. Show that $\mathcal{K}^0 \in \textbf{TxtExExact}$.

4-19   Suppose that (not necessarily computable) $\textbf{F} \colon \mathrm{SEQ} \to N$ identifies $\mathcal{L} \subseteq \mathcal{E}$ exactly. Show that for all $L \in \mathcal{E}$, $L \in \mathcal{L}$ if and only if there is a locking sequence for **F** on L.

4-20   (*Advanced*) Show that $\mathcal{L} \in \textbf{TxtExExact}$ if and only if $\mathcal{L} \in \textbf{TxtEx}$ and $\mathcal{L}$ is arithmetically indexable.

Hint: Use Exercise 4-19.

4-21 (***Advanced***) We define a success criterion in the spirit of exact identification but somewhat weaker.[5] Given scientist **F** and $\mathcal{L} \subseteq \mathcal{E}$, **F** *exactly identifies $\mathcal{L}$ in the weak sense* just in case **F** identifies $\mathcal{L}$ and **F** identifies no language in the complement of $\mathcal{L}$. The class of all $\mathcal{L} \subseteq \mathcal{E}$ such that some computable $\mathbf{M} : \mathrm{SEQ} \to N$ identifies $\mathcal{L}$ exactly in the weak sense is denoted by **TxtExWeakExact**. Prove:

(a) $\mathcal{L} \in$ **TxtExWeakExact** if and only if $\mathcal{L} \in$ **TxtEx** and $\mathcal{L}$ is Π_1^1 indexable.

(b) There is $\mathcal{L} \in$ **TxtExWeakExact** such that $\mathcal{L}$ is not Σ_1^1 indexable.

Conclude that **TxtExExact** $\subset$ **TxtExWeakExact**.

---

[5] For the background to this exercise, see Rogers [158, Chapters 14,16] or Shoenfield [176, Chapters 6,7].

Part II

Fundamental Paradigms Generalized

5 Strategies for Learning

The paradigms **TxtEx** and **Ex** allow scientists to be any computable device whatsoever. This conception seems excessively general if only because human scientists (and the computers they build) operate under resource constraints involving time and memory. In addition, real scientists are apt to impose various methodological constraints upon their theorizing, for example, requiring that present hypotheses account for all available data. In the present chapter we formalize and investigate such constraints by considering the inductive competence of alternative subsets of the class of computable scientists. Any such subset is called a *strategy*, and the principal question it invites is whether every identifiable collection of languages or functions is identified by a member of the strategy. We shall see that the answer is often negative, even for strategies that appear to embody a rational canon of hypothesis selection. In this sense, many of the strategies to be defined below are restrictive constraints on scientists.

In terms of paradigms, the present chapter may be conceived as exploring alternative conceptions of *scientist*, while leaving untouched the interpretations of *theoretically possible reality, data* etc. that we introduced in Chapters 3 and 4. Let us also note the connection of strategies to language development in children. To the extent that human children are essentially identically endowed for language acquisition (which seems manifestly to be the case), their learning methods are drawn from an extremely narrow strategy in the sense defined above. So it is suggestive to examine the inductive capacity of diverse constraints on scientists in hopes of finding one that allows identification of just the languages children can assimilate. (See Section 3.1.2 for more discussion.)

In what follows, we first consider strategies for the identification of languages, and then of functions.

§5.1 Strategies for language identification: Introduction

We divide strategies for language learning into four groups:

1. constraints on potential conjectures,
2. constraints on the information available to a scientist,
3. constraints on convergence, and

4. constraints on the relation between conjectures.

The next four sections treat each of these in turn.

Relative to any given constraint a further distinction often arises. As an example, consider the requirement that conjectures must be consistent with the data that give rise to them. Formally, scientists satisfying this requirement have the property that on evidential state σ they output the index of a language that contains *content*(σ). Observe, however, that this requirement can be interpreted in the following two different ways.

1. *Global consistency:* A collection of languages, $\mathcal{L}$, is identifiable by a globally consistent scientist just in case there exists an **M** that is consistent on all $\sigma \in$ SEQ and **M** identifies $\mathcal{L}$. Such collections of languages are denoted $[\mathbf{TxtEx}]^{\text{consistent}}$.

2. *Class consistency:* A collection of languages $\mathcal{L}$ is identifiable by a class-consistent scientist just in case there exists an **M** that is consistent on all evidential states drawn from languages in $\mathcal{L}$ and **M** identifies $\mathcal{L}$. Such collections of languages are denoted $[\mathbf{TxtEx}]^{\text{class-consistent}}$.

Of course, the question immediately arises whether $[\mathbf{TxtEx}]^{\text{consistent}}$ is a proper subset of $[\mathbf{TxtEx}]^{\text{class-consistent}}$. (See Proposition 5.13 below.) For many strategies, considering both the global and class versions is meaningful, whereas for other strategies only one version makes sense.

§5.2 Constraints on potential conjectures

From the premise that **M** identifies $\mathcal{L} \subseteq \mathcal{E}$, one can deduce no information about the nature of $\mathbf{M}(\sigma)$ for any particular $\sigma \in$ SEQ. For example, is $\mathbf{M}(\sigma)$ consistent with σ? This section considers the effects on identification of various constraints on ways in which learners respond to evidential states.

§5.2.1 Totality

The most elementary constraint on a conjecture is that it exist. This requirement may be formulated as follows.

5.1 Definition

(a) **M** is *always defined on* L just in case, for every σ with *content*$(\sigma) \subseteq L$, we have $\mathbf{M}(\sigma)\!\downarrow$.

(b) **M** is *always defined on* $\mathcal{L}$ just in case **M** is always defined on each $L \in \mathcal{L}$.

(c) **M** is *always defined* just in case **M** is always defined on each $L \subseteq \mathcal{E}$.

Clearly "**M** is always defined" is the same as "**M** is total." As discussed in the introduction, we may distinguish the global and the class versions of this strategy. The collections of languages identifiable by the two versions are recorded in the next definition.

5.2 Definition

(a) $[\mathbf{TxtEx}]^{\text{all-def}} = \{ \mathcal{L} \mid \mathcal{L} \subseteq \mathbf{TxtEx}(\mathbf{M}) \text{ for some always defined } \mathbf{M} \}$.

(b) $[\mathbf{TxtEx}]^{\text{class-all-def}} = \{ \mathcal{L} \mid \mathcal{L} \subseteq \mathbf{TxtEx}(\mathbf{M}) \text{ for some } \mathbf{M} \text{ always defined on } \mathcal{L} \}$.

As might be expected from Proposition 4.15, requiring that scientists always be defined is not restrictive. The following proposition is simply a restatement of Proposition 4.15.

5.3 Proposition $[\mathbf{TxtEx}]^{\textit{all-def}} = [\mathbf{TxtEx}]^{\textit{class-all-def}} = \mathbf{TxtEx}$.

It will simplify the formulation of definitions and results in this chapter to limit attention to scientists that are defined on all inputs. We thus enter the following convention.

Convention: Just for Chapter 5, the term "scientist" applies only to total functions from SEQ to N (in the language identification paradigm), or to total functions from SEG to N (in the function identification paradigm).

§5.2.2 Consistency

Our next strategy captures a natural constraint on hypothesis selection, namely, that each conjecture made by a learner be consistent with the the data seen thus far.

5.4 Definition (Angluin [6])

(a) **M** is said to be *consistent* on L just in case, for every σ with $content(\sigma) \subseteq L$, we have $content(\sigma) \subseteq W_{\mathbf{M}(\sigma)}$.

(b) **M** is *consistent* on $\mathcal{L}$ just in case **M** is consistent on each $L \in \mathcal{L}$.

(c) **M** is *consistent* just in case **M** is consistent on each $L \subseteq \mathcal{E}$.

We first consider the global version of consistency.

5.5 Definition $[\mathbf{TxtEx}]^{\text{consistent}} = \{ \mathcal{L} \mid \mathcal{L} \subseteq \mathbf{TxtEx}(\mathbf{M}) \text{ for some consistent } \mathbf{M} \}$.

It is easy to verify that the collection of all finite languages can be identified by a consistent scientist. Consistency appears to be a rational strategy. However, the following proposition demonstrates that consistency restricts **TxtEx**.

5.6 Proposition *Suppose* $\mathcal{L} \subseteq \mathcal{E}$ *is consistently identifiable. Then* $\mathcal{L}$ *is a collection of recursive languages.*

Proof: Suppose $L \in \mathcal{L}$. By the locking sequence lemma (Theorem 3.22), there is a sequence σ such that $content(\sigma) \subseteq L$, $W_{\mathbf{M}(\sigma)} = L$, and for each $\tau \in$ SEQ with $content(\tau) \subseteq L$, we have that $\mathbf{M}(\sigma \diamond \tau) = \mathbf{M}(\sigma)$.

Suppose $x \in L$. Then $\mathbf{M}(\sigma \diamond x) = \mathbf{M}(\sigma)$, since σ is a locking sequence for L. Now suppose $x \notin L$. Then, since $\mathbf{M}$ is consistent, $\mathbf{M}(\sigma \diamond x)$ is not an index for L, and hence $\mathbf{M}(\sigma \diamond x) \neq \mathbf{M}(\sigma)$. Thus $x \in L$ if and only if $\mathbf{M}(\sigma \diamond x) = \mathbf{M}(\sigma)$. Since $\mathbf{M}$ is total, this constitutes an effective test for membership in L. ∎

There are certainly $\mathcal{L} \in$ **TxtEx** that include nonrecursive languages. One such collection is $\{ K \}$! Hence Proposition 5.6 yields the following corollary.

5.7 Corollary $[\mathbf{TxtEx}]^{consistent} \subset \mathbf{TxtEx}$.

Proposition 5.6 suggests the following question: If attention is limited to the recursive languages, does consistency still restrict **TxtEx**? The next proposition provides an affirmative answer.

5.8 Proposition *There is an* $\mathcal{L} \subseteq \mathcal{REC}$ *such that* $\mathcal{L} \in (\mathbf{TxtEx} - [\mathbf{TxtEx}]^{consistent})$.

Our proof of the proposition uses the following lemma and definition. The lemma is a standard exercise.

5.9 Lemma *For each 0–1 valued recursive function* $h(\cdot, \cdot)$, *there is a recursive set* S *which differs from each of the recursive sets* $\{ x \mid h(i, x) = 1 \}$ *where* $i = 0, 1, \cdots$.

5.10 Definition $\mathcal{L} \subseteq \mathcal{E}$ is said to be *r.e. indexable* just in case there is $S \in \mathcal{E}$ such that $\mathcal{L} = \{ W_i \mid i \in S \}$; in this case S is said to be an *r.e. index set for* $\mathcal{L}$. Similarly, $\mathcal{C} \subseteq \mathcal{P}$ is said to be *r.e. indexable* just in case there is $S \in \mathcal{E}$ such that $\mathcal{C} = \{ \varphi_i \mid i \in S \}$ and S is said to be an *r.e. index set for* $\mathcal{C}$.

Although the recursive sets are r.e. indexable (see Rogers [158, Page 73]), Lemma 5.9 says that the collection of characteristic functions of recursive sets is not r.e. indexable.

Proof (of Proposition 5.8): For each $i \in N$, define $L_i = \{\langle i, x \rangle \mid x \in W_i\}$. Let $\mathcal{L} = \{L_i \mid W_i \text{ is recursive}\}$. Clearly, $\mathcal{L} \in \textbf{TxtEx}$.

Suppose, however, that a consistent scientist $\textbf{M}$ identifies $\mathcal{L}$. Let h be the function defined by the following equation:

$$h(\langle \sigma, i \rangle, x) = \begin{cases} 1, & \text{if } \textbf{M}(\sigma \diamond \langle i, x \rangle) = \textbf{M}(\sigma); \\ 0, & \text{otherwise.} \end{cases}$$

Since $\textbf{M}$ must be total, h is clearly total recursive. Thus h satisfies the hypothesis of Lemma 5.9, so there is a recursive set S such that no $f_{\langle \sigma, i \rangle} = \lambda x . h(\langle \sigma, i \rangle, x)$ is a characteristic function of S. But let i' be an index for S, and let σ' be a locking sequence for $\textbf{M}$ on $L_{i'}$. Suppose $x \in W_{i'}$. Then $\textbf{M}(\sigma' \diamond \langle i', x \rangle) = \textbf{M}(\sigma')$, which implies that $h(\langle \sigma', i' \rangle, x) = 1$. Now suppose $x \notin W_{i'}$. Then $\textbf{M}(\sigma' \diamond \langle i', x \rangle) \neq \textbf{M}(\sigma')$, since $\textbf{M}$ is consistent so that $h(\langle \sigma', i' \rangle, x) = 0$. Thus $f_{\langle \sigma', i' \rangle} = \lambda x . h(\langle \sigma', i' \rangle, x)$ is the characteristic function of S, contradicting the choice of S. ∎

We now consider the class version of consistency in which a scientist is required to be consistent only on the evidential states drawn from the languages under consideration.

5.11 Definition (Bārzdiņš [13]) $[\textbf{TxtEx}]^{\text{class-consistent}} = \{\mathcal{L} \mid \mathcal{L} \subseteq \textbf{TxtEx}(\textbf{M}) \text{ for some } \textbf{M} \text{ consistent on } \mathcal{L}\}$.

We leave it to the reader to show the following proposition which establishes that the class version of consistency also restricts $\textbf{TxtEx}$.

5.12 Proposition (Bārzdiņš [13]) $[\textbf{TxtEx}]^{\text{class-consistent}} \subset \textbf{TxtEx}$.

A natural question is how the global and class versions of consistency compare. As the $\mathcal{L}$ of the proof of 5.8 is readily seen to be in $[\textbf{TxtEx}]^{\text{class-consistent}}$, that proof also yields the following.

5.13 Proposition $[\textbf{TxtEx}]^{\text{consistent}} \subset [\textbf{TxtEx}]^{\text{class-consistent}}$.

§5.2.3 Accountability

We next consider scientists whose hypotheses always include some prediction about the state of affairs outside the data thus far seen.

5.14 Definition

(a) **M** is said to be *accountable on* L just in case, for every σ with *content*$(\sigma) \subseteq L$, we have that $W_{\mathbf{M}(\sigma)} - content(\sigma)$ is nonempty.

(b) **M** is said to be *accountable on* $\mathcal{L}$ just in case **M** is accountable on each $L \in \mathcal{L}$.

(c) **M** is *accountable* just in case **M** is accountable on each $L \subseteq \mathcal{E}$.

Thus the hypotheses of accountable learners are always subject to further confirmation. The next definition considers the global and the class versions of accountability.

5.15 Definition

(a) $[\mathbf{TxtEx}]^{\text{account}} = \{\, \mathcal{L} \mid \mathcal{L} \subseteq \mathbf{TxtEx}(\mathbf{M}) \text{ for some accountable } \mathbf{M} \,\}$.

(b) $[\mathbf{TxtEx}]^{\text{class-account}} = \{\, \mathcal{L} \mid \mathcal{L} \subseteq \mathbf{TxtEx}(\mathbf{M}) \text{ for some } \mathbf{M} \text{ accountable on } \mathcal{L} \,\}$.

It is easy to see that $[\mathbf{TxtEx}]^{\text{account}} \subseteq [\mathbf{TxtEx}]^{\text{class-account}} \subseteq \mathbf{TxtEx}$ and that no accountable scientists can identify any finite language. This suggests the following question. If attention is restricted to infinite languages, are there identifiable collections of languages that cannot be identified by class-accountable scientists? The next proposition provides an affirmative answer.

5.16 Proposition *There is an* $\mathcal{L} \in \mathbf{TxtEx} - [\mathbf{TxtEx}]^{\text{class-account}}$ *such that every* $L \in \mathcal{L}$ *is infinite.*

Proof: Recall from Chapter 2 that for each L and x, $\text{col}_x(L) = \{\, y \mid \langle x, y \rangle \in L \,\}$. Let

$$\mathcal{L} \;=\; \{\, L \in \mathcal{E} \mid L \text{ is infinite, } card(\text{col}_0(L)) \leq 2, \text{ and } W_{max(\text{col}_0(L))} = L \,\}.$$

Clearly, $\mathcal{L} \in \mathbf{TxtEx}$.

Suppose by way of contradiction that a class-accountable scientist **M** identifies $\mathcal{L}$. By Kleene's recursion theorem (Theorem 2.3) there exists an index e such that W_e may be defined in stages $s = 0, 1, 2, \ldots$, as below. For each s, W_e^s denotes the finite portion of W_e enumerated as of the beginning of stage s. In each stage s, we determine a number y_{s+1}, finite sets S_{s+1} and X_{s+1}, and sequence σ_{s+1}. We begin with $y_0 = \langle 1, 0 \rangle$, $S_0 = \{\, \langle 0, e \rangle, y_0 \,\}$, $X_0 = \emptyset$, σ_0 chosen so that $content(\sigma_0) = S_0$, and $W_e^0 = S_0$. Go to stage 0.

Begin (*Stage s*)
Search for the least $\langle t, z \rangle$, if any, such that $z \in (W_{\mathbf{M}(\sigma_s), t} - S_s)$.

If $\langle t, z \rangle$ is ever found, then:

set $X_{s+1} = X_s \cup \{ z \}$,

set y_{s+1} to the least number of the form $\langle 1, w \rangle$ that is not in the finite set $S_s \cup X_{s+1}$,

set $S_{s+1} = S_s \cup \{ y_{s+1} \}$,

set σ_{s+1} be the least extension of σ_s such that $content(\sigma_{s+1}) = S_{s+1}$,

set $W_e^{s+1} = W_e^s \cup \{ y_{s+1} \}$, and

go to stage $s + 1$.

End *(Stage s)*

To show that **M** fails to accountably identify $\mathcal{L}$, we consider two cases.

Case 1: All stages of the construction halt. Let $L = W_e$. It is easy to see that $L \in \mathcal{L}$ and $(\bigcup_i X_i) \cap W_e = \emptyset$. Let $T = \bigcup_i \sigma_i$. Observe that T is a text for L. But for each i we have $W_{\mathbf{M}(\sigma_i)} \cap X_{i+1} \neq \emptyset$. Thus **M** fails to identify L.

Case 2: Some stage s starts but does not halt. By Kleene's recursion theorem there exists an $e' > e$ such that $W_{e'} = W_e \cup \{ \langle 0, e' \rangle \} \cup \{ \langle 2, w \rangle \mid w \in N \}$. Clearly, $W_{e'} \in \mathcal{L}$. However, $W_{\mathbf{M}(\sigma_s)} \subseteq S_s = content(\sigma_s) = W_e \subseteq W_{e'}$. Thus, **M** fails to be accountable on $W_{e'}$. ∎

The global version of accountability turns out to be more restrictive than the class version. To show this, let us first recall from Chapter 4 that $\mathcal{SD} = \{ f \in \mathcal{R} \mid \varphi_{f(0)} = f \}$ and introduce the following.

5.17 Definition $\mathcal{L}_{\mathcal{SD}} = \{ L \mid L$ is single valued and represents some element of $\mathcal{SD} \}$.

5.18 Proposition $\mathcal{L}_{\mathcal{SD}} \in ([\mathbf{TxtEx}]^{class\text{-}account} - [\mathbf{TxtEx}]^{account})$.

Proof: We first show that $\mathcal{L}_{\mathcal{SD}} \in [\mathbf{TxtEx}]^{class\text{-}account}$. By the S-m-n Theorem (Theorem 2.1), there is a recursive g such that, for all i, $W_{g(i)} = \{ \langle x, \varphi_i(x) \rangle \mid x \in domain(\varphi_i) \}$. Let G_N be an index for N. Consider the scientist **M** that behaves as follows on each σ:

$$\mathbf{M}(\sigma) = \begin{cases} g(min(col_0(content(\sigma)))), & \text{if } col_0(content(\sigma)) \neq \emptyset; \\ G_N, & \text{otherwise.} \end{cases}$$

It is easy to verify that **M** is accountable on $\mathcal{L}_{\mathcal{SD}}$ and that is identifies $\mathcal{L}_{\mathcal{SD}}$.

Now suppose by way of contradiction that an accountable scientist **M** identifies $\mathcal{L}_{\mathcal{SD}}$. Through an implicit use of Kleene's recursion theorem (Theorem 2.3), we exhibit a $W_e \in \mathcal{L}_{\mathcal{SD}}$ which **M** fails to identify. We construct a text for this W_e in stages.

Stage 0: $\sigma^0 = \langle 0, e \rangle$.

Stage $n + 1$: Let $\langle m, s \rangle$ be the least number such that $m \in W_{\mathbf{M}(\sigma^n)} - content(\sigma^n)$ is found in $\leq s$ steps. (Such a number must exist, since $\mathbf{M}$ is accountable.) If (i) $\pi_1(m) < |\sigma^n|$, then let $\sigma^{n+1} = \sigma^n \diamond \langle |\sigma^n|, 0 \rangle$. Else if (ii) $\pi_1(m) \geq |\sigma^n|$, then let $\sigma^{n+1} = \sigma^n \diamond \langle |\sigma^n|, 0 \rangle \diamond \cdots \diamond \langle \pi_1(m), 1 \dot{-} \pi_2(m) \rangle$.

Let $T = \bigcup_n \sigma^n$ and $W_e = content(T)$. It is clear that $W_e \in \mathcal{L}_{\mathcal{SD}}$. It is also clear that $\mathbf{M}$ fails to identify T, since for each n, either (i) $W_{\mathbf{M}(\sigma^n)} \notin \mathcal{L}_{\mathcal{SD}}$ (by not being single valued), or else (ii) $W_{\mathbf{M}(\sigma^n)} \not\supseteq content(\sigma^{n+1})$. ∎

§5.2.4 Prudence

Suppose scientist $\mathbf{M}$ is defined on $\sigma \in \text{SEQ}$. We say that $\mathbf{M}$ makes a "wild guess" if $\mathbf{M}$ does not identify $W_{\mathbf{M}(\sigma)}$. Here we consider scientists that never respond to their data with a wild guess.

5.19 Definition

(a) $\mathbf{M}$ is said to be *prudent* just in case for all $\sigma \in \text{SEQ}$, if $\mathbf{M}(\sigma)$ is defined, then $\mathbf{M}$ identifies $W_{\mathbf{M}(\sigma)}$.

(b) $[\mathbf{TxtEx}]^{\text{prudent}} = \{ \mathcal{L} \mid \mathcal{L} \subseteq \mathbf{TxtEx}(\mathbf{M}) \text{ for some prudent } \mathbf{M} \}$.

In other words, prudent learners only conjecture grammars for languages they are prepared to learn. It is easy to verify that the collection of finite languages, and the collection of co-singleton languages, can be identified by prudent scientists.

If "prestorage" models of linguistic development are correct, then children acquiring language may well be prudent learners. A prestorage model posits an internal list of candidate grammars that coincides exactly with the natural languages. Language acquisition amounts to the selection of a grammar from this list in response to linguistic input. Such a prestorage learner is prudent in as much as his or her linguistic hypotheses are limited to grammars from the list, that is, to grammars corresponding to natural (i.e., learnable) languages. The next proposition reveals that prudence has no impact on learnability.

5.20 Proposition (Fulk [71]) $\mathbf{TxtEx} = [\mathbf{TxtEx}]^{prudent}$.

The proposition is an immediate corollary of the following lemmas. We defer the proofs of these lemmas to Section 5.4.1. To help state these lemmas, we introduce the following definition.

5.21 Definition $\mathcal{L} \in \mathbf{TxtEx}$ is called *r.e. extendible* just in case there is an r.e. indexable $\mathcal{L}' \in \mathbf{TxtEx}$ such that $\mathcal{L} \subseteq \mathcal{L}'$.

5.22 Lemma $\mathbf{TxtEx} = [\mathbf{TxtEx}]^{prudent}$ *if and only if every* $\mathcal{L} \in \mathbf{TxtEx}$ *is r.e. extendible.*

5.23 Lemma *Every* $\mathcal{L} \in \mathbf{TxtEx}$ *is r.e. extendible.*

§5.3   Constraints on the use of information

Each initial sequence $T[n]$ of a text T provides partial information about the identity of $content(T)$. The information embodied in $T[n]$ may be factored into two components:

(i) $content(T[n])$, that is, the subset of $content(T)$ available to the scientist by the nth moment, and

(ii) the order in which $content(T[n])$ occurs in $T[n]$.

Human learners operate under processing constraints that prevent them from fully exploiting either kind of information. The notion of memory limitation studied in Chapters 3 and 4 is an example of a strategy modeling the first kind of restriction. The next two strategies capture the second kind of limitation.

§5.3.1   Set-driven scientists

A set-driven scientist is insensitive to the order in which data are presented.

5.24 Definition (Wexler and Culicover [194])

(a) $\mathbf{M}$ is *set driven* just in case for all $\sigma, \tau \in \mathrm{SEQ}$, if $content(\sigma) = content(\tau)$, then $\mathbf{M}(\sigma) = \mathbf{M}(\tau)$.

(b) $[\mathbf{TxtEx}]^{\text{set-driven}} = \{ \mathcal{L} \mid \mathcal{L} \subseteq \mathbf{TxtEx}(\mathbf{M}) \text{ for some set-driven } \mathbf{M} \}$.

Note that we consider only the global version of set-drivenness. It is easy to verify that $\mathcal{FIN}$, the collection of finite languages, is identified by a set-driven scientist.

Identification of a language L requires identification of every text for L, and these texts constitute every possible ordering of L. This consideration encourages the belief that the internal order of a finite sequence plays little role in identifiability. However, the next proposition shows the belief to be unjustified.

5.25 Proposition (Schäfer-Richter [167], Fulk [69]) $[\mathbf{TxtEx}]^{set\text{-}driven} \subset \mathbf{TxtEx}$.

Proof: For each j, define $L_j = \{ \langle j, x \rangle \mid x \in N \}$ and, for each j and n, define $\sigma^{j,n} = \langle j, 0 \rangle \diamond \langle j, 1 \rangle \diamond \cdots \diamond \langle j, n \rangle$. Let $\mathbf{M}_0, \mathbf{M}_1, \mathbf{M}_2, \ldots$ denote an enumeration of all scientists. For each j, let

$$
L'_j = \begin{cases}
content(\sigma^{j,n}), & \text{if } \langle n, s \rangle \text{ is the least pair, if any, such that} \\
& \qquad \mathbf{M}_j(\sigma^{j,n}) = i \text{ and } W_{i,s} \supset content(\sigma^{j,n}); \\
\{ \langle j, 0 \rangle \}, & \text{otherwise.}
\end{cases}
$$

Let $\mathcal{L} = \{ L_j, L'_j \mid j \in N \}$. It is easy to see that $\mathcal{L} \in \mathbf{TxtEx}$.

Suppose by way of contradiction that $\mathbf{M}_j$ is a set-driven scientist that identifies $\mathcal{L}$. $\mathbf{M}_j$ thus identifies the text $T = \langle j, 0 \rangle \diamond \langle j, 1 \rangle \diamond \cdots \diamond \langle j, n \rangle \diamond \cdots$. So there must be an $n \in N$ and an index i for L_j such that $\mathbf{M}_j(\sigma^{j,n}) = i$. In particular, there must be a least $\langle n, s \rangle$ such that $\mathbf{M}_j(\sigma^{j,n}) = i$ and $W_{i,s} \supset content(\sigma^{j,n})$. But then $\mathbf{M}_j$ does not identify $content(\sigma^{j,n})$, since on the text $T' = \sigma^{j,n} \diamond \langle j, n \rangle \diamond \langle j, n \rangle \diamond \cdots$, $\mathbf{M}_j$ must conjecture i in the limit, since $\mathbf{M}_j$ is set driven. Thus $\mathbf{M}_j$ fails to identify $\mathcal{L}$, a contradiction. ∎

§5.3.2 Rearrangement-independent scientists

Set-driven scientists ignore the order in which data arrive and base their conjectures only on the content of the data seen at any given time. The following definition introduces a less stringent variation on set-drivenness.

5.26 Definition (Schäfer-Richter [167], Fulk [69, 71])

(a) $\mathbf{M}$ is *rearrangement-independent* just in case for every $\sigma, \tau \in \mathrm{SEQ}$ with $content(\sigma) = content(\tau)$ and $|\sigma| = |\tau|$, we have $\mathbf{M}(\sigma) = \mathbf{M}(\tau)$.

(b) $[\mathbf{TxtEx}]^{rearrangement\text{-}independent} = \{ \mathcal{L} \mid \mathcal{L} \subseteq \mathbf{TxtEx}(\mathbf{M}) \text{ for some rearrangement-independent } \mathbf{M} \}$.

Unlike set-drivenness, rearrangement independence turns out not to be restrictive; we delay the proof of this fact to the next section.

§5.4 Constraint on convergence

Suppose that a scientist $\mathbf{M}$ identifies $\mathcal{L} \subseteq \mathcal{E}$. Then for each $L \in \mathcal{L}$ and each text T for L, $\mathbf{M}$ must converge to some index for L. This $\mathbf{M}$ does not necessarily converge to the same index on different texts for the same language in $\mathcal{L}$, nor need **M** necessarily converge on texts for languages outside $\mathcal{L}$. We next consider two constraints on convergence that limit the freedom of scientists in these ways.

§5.4.1 Order independence

As the first constraint on convergence we consider scientists that converge to the same index on every text for a language.

5.27 Definition (Blum and Blum [18])

(a) **M** is *order-independent on* L just in case for all texts T, T' for L, if $\mathbf{M}(T){\downarrow}$, then $\mathbf{M}(T'){\downarrow} = \mathbf{M}(T)$.

(b) **M** is *order-independent on* $\mathcal{L}$ just in case **M** is order-independent on each $L \in \mathcal{L}$.

(c) **M** is *order-independent* just in case **M** is order-independent on each $L \subseteq \mathcal{E}$.

Thus an order-independent scientist is relatively insensitive to the choice of text for a language on which it is order-independent: any such text eventually leads it to the same index. Note that different texts for the same language may cause an order-independent scientist to examine different amounts of input before convergence begins (just as for order-dependent scientists).

5.28 Definition (Blum and Blum [18])

(a) $[\mathbf{TxtEx}]^{\text{order-independent}} = \{\, \mathcal{L} \mid \mathcal{L} \subseteq \mathbf{TxtEx}(\mathbf{M}) \text{ for some order-independent } \mathbf{M} \,\}$.

(b) $[\mathbf{TxtEx}]^{\text{class-order-independent}} = \{\, \mathcal{L} \mid \mathcal{L} \subseteq \mathbf{TxtEx}(\mathbf{M}) \text{ for some } \mathbf{M} \text{ order-independent on } \mathcal{L} \,\}$.

Clearly, $[\mathbf{TxtEx}]^{\text{order-independent}} \subseteq [\mathbf{TxtEx}]^{\text{class-order-independent}} \subseteq \mathbf{TxtEx}$. The effect of order independence on scientists may at first appear to be restrictive because of the following consideration. An order-independent learning policy seems to require the ability to determine the equivalence of distinct indexes, but the equivalence question cannot in general be answered by a computational process, indeed, the set $\{\, \langle i, j \rangle \mid W_i = W_j \,\}$ is not even r.e. (see Rogers [158, Section 5.2]). Contrary to expectation, order independence turns out not to be restrictive. This follows from the following extension of a result of Blum and Blum [18] by Fulk [71].

5.29 Proposition (Fulk [71]) *Given any scientist* **M**, *one can effectively construct scientist* **M'** *such that all the following conditions hold.*

1. **TxtEx(M)** $\subseteq$ **TxtEx(M')**.

2. **M'** *is order-independent.*

3. **M'** *is rearrangement-independent.*

4. *If there exists a locking sequence for* **M'** *on* L, *then* **M'** *identifies* L.

5. *If* **M'** *identifies* L, *then all texts for* L *contain a locking sequence for* **M'** *on* L.

5.30 Corollary (Blum and Blum [18]) $[\textbf{TxtEx}]^{order\text{-}independent} = \textbf{TxtEx}$.

5.31 Corollary (Fulk [69], Schäfer-Richter [167])
$[\textbf{TxtEx}]^{rearrangement\text{-}independent} = \textbf{TxtEx}$.

To help prove Proposition 5.29, we introduce the following weakening of the notion of locking sequence.

5.32 Definition (Fulk [69]) *Given a scientist* **M** *and a language* L, *we say that* σ *is a* stabilizing sequence *for* **M** *on* L *just in case*

(a) $content(\sigma) \subseteq L$, *and*

(b) $(\forall \tau \mid content(\tau) \subseteq L) \ [\mathbf{M}(\sigma) = \mathbf{M}(\sigma \diamond \tau)]$.

So, a stabilizing sequence on L is like a locking sequence on L, except that **M**'s conjecture on it need not be an index for L. The proof of the following lemma is left to the reader.

5.33 Lemma *If* **M** *identifies* L, *then every stabilizing sequence for* **M** *on* L *is also a locking sequence for* **M** *on* L.

The next two definitions introduce some terminology we use in describing how to search for stabilizing sequences.

5.34 Definition For each $\sigma \in$ SEQ, *visible*(σ) denotes the set $\{ \sigma' < |\sigma| \mid content(\sigma') \subseteq content(\sigma) \}$.

Note that the usage "$\sigma' < |\sigma|$" in the above definition implicitly identifies an initial sequence with its canonical indexing and thereby induces a linear ordering on elements of SEQ. Also note that for each $\sigma \in$ SEQ, the cardinality of $visible(\sigma)$ is finite and $visible(\sigma)$ can be effectively computed from σ. Furthermore, $visible(\sigma)$ depends only on the content and length of σ.

5.35 Definition Given a scientist **M** and a $\sigma \in$ SEQ, σ_0 is called a *candidate stabilizing sequence* for **M** at σ just in case:

(a) $content(\sigma_0) \subseteq content(\sigma)$, and

(b) $(\forall \sigma' \in visible(\sigma))[\sigma_0 \subseteq \sigma' \Rightarrow \mathbf{M}(\sigma_0) = \mathbf{M}(\sigma')]$.

The following two claims summarize the properties of candidate stabilizing sequences. The proof of the first claim is immediate and is left to the reader.

5.36 Claim

(a) *Given* $\mathbf{M}, \sigma$, *and* σ_0, *it is effectively decidable whether* σ_0 *is a candidate stabilizing sequence for* **M** *at* σ.

(b) *Given* **M** *and* σ, *there is a candidate stabilizing sequence for* **M** *at* σ.

(c) *If* σ_0 *is a stabilizing sequence for* **M** *on* L, *then* σ_0 *is a candidate stabilizing sequence for every sequence* σ *such that* $content(\sigma_0) \subseteq content(\sigma) \subseteq L$.

(d) *If* $content(\sigma_0) \subseteq content(\sigma)$ *and* σ_0 *is not a candidate stabilizing sequence for* **M** *at* σ, *then for all* $\tau \supseteq \sigma$, σ_0 *is not a candidate stabilizing sequence for* **M** *at* τ.

5.37 Claim *Given a scientist* **M** *and text* T *such that* σ *is a candidate stabilizing sequence for* **M** *at* $T[n]$ *for infinitely many* n, *then* σ *is a stabilizing sequence for* **M** *on* $content(T)$.

Proof: Suppose by way of contradiction that σ is not a stabilizing sequence for **M** on $content(T)$. Then there exists a σ' such that $content(\sigma') \subseteq content(T)$, $\sigma \subseteq \sigma'$, and $\mathbf{M}(\sigma) \neq \mathbf{M}(\sigma')$. But, for all but finitely many n, $\sigma' \in visible(T[n])$. Hence, for all but finitely many n, σ fails to be a candidate stabilizing sequence for **M** at $T[n]$, a contradiction. ∎

As a corollary to the above two claims we have

5.38 Corollary *Suppose* **M** *and* T *are given. Then the following are equivalent:*

(a) σ_0 is a stabilizing sequence for **M** on content(T).

(b) σ_0 is a candidate stabilizing sequence for **M** at all but finitely many initial segments of T.

(c) σ_0 is a candidate stabilizing sequence for **M** at infinitely many initial segments of T.

Proof (Proposition 5.29): Let $pad(.,.)$ be a recursive one-to-one padding function such that for $i, j \in N$, $W_{pad(i,j)} = W_i$ (see Chapter 2). Let **M**$'$ be a scientist such that for each $\sigma \in$ SEQ, **M**$'(\sigma) = pad(\mathbf{M}(\sigma_0), \sigma_0)$, where σ_0 is the least candidate stabilizing sequence for **M** at σ. By Claim 5.36, the search for σ_0 is effective and always succeeds.

So by Corollary 5.38, we have

5.39 Claim   For any text T, **M**$'(T){\downarrow} = pad(\mathbf{M}(\sigma_0), \sigma_0)$ if and only if σ_0 is the least stabilizing sequence for **M** on content(T). Moreover, if there exists no stabilizing sequence for **M** on content(T), then **M**$'(T){\uparrow}$.

We now show that **M**$'$ satisfies all the properties claimed in the proposition.

1. Fix an $L \in$ **TxtEx(M)** and let T be an arbitrary text for L. By Theorem 3.22 there exists a locking sequence for **M** on L. Hence there is also a stabilizing sequence for **M** on L. Let σ_0 be the least stabilizing sequence for **M** on L. Then by Claim 5.39 we have that **M**$'(T){\downarrow} = pad(\mathbf{M}(\sigma_0), \sigma_0)$, but by Lemma 5.33, σ_0 is also a locking sequence for **M** on L. Hence, $W_{\mathbf{M}'(T)} = W_{pad(\mathbf{M}(\sigma_0), \sigma_0)} = W_{\mathbf{M}(\sigma_0)} = L$.

2. By Claim 5.39, if **M**$'$ converges on T, then the value of **M**$'(T)$ depends only on content(T). Thus **M**$'$ is order-independent.

3. It is clear from the construction that **M**$'$ is rearrangement-independent, because the least candidate stabilizing sequence for **M** at σ depends only on content(σ) and $|\sigma|$.

4. Suppose σ is a locking sequence for **M**$'$ on L. Then **M**$'$ identifies all texts for L that extend σ. Since **M**$'$ is order-independent, it follows that **M**$'$ identifies L.

5. Suppose **M**$'$ identifies L. Let σ_0 be the least stabilizing sequence for **M** on L and let T be an arbitrary text for L. Choose an n_0 so large that
   (a) $(\forall \sigma \leq \sigma_0)[content(\sigma) \subseteq L \Leftrightarrow content(\sigma) \subseteq content(T[n_0])]$, and
   (b) $(\forall \sigma < \sigma_0)[\sigma$ is not a candidate stabilizing sequence for $T[n_0]]$.
Such an n_0 must exist. (For (b), use Corollary 5.38). By Claim 5.36, we thus have that, for all $\tau \supseteq T[n_0]$ with content(τ) $\subseteq L$, σ_0 is the least candidate stabilizing sequence for **M** at τ. Thus $T[n_0]$ is a locking sequence for **M**$'$ on L. ∎

We now return to the proofs of Lemmas 5.22 and 5.23.

Proof (Lemma 5.22): Suppose first that **TxtEx** = [**TxtEx**]^{prudent}. Fix an $\mathcal{L} \in$ **TxtEx**. We argue that $\mathcal{L}$ is r.e. extendible. Let **M** be a prudent scientist that identifies $\mathcal{L}$. Then $S = \{\, \mathbf{M}(\sigma) \mid \sigma \in \text{SEQ} \,\}$ is an r.e. set. Since **M** is prudent, **M** identifies $\mathcal{L}' = \{\, W_i \mid i \in S \,\}$. Clearly, $\mathcal{L}'$ is r.e. indexable and a superset of $\mathcal{L}$.

Now suppose that every $\mathcal{L} \in$ **TxtEx** is r.e extendible. Fix an $\mathcal{L} \in$ **TxtEx** and let $\mathcal{L}' \in$ **TxtEx** be a superset of $\mathcal{L}$ that is r.e. indexable, say by the r.e. set S. Without loss of generality we take S to be infinite. By Proposition 5.29, there is a total order-independent scientist, **M**, that identifies $\mathcal{L}'' \supseteq \mathcal{L}'$. We show how to construct a prudent scientist **M**$'$ that identifies $\mathcal{L}'$ (and hence $\mathcal{L}$). Let $s_0, s_1, \ldots$ be a one-one recursive enumeration of S. Let T^i be a text for W_{s_i} that can be obtained recursively from i. Now, for each σ, define

$$\mathbf{M}'(\sigma) \;=\; min\left(\{\, s_{|\sigma|} \,\} \cup \{\, s_i \mid i \leq |\sigma| \text{ and } \mathbf{M}(T^i[|\sigma|]) = \mathbf{M}(\sigma) \,\} \right).$$

Since **M** is order-independent and identifies $\mathcal{L}'$, **M**$'$ will converge on any text T for $L \in \mathcal{L}'$ to an s_i such that $W_{s_i} = L$. Also, every index in S is an index for a language in $\mathcal{L}'$, and **M**$'$ outputs only indexes from S. Thus **M**$'$ is prudent and identifies $\mathcal{L}'$. ∎

Proof (Lemma 5.23): Our goal is to show that every $\mathcal{L} \in$ **TxtEx** is r.e extendible. Fix an $\mathcal{L} \in$ **TxtEx**. By Proposition 5.29, $\mathcal{L}$ is identifiable by some scientist **M** such that **M** identifies L if and only if there is a locking sequence for **M** on L. Without loss of generality we assume that $\emptyset \in \mathcal{L}$. We exhibit an r.e. indexable collection $\mathcal{L}'$ such that $\mathcal{L}' \in$ **TxtEx** and $\mathcal{L}' \supseteq \mathcal{L}$. There are two cases:

Case 1: **M** identifies N. Define a recursive function f by

$$W_{f(\sigma)} \;=\; \begin{cases} \emptyset, & \text{if } content(\sigma) \not\subseteq W_{\mathbf{M}(\sigma)}; \\ W_{\mathbf{M}(\sigma)}, & \text{if } \sigma \text{ is a locking sequence for } \mathbf{M} \text{ on } W_{\mathbf{M}(\sigma)}; \\ N, & \text{otherwise.} \end{cases}$$

To see that f defined in this way is recursive, we argue informally. Given σ, to enumerate $W_{f(\sigma)}$, compute $\mathbf{M}(\sigma)$ and enumerate nothing in $W_{f(\sigma)}$ until, if ever, a stage s is reached such that $W_{\mathbf{M}(\sigma),s}$ contains all of $content(\sigma)$. At this point begin enumerating all of $W_{\mathbf{M}(\sigma)}$ into $W_{f(\sigma)}$ until, if ever, there is discovered a sequence γ such that $\gamma \supseteq \sigma$, $content(\gamma) \subseteq W_{\mathbf{M}(\sigma)}$ and $\mathbf{M}(\gamma) \neq \mathbf{M}(\sigma)$. If such a γ exists, then begin enumerating all of N into $W_{f(\sigma)}$.

Since f is recursive, $S = \{\, f(\sigma) \mid \sigma \in \text{SEQ} \,\}$ is r.e. On the other hand, since $\emptyset$ and N are identified by **M** and since **M** identifies every L such that there is a locking sequence for **M** on L, **M** identifies every language with an index in S.

Case 2: **M** does not identify N. Define a recursive function f by

$$
W_{f(\sigma)} \;=\;
\begin{cases}
\emptyset, & \text{if } content(\sigma) \not\subseteq W_{\mathbf{M}(\sigma)}; \\[6pt]
W_{\mathbf{M}(\sigma)}, & \text{if } \sigma \text{ is a locking sequence for } \mathbf{M} \text{ on } W_{\mathbf{M}(\sigma)}; \\[6pt]
\{0, 1, \ldots, y\}, & \text{otherwise, where } y \text{ is the maximum element} \\
& \text{enumerated in } W_{f(\sigma)} \text{ when it is discovered} \\
& \text{that } \sigma \text{ is not a locking sequence for } W_{f(\sigma)}.
\end{cases}
$$

We leave it to the reader to argue that f defined in this way is recursive.

Suppose G_i is a grammar (effectively obtained from i) for $\{x \mid x \leq i\}$. Let $S = \{f(\sigma) \mid \sigma \in \mathrm{SEQ}\} \cup \{G_i \mid i \in N\}$. Clearly, S is an r.e. index set for some collection of languages, $\mathcal{L}'$. Note that S contains all languages identified by **M**, together with all initial segments of N. Let r be a total recursive function such that for every $\sigma \in \mathrm{SEQ}$, $W_{r(\sigma)} = content(\sigma)$. To see that $\mathcal{L}' \in \mathbf{TxtEx}$, define scientist **M**′ as follows:

$$
\mathbf{M}'(\sigma) \;=\;
\begin{cases}
r(\sigma), & \text{if } content(\sigma) \text{ is an initial segment of } N; \\
\mathbf{M}(\sigma), & \text{otherwise.}
\end{cases}
$$

Since **M** does not identify N, **M**′ identifies all that **M** does, together with all initial segments of N. ∎

§5.4.2 Reliability

A scientist that occasionally converges to an incorrect language may be termed "unreliable."

5.40 Definition (Minicozzi [132])

(a) **M** is *reliable* on L just in case for any text T for L, if $\mathbf{M}(T)\!\downarrow$, then $W_{\mathbf{M}(T)} = L$.

(b) **M** is *reliable* on $\mathcal{L}$ just in case **M** is reliable on each $L \in \mathcal{L}$.

(c) **M** is *reliable* just in case **M** is reliable on each $L \subseteq \mathcal{E}$.

Thus a scientist that does not converge on any text is reliable. Only the global version of reliability yields a useful strategy.

5.41 Definition $[\mathbf{TxtEx}]^{\text{reliable}} = \{\mathcal{L} \mid \mathcal{L} \subseteq \mathbf{TxtEx}(\mathbf{M}) \text{ for some reliable } \mathbf{M}\}$.

It is easy to see that the collection of finite languages is identifiable by a reliable scientist. On the other hand, the obvious scientist for identifying $\{N - \{x\} \mid x \in N\}$

— namely, the one that responds to $\sigma \in$ SEQ with a canonical index for N minus the least number missing from $content(\sigma)$ — is not reliable as it converges on a text for the even numbers but fails to identify them.

Reliability is a useful property of scientists. A reliable scientist never fails to signal the inaccuracy of a previous conjecture. To explain, let **M** be a reliable scientist, let T be a text for some language, and suppose that for some $i, n \in N$, $\mathbf{M}(T[n]) = i$. If $W_i \neq content(T)$ — that is, if i is incorrect — then for some $m > n$ we have $\mathbf{M}(T[m]) \neq i$. (This is the case, because otherwise **M** converges on T to the incorrect index i, contradicting **M**'s reliability.) The new index $\mathbf{M}(T[m])$ signals the incorrectness of i. It might thus be hoped that every identifiable collection of languages is identified by a reliable scientist. However, reliability turns out to be quite a debilitating constraint on scientists, as shown by the following proposition.

5.42 Proposition *Suppose some reliable scientist* **M** *identifies* $L \in \mathcal{E}$. *Then* L *is finite.*

Proof: This is a straightforward locking sequence argument. Let σ be a locking sequence for **M** on L. Then, if $T = \sigma \diamond \# \diamond \# \diamond \cdots$, **M** converges on T to an index for L. Thus $L = content(T) = content(\sigma)$, which is finite. ∎

5.43 Corollary $[\mathbf{TxtEx}]^{reliable} \subset \mathbf{TxtEx}$.

§5.5 Constraints on the relation between conjectures

The successive conjectures emitted by an arbitrary scientist need stand in no particular relation to each other. We now deal with strategies resulting from imposition of such a relation.

§5.5.1 Conservatism

A seemingly rational constraint is captured by the following strategy.

5.44 Definition (Angluin [6])

(a) **M** is *conservative on* L just in case for all σ and τ such that $\sigma \subseteq \tau$ and $content(\tau) \subseteq L$, if $content(\tau) \subseteq W_{\mathbf{M}(\sigma)}$, then $\mathbf{M}(\tau) = \mathbf{M}(\sigma)$.

(b) **M** is *conservative on* $\mathcal{L}$ just in case **M** is conservative on each $L \in \mathcal{L}$.

(c) **M** is *conservative* just in case **M** is conservative on each $L \subseteq \mathcal{E}$.

5.45 Definition

(a) $[\mathbf{TxtEx}]^{\text{conservative}} = \{\, \mathcal{L} \mid \mathcal{L} \subseteq \mathbf{TxtEx}(\mathbf{M}) \text{ for some conservative } \mathbf{M} \,\}$.

(b) $[\mathbf{TxtEx}]^{\text{class-conservative}} = \{\, \mathcal{L} \mid \mathcal{L} \subseteq \mathbf{TxtEx}(\mathbf{M}) \text{ for some } \mathbf{M} \text{ conservative on } \mathcal{L} \,\}$.

A conservative scientist thus never abandons a locally successful conjecture, that is, a conjecture that generates all the data seen to date. It is easy to verify that the collection of all finite languages and the collection of all co-singleton languages can be identified by conservative scientists.

The following proposition implies that conservatism is restrictive.

5.46 Proposition (Angluin [6]) $[\mathbf{TxtEx}]^{conservative} \subset \mathbf{TxtEx}$.

Proof: This argument is essentially the same as that for Proposition 5.25. Consider the class $\mathcal{L}$ defined in that proof and suppose that $\mathbf{M}_j$ is a conservative scientist that identifies $\mathcal{L}$. As argued in the proof of Proposition 5.25, $\mathbf{M}_j$ must identify the text $T = \langle j, 0\rangle \diamond \langle j, 1\rangle \diamond \langle j, 2\rangle \diamond \cdots$, for L_j. Thus there is a least pair $\langle n, s\rangle$ such that $\mathbf{M}_j(T[n]) = i$ and $W_{i,s} \supset content(T[n])$. So $L'_j = content(T[n])$ is not identified by $\mathbf{M}_j$, since on the text $\langle j, 0\rangle \diamond \langle j, 1\rangle \diamond \cdots \diamond \langle j, n\rangle \diamond \langle j, n\rangle \diamond \cdots$, $\mathbf{M}_j$ must continue to output i by the conservativeness of $\mathbf{M}_j$. ∎

It turns out that both global and class versions of conservatism render the same collections of languages identifiable, as implied by the next proposition. Its proof is discussed in Exercise 5-21.

5.47 Proposition $[\mathbf{TxtEx}]^{conservative} = [\mathbf{TxtEx}]^{class\text{-}conservative}$.

§5.5.2 Generalization strategies

We now consider a collection of strategies that require scientists to "improve" upon their successive conjectures. A scientist can begin by hypothesizing an index for a language smaller than the target language and then build to the target language. Such strategies are referred to as generalization strategies, and they model bottom-up or specific-to-general searches in artificial systems for empirical inquiry. For example, see systems such as Muggleton and Feng's Golem [134].

Three different generalization strategies have been proposed.

5.48 Definition (Jantke [99])

(a) **M** is said to be *strong-monotonic on* L just in case, for each τ with $content(\tau) \subseteq L$ and each $\sigma \subseteq \tau$, we have $W_{\mathbf{M}(\sigma)} \subseteq W_{\mathbf{M}(\tau)}$.

(b) **M** is said to be *strong monotonic on* $\mathcal{L}$ just in case **M** is strong-monotonic on each $L \in \mathcal{L}$.

(c) **M** is *strong monotonic* just in case **M** is strong monotonic on each $L \subseteq \mathcal{E}$.

So, a strong-monotonic scientist, upon being fed a text for a language, outputs a chain of hypotheses such that if index j is hypothesized after index i, then $W_i \subseteq W_j$. A consequence of this requirement is that if a scientist incorrectly hypothesizes that a particular element belongs to the target language, then it cannot revise this assumption by emitting a hypothesis that excludes this element.

5.49 Definition

(a) $[\mathbf{TxtEx}]^{\text{strong-monotonic}} = \{\, \mathcal{L} \mid \mathcal{L} \subseteq \mathbf{TxtEx}(\mathbf{M}) \text{ for some strong-monotonic } \mathbf{M} \,\}$.

(b) $[\mathbf{TxtEx}]^{\text{class-strong-monotonic}} = \{\, \mathcal{L} \mid \mathcal{L} \subseteq \mathbf{TxtEx}(\mathbf{M}) \text{ for some } \mathbf{M} \text{ strong-monotonic on } \mathcal{L} \,\}$.

Exercise 5-15 shows:

$$[\mathbf{TxtEx}]^{\text{strong-monotonic}} = [\mathbf{TxtEx}]^{\text{class-strong-monotonic}}.$$

We thus consider only the global version in the sequel.

Wiehagen [200] suggested that the requirement of strong monotonicity is too stringent. He proposed the weaker notion of *monotonic strategy*, which simply requires that a scientist's successive hypotheses be more general only with respect to the target language. More precisely:

5.50 Definition (Wiehagen [200])

(a) **M** is said to be *monotonic on* L just in case, for each τ with $content(\tau) \subseteq L$ and each $\sigma \subseteq \tau$, we have $W_{\mathbf{M}(\sigma)} \cap L \subseteq W_{\mathbf{M}(\tau)} \cap L$.

(b) **M** is said to be *monotonic on* $\mathcal{L}$ just in case **M** is monotonic on each $L \in \mathcal{L}$.

Thus a monotonic strategy is allowed to correct its mistaken assumption that certain nonelements of L belong to L, but once it has correctly concluded that an element of L belongs to L it is not allowed to output a hypothesis that contradicts such a conclusion. The reader should note that we deliberately omitted the third clause in the above definition because the global version of monotonicity is equivalent to the requirement of strong monotonicity. (See Exercise 5-19.) For this reason, in the next definition we introduce only the class version of monotonicity and, in keeping with the usage in the literature, refer to the class as $[\mathbf{TxtEx}]^{\text{monotonic}}$ instead of $[\mathbf{TxtEx}]^{\text{class-monotonic}}$.

5.51 Definition $[\mathbf{TxtEx}]^{\text{monotonic}} = \{\, \mathcal{L} \mid \mathcal{L} \subseteq \mathbf{TxtEx}(\mathbf{M})$ for some $\mathbf{M}$ monotonic on $\mathcal{L}\,\}$.

The third generalization strategy, referred to as *weak monotonic*, allows a scientist to expel elements from its hypothesis only if it encounters elements in its evidential state that cannot be accounted for by its current hypothesis. More precisely:

5.52 Definition (Lange and Zeugmann [119])

(a) $\mathbf{M}$ is said to be *weak monotonic on* L just in case, for each τ with $\mathit{content}(\tau) \subseteq L$ and each $\sigma \subseteq \tau$ with $\mathit{content}(\tau) \subseteq W_{\mathbf{M}(\sigma)}$, we have that $W_{\mathbf{M}(\sigma)} \subseteq W_{\mathbf{M}(\tau)}$.

(b) $\mathbf{M}$ is said to be *weak monotonic on* $\mathcal{L}$ just in case $\mathbf{M}$ is weak monotonic on each $L \in \mathcal{L}$.

(c) $\mathbf{M}$ is *weak monotonic* just in case $\mathbf{M}$ is weak monotonic on each $L \subseteq \mathcal{E}$.

So, if a weak-monotonic scientist conjectures index j after index i and the set of elements seen by the scientist when index j is conjectured is a subset of W_i, then $W_i \subseteq W_j$. The collections of languages identified by the global and the class versions of weak-monotonic scientists are introduced in the next definition.

5.53 Definition

(a) $[\mathbf{TxtEx}]^{\text{weak-monotonic}} = \{\, \mathcal{L} \mid \mathcal{L} \subseteq \mathbf{TxtEx}(\mathbf{M})$ for some weak-monotonic $\mathbf{M}\,\}$.

(b) $[\mathbf{TxtEx}]^{\text{class-weak-monotonic}} = \{\, \mathcal{L} \mid \mathcal{L} \subseteq \mathbf{TxtEx}(\mathbf{M})$ for some $\mathbf{M}$ weak-monotonic on $\mathcal{L}\,\}$.

It is easy to see that

$$[\mathbf{TxtEx}]^{\text{weak-monotonic}} \quad \subseteq \quad [\mathbf{TxtEx}]^{\text{class-weak-monotonic}}.$$

Equality follows using the following fact. (See Exercise 5-21.)

$$[\mathbf{TxtEx}]^{\text{class-weak-monotonic}} \quad \subseteq \quad [\mathbf{TxtEx}]^{\text{conservative}}.$$

We note that there is a similarity between weak-monotonicity and conservativeness. A conservative scientist can only change her hypothesis if the current hypothesis does not account for some data; a weak-monotonic scientist must keep generalizing until the current hypothesis fails to account for some data. A nontrivial proof shows that weak-monotonic scientists and conservative scientists identify the same collections of languages. (See Exercise 5-21.)

We now consider the interplay between the three generalization strategies defined above. It is easy to verify the following proposition.

5.54 Proposition

(a) $[\mathbf{TxtEx}]^{strong\text{-}monotonic} \subseteq [\mathbf{TxtEx}]^{monotonic} \subseteq \mathbf{TxtEx}$.

(b) $[\mathbf{TxtEx}]^{strong\text{-}monotonic} \subseteq [\mathbf{TxtEx}]^{weak\text{-}monotonic} \subseteq \mathbf{TxtEx}$.

(c) $[\mathbf{TxtEx}]^{conservative} \subseteq [\mathbf{TxtEx}]^{class\text{-}conservative} \subseteq [\mathbf{TxtEx}]^{class\text{-}weak\text{-}monotonic}$.

(d) $[\mathbf{TxtEx}]^{conservative} \subseteq [\mathbf{TxtEx}]^{weak\text{-}monotonic} \subseteq [\mathbf{TxtEx}]^{class\text{-}weak\text{-}monotonic}$.

The next result shows that there are collections of languages that can be identified by monotonic scientists but cannot be identified by any weak-monotonic scientists.

5.55 Proposition $[\mathbf{TxtEx}]^{monotonic} - [\mathbf{TxtEx}]^{weak\text{-}monotonic} \neq \emptyset$.

Before proving this proposition, we note the following corollary that follows from the above proposition and Proposition 5.54.

5.56 Corollary

(a) $[\mathbf{TxtEx}]^{strong\text{-}monotonic} \subset [\mathbf{TxtEx}]^{monotonic}$.

(b) $[\mathbf{TxtEx}]^{weak\text{-}monotonic} \subset \mathbf{TxtEx}$.

Proof (Proposition 5.55): Let $\mathbf{M}_0, \mathbf{M}_1, \ldots$ be an enumeration of total computable scientists along the lines of Corollary 4.16. For each j and m, let $L_j = \{\, \langle j, x \rangle \mid x \in N \,\}$ and $L_j^m = \{\, \langle j, x \rangle \mid x < m \,\}$. For each j, let T_j denote the text $\langle j, 0 \rangle \diamond \langle j, 1 \rangle \diamond \cdots \diamond \langle j, n \rangle \diamond \cdots$ and let

$$S_j \;=\; \{\, \langle m, n \rangle \mid m > 0 \text{ and } L_j^{m+1} \subseteq W_{\mathbf{M}_j(T_j[m]),n} \,\}.$$

Note that S_j is recursive. Now define the collection of languages:

$$\mathcal{L} \;=\; \{\, L_j \mid S_j = \emptyset \,\} \cup \{\, L_j^m \mid S_j \neq \emptyset \text{ and } m = \pi_1(min(S_j)) \,\}.$$

We show that $\mathcal{L} \in ([\mathbf{TxtEx}]^{monotonic} - [\mathbf{TxtEx}]^{weak\text{-}monotonic})$.

We first exhibit a monotonic scientist that identifies $\mathcal{L}$. Let G_N be an index for N. Let $G_\emptyset$ be an index for $\emptyset$. Let G_j be an index for L_j that can be effectively obtained from j. Let G_j^m denote an index for L_j^m that can be effectively obtained from j and m. Let $S_j^s = S_j \cap \{\, x \mid x \leq s \,\}$. Now let $\mathbf{M}$ be a scientist that, for each σ,

$$
\mathbf{M}(\sigma) \;=\; \begin{cases}
G_N, & \text{if } content(\sigma) = \emptyset; \\[4pt]
G_j, & \text{if } \emptyset \subset content(\sigma) \subseteq L_j \text{ and } S_j^{|\sigma|} = \emptyset; \\[4pt]
G_j^m, & \text{if } \emptyset \subset content(\sigma) \subseteq L_j \text{ and } S_j^{|\sigma|} \neq \emptyset, \\
& \quad \text{where } m = \pi_1(min(S_j^{|\sigma|})); \\[4pt]
G_\emptyset, & \text{otherwise.}
\end{cases}
$$

It is easy to verify that $\mathbf{M}$ is monotonic and identifies $\mathcal{L}$.

Next we show that no weak-monotonic scientist identifies $\mathcal{L}$. Suppose scientist $\mathbf{M}_j$ identifies $\mathcal{L}$. Consider the language L_j. Clearly, $S_j \neq \emptyset$, because otherwise $L_j \in \mathcal{L}$ and $\mathbf{M}_j$ does not identify L_j. Let $\langle m, n \rangle = min(S_j)$, hence $L_j^m \in \mathcal{L}_j$. Suppose σ is an extension of $T_j[m]$ such that $content(\sigma) = L_j^m$ and $W_{\mathbf{M}_j(\sigma)} = L_j^m$. Such a σ exists as $L_j^m \in \mathcal{L}$ and $\mathbf{M}_j$ identifies $\mathcal{L}$. Thus we have $W_{\mathbf{M}_j(\sigma)} = L_j^m \not\supseteq W_{\mathbf{M}_j(T[m])}$, which violates the weak-monotonicity property for identification of L_j^m by $\mathbf{M}_j$. Thus $\mathbf{M}_j$ fails to be weak monotonic. ∎

The next proposition shows that there are collections of languages that can be identified by weak-monotonic scientists but not identified by any monotonic scientists.

5.57 Proposition $[\mathbf{TxtEx}]^{weak\text{-}monotonic} - [\mathbf{TxtEx}]^{monotonic} \neq \emptyset$.

The above proposition (together with Proposition 5.54) implies the following corollary.

5.58 Corollary

(a) $[\mathbf{TxtEx}]^{strong\text{-}monotonic} \subset [\mathbf{TxtEx}]^{weak\text{-}monotonic}$.

(b) $[\mathbf{TxtEx}]^{monotonic} \subset \mathbf{TxtEx}$.

Proof (Proposition 5.57): This argument is based on a technique due to Lange and Zeugmann [119].

For each m and n, we define:

$$
\begin{aligned}
L_1 &= \{\, \langle 0, x \rangle \mid x \in N \,\}. \\
L_2^m &= \{\, \langle 0, x \rangle \mid x \leq m \,\} \cup \{\, \langle 1, x \rangle \mid x > m \,\}. \\
L_3^{m,n} &= \{\, \langle 0, x \rangle \mid x \leq m \ \vee\ x > n \,\} \cup \{\, \langle 1, x \rangle \mid m < x \leq n \,\}.
\end{aligned}
$$

We also define $\mathcal{L} = \{ L_1,\ L_2^0,\ L_2^1,\ L_2^2,\ \ldots \} \cup \{ L_3^{m,n} \mid m < n \}$.

It is easy to verify that $\mathcal{L} \in [\mathbf{TxtEx}]^{\text{weak-monotonic}}$.

We next show that $\mathcal{L} \notin [\mathbf{TxtEx}]^{\text{monotonic}}$. Consider any scientist $\mathbf{M}$ that identifies $\mathcal{L}$. Let σ be such that $content(\sigma) = \{ \langle 0, x \rangle \mid x \leq m \}$, for some $m \in N$, and $W_{\mathbf{M}(\sigma)} = L_1$. (Note that there exists such a σ, since $\mathbf{M}$ identifies L_1.)

Let $\sigma' \supseteq \sigma$ be such that $content(\sigma') = \{ \langle 0, x \rangle \mid x \leq m \} \cup \{ \langle 1, x \rangle \mid m < x \leq n \}$, for some $n > m$, and $W_{\mathbf{M}(\sigma')} = L_2^m$. (Note that there exists such a σ', since $\mathbf{M}$ identifies L_2^m.)

Let $\sigma'' \supseteq \sigma'$ be such that $content(\sigma'') \subseteq L_3^{m,n}$ and $W_{\mathbf{M}(\sigma'')} = L_3^{m,n}$. (Note that there exists such a σ'', since $\mathbf{M}'$ identifies $L_3^{m,n}$.)

We finally claim that $\mathbf{M}$ fails to be monotonic while identifying $L_3^{m,n}$. To see this it is sufficient to observe that $\langle 0, n+1 \rangle \in L_3^{m,n} \cap W_{\mathbf{M}(\sigma)} \cap W_{\mathbf{M}(\sigma'')}$ but $\langle 0, n+1 \rangle \notin W_{\mathbf{M}(\sigma')}$. ∎

§5.5.3 Specialization strategies

Generalization strategies improve upon their successive conjectures by emitting indexes for larger and larger languages. Alternatively, a scientist can begin with an index for a language larger than the target language and then "cut down" her hypotheses to converge to an index for the target language. Such strategies are referred to as specialization strategies; they may be viewed as models for top-down or general-to-specific searches in artificial systems of empirical inquiry (see for example, Shapiro's MIS [171] and Quinlan's FOIL [157]).

Three specialization strategies can be defined as duals to the three generalization strategies. We consider only the dual of weak-monotonic scientists. Duals of strong-monotonic scientists and monotonic scientists are considered in the exercises.

5.59 Definition (Kapur [103])

(a) $\mathbf{M}$ is *dual-weak-monotonic on L* just in case, for each τ with $content(\tau) \subseteq L$ and each $\sigma \subseteq \tau$ with $content(\tau) \subseteq W_{\mathbf{M}(\sigma)}$, we have $W_{\mathbf{M}(\sigma)} \supseteq W_{\mathbf{M}(\tau)}$.

(b) $\mathbf{M}$ is *dual-weak-monotonic on $\mathcal{L}$* just in case $\mathbf{M}$ is dual-weak-monotonic on each $L \in \mathcal{L}$.

(c) $\mathbf{M}$ is *dual-weak-monotonic* just in case $\mathbf{M}$ is dual-weak-monotonic on each $L \subseteq \mathcal{E}$.

(d) $[\mathbf{TxtEx}]^{\text{dual-weak-monotonic}} = \{ \mathcal{L} \mid \mathcal{L} \subseteq \mathbf{TxtEx}(\mathbf{M})$ for some dual-weak-monotonic $\mathbf{M} \}$.

(e) $[\mathbf{TxtEx}]^{\text{class-dual-weak-monotonic}} = \{\, \mathcal{L} \mid \mathcal{L} \subseteq \mathbf{TxtEx}(\mathbf{M})$ for some $\mathbf{M}$ dual-weak-monotonic on $\mathcal{L}\,\}$.

Clearly, $[\mathbf{TxtEx}]^{\text{dual-weak-monotonic}} \subseteq [\mathbf{TxtEx}]^{\text{class-dual-weak-monotonic}}$. The next result shows the surprising fact that every identifiable collection of languages can also be identified by a dual-weak-monotonic scientist.

5.60 Proposition $\mathbf{TxtEx} \subseteq [\mathbf{TxtEx}]^{\textit{dual-weak-monotonic}}$.

Proof (After Kinber and Stephan [109]):   Fix $\mathbf{M}$. We assume, without loss of generality (by Proposition 5.29), that $\mathbf{M}$ identifies T if and only if T contains a locking sequence for $\mathbf{M}$ on $content(T)$. By the s-m-n theorem, there is a recursive f such that, for all e and σ,

$$
W_{f(e,\sigma)} \;=\; \begin{cases} \emptyset, & \text{if } content(\sigma) \not\subseteq W_e; \\ W_e, & \text{if } \sigma \text{ is a locking sequence for } \mathbf{M} \text{ on } W_e; \\ N, & \text{otherwise.} \end{cases}
$$

We inductively define $\mathbf{M}'$ so that, for each σ, there is a $\tau_\sigma \subseteq \sigma$ such that $\mathbf{M}'(\sigma) = f(\mathbf{M}(\tau_\sigma), \tau_\sigma)$. Define $\mathbf{M}'(\emptyset) = W_{f(\mathbf{M}(\emptyset),\emptyset)}$. Given σ and x, define

$$
\mathbf{M}'(\sigma \diamond x) \;=\; \begin{cases} f(\mathbf{M}(\sigma \diamond x), \sigma \diamond x), & \text{if there exists a } \gamma \supseteq \tau_\sigma \text{ such that} \\ & \quad content(\gamma) \subseteq content(\sigma) \cup \{\,x\,\}, \\ & \quad |\gamma| \leq |\sigma|, \text{ and } \mathbf{M}(\tau_\sigma) \neq \mathbf{M}(\gamma); \\ \mathbf{M}'(\sigma), & \text{otherwise.} \end{cases}
$$

Claim: $\mathbf{M}'$ identifies each language identified by $\mathbf{M}$. To see this, first suppose $\mathbf{M}$ identifies T and suppose that $T[n]$ is a locking sequence for $\mathbf{M}$ on T. Once $\mathbf{M}'$ outputs $f(\mathbf{M}(T[n']), T[n'])$ for some $n' > n$, it never changes its mind. Thus $\mathbf{M}'$ converges on T. Suppose $\mathbf{M}'$ converges to $f(\mathbf{M}(T[n'']), T[n''])$. Then $T[n'']$ must be a locking sequence for $\mathbf{M}$ on $content(T)$. It follows that $\mathbf{M}'$ identifies T. Thus the claim is shown.

Claim: $\mathbf{M}'$ is dual-weak-monotonic. To see this, first suppose $\sigma \subseteq \sigma'$ and $\mathbf{M}'(\sigma) \neq \mathbf{M}'(\sigma')$. This implies that there is a γ such that $\tau_\sigma \subseteq \gamma$, $content(\gamma) \subseteq content(\tau_{\sigma'})$, and $\mathbf{M}(\tau_\sigma) \neq \mathbf{M}(\gamma)$. It follows that either $content(\gamma) \not\subseteq W_{\mathbf{M}(\tau_\sigma)} = W_{\mathbf{M}'(\sigma)}$ or $W_{\mathbf{M}'(\sigma)} = N$. In both cases, the dual-weak-monotonic property of $\mathbf{M}'$ is not violated, hence, the claim and the theorem follow. ∎

§5.6 Strategies for function identification

We now turn our attention to strategies for function identification. As in the case of languages, we consider both the global and class versions where they are meaningful. *Notation:* Recall from Chapter 4 that $f[n]$ denotes both the partial function $\{(x, f(x)) \mid x < n\}$ and the initial segment of length n of the canonical text for f. Also recall from Definition 4.18 that INIT $= \{f[n] \mid f \in \mathcal{F}$ and $n \in N\}$.

§5.6.1 Consistency

The next definition formalizes consistency in the context of function identification.

5.61 Definition (Bārzdiņš [13], Blum and Blum [18])

(a) **M** is *consistent* on f just in case for all n, $f[n] \subseteq \varphi_{\mathbf{M}(f[n])}$.

(b) **M** is *consistent* on $\mathcal{S} \subseteq \mathcal{R}$ just in case **M** is consistent on each $f \in \mathcal{S}$.

(c) **M** is *consistent* just in case **M** is consistent on $\mathcal{R}$.

(d) $[\mathbf{Ex}]^{\text{consistent}} = \{\mathcal{S} \mid \mathcal{S} \subseteq \mathbf{Ex}(\mathbf{M})$ for some consistent **M** $\}$.

(e) $[\mathbf{Ex}]^{\text{class-consistent}} = \{\mathcal{S} \mid \mathcal{S} \subseteq \mathbf{Ex}(\mathbf{M})$ for some **M** consistent on $\mathcal{S}\}$.

Just as in the language paradigm, consistency has the ring of rationality. However, similarly to before, implementing the strategy can entail a loss of inductive power.

5.62 Proposition $[\mathbf{Ex}]^{\textit{consistent}} \subset [\mathbf{Ex}]^{\textit{class-consistent}} \subset \mathbf{Ex}$.

Proof: Clearly, $[\mathbf{Ex}]^{\text{consistent}} \subseteq [\mathbf{Ex}]^{\text{class-consistent}} \subseteq \mathbf{Ex}$.

We first show that $[\mathbf{Ex}]^{\text{consistent}} \subset [\mathbf{Ex}]^{\text{class-consistent}}$.

Consider the collection of self-describing functions $\mathcal{SD} = \{f \in \mathcal{R} \mid \varphi_{f(0)} = f\}$. It is easy to show that $\mathcal{SD} \in [\mathbf{Ex}]^{\text{class-consistent}}$. Suppose by way of contradiction that a scientist **M** that is consistent (on $\mathcal{R}$) identifies $\mathcal{SD}$. Then, by Kleene's recursion theorem (Theorem 2.3), there exists an index e such that, for all x,

$$\varphi_e(x) = \begin{cases} e, & \text{if } x = 0; \\ 0, & \text{if } x > 0 \text{ and } \mathbf{M}(\varphi_e[x] \diamond (x, 0)) \neq \mathbf{M}(\varphi_e[x]); \\ 1, & \text{otherwise.} \end{cases}$$

It is clear that $\varphi_e \in \mathcal{SD}$. Also, since **M** is consistent, for each $x > 0$, either $\mathbf{M}(\varphi_e[x] \diamond (x, 0)) \neq \mathbf{M}(\varphi_e[x])$ or $\mathbf{M}(\varphi_e[x] \diamond (x, 1)) \neq \mathbf{M}(\varphi_e[x])$. Hence, for each $x > 0$, $\mathbf{M}(\varphi_e[x + 1]) \neq \mathbf{M}(\varphi_e[x])$. It follows that $\varphi_e \notin \mathbf{Ex}(\mathbf{M})$, a contradiction.

We next show that $\mathbf{Ex} - [\mathbf{Ex}]^{\text{class-consistent}} \neq \emptyset$.
Define:

$$\mathcal{SD}' = \{ f \mid (\forall x)[f(x) < f(x+1)] \wedge \varphi_{f(0)} = f \}$$

$$\cup$$

$$\{ f \mid (\exists x)[f(x+1) < f(x)] \wedge \varphi_{f(min(\{ x+1 \mid f(x+1) < f(x) \}))} = f \}.$$

We leave it to the reader to verify that $\mathcal{SD}' \in \mathbf{Ex}$. We argue that $\mathcal{SD}' \notin [\mathbf{Ex}]^{\text{class-consistent}}$. Suppose by way of contradiction that a scientist $\mathbf{M}$ that is consistent on $\mathcal{SD}'$ identifies $\mathcal{SD}'$. Then by Kleene's recursion theorem (Theorem 2.3), there exists an index e such that, for all x,

$$\varphi_e(x) =$$

$$\begin{cases} e, & \text{if (i) } x = 0; \\ \varphi_e(x-1) + 1, & \text{if (ii) } x > 0 \text{ and } \mathbf{M}(\varphi_e[x] \diamond (x, \varphi_e(x-1)+1)) \neq \mathbf{M}(\varphi_e[x]); \\ \varphi_e(x-1) + 2, & \text{if (iii) } x > 0, \text{ not (ii), and } \mathbf{M}(\varphi_e[x] \diamond (x, \varphi_e(x-1)+2)) \neq \\ & \quad \mathbf{M}(\varphi_e[x]); \\ \uparrow, & \text{(iv) otherwise.} \end{cases}$$

Suppose φ_e is total. Then $\varphi_e \in \mathcal{SD}'$, and for all $x > 0$, $\mathbf{M}(\varphi_e[x]) \neq \mathbf{M}(\varphi_e[x+1])$. Hence, $\varphi_e \notin \mathbf{Ex}(\mathbf{M})$, a contradiction. Therefore, φ_e is not total. Suppose x is the least number such that $\varphi_e(x)$ is not defined. Then $\mathbf{M}(\varphi_e[x] \diamond (x, \varphi_e(x-1)+1)) = \mathbf{M}(\varphi_e[x])$ and $\mathbf{M}(\varphi_e[x] \diamond (x, \varphi_e(x-1)+2)) = \mathbf{M}(\varphi_e[x])$. Let $z \in \{1, 2\}$ be such that $\varphi_{\mathbf{M}(\varphi_e[x])}(x) \neq \varphi_e(x-1) + z$. Again, by Kleene's recursion theorem, there exists an index e_1 such that, for all x,

$$\varphi_{e_1}(y) = \begin{cases} \varphi_e(y), & \text{if } y < x; \\ \varphi_e(x-1) + z, & \text{if } y = x; \\ \varphi_e(x-1) + z + e_1 + 1, & \text{if } y = x+1; \\ e_1, & \text{if } y = x+2; \\ 0, & \text{otherwise.} \end{cases}$$

It is easy to verify that $\varphi_{e_1} \in \mathcal{SD}'$. However, since $\varphi_{\mathbf{M}(\varphi_{e_1}[x+1])}(x) \neq \varphi_{e_1}(x)$, $\mathbf{M}$ is not consistent on φ_{e_1}. This is a contradiction. It follows that no such $\mathbf{M}$ can exist. ∎

§5.6.2 Popperian

As discussed in the context of languages, scientific practice usually demands the testability of hypotheses, a constraint that was labeled "accountability" in Section 5.2.3. We now formulate a similar requirement for the paradigm of function learning.

5.63 Definition (Case and Ngo-Manguelle [34])

(a) **M** is *Popperian* on f just in case for all n, $\varphi_{\mathbf{M}(f[n])} \in \mathcal{R}$.

(b) **M** is *Popperian* on $\mathcal{S} \subseteq \mathcal{R}$ just in case **M** is Popperian on each $f \in \mathcal{S}$.

(c) **M** is *Popperian* just in case **M** is Popperian on $\mathcal{R}$.

(d) $[\mathbf{Ex}]^{\text{Popperian}} = \{\, \mathcal{S} \mid \mathcal{S} \subseteq \mathbf{Ex}(\mathbf{M}) \text{ for Popperian } \mathbf{M} \,\}$.

(e) $[\mathbf{Ex}]^{\text{class-Popperian}} = \{\, \mathcal{S} \mid \mathcal{S} \subseteq \mathbf{Ex}(\mathbf{M}) \text{ for some } \mathbf{M} \text{ Popperian on } \mathcal{S} \,\}$.

An index for a total computable function is a testable hypothesis, since it is possible to test its accuracy against the data provided by a finite sequence. Such testability motivates the terminology "Popperian," since Popper (e.g, [153]) insisted on this aspect of scientific practice. Requiring the testability of hypotheses appears to be a useful requirement. However, like many other seemingly rational constraints, both versions of Popperian scientists pay a price for their rationality, as implied by the next result.

5.64 Proposition $[\mathbf{Ex}]^{\text{Popperian}} \subset [\mathbf{Ex}]^{\text{class-Popperian}} \subset \mathbf{Ex}$.

Proof: Clearly, $[\mathbf{Ex}]^{\text{Popperian}} \subseteq [\mathbf{Ex}]^{\text{class-Popperian}} \subseteq \mathbf{Ex}$.

We first show that $[\mathbf{Ex}]^{\text{class-Popperian}} - [\mathbf{Ex}]^{\text{Popperian}} \neq \emptyset$.

Consider again the collection of self-describing computable functions $\mathcal{SD} = \{\, f \in \mathcal{R} \mid \varphi_{f(0)} = f \,\}$. Clearly, $\mathcal{SD} \in [\mathbf{Ex}]^{\text{class-Popperian}}$. Suppose by way of contradiction that **M** is Popperian (on $\mathcal{R}$) and identifies $\mathcal{S}$. Then, by Kleene's recursion theorem (Theorem 2.3), there exists an e such that, for all x,

$$\varphi_e(x) = \begin{cases} e, & \text{if } x = 0; \\ \varphi_{\mathbf{M}(\varphi_e[x])}(x) + 1, & \text{if } x > 0. \end{cases}$$

Since **M** is Popperian, φ_e is total and thus $\varphi_e \in \mathcal{SD}$. Also, for all $x > 0$, $\varphi_e(x) \neq \varphi_{\mathbf{M}(\varphi_e[x])}(x)$. Thus $\varphi_e \notin \mathbf{Ex}(\mathbf{M})$, a contradiction. Hence, $\mathcal{SD} \notin [\mathbf{Ex}]^{\text{Popperian}}$.

Let $\mathcal{SD}'$ be as defined in the proof of Proposition 5.62 on page 116. Clearly, $\mathcal{SD}' \in \mathbf{Ex}$. By Exercise 5-22 $\mathcal{SD}' \notin [\mathbf{Ex}]^{\text{class-Popperian}}$. ∎

We describe a nice characterization of $[\mathbf{Ex}]^{\text{Popperian}}$. First, recall from Definition 5.10 that $\mathcal{S} \subseteq \mathcal{R}$ is said to be *r.e. indexable* exactly when there is an $S \in \mathcal{E}$ such that $\mathcal{S} = \{\, \varphi_i \mid i \in S \,\}$. We define the class

$$\mathbf{Enum} = \{\, \mathcal{S} \mid (\exists \mathcal{S}' \supseteq \mathcal{S})[\mathcal{S}' \text{ is r.e. indexable}] \,\}.$$

The characterization of $[\mathbf{Ex}]^{\text{Popperian}}$ says that the collections of functions that Popperian scientists can identify are precisely the collections of functions that are subsets of r.e. indexable collections of functions.

5.65 Proposition (Bārzdiņš and Freivalds [15], Case and Smith [35])
Enum $= [\mathbf{Ex}]^{\text{Popperian}}$.

Proof: Suppose $\mathcal{S} \in [\mathbf{Ex}]^{\text{Popperian}}$. Fix a Popperian scientist $\mathbf{M}$ that identifies each function in $\mathcal{S}$. Let $\mathcal{S}' = \{\varphi_{\mathbf{M}(\sigma)} \mid \sigma \in \text{SEG}\}$. It is easy to see that $\mathcal{R} \supseteq \mathcal{S}' \supseteq \mathcal{S}$ and that $\mathcal{S}'$ is r.e. indexable.

Suppose $\mathcal{S}' \neq \emptyset$ is an r.e. indexable class of total functions. Choose a $g \in \mathcal{R}$ such that $\{\varphi_{g(i)} \mid i \in N\} = \mathcal{S}'$. Let $\mathbf{M}$ be a scientist that, for each $\sigma \in \text{INIT}$,

$$\mathbf{M}(\sigma) \;=\; g\left(\min(\{\,|\sigma|\,\} \cup \{\,i < |\sigma| \;\mid\; \sigma = \varphi_{g(i)}[|\sigma|]\,\})\right).$$

It is easy to verify that $\mathbf{M}$ is Popperian and that $\mathcal{S}' \subseteq \mathbf{Ex}(\mathbf{M})$. ∎

§5.6.3 Reliability

Reliable scientists were first studied by Minicozzi [132]. Reliability in the context of languages guarantees that if a scientist converges on a text for a language, then the scientist converges to an index for that language. The following formalizes reliability in the context of functions.

5.66 Definition (Minicozzi [132])

(a) $\mathbf{M}$ is *reliable* on f just in case $\mathbf{M}(f)\!\downarrow \Rightarrow \varphi_{\mathbf{M}(f)} = f$.

(b) $\mathbf{M}$ is *reliable* on $\mathcal{S} \subseteq \mathcal{R}$ just in case $\mathbf{M}$ is reliable on each $f \in \mathcal{S}$.

(c) $\mathbf{M}$ is *recursive-reliable* just in case $\mathbf{M}$ is reliable on $\mathcal{R}$.

(d) $[\mathbf{Ex}]^{\text{rec-reliable}} = \{\mathcal{S} \mid \mathcal{S} \subseteq \mathbf{Ex}(\mathbf{M})$ for some recursive-reliable $\mathbf{M}\}$.

The next proposition shows that recursive-reliable scientists pay a price for this useful property.

5.67 Proposition $[\mathbf{Ex}]^{\text{rec-reliable}} \subset \mathbf{Ex}$.

Proof: Clearly, $[\mathbf{Ex}]^{\text{rec-reliable}} \subseteq \mathbf{Ex}$. Below we argue that $\mathbf{Ex} - [\mathbf{Ex}]^{\text{rec-reliable}} \neq \emptyset$. Our argument uses the following claim.

5.68 Claim *Suppose* **M** *is recursive-reliable. Then for all* $\sigma \in$ INIT, *there exists a* $\tau \in$ INIT *such that* $\sigma \subseteq \tau$ *and* $\mathbf{M}(\sigma) \neq \mathbf{M}(\tau)$. *Moreover, there is a recursive function t such that, given* σ, $t(\sigma) =$ *a* τ *as above.*

Proof (Claim 5.68): If such a τ does not exist then **M** converges to $\mathbf{M}(\sigma)$ on all functions consistent with σ. However, $\mathbf{M}(\sigma)$ can be an index for at most one function consistent with σ. This contradicts the fact that **M** is recursive-reliable. The moreover clause is obvious. $\square$

Recall that $\mathcal{SD} = \{\, f \mid \varphi_{f(0)} = f \,\} \in \mathbf{Ex}$. Fix a recursive-reliable scientist **M**. We show that **M** fails to identify $\mathcal{SD}$. By Kleene's recursion theorem (Theorem 2.3), there exists an e such that φ_e may be defined as follows: let σ_0 be such that $content(\sigma_0) = \{\, (0, e) \,\}$, $\sigma_{i+1} = t(\sigma_i)$ (for $i \in N$), and $\varphi_e = \bigcup_i content(\sigma_i)$. Clearly, $\varphi_e \in \mathcal{SD}$. Also, $\mathbf{M}(\varphi_e)\!\uparrow$. Thus, $\mathcal{SD} \not\subseteq \mathbf{Ex}(\mathbf{M})$. ∎

§5.6.4 Decisiveness

In the course of identification a scientist may conjecture a hypothesis, abandon it after seeing more data, and revert to the abandoned hypothesis once again. A sensible strategy would be to consider only those scientists that never go back to an abandoned conjecture.

5.69 Definition

(a) **M** is *decisive* on f just in case, for all $l, m, n \in N$ with $l < m < n$ and $\varphi_{\mathbf{M}(f[l])} \neq \varphi_{\mathbf{M}(f[m])}$, we have $\varphi_{\mathbf{M}(f[l])} \neq \varphi_{\mathbf{M}(f[n])}$.

(b) **M** is *decisive* on $\mathcal{S}$ just in case **M** is decisive on each $f \in \mathcal{S}$.

(c) **M** is *decisive* just in case **M** is decisive on $\mathcal{R}$.

(d) $[\mathbf{Ex}]^{\text{decisive}} = \{\, \mathcal{S} \mid \mathcal{S} \subseteq \mathbf{Ex}(\mathbf{M}) \text{ for some decisive } \mathbf{M} \,\}$.

(e) $[\mathbf{Ex}]^{\text{class-decisive}} = \{\, \mathcal{S} \mid \mathcal{S} \subseteq \mathbf{Ex}(\mathbf{M}) \text{ for some } \mathbf{M} \text{ decisive on } \mathcal{S} \,\}$.

We shall now see that scientists can adopt a decisive strategy without loss of inductive competence.

5.70 Proposition (Schäfer-Richter [167]) $[\mathbf{Ex}]^{\text{decisive}} = [\mathbf{Ex}]^{\text{class-decisive}} = \mathbf{Ex}$.

Proof: Clearly, $[\mathbf{Ex}]^{\text{decisive}} \subseteq [\mathbf{Ex}]^{\text{class-decisive}} \subseteq \mathbf{Ex}$. We show that $\mathbf{Ex} \subseteq [\mathbf{Ex}]^{\text{decisive}}$.

Suppose scientist $\mathbf{M}$ is given. We describe a scientist $\mathbf{M}'$ such that $\mathbf{Ex}(\mathbf{M}) \subseteq \mathbf{Ex}(\mathbf{M}')$ and $\mathbf{M}'$ is decisive. Let $h: N \times \text{INIT} \to N$ be a recursive function that satisfies the following equation.

$$\varphi_{h(i,\sigma)}(x) = \begin{cases} \sigma(x), & \text{if } x < |\sigma|; \\ \varphi_i(x), & \text{if } x \geq |\sigma|, \ \sigma \subseteq \varphi_i, \ (\forall y \leq x)[\varphi_i(y)\downarrow], \text{ and} \\ & \quad (\forall y \in \{\, |\sigma|, \ldots, x+1 \,\})[\, \mathbf{M}(\sigma) = \mathbf{M}(\varphi_i[y]) \,]; \\ \uparrow, & \text{otherwise.} \end{cases}$$

For each $\mathbf{M}$ and each $\sigma \in \text{INIT}$, define

$$\text{convpoint}(\mathbf{M}, \sigma) = min(\{\, x \leq |\sigma| \mid (\forall y \in \{\, x, \ldots, |\sigma| \,\})[\, \mathbf{M}(\sigma[y]) = \mathbf{M}(\sigma) \,] \,\}).$$

Now let $\mathbf{M}'$ be a scientist such that, for all $\sigma \in \text{INIT}$, $\mathbf{M}'(\sigma) = h(\mathbf{M}(\sigma[m]), \sigma[m])$, where $m = \text{convpoint}(\mathbf{M}, \sigma)$. We claim that $\mathbf{Ex}(\mathbf{M}) \subseteq \mathbf{Ex}(\mathbf{M}')$ and $\mathbf{M}'$ is decisive.

Note that if $f \in \mathbf{Ex}(\mathbf{M})$, then $\mathbf{M}'(f)$ converges to $h(i, f[m])$, where $i = \mathbf{M}(f)$ and m is the convergence point for $\mathbf{M}$ on f. Moreover, $\varphi_{h(i, f[m])} = \varphi_i$. Thus $f \in \mathbf{Ex}(\mathbf{M}')$.

To see that $\mathbf{M}'$ is decisive, suppose f and $l < m < n$ are given such that $\mathbf{M}'(f[l]) \neq \mathbf{M}'(f[m]) \neq \mathbf{M}'(f[n])$. Let $n' = \text{convpoint}(\mathbf{M}, f[n])$ and $l' = \text{convpoint}(\mathbf{M}, f[l])$. Clearly, $n' \geq m$ and $l' \leq l$. Now $\mathbf{M}'(f[n]) = h(\mathbf{M}(f[n']), f[n'])$ and thus $f[m] \subseteq f[n'] \subseteq \varphi_{\mathbf{M}(f[n])}$ (by construction of h). However, $\mathbf{M}'(f[l]) = h(\mathbf{M}(f[l']), f[l'])$. Thus, $f[m] \not\subseteq \varphi_{\mathbf{M}'(f[l])}$, since, in the construction of $h(\mathbf{M}(f[l']), f[l'])$, either a mind change would be observed before input m or $\varphi_{\mathbf{M}'(f[l'])}$ is convergently different from $f[m]$. Therefore, $\mathbf{M}'$ is decisive.   ∎

§5.7 Bibliographic notes

The question of consistency has been independently considered by Bārzdiņš [13] and by Blum and Blum [18] in the context of functions. The reader can find additional material on consistent strategies in Wiehagen and Liepe [202], Jantke and Beick [100], Zeugmann [206], and Fulk [70]. Consistency in the context of languages has been addressed by Angluin [6]. Wiehagen and Zeugmann [203] present an interesting perspective on the power of inconsistent strategies in the context of more practical domains.

The notion of set-driven scientists was introduced by Wexler and Culicover [194]. Schäfer-Richter [167], and later Fulk [69], independently established that set-drivenness is a restriction on computable scientists. The notion of rearrangement-independence was introduced as a weakening of set-drivenness by Schäfer-Richter [167] and by Fulk [69].

The question of order-independence was first considered by Blum and Blum [18]. They showed that order-independence is not a restriction on **TxtEx**. The proof presented in this chapter is due to Fulk [69, 71]. In the proof he showed that not only can a scientist be converted into an order-independent scientist without any loss in learning ability, but the resulting order-independent scientist can also be made to satisfy several additional properties such as rearrangement-independence. The reader is referred to Lange and Zeugmann [121] for a treatment of order-independence and set-drivenness in the context of uniformly decidable families of recursive languages. A related result is also due to Jain [84].

The notion of prudence was introduced by Wexler and Culicover. Fulk [69, 71] showed that prudence is not a restriction on identification. The reader is referred to Kurtz and Royer [115] and to Jain and Sharma [91] for additional results on prudence.

The question of identification by reliable scientists was considered by Minicozzi [132]. The reader is directed to papers by Case, Jain, and Ngo-Manguelle [28] and by Kinber and Zeugmann [110, 111] for additional material on reliability.[1]

Angluin [6] began the investigation of conservative scientists. The study of monotonicity was initiated by Jantke [99] who also defined the notion of strong-monotonic strategies. Wiehagen [200] introduced monotonic strategies and Lange and Zeugmann [119] defined weak-monotonic strategies. The duals of these strategies were proposed by Kapur [103]. Lange, Kapur, and Zeugmann have obtained numerous results on the relative learning abilities of these strategies in the context of identifying uniformly decidable families of recursive languages, e.g., see [122], [209], and [120]. A survey of this work can be found in [208]. The study of monotonicity for r.e. languages is due to Jain and Sharma [88, 96], where the distinction between global and class versions of a strategy is formalized. Kinber and Stephan [109] also independently investigated monotonicity in the context of r.e. languages.

---

[1] In our discussion of strategies, we have required that the underlying realities a scientists investigates are to be modeled by recursively enumerable languages or computable functions. In the case of reliability, it is mathematically interesting to modify this requirement and consider the behavior of scientists on non-r.e. "languages" and non-recursive functions. For example, in the language case one can require, not unreasonably, that a reliable scientist should fail to converge on any text that has a non-r.e. set as its content. In the language case, this strengthened reliability requirement turns out to be equivalent to ordinary reliability. In the function case, matters are quite different and rather involved. For this reason, we have called the strategy discussed in Definition 5.66 as recursive-reliable to distinguish it from the notion of reliable scientists in the literature reserved for this stricter notion of reliability. Case, Jain, and Ngo-Manguelle [28] discuss these subtle issues. Fortunately, for other strategies discussed in this chapter, both for languages and functions, the analogous stricter version of global strategies do not place any additional constraint on identifiability.

§5.8 Exercises

5-1 No natural language, it appears, includes a longest sentence. If this universal feature of natural language corresponds to an innate constraint on children's linguistic hypotheses, then children would be barred from conjecturing a grammar for a finite language. Such a constraint on potential conjectures amounts to a strategy. To formulate it, let us call $\mathbf{M}$ *nontrivial* on a language L just in case for all σ such that $content(\sigma) \subseteq L$, $W_{\varphi(\sigma)}$ is infinite. $\mathbf{M}$ is *nontrivial* on $\mathcal{L}$ just in case $\mathbf{M}$ is nontrivial on each $L \in \mathcal{L}$. $\mathbf{M}$ is *nontrivial* just in case $\mathbf{M}$ is nontrivial on each $L \subseteq \mathcal{E}$. Define:

$$[\mathbf{TxtEx}]^{\text{non-trivial}} \quad = \quad \{\, \mathcal{L} \mid \mathcal{L} \subseteq \mathbf{TxtEx}(\mathbf{M}) \text{ for some nontrivial } \mathbf{M} \,\}.$$

$$[\mathbf{TxtEx}]^{\text{class-nontrivial}} \quad = \quad \left\{\, \mathcal{L} \;\middle|\; \begin{array}{l} \mathcal{L} \subseteq \mathbf{TxtEx}(\mathbf{M}) \text{ for some} \\ \mathbf{M} \text{ that is nontrivial on } \mathcal{L} \end{array} \right\}.$$

Clearly, no nontrivial scientist can identify any finite language. In contrast, their behavior on collections of infinite languages is less evident. To explore the matter, show the following.

(a) There is $\mathcal{L} \subseteq \mathcal{E}$ such that (i) every $L \in \mathcal{L}$ is infinite, and (ii) $\mathcal{L} \in (\mathbf{TxtEx} - [\mathbf{TxtEx}]^{\text{nontrivial}})$.

(b) $[\mathbf{TxtEx}]^{\text{non-trivial}} = [\mathbf{TxtEx}]^{\text{account}}$.

(c) $[\mathbf{TxtEx}]^{\text{class-nontrivial}} \subset [\mathbf{TxtEx}]^{\text{class-account}}$.

5-2 Show that $[\mathbf{TxtEx}]^{\text{class-consistent}} \subset \mathbf{TxtEx}$.

5-3 $\mathbf{M}$ is called *nonexcessive* just in case for all $\sigma \in \text{SEQ}$, $W_{\mathbf{M}(\sigma)} \neq N$. $[\mathbf{TxtEx}]^{\text{nonexcessive}}$ denotes $\{\, \mathcal{L} \subseteq \mathcal{E} \mid \text{there exists a nonexcessive } \mathbf{M} \text{ that identifies } \mathcal{L} \,\}$. Prove: For all $\mathcal{L} \subseteq \mathcal{E}$, if $N \notin \mathcal{L}$, then $\mathcal{L} \in [\mathbf{TxtEx}]^{\text{nonexcessive}}$ if and only if $\mathcal{L} \in \mathbf{TxtEx}$.

5-4 (J. Canny) $\mathbf{M}$ is said to be *weakly nontrivial* just in case for all infinite $L \in \mathbf{TxtEx}(\mathbf{M})$, $W_{\mathbf{M}(T[n])}$ is infinite for all $n \in N$ and all texts T for L. Nontriviality implies weak nontriviality. $[\mathbf{TxtEx}]^{\text{weak-nontriv}}$ denotes $\{\, \mathcal{L} \subseteq \mathcal{E} \mid \text{there exists a weakly nontrivial } \mathbf{M} \text{ that identifies } \mathcal{L} \,\}$. Show that for some collection $\mathcal{L} \subseteq \mathcal{E}$ of infinite languages, $\mathcal{L} \in \mathbf{TxtEx} - [\mathbf{TxtEx}]^{\text{weak-nontriv}}$.

5-5 **M** is said to be *conditionally consistent* just in case for all $\sigma \in$ SEQ, if $\mathbf{M}(\sigma)\downarrow$, then *content*$(\sigma) \subseteq W_{\mathbf{M}(\sigma)}$. $[\mathbf{TxtEx}]^{\text{cond-consistent}}$ denotes $\{\, \mathcal{L} \subseteq \mathcal{E} \mid$ there exists a conditionally consistent scientist **M** that identifies $\mathcal{L} \,\}$.

Refute the following variant of Proposition 5.6: If conditionally consistent **M** identifies $\mathcal{L} \subseteq \mathcal{E}$, then $\mathcal{L} \subseteq \mathcal{REC}$.

5-6 Show that $\{\, K \cup \{\, x \,\} \mid x \in \overline{K} \,\} \in [\mathbf{TxtEx}]^{\text{prudent}}$.

5-7 $L \in \mathcal{E}$ is called *total* just in case for all $x \in N$ there is $y \in N$ such that $\langle x, y \rangle \in L$. Note that a total language need not represent a function (since it need not be single valued). **M** is called *total-minded* just in case for all $\sigma \in$ SEQ, if $\mathbf{M}(\sigma)\downarrow$ then $W_{\mathbf{M}(\sigma)}$ is total. $[\mathbf{TxtEx}]^{\text{tot-minded}}$ denotes $\{\, \mathcal{L} \subseteq \mathcal{E} \mid$ there exist a total-minded scientist **M** that identifies $\mathcal{L} \,\}$. Prove: There is $\mathcal{L} \subseteq \mathcal{E}$ such that (a) every $L \in \mathcal{L}$ is total, and (b) $\mathcal{L} \in (\mathbf{TxtEx} - [\mathbf{TxtEx}]^{\text{tot-minded}})$. *Hint:* Use Rogers [158], Theorem 5-XVI: the single-valuedness theorem.

5-8 Prove that if $\mathcal{L}$ contains only infinite languages, then $\mathcal{L} \in \mathbf{TxtEx}$ if and only if $\mathcal{L} \in [\mathbf{TxtEx}]^{\text{set-driven}}$.

5-9 Give a proof of Lemma 5.33.

5-10 Show the following:

(a) $[\mathbf{TxtEx}]^{\text{consistent}} \not\subseteq [\mathbf{TxtEx}]^{\text{conservative}}$.

(b) $[\mathbf{TxtEx}]^{\text{conservative}} \not\subseteq [\mathbf{TxtEx}]^{\text{consistent}}$.

5-11 **M** is said to be *gradualist* just in case for all $\sigma \in$ SEQ, $\{\, \mathbf{M}(\sigma \diamond n) \mid n \in N \,\}$ is finite. $[\mathbf{TxtEx}]^{\text{gradualist}}$ denotes $\{\, \mathcal{L} \subseteq \mathcal{E} \mid$ there exists a gradualist scientist **M** that identifies $\mathcal{L} \,\}$. Show that $[\mathbf{TxtEx}]^{\text{gradualist}} = \mathbf{TxtEx}$.

5-12 **M** is called *cautious* just in case for all $\sigma, \tau \in$ SEQ, $W_{\mathbf{M}(\sigma\tau)}$ is not a proper subset of $W_{\mathbf{M}(\sigma)}$. Note that cautious scientists behave as if they never overgeneralize. Compare this strategy with conservative scientists that do not over generalize on languages they identify, but may over generalize on languages they do not identify. $[\mathbf{TxtEx}]^{\text{cautious}}$ denotes $\{\, \mathcal{L} \subseteq \mathcal{E} \mid$ there exists a cautious scientist **M** such that $\mathcal{L} \subseteq \mathbf{TxtEx}(\mathbf{M}) \,\}$. Show that $[\mathbf{TxtEx}]^{\text{cautious}} \subset \mathbf{TxtEx}$.

5-13   Show that $[\mathbf{TxtEx}]^{\text{cautious}} \not\subseteq [\mathbf{TxtEx}]^{\text{conservative}}$.

5-14   A scientist that converges on every text may be termed "confident."   **M** is *confident* on L just in case for all texts T for L, $\mathbf{M}(T){\downarrow}$. **M** is *confident* on $\mathcal{L}$ just in case **M** is confident on each $L \in \mathcal{L}$. **M** is *confident* just in case **M** is confident on $L \subseteq \mathcal{E}$. $[\mathbf{TxtEx}]^{\text{confident}} = \{\, \mathcal{L} \mid (\exists \mathbf{M})[\mathbf{M} \text{ is confident and } \mathcal{L} \subseteq \mathbf{TxtEx}(\mathbf{M})]\,\}$.

Show the following:

(a) Let a confident scientist **M** be given. Then for every $L \in \mathcal{E}$, there is $\sigma \in \text{SEQ}$ such that (i) $content(\sigma) \subseteq L$, and (ii) for all $\tau \in \text{SEQ}$ such that $content(\tau) \subseteq L$, $\mathbf{M}(\sigma \diamond \tau) = \mathbf{M}(\sigma)$.

(b) $[\mathbf{TxtEx}]^{\text{confident}} \subset \mathbf{TxtEx}$.

5-15   Show the following:

(a) $[\mathbf{TxtEx}]^{\text{class-strong-monotonic}} = [\mathbf{TxtEx}]^{\text{strong-monotonic}}$.

(b) $[\mathbf{TxtEx}]^{\text{class-weak-monotonic}} = [\mathbf{TxtEx}]^{\text{weak-monotonic}}$.

5-16   (Kapur [103])   Define the dual of a strong-monotonic scientist as follows.

5.71 Definition

(a) **M** is *dual-strong-monotonic* on L just in case, for all τ with $content(\tau) \subseteq L$ and all σ with $\sigma \subseteq \tau$, we have $W_{\mathbf{M}(\sigma)} \supseteq W_{\mathbf{M}(\tau)}$.

(b) **M** is *dual-strong-monotonic* on $\mathcal{L}$ just in case **M** is dual-strong-monotonic on each $L \in \mathcal{L}$.

(c) **M** is *dual-strong-monotonic* just in case it is dual-strong-monotonic on each $L \subseteq \mathcal{E}$.

(d) $[\mathbf{TxtEx}]^{\text{dual-strong-monotonic}} = \{\, \mathcal{L} \mid \mathcal{L} \subseteq \mathbf{TxtEx}(\mathbf{M}) \text{ for some dual-strong-monotonic } \mathbf{M} \,\}$.

(e) $[\mathbf{TxtEx}]^{\text{class-dual-strong-monotonic}} = \{\, \mathcal{L} \mid \mathcal{L} \subseteq \mathbf{TxtEx}(\mathbf{M}) \text{ for some } \mathbf{M} \text{ that is dual-strong-monotonic on } \mathcal{L} \,\}$.

Show that $[\mathbf{TxtEx}]^{\text{class-dual-strong-monotonic}} = [\mathbf{TxtEx}]^{\text{dual-strong-monotonic}}$.

5-17   (Kapur [103])   Define the dual of a monotonic scientist as follows.

5.72 Definition

(a) **M** is *dual-monotonic* on L just in case, for each τ with $content(\tau) \subseteq L$ and each σ with $\sigma \subseteq \tau$ we have that $\overline{W_{\mathbf{M}(\sigma)}} \cap \overline{L} \subseteq \overline{W_{\mathbf{M}(\tau)}} \cap \overline{L}$.

(b) **M** is *dual-monotonic on $\mathcal{L}$* just in case **M** is dual-monotonic on each $L \in \mathcal{L}$.

(c) **M** is *dual-monotonic* just in case **M** is dual-monotonic on each $L \subseteq \mathcal{E}$.

(d) $[\mathbf{TxtEx}]^{\text{dual-monotonic}} = \{\, \mathcal{L} \subseteq \mathcal{E} \mid \mathcal{L} \subseteq \mathbf{TxtEx}(\mathbf{M})$ for some dual-monotonic **M** $\}$.

(e) $[\mathbf{TxtEx}]^{\text{class-dual-monotonic}} = \{\, \mathcal{L} \subseteq \mathcal{E} \mid \mathcal{L} \subseteq \mathbf{TxtEx}(\mathbf{M})$ for some **M** that is dual-monotonic on $\mathcal{L}$ $\}$.

What is the relationship between $[\mathbf{TxtEx}]^{\text{dual-monotonic}}$ and $[\mathbf{TxtEx}]^{\text{class-dual-monotonic}}$?
What is the relationship between $[\mathbf{TxtEx}]^{\text{dual-monotonic}}$ and $[\mathbf{TxtEx}]^{\text{dual-strong-monotonic}}$?

5-18 Show that $[\mathbf{TxtEx}]^{\text{class-dual-weak-monotonic}} = [\mathbf{TxtEx}]^{\text{dual-weak-monotonic}}$.

5-19 In the discussion following Definition 5.50 we mentioned that the the global version of monotonicity is equivalent to strong monotonicity. This exercise establishes this fact.

(a) Define $[\mathbf{TxtEx}]^{\text{global-monotonic}}$, a global version on monotonicity.[2]

(b) Prove that $[\mathbf{TxtEx}]^{\text{global-monotonic}} = [\mathbf{TxtEx}]^{\text{strong-monotonic}}$ by showing that every machine which is monotonic on N is also strong monotonic.

5-20

(a) Show that $[\mathbf{TxtEx}]^{\text{dual-monotonic}} - [\mathbf{TxtEx}]^{\text{dual-strong-monotonic}} \neq \emptyset$.

(b) Show that $\mathbf{TxtEx} - [\mathbf{TxtEx}]^{\text{dual-monotonic}} \neq \emptyset$.

(c) Use Proposition 5.60 and parts (a) and (b) to deduce: $[\mathbf{TxtEx}]^{\text{dual-strong-monotonic}} \subset [\mathbf{TxtEx}]^{\text{dual-monotonic}} \subset \mathbf{TxtEx} = [\mathbf{TxtEx}]^{\text{dual-weak-monotonic}}$.

5-21 Show that $[\mathbf{TxtEx}]^{\text{class-weak-monotonic}} \subseteq [\mathbf{TxtEx}]^{\text{conservative}}$. Thus conclude that the classes $[\mathbf{TxtEx}]^{\text{class-weak-monotonic}}$, $[\mathbf{TxtEx}]^{\text{weak-monotonic}}$, $[\mathbf{TxtEx}]^{\text{conservative}}$, and $[\mathbf{TxtEx}]^{\text{class-conservative}}$ are all equal.

---

[2] Unlike for other criteria based on strategies, for monotonic identification we used $[\mathbf{TxtEx}]^{\text{monotonic}}$ to denote class monotonicity instead of global monotonicity; hence this special notation for global monotonicity.

5-22 Let $\mathcal{SD}'$ be as defined in the proof of Proposition 5.62 on page 116. Show that $\mathcal{SD}' \notin [\mathbf{Ex}]^{\text{class-Popperian}}$.

5-23 Show that $[\mathbf{Ex}]^{\text{Popperian}} \subseteq [\mathbf{Ex}]^{\text{consistent}}$.

6 Criteria of Learning

In Chapter 5 we considered several conceptions of "scientist." In the present chapter we examine alternative criteria of scientific success.

The **Ex** and **TxtEx** paradigms require the learner's conjectures to converge to some one index for the function or language being learned. This models both the accuracy and stability of successful learning. However, not all theorists take such a requirement to be necessary for learning, although most accept its sufficiency. It is noted, for example, that physicists sometimes employ explanations that are predictively inaccurate for certain experiments. In particular, Newtonian mechanics was used for explanation long after it was recognized that the theory failed to accurately predict dispersion in the X-ray region. Similarly, in the developmental context it might be doubted that children stabilize to a grammar that exactly models the parents' language — or even stabilize to a single grammar at all. Accordingly, more liberal conceptions of accuracy and stability have been proposed for learning, enforcing weaker requirements in these respects. The present chapter reviews some elementary success criteria of this nature. More sophisticated criteria are discussed in Chapter 7. In each case we conceive of the new criterion as giving rise to a novel paradigm of inductive inference. In what follows, extensions of **Ex** are considered first, followed by extensions of **TxtEx**.

§6.1 Criteria for function identification

§6.1.1 Anomalous Ex-identification

Our initial focus will be on relaxing the strict accuracy required for success within the paradigm **Ex**. One means of weakening this requirement is to define a proximity measure between functions, and then allow learners to converge to indexes that are for functions "sufficiently close" to the target. A simple proximity measure involves counting the number of points on which two functions give different results. For finite n we thus consider two functions to be "n-close" if they are equal on all but at most n arguments. (They are considered *un*equal on an argument if only one of them is defined there.) Two functions are called "finitely" close if they are n-close for some n. These ideas are formalized in the following definition, which is recalled from Chapter 2.

6.1 Definition Let $\xi \in \mathcal{P}$, $f \in \mathcal{R}$, and $n \in N$.

(a) We say that $\xi =^n f$ (read: ξ is an *n-variant* of f) just in case $card(\{\, x \mid \xi(x) \neq f(x)\,\}) \leq n$.

(b) We say that $\xi =^* f$ just in case $card(\{\, x \mid \xi(x) \neq f(x)\,\})$ is finite; we refer to ξ as a *finite variant* of f.

In the definition it is helpful to think of an index i for ξ as a "possibly anomalous explanation" for f, that is, an explanation whose prediction may include a finite number of anomalies. In this case, i is called an *n-error* (or *-error*) index for f. We distinguish two kinds of errors that i may embody in explaining f. If $\xi(x)$ is undefined, then i commits an error of *omission* at x. If $\xi(x)\!\downarrow\ \neq f(x)$, then i commits an error of *commission* at x.

Definition 6.1 suggests the following criterion of learning, in which it suffices to converge to an index for a function that is proximate to the target. (The $*$ case of the new paradigm was introduced by Blum and Blum [18], the other cases by Case and Smith [35].)

6.2 Definition (Blum and Blum [18], Case and Smith [35]) Let $a \in (N \cup \{*\})$.

(a) $\mathbf{M}$ $\mathbf{Ex}^a$-*identifies* f (written: $f \in \mathbf{Ex}^a(\mathbf{M})$) just in case $\mathbf{M}(f)\!\downarrow$ and $\varphi_{\mathbf{M}(f)} =^a f$.

(b) $\mathbf{M}$ $\mathbf{Ex}^a$-*identifies* $\mathcal{S}$ just in case $\mathcal{S} \subseteq \mathbf{Ex}^a(\mathbf{M})$.

(c) $\mathbf{Ex}^a = \{\,\mathcal{S} \mid \mathcal{S} \subseteq \mathbf{Ex}^a(\mathbf{M})$ for some $\mathbf{M}\,\}$.

$\mathbf{Ex}^0$, of course, is the same as $\mathbf{Ex}$. Note that in $\mathbf{Ex}^a$, for $a \in N$, the parameter 'a' is an upper bound on the number of errors allowed in the final hypothesis, not an exact number of required errors. Indeed, were a interpreted in the latter sense, $\mathbf{Ex}^a$ would collapse to the original paradigm $\mathbf{Ex}$ (see Exercise 6-2).

The success criterion for $\mathbf{Ex}^*$ can be formulated this way: $\mathbf{M}$ $\mathbf{Ex}^*$-identifies $\mathcal{S}$ just in case for every $f \in \mathcal{S}$ there is $m \in N$ such that $\mathbf{M}$ $\mathbf{Ex}^m$-identifies f. Thus, $\mathbf{M}$'s errors must be bounded on each function in $\mathcal{S}$. The bound itself, however, might grow without limit across different members of $\mathcal{S}$.

A simple modification of the proof of Proposition 4.15 yields:

6.3 Proposition *For every collection $\mathcal{S}$ of functions, and any $a \in (N \cup \{*\})$, $\mathcal{S}$ is $\mathbf{Ex}^a$ identifiable just in case some total scientist $\mathbf{Ex}^a$-identifies $\mathcal{S}$.*

It also follows that there is a recursively enumerable sequence of total computable scientists $\mathbf{M}_0, \mathbf{M}_1, \ldots$, such that for all $\mathcal{C} \in \mathbf{Ex}^a$, there is an i such that $\mathcal{C} \subseteq \mathbf{Ex}^a(\mathbf{M}_i)$.

Analogous results hold for each of the paradigms treated in this chapter (see Exercise 6-1). As a consequence, to show the *un*learnability of a certain collection of functions we shall often reason only about the behavior of total scientists, leaving this step of the argument implicit.

It is clear from Definition 6.2 that, for each $m \in N$, $\mathbf{Ex}^m \subseteq \mathbf{Ex}^{m+1}$. To show that the containment is proper, we introduce a variant of the "self-describing" functions $\mathcal{SD}$ introduced in Definition 4.24.

6.4 Definition Let $a \in (N \cup \{*\})$. $\mathcal{ASD}^a$ is the set of all $f \in \mathcal{R}$ such that $f(0)$ is an index for an a-variant of f, that is, $\varphi_{f(0)} =^a f$.

The symbol $\mathcal{ASD}$ is read as "almost self-describing." It is clear that $\mathcal{ASD}^0 = \mathcal{SD}$, and that $f \in \mathcal{ASD}^*$ just in case $f(0)$ is a $*$-error index for f. By Lemma 2.4, for all $a \in (N \cup \{*\})$, $\mathcal{ASD}^a \neq \emptyset$. The following result shows that $\mathcal{ASD}^{m+1}$ is an example of an $\mathbf{Ex}^{m+1}$-identifiable collection of functions that no scientist can $\mathbf{Ex}^m$-identify.

6.5 Proposition (Case and Smith [35]) *For each* $m \in N$, $\mathcal{ASD}^{m+1} \in (\mathbf{Ex}^{m+1} - \mathbf{Ex}^m)$.

Proof: Fix m. Clearly, $\mathcal{ASD}^{m+1} \in \mathbf{Ex}^{m+1}$. To show the proposition, it thus suffices to prove that $\mathcal{ASD}^{m+1} \notin \mathbf{Ex}^m$.

Suppose by way of contradiction that scientist $\mathbf{M}$ $\mathbf{Ex}^m$-identifies $\mathcal{ASD}^{m+1}$. Without loss of generality we may assume that $\mathbf{M}$ is total (since an analog of Proposition 4.15 holds for $\mathbf{Ex}^m$-identification). We now show the existence of a total computable function $f \in \mathcal{ASD}^{m+1}$ such that $\mathbf{M}$ fails to $\mathbf{Ex}^m$-identify f. The proof of this employs a technique that is frequently used in sequel, hence we discuss the idea behind the proof in some detail.

We use Kleene's recursion theorem (Theorem 2.3) to construct a program with index e such that the (partial) function φ_e is defined in stages. At the start of the construction, we initialize $\varphi_e(0) = e$. The construction is arranged so that if it ever reaches stage s, then at the beginning of that stage the domain of φ_e will be $\{0, \ldots, x_s - 1\}$, a finite initial segment of N. In stage s, the construction dovetails between the following two processes until, if ever, the search in b succeeds.

a.   Hold back defining φ_e on the $m + 1$ many arguments $x_s, \ldots, x_s + m$ and, for $x = x_s + m + 1, x_s + m + 2, \ldots$ in turn, extend φ_e to take the value 0.

b.   Search for a suitable extension of φ_e as defined thus far that forces the scientist $\mathbf{M}$ to change its mind.

All of the extensions considered in b will be in $\mathcal{ASD}^{m+1}$. If the search for a suitable extension succeeds in infinitely many stages, we then take f to be φ_e, which will turn out to belong to $\mathcal{ASD}^{m+1}$. But $\mathbf{M}$ on such an f fails to converge. On the other hand, if at some stage, no suitable extension can be found, then $\mathbf{M}$ converges to the same program, p, for each of the extensions considered in b. But in this case we arrange that, among these extensions, there is one that differs from φ_p on each of the $m + 1$-many arguments $x_s, \ldots, x_s + m$; hence $\mathbf{M}$ fails to converge to an m-error index for that particular extension.

Here is the formal construction.

Let $\varphi_e(0) = e$. Let x_s denote the least x such that $\varphi_e(x)$ has not been defined before stage s. Thus, $x_0 = 1$. Go to stage 0.

Begin (*Stage s*)

For each $y \leq m + 1$, define the function f_y as follows.

$$f_y(x) = \begin{cases} \varphi_e(x), & \text{if } x < x_s; \\ y, & \text{if } x_s \leq x \leq x_s + m; \\ 0, & \text{if } x_s + m < x. \end{cases}$$

Dovetail between a and b below until, if ever, the search in b succeeds.

    a.   For $i = 1$ to ∞, set $\varphi_e(x_s + m + i) = 0$.

    b.   Search for a $y \leq m+1$ and an $n \geq x_s + m + 1$ such that $\mathbf{M}(\varphi_e[x_s]) \neq \mathbf{M}(f_y[n])$.

If and when the search in b succeeds, let y and n be as discovered in the search and set $\varphi_e(x) = f_y(x)$ for each $x < n$ for which φ_e has yet to be defined. (*Hence,* $\varphi_e[n] = f_y[n]$.)

Go on to stage $s + 1$.

End (*Stage s*)

Consider the following two cases.

Case 1: Infinitely many stages are executed. In this case, let $f = \varphi_e$. It is clear by construction that $f \in \mathcal{ASD}^{m+1}$. But scientist $\mathbf{M}$ makes infinitely many mind changes on this f, hence $\mathbf{M}$ fails to $\mathbf{Ex}^m$-identify f.

Case 2: Some stage s starts but never terminates. For each $y \leq m + 1$, let f_y be as defined in stage s and let $p = \mathbf{M}(\varphi_e[x_s])$. By construction, for each y, $f_y \in \mathcal{ASD}^{m+1}$. Also, since stage s never terminates, we have that, for each $y \leq m+1$, $\mathbf{M}(f_y)\downarrow = p$. But since $card(\{\,\varphi_p(x_s + i) \mid i \leq m\,\}) \leq m+1$, it follows that there is at least one $y' \leq m+1$

such that $f_{y'}$ differs from φ_p on each of $x_s, \ldots, x_s + m$. Take $f = f_{y'}$. Then f is an element of $\mathcal{ASD}^{m+1}$ that **M** fails to $\mathbf{Ex}^m$-identify.

From the above two cases it follows that $\mathcal{ASD}^{m+1} \notin \mathbf{Ex}^m$.   ∎

The following corollary says that if the finite number of errors allowed in the final hypothesis is not bounded, then more collections of functions can be learned than otherwise.

6.6 Corollary (Case and Smith [35]) $\mathcal{ASD}^* \in (\mathbf{Ex}^* - \cup_{m \in N} \mathbf{Ex}^m)$.

Proof: It is clear that $\mathcal{ASD}^* \in \mathbf{Ex}^*$. Suppose by way of contradiction that $\mathcal{ASD}^* \in \cup_{m \in N} \mathbf{Ex}^m$. Then there exists an m such that $\mathcal{ASD}^* \in \mathbf{Ex}^m$, hence, any subset of $\mathcal{ASD}^*$ is also in $\mathbf{Ex}^m$. But $\mathcal{ASD}^{m+1}$ is a subset of $\mathcal{ASD}^*$, which is not in $\mathbf{Ex}^m$. This is a contradiction.   ∎

It is immediate from Proposition 6.5 that allowing more errors increases learning power. We note this fact in the form of an "anomaly hierarchy," one of many such hierarchies to be encountered in this and later chapters.

6.7 Corollary $\mathbf{Ex}^0 \subset \mathbf{Ex}^1 \subset \mathbf{Ex}^2 \subset \cdots \subset \mathbf{Ex}^*$.

§6.1.2 Behaviorally correct function identification

Turning from accuracy to stability, we wish now to relax the **Ex** requirement that scientists converge to a single index for the target function. The simplest alternative is to require only that a scientist eventually ceases to produce incorrect indexes, leaving her the liberty of forever changing the particular index used to name the target function. This criterion was first introduced by Bārzdiņš [14] and later considered by Case and Smith [35] (see also Feldman[58]). It is formalized as follows.

6.8 Definition (Bārzdiņš [14], Case and Smith [35])

(a) **M** *Bc-identifies* f (written: $f \in \mathbf{Bc}(\mathbf{M})$) just in case for all but finitely many n, $\varphi_{\mathbf{M}(f[n])} = f$.

(b) $\mathbf{Bc} = \{ \mathcal{S} \mid \mathcal{S} \subseteq \mathbf{Bc}(\mathbf{M}) \text{ for some } \mathbf{M} \}$.

Bc is read as "behaviorally correct." Thus, scientist **M Bc**-identifies f just in case **M**, fed the graph of f, produces an infinite sequence of hypotheses, $p_0, p_1, p_2, \ldots$, such that for all but finitely many n, p_n is an index for f. It follows immediately that $\mathbf{Ex} \subseteq \mathbf{Bc}$. We leave the proof of the following fact to Exercise 6-4.

6.9 Proposition (J. Steel cited in Case and Smith [35]) Ex* $\subseteq$ Bc.

There remains the obvious question of whether **Bc** is strictly weaker than **Ex***. The following proposition provides an affirmative answer.

6.10 Proposition (Case and Smith [35]) Bc $-$ Ex* $\neq$ $\emptyset$.

Proof: Let $\mathcal{S} = \{ f \in \mathcal{R} \mid (\overset{\infty}{\forall} n)[\varphi_{f(n)} = f] \}$. Thus $\mathcal{S}$ is the collection of computable functions f such that, for all but finitely many n, $f(n)$ is an index for f. By Lemma 2.4, $\mathcal{S}$ is nonempty.

Clearly, $\mathcal{S} \in$ **Bc**. Fix an arbitrary scientist **M**. Below we exhibit a function $f \in (\mathcal{S} - $ **Ex**$^*(\mathbf{M}))$. It will thus follow that $\mathcal{S} \notin$ **Ex***. Without loss of generality, we assume that **M** is total.

By the operator recursion theorem (Theorem 2.6), there is a 1-1, recursive function p such that the behavior of programs with indexes $p(0), p(1), p(2), \ldots$ are as described in stages below. We arrange things so that one of the $\varphi_{p(i)}$'s witnesses the failure of **M** to **Ex***-identify $\mathcal{S}$.

In the following construction $\varphi^s_{p(n)}$ denotes the part of $\varphi_{p(n)}$ defined before stage s. Let x_s denote the least x such that $\varphi_{p(0)}$ has not been defined before stage s. For each n, set $\varphi^0_{p(n)} = \emptyset$. If the construction reaches stage s, then the domain of $\varphi^s_{p(0)}$ will be $\{ 0, \ldots, x_s - 1 \}$, a finite initial segment of N, and $\varphi^s_{p(2s+1)}$ and $\varphi^s_{p(2s+2)}$ will be completely undefined. Go to stage 0.

Begin (*Stage s*)

Let $q_s = \mathbf{M}(\varphi_{p(0)}[x_s])$ and, for each $x < x_s$, set $\varphi_{p(2s+1)}(x) = \varphi_{p(0)}(x)$ and $\varphi_{p(2s+2)}(x) = \varphi_{p(0)}(x)$. (*Hence, $\varphi_{p(0)}[x_s] = \varphi_{p(2s+1)}[x_s] = \varphi_{p(2s+2)}[x_s]$.*)

For $y = x_s$ to ∞ **do**

Set $\varphi_{p(2s+1)}(y) = p(2s + 1)$ and $\varphi_{p(2s+2)}(y) = p(2s + 2)$.

Condition 1. $\mathbf{M}(\varphi_{p(2s+1)}[y]) \neq q_s$.

Then, for each $x \in \{ x_s, \ldots, y - 1 \}$, set $\varphi_{p(0)}(x) = \varphi_{p(2s+1)}(x)$ and henceforth make $\varphi_{p(2s+1)}$ follow $\varphi_{p(0)}$ so that $p(2s + 1)$ is an index for $\varphi_{p(0)}$. Go on to stage $s + 1$.

Condition 2. Condition 1 fails, but $\mathbf{M}(\varphi_{p(2s+2)}[y]) \neq q_s$.

Then, for each $x \in \{ x_s, \ldots, y - 1 \}$, set $\varphi_{p(0)}(x) = \varphi_{p(2s+2)}(x)$ and, henceforth, make $\varphi_{p(2s+2)}$ follow $\varphi_{p(0)}$ so that $p(2s + 2)$ is an index for $\varphi_{p(0)}$. Go on to stage $s + 1$. (*Note that if neither condition succeeds, then the* **For** *loop continues.*)

Endfor

End (*Stage s*)

Consider the following two cases.

Case 1: All stages terminate. In this case, let $f = \varphi_{p(0)}$. Clearly, the range of f contains indexes only for f. Hence, $f \in \mathcal{S}$. However, **M** on f makes infinitely many mind changes; hence, $\mathbf{M}(f)\uparrow$.

Case 2: Some stage s starts but fails to terminate. In this case let $f_1 = \varphi_{p(2s+1)}$ and $f_2 = \varphi_{p(2s+2)}$. Clearly, both f_1 and f_2 are in $\mathcal{S}$ and, for infinitely many x, $f_1(x) \neq f_2(x)$. However, $\mathbf{M}(f_1) = \mathbf{M}(f_2) = \mathbf{M}(\varphi_{p(0)}[x_s])$. Thus **M** fails to **Ex***-identify at least one of f_1 and f_2.

From the above cases it follows that $\mathcal{S} \notin \mathbf{Ex}^*(\mathbf{M})$. ∎

6.11 Corollary $\mathcal{R} \notin \mathbf{Ex}^*$.

§6.1.3 Behaviorally correct function identification with anomalies

The previous two subsections investigated two ways of liberalizing the **Ex** criterion of successful learning. These two means are combined in the following definition.

6.12 Definition (Case and Smith [35]) Let $a \in (N \cup \{*\})$.

(a) **M** $\mathbf{Bc}^a$-*identifies* f (written: $f \in \mathbf{Bc}^a(\mathbf{M})$) just in case for all but finitely many n, $\varphi_{\mathbf{M}(f[n])} =^a f$.

(b) $\mathbf{Bc}^a = \{ \mathcal{S} \mid \mathcal{S} \subseteq \mathbf{Bc}^a(\mathbf{M})$ for some **M** $\}$.

Thus, a scientist $\mathbf{Bc}^a$-identifies function f just in case, being fed the graph of f, she produces an infinite sequence of hypotheses, $p_0, p_1, p_2, \ldots$ such that for all but finitely many n, p_n is an index for an a-variant of f. It is easy to see that $\mathbf{Bc} \subseteq \mathbf{Bc}^1 \subseteq \mathbf{Bc}^2 \subseteq \cdots$. The next proposition shows that these containments are strict.

6.13 Proposition (Case and Smith [35])

(a) *For each* $m \in N$, $\mathbf{Bc}^{m+1} - \mathbf{Bc}^m \neq \emptyset$

(b) $\mathbf{Bc}^* - \cup_{m \in N} \mathbf{Bc}^m \neq \emptyset$.

6.14 Corollary $\mathbf{Bc}^0 \subset \mathbf{Bc}^1 \subset \mathbf{Bc}^2 \subset \cdots \subset \mathbf{Bc}^*$.

Proof (of Proposition 6.13): *Proof for part (a).* Fix an $m \in N$. Define

$$\mathcal{S}^{m+1} \;=\; \{\, f \in \mathcal{R} \mid (\overset{\infty}{\forall} n)[\varphi_{f(n)} =^{m+1} f]\,\}.$$

Clearly, $\mathcal{S}^{m+1} \in \mathbf{Bc}^{m+1}$. We show that $\mathcal{S}^{m+1} \notin \mathbf{Bc}^m$.

Fix an arbitrary scientist $\mathbf{M}$. We argue that $\mathbf{M}$ fails to $\mathbf{Bc}^m$-identify some $f \in \mathcal{S}^{m+1}$. Without loss of generality, assume that $\mathbf{M}$ is a total scientist.

By implicit use of the operator recursion theorem (Theorem 2.6), we describe a repetition-free r.e. sequence of programs $p(0), p(1), p(2), \ldots$ such that, for some i, $\varphi_{p(i)} \in (\mathcal{S}^{m+1} - \mathbf{Bc}^m(\mathbf{M}))$. Here is an informal effective construction of the $\varphi_{p(i)}$'s.

For each $i \in N$, $\varphi^s_{p(i)}$ denotes the part of $\varphi_{p(i)}$ defined before stage s. Let x_s denote the least x such that $\varphi_{p(0)}(x_s)$ has not been defined before stage s. If the construction reaches stage s, then the domain of $\varphi^s_{p(0)}$ will be $\{\,0, \ldots, x_s - 1\,\}$, a finite initial segment of N, and $\varphi^s_{p(s)}$ will be completely undefined. For each $i \in N$, set $\varphi^0_{p(i)} = \emptyset$. Go to stage 0.

Begin *(Stage s)*

For each $x < x_s$, set $\varphi_{p(s)}(x) = \varphi_{p(0)}(x)$.

Dovetail between a and b until, if ever, the search in b succeeds.

a.   For $i = 0$ to ∞, set $\varphi_{p(s)}(x_s + i) = p(s)$.

b.   Search for $n, y_0, y_1, \ldots, y_m$ such that $x_s \le n < y_0 < y_1 < \cdots < y_m$ and, for each $i \le m$, $\varphi_{\mathbf{M}(\sigma)}(y_i)\!\downarrow$, where $\sigma = \varphi_{p(0)}[x_s] \diamond (x_s, p(s)) \diamond (x_s + 1, p(s)) \diamond \cdots \diamond (n, p(s))$.

If and when the search in b succeeds, let $y_0, y_1, \ldots, y_m$ be the $m+1$ points on which $\mathbf{M}$'s conjecture on evidential state $\sigma = \varphi_{p(0)}[x_s] \diamond (x_s, p(s)) \diamond (x_s + 1, p(s)) \diamond \cdots \diamond (n, p(s))$ converges.

(We now force $\varphi_{p(0)}$ to differ from $\mathbf{M}$'s conjecture on these $m + 1$ points.)

Let x be the maximum element on which $\varphi_{p(s)}$ has been thus far defined and let $x' = max(\{\, x, y_m\,\})$.

For each $y \in \{\, y_0, \ldots, y_m\,\}$, set $\varphi_{p(0)}(y) = p(0)$, if $\varphi_{\mathbf{M}(\sigma)}(y) \ne p(0)$, and set $\varphi_{p(0)}(y) = p(s)$, otherwise.

For each $y \in (\{\, x_s, \ldots, x'\,\} - \{\, y_0, \ldots, y_m\,\})$, set $\varphi_{p(0)}(y) = p(s)$.

For each $y \in \{\, x, \ldots, x'\,\}$, set $\varphi_{p(s)}(y) = p(s)$.

(Note that at this point in the definitions of $\varphi_{p(0)}$ and $\varphi_{p(s)}$, these two functions are $(m + 1)$-variants.)

Henceforth, make $\varphi_{p(s)}$ behave exactly like $\varphi_{p(0)}$ on arguments greater than x'.

(*This ensures that $p(s)$ is an $(m+1)$-error index for $\varphi_{p(0)}$.*)

Go on to stage $s+1$.

End (*Stage s*)

Consider the following two cases.

Case 1: Infinitely many stages are executed. In this case, let $f = \varphi_{p(0)}$. It is clear that $f \in \mathcal{R}$ and everything in its range is either an index for f or an $(m+1)$-error index for f. Hence, $f \in \mathcal{S}^{m+1}$. But, for each s, there is a σ such that $\varphi_{p(0)}^{s} \subset \sigma \subset f$ and **M**'s conjecture on σ makes at least $m+1$ mistakes in computing f. Hence, $f \notin \mathbf{Bc}^{m}(\mathbf{M})$.

Case 2: Some stage s starts but never terminates. In this case, $\varphi_{p(s)} \in \mathcal{R}$ and, for all but finitely many x, $\varphi_{p(s)}(x) = p(s)$. Let $f = \varphi_{p(s)}$. Clearly, $f \in \mathcal{S}^{m+1}$. Also, for each σ such that $\varphi_{p(0)}^{s} \subset \sigma \subset f$, **M**'s conjecture on σ computes only a finite function because the search for $y_0, \ldots, y_m$ in step b fails. Hence, $f \notin \mathbf{Bc}^{m}(\mathbf{M})$.

The proof of part (b) can be worked out on lines similar to the proof of Corollary 6.6. ∎

$\mathbf{Bc}^{*}$ is the weakest criterion of success considered so far in our discussion. Although further liberalization could be envisioned, the following proposition shows that no further weakening is necessary.

6.15 Proposition (L. Harrington cited in Case and Smith [35]) $\mathcal{R} \in \mathbf{Bc}^{*}$.

Proof: Let $\mathbf{M}_H$ be a scientist which, on input σ, outputs a program with index e_σ, where, for each x,

$$
\varphi_{e_\sigma}(x) \;=\; \begin{cases} \varphi_p(x), & \text{if (i) } p \text{ is the least number } \le |\sigma| \text{ such that} \\ & \quad max(\{\,\Phi_p(y) \mid y < |\sigma|\,\}) \le x \text{ and } \varphi_p[|\sigma|] = \sigma; \\ 0, & \text{if (ii) no such } p \le |\sigma| \text{ exists that satisfies the} \\ & \quad \text{condition in clause (i).} \end{cases}
$$

Fix an arbitrary $f \in \mathcal{R}$. We show that $\mathbf{M}_H$ $\mathbf{Bc}^{*}$-identifies f. Let p_0 be the least index for f. Choose n_0 so large that (a) $p_0 \le n_0$ and (b) for each $p \le p_0$, $\varphi_p[n_0] \ne f[n_0]$. *Claim:* For each $n \ge n_0$, $\varphi_{e_{f[n]}} =^{*} f$. To see this, take $x_n = max(\{\,\Phi_{p_0}(y) \mid y < n\,\})$ and consider an $x \ge x_n$. By our choices of n_0, n, x_n, and x it follows that, on input x, p_0 is the p found in clause (i) of the definition of $\varphi_{e_{f[n]}}(x)$, and hence,

$$
f(x) \;=\; \varphi_{p_0}(x) \;=\; \varphi_{e_{f[n]}}(x) \;=\; \varphi_{\mathbf{M}_H(f[n])}(x).
$$

Therefore, the claim follows. Thus, $\mathbf{M}_H$ $\mathbf{Bc}^{*}$ identifies f. ∎

§6.1.4 Vacillatory function identification

The **Bc** criterion might appear overly liberal in allowing scientists to announce ever larger indexes for the target function. A more modest relaxation of **Ex** countenances endless shifts in hypotheses, but only within a fixed, finite set of alternatives. Thus, for scientist **M** to identify function f in this sense, there must be a finite set D_f of indexes with two properties: first, all but finitely many of **M**'s conjectures about f must be drawn from D_f; second, every index in D_f must be for f. It is easy to see that this new identification criterion is implied by **Ex**-identification (taking D_f to be a singleton set) and implies **Bc**-identification. In order to facilitate comparison with earlier paradigms, we also incorporate anomalies into this success criterion. The formal definition is as follows.

6.16 Definition (Bārzdiņš and Podnieks [16], Case and Smith [35]) Let $a \in (N \cup \{*\})$.

(a) **M Fex**^{a}-*identifies* f (written: $f \in \mathbf{Fex}^a(\mathbf{M})$) just in case there exists a nonempty finite set D_f of a-error indexes for f such that for all but finitely many n, $\mathbf{M}(f[n]) \in D_f$.

(b) $\mathbf{Fex}^a = \{\, \mathcal{S} \mid \mathcal{S} \subseteq \mathbf{Fex}^a(\mathbf{M}) \text{ for some } \mathbf{M} \,\}$.

So, for an **M** to **Fex**^{a}-identify f, there must be some finite set D_f of indexes to which **M**'s conjectures must ultimately be limited — and D_f must consist only of indexes for a-variants of f. Clearly, $\mathbf{Ex}^a \subseteq \mathbf{Fex}^a$ for all $a \in (N \cup \{*\})$. Surprisingly, the inclusion is nowhere proper.

6.17 Proposition (Bārzdiņš and Podnieks [16], Case and Smith [35]) *For each* $a \in (N \cup \{*\})$, $\mathbf{Ex}^a = \mathbf{Fex}^a$.

Proof: Let $n \in N$. We argue $\mathbf{Ex}^n = \mathbf{Fex}^n$. The $*$ case is discussed later.

As previously noted, $\mathbf{Ex}^n \subseteq \mathbf{Fex}^n$, hence it suffices to show that $\mathbf{Fex}^n \subseteq \mathbf{Ex}^n$. We do this by showing how to effectively transform any scientist **M** into a corresponding scientist **M**′ such that $\mathbf{Fex}^n(\mathbf{M}) \subseteq \mathbf{Ex}^n(\mathbf{M}')$.

We employ an internal simulation argument that uses a cancellation technique. **M**′ behaves as follows.

On input σ, **M**′ simulates **M** on σ to find all the distinct indexes that **M** outputs on the initial sequences of σ. Let these indexes be $p_0, p_1, \ldots, p_k$. **M**′ then *cancels* any index p_i, $i \leq k$, from this list that are found to be convergently different from σ at more than n arguments in less than or equal to $|\sigma|$ steps. More precisely, **M**′ cancels any index p_i for which $card(\{\, x < |\sigma| \mid \Phi_{p_i}(x) \le |\sigma| \text{ and } \varphi_{p_i}(x) \ne \hat{\sigma}(x)\,\}) > n$. (Recall that $\hat{\sigma}$ is the finite function with graph $content(\sigma)$.) Clearly, each of the uncanceled indexes makes only up to n errors of commission. For each uncanceled p_i, let E_{p_i} denote the set of these $\le n$ points for which it can be detected in $\le |\sigma|$ steps that p_i makes an error of commission. More precisely, $E_{p_i} = \{\, x < |\sigma| \mid \Phi_p(x) \le |\sigma| \text{ and } \varphi_p(x) \ne \hat{\sigma}(x)\,\}$.

Now, for each uncanceled p_i, let q_i be an index of a program that behaves exactly like the program with index p_i but is patched to agree with σ on arguments in E_{p_i}. To be precise, q_i is defined as follows:

$$\varphi_{q_i}(x) \;=\; \begin{cases} \hat{\sigma}(x), & \text{if } x \in E_{p_i}; \\ \varphi_{p_i}(x), & \text{otherwise.} \end{cases}$$

Finally, let p be an index of a program formed from each of these q_i's (derived from the uncanceled p_i's) whose behavior is described as follows. The program with index p on any input y simulates each of the programs with indexes q_i's on input y and outputs the same value as the (lexicographically least) q_i, which converges first. $\mathbf{M}'$ on input σ outputs p.

We now argue that $\mathbf{Fex}^n(\mathbf{M}) \subseteq \mathbf{Ex}^n(\mathbf{M}')$. Let $f \in \mathbf{Fex}^n(\mathbf{M})$. Then any index q output infinitely often by $\mathbf{M}$ on f is such that $\varphi_q =^n f$. Choose m_0 to be so large that the following hold:

1. If program q is ever output by $\mathbf{M}$ on f, then q has been output at least once by $\mathbf{M}$ on $f[m_0]$, that is, $\{\,\mathbf{M}(\sigma) \mid \sigma \subset f\,\} = \{\,\mathbf{M}(\sigma) \mid \sigma \subseteq f[m_0]\,\}$.

2. If, for some $q \in \{\,\mathbf{M}(\sigma) \mid \sigma \subset f\,\}$, we have $card(\{\, x \mid \varphi_q(x){\downarrow} \ne f(x)\,\}) > n$, then q is cancelled by $\mathbf{M}'$ after it has seen $f[m_0]$.

3. For each $q \in \{\,\mathbf{M}(\sigma) \mid \sigma \subset f\,\}$ that is never cancelled, we have that q's at most n convergent anomalies (if any) are discovered in $\le m_0$ steps, and these anomalies are all less than m_0.

Clearly, such an m_0 exists. Also, after $\mathbf{M}'$ has seen $f[m_0]$, $\mathbf{M}'$ performs no new cancelations. Hence, in the limit $\mathbf{M}'$ on f outputs an index p that simulates a collection of indexes q_i, none of which makes an error of commission and at least one of which makes no more than n errors of omission. Hence, $\varphi_p =^n f$.

A proof of the $a = *$ case can be worked out by modifying the above argument. The modification is based on the following observation. For the $a = *$ case, the main problem arises in determining when a program has made enough convergent errors (so that it can be cancelled). For this, the machine $\mathbf{M}'$, upon seeing $f[m]$, cancels a program, p, just in case it can be determined in $\le m$ steps that p makes more convergent errors on inputs

$\leq m$ than the number of times p has been output by $\mathbf{M}$ on initial segments of $f[m]$. We leave the details of the proof to the reader. ∎

§6.2 Criteria of language identification

Here we consider generalizations of the **TxtEx** criterion of language learning that parallel the generalizations of **Ex** in the previous section. We begin by allowing a finite number of errors into the scientist's final hypothesis.

§6.2.1 Anomalous TxtEx-identification

Terminology: Recall from Chapter 2 that $L_1 =^n L_2$ means that $card(L_1 \triangle L_2) \leq n$ and such L_1 and L_2 are called *n-variants*. Also recall that $L_1 =^* L_2$ means that $card(L_1 \triangle L_2)$ is finite, and such L_1 and L_2 are called *finite-variants*. For each $a \in (N \cup \{*\})$ and each L_1 and L_2 with $L_1 =^a L_2$, we refer to an index i for L_1 as an *a-error index* for L_2. If $x \in (W_i - L)$, then we refer to x as an *error of commission* with respect to i and L. Similarly, $x \in (L - W_i)$ is an *error of omission*.

We now liberalize **TxtEx** to allow for a finite number of such errors.

6.18 Definition (Osherson and Weinstein [143], Case and Lynes [33]) Let $a \in (N \cup \{*\})$.

(a) $\mathbf{M}$ **TxtEx**^{a}-*identifies* L just in case for each text T for L, $\mathbf{M}(T)\downarrow$ and $W_{\mathbf{M}(T)} =^a L$.

(b) $\mathbf{M}$ **TxtEx**^{a}-*identifies* $\mathcal{L}$ just in case $\mathbf{M}$ **TxtEx**^{a}-identifies each $L \in \mathcal{L}$.

(c) **TxtEx**$^a = \{ \mathcal{L} \mid \mathcal{L} \subseteq \mathbf{TxtEx}^a(\mathbf{M})$ for some $\mathbf{M} \}$.

The definition implies that $\mathbf{TxtEx} = \mathbf{TxtEx}^0 \subseteq \mathbf{TxtEx}^1 \subseteq \mathbf{TxtEx}^2 \subseteq \cdots \subseteq \mathbf{TxtEx}^*$. To show that the hierarchy is in fact strict we rely on a technique that will repeatedly appear in the sequel. It consists of translating results about function identification to the language setting. In the present case Proposition 6.5 and Corollary 6.6 are used to prove the following.

6.19 Proposition (Case and Lynes [33])

(a) $\mathbf{TxtEx}^{m+1} - \mathbf{TxtEx}^m \neq \emptyset$.

(b) $\mathbf{TxtEx}^* - \bigcup_{m \in N} \mathbf{TxtEx}^m \neq \emptyset$.

Proof: For each $f \in \mathcal{R}$, let L_f denote the single-valued total language: $\{ \langle n, f(n) \rangle \mid n \in N \}$. For each $\mathcal{S} \subseteq \mathcal{R}$, let $\mathcal{L}_\mathcal{S}$ denote the collection of single-valued total languages $\{ L_f \mid f \in \mathcal{S} \}$.

Let p_1 be a recursive function that translates an index for a (partial) recursive function ψ into an index for the corresponding single-valued language L_ψ. Formally, for all $i, x \in N$,

$$\varphi_{p_1(i)}(x) \;=\; \begin{cases} 1, & \text{if } \varphi_i(\pi_1(x)) = \pi_2(x); \\ \uparrow, & \text{otherwise.} \end{cases}$$

Similarly, let p_2 be a recursive function that translates an index for a language L into an index for a partial recursive function represented by L. Formally, for all $i, x \in N$,

$$\varphi_{p_2(i)}(x) \;=\; \begin{cases} \pi_2(z), & \text{if, for some } z \in W_i, \ \pi_1(z) = x; \\ \uparrow, & \text{otherwise.} \end{cases}$$

In the first condition of the above definition of $\varphi_{p_2(i)}(x)$, we assume that the z used is the first appropriate one produced by some uniform enumeration of W_i.

Let $a \in (N \cup \{*\})$ and let $f \in \mathcal{R}$. It is easy to verify that if i is an index for an a-variant of f such that i *does not* make any convergent errors (with respect to f), then $p_1(i)$ is an index for an a-variant of the single-valued total language L_f. Similarly, if j is an index for an a-variant for the single-valued total language L, then $p_2(j)$ is an index for an a-variant of the recursive function represented by L.

Choose an $\mathcal{S} \in (\mathbf{Ex}^{m+1} - \mathbf{Ex}^m)$. (By Proposition 6.5, such an $\mathcal{S}$ exists.) We argue that $\mathcal{L}_\mathcal{S} \in \mathbf{TxtEx}^{m+1} - \mathbf{TxtEx}^m$.

Claim: $\mathcal{L}_\mathcal{S} \in \mathbf{TxtEx}^{m+1}$. *Proof:* Let $\mathbf{M}$ be a scientist that searches a text for an element of the form $\langle 0, z \rangle$ and keeps on emitting $p_1(z')$, where z' is a program obtained by patching the convergent errors of z with respect to the function represented by the input language. Clearly, $\mathbf{M}$ $\mathbf{TxtEx}^{m+1}$-identified $\mathcal{L}_\mathcal{S}$. Hence, the claim follows.

Claim: $\mathcal{L}_\mathcal{S} \notin \mathbf{TxtEx}^m$. *Proof:* Suppose by way of contradiction that a scientist $\mathbf{M}$ $\mathbf{TxtEx}^m$-identifies $\mathcal{L}_\mathcal{S}$. Let $t : (N \times N \cup \{\#\}) \to (N \cup \{*\})$ be such that $t((x, y)) = \langle x, y \rangle$ and $t(\#) = \#$. Extend t to SEG $\to$ SEQ by taking $t(\sigma)$ to be the result of applying t to each element of σ. Now, let $\mathbf{M}'$ be a scientist such that, for each segment σ, $\mathbf{M}'(\sigma) = p_2(\mathbf{M}(t(\sigma)))$. Since $\mathbf{M}$ $\mathbf{TxtEx}^m$-identifies $\mathcal{L}_\mathcal{S}$, it follows that $\mathbf{M}'$ must $\mathbf{Ex}^m$-identify $\mathcal{S}$, a contradiction. Hence, the claim and part (a) follows.

A similar proof works for part (b) using $\mathcal{ASD}^*$ of Corollary 6.6. ∎

6.20 Corollary $\mathbf{TxtEx} \subset \mathbf{TxtEx}^1 \subset \mathbf{TxtEx}^2 \subset \cdots \subset \mathbf{TxtEx}^*$.

§6.2.2 Behaviorally correct language identification

The next definition liberalizes the stability requirement for **TxtEx** just as we did for **Ex**.

6.21 Definition (Osherson and Weinstein [143], Case and Lynes [33]) Let $a \in (N \cup \{*\})$.

(a) **M TxtBc^a-*identifies*** L (written: $L \in \mathbf{TxtBc}^a(\mathbf{M})$) just in case, for all texts T for L, for all but finitely many n, $W_{\mathbf{M}(T[n])} =^a L$.

(b) $\mathbf{TxtBc}^a = \{\, \mathcal{L} \mid \mathcal{L} \subseteq \mathbf{TxtBc}^a(\mathbf{M}) \text{ for some } \mathbf{M} \,\}$.

(c) $\mathbf{TxtBc}^0$ is abbreviated to **TxtBc**.

Thus a scientist **M TxtBc^a**-identifies language L just in case **M**, fed any text for L, produces an infinite sequence of hypotheses, all but finitely many of which are for a-variants of L. Successive conjectures need not be identical, nor even for the same language; and different texts may lead to different sequences.

The definition gives rise to a strict hierarchy, as described in the following corollary. Its proof follows a modification of the proof of Proposition 6.13 and is left for the reader. A different proof for this can be obtained using Proposition 6.24 below.

6.22 Corollary $\mathbf{TxtBc} \subset \mathbf{TxtBc}^1 \subset \mathbf{TxtBc}^2 \subset \cdots \subset \mathbf{TxtBc}^*$.

In the case of functions, Propositions 6.9 and 6.10 reveal that **Bc** properly contains **Ex***. Is the situation similar when we pass to **TxtBc** and **TxtEx***? The following proposition shows that the latter paradigms are in fact incomparable.

6.23 Proposition

(a) $\mathbf{TxtBc} \not\subseteq \mathbf{TxtEx}^*$.

(b) $\mathbf{TxtEx}^* \not\subseteq \mathbf{TxtBc}$.

Proof: Part (a) is an immediate consequence of Proposition 6.10. Part (b) is taken up in Exercise 6-9. ∎

The above proposition shows that the instability allowed in **TxtBc** fails to compensate for the finite, but unbounded, number of errors allowed in **TxtEx***. A subtler picture emerges when we consider bounded numbers of errors, as embodied in the criteria **TxtEx^m**.

6.24 Proposition (Case and Lynes [33])

(a) $\{ L \mid L =^{2m+1} N \} \in (\textbf{TxtEx}^{2m+1} - \textbf{TxtBc}^m)$.

(b) *For each* $m \le 2m'$, $\textbf{TxtEx}^m \subseteq \textbf{TxtBc}^{m'}$.

Proof: We prove part (b). A proof of part (a) can be worked out by employing an analog of the locking sequence lemma (Theorem 3.22) for $\textbf{TxtBc}^a$-identification (see Exercise 6-9).

Suppose scientist $\textbf{M}$ $\textbf{TxtEx}^{2m}$-identifies $\mathcal{L}$. We construct a scientist $\textbf{M}'$ which $\textbf{TxtBc}^m$-identifies $\mathcal{L}$.

By the s-m-n theorem (Theorem 2.1), for each σ, there is an index p_σ such that

$$W_{p_\sigma} = \Big(W_p \cup content(\sigma) \Big) - \Big(\text{the } m \text{ least numbers in } (W_{p,|\sigma|} - content(\sigma)) \Big),$$

where in the second part if $(W_{p,|\sigma|} - content(\sigma))$ has fewer than m elements, we just take $(W_{p,|\sigma|} - content(\sigma))$. For each σ, we take $\textbf{M}'(\sigma) = p_\sigma$.

Let T be a text for $L \in \mathcal{L}$ and let p be the index to which $\textbf{M}$ converges on T. Hence, $W_p =^{2m} L$. Let n_0 be such that, for all $n \ge n_0$,

(a) $\textbf{M}(T[n]) = p$,

(b) $L - W_p \subseteq content(T[n])$ and $W_p - L \subseteq W_{p,n}$, and

(c) $\{ x \in L \mid x \le max(W_p - L) \} \subseteq content(T[n_0])$.

Clearly, such an n_0 exists. Note that, for each $n > n_0$, $\textbf{M}'$ patches all the errors of omission of $\textbf{M}$.

Now fix an $n \ge n_0$. Let $\textbf{M}(T[n]) = p$. Consider the following two cases:

Case 1: $card(W_p - L) \ge m$. That is, the number of mistakes of commission in p is $\ge m$. Then, $p_{T[n]}$ removes m of these mistakes of commission, leaving a residue of $\le m$ errors.

Case 2: $card(W_p - L) = m'$ and $m' < m$. That is, the number m' of mistakes of commission in p is $< m$. Then, $p_{T[n]}$ removes all these errors of commission, but potentially creates up to $m - m'$ new errors of omission. However, this number, $m - m'$, is still $\le m$.

In both cases, $p_{T[n]}$ has $\le m$ errors, hence $\textbf{M}'$ $\textbf{TxtBc}^m$-identifies $L \in \mathcal{L}$. ∎

§6.2.3 Vacillatory language identification

Recall the vacillatory criterion of success for functions introduced in Section 6.1.4. To be successful in the vacillatory sense, the learner's conjectures must eventually remain within some fixed, finite set of indexes — where each index is for a function sufficiently close to the target. We adapt this notion to the case of languages.

6.25 Definition (Case [25], Osherson and Weinstein [143]) Let $a \in (N \cup \{*\})$ and $b \in (N^+ \cup \{*\})$.

(a) We say that $\mathbf{M}$ on T *finitely converges to* a finite set D just in case, for all but finitely many n, $\mathbf{M}(T[n]) \in D$.

(b) $\mathbf{M}$ $\mathbf{TxtFex}_b^a$-*identifies* L (written: $L \in \mathbf{TxtFex}_b^a(\mathbf{M})$) just in case for all texts T for L there is a finite, nonempty set D of cardinality at most b such that $\mathbf{M}$ finitely converges to D and, for each $i \in D$, $W_i =^a L$.

(c) $\mathbf{TxtFex}_b^a = \{\, \mathcal{L} \mid \mathcal{L} \subseteq \mathbf{TxtFex}_b^a(\mathbf{M})$ for some $\mathbf{M} \,\}$.

Thus, $\mathbf{M}$ $\mathbf{TxtFex}_b^a$-identifies L just in case for every text T for L there is a nonempty, finite set D_T of no more than b indexes for a-variants of L such that all but finitely many of $\mathbf{M}$'s conjectures are drawn from D_T.

For the function case, Proposition 6.17 showed that there is nothing to be gained from allowing scientists to vacillate. The situation is different for languages. Indeed, we now prove that there are collections of languages for which 0-error indexes can be learned if the scientist may vacillate among $n + 1$ conjectures, but for which even $*$-error indexes cannot be learned if vacillation is limited to sets of size n.

6.26 Proposition (Case [25])

(a) *For* $n \in N^+$, $\mathbf{TxtFex}_{n+1}^0 - \mathbf{TxtFex}_n^* \neq \emptyset$.

(b) *For* $a \in (N \cup \{*\})$, $\mathbf{TxtFex}_*^a - \cup_{n \in N^+} \mathbf{TxtFex}_n^a \neq \emptyset$.

As an immediate corollary we obtain:

6.27 Corollary *Let* $a \in (N \cup \{*\})$. *Then* $\mathbf{TxtFex}_1^a \subset \mathbf{TxtFex}_2^a \subset \mathbf{TxtFex}_3^a \subset \cdots \subset \mathbf{TxtFex}_*^a$.

Proof (of Proposition 6.26): We prove only part (a). The argument for part (b) can be worked out using the proof of part (a) in a way similar to the proof of Corollary 6.6.

Notation: Define $\mathrm{Last}_n(\mathbf{M}, \sigma) = \{\, \mathbf{M}(\tau) \mid \sigma[m] \subseteq \tau \subseteq \sigma \,\}$, where m is the least number $\leq |\sigma|$ such that $card(\{\, \mathbf{M}(\tau) \mid \sigma[m] \subseteq \tau \subseteq \sigma \,\}) \leq n$. Intuitively, $\mathrm{Last}_n(\mathbf{M}, \sigma)$ denotes the set of the last n distinct indexes output by $\mathbf{M}$ when it is fed evidential state

σ. If the number of distinct indexes output by $\mathbf{M}$ on σ is less than n, then $\mathrm{Last}_n(\mathbf{M}, \sigma)$ is the entire set of indexes output by $\mathbf{M}$ on σ.

For each $n \in N$, define the collection of languages

$$\mathcal{L}_{n+1} \quad = \quad \left\{ L \in \mathcal{E} \;\middle|\; \begin{array}{l} L \text{ is infinite, } card(\pi_2(L)) \leq m{+}1, \text{ and, for} \\ \text{all but finitely many } z \in L, \; W_{\pi_2(z)} = L \end{array} \right\}.$$

It is easy to verify that $\mathcal{L}_{n+1} \in \mathbf{TxtFex}^0_{n+1}$. It remains to show that $\mathcal{L}_{n+1} \notin \mathbf{TxtFex}^*_n$.

Fix an arbitrary scientist $\mathbf{M}$. By a padded version of the $(n + 1)$-ary recursion theorem (Theorem 2.5), there are distinct programs $e_0, e_1, \cdots, e_n$ defining r.e. sets W_{e_0}, $W_{e_1}, \ldots, W_{e_n}$, respectively, which are constructed as follows. All of the W_{e_i}'s will be in $\mathcal{L}_{n+1}$ and one of the W_{e_i}'s will witness that $\mathbf{M}$ fails to $\mathbf{TxtFex}^*_n$-identify $\mathcal{L}_{n+1}$. It will thus follow that $\mathcal{L}_{n+1} \notin \mathbf{TxtFex}^*_n$.

Let $\sigma_0 = \emptyset$. Go to stage 0.

Begin *(Stage s)*

For each $i \leq n$, enumerate $\langle s, e_0 \rangle$ into W_{e_i}.

(This guarantees in Case 1 below that the W_{e_i} are all infinite.)

Set $\sigma = \sigma_s \diamond \langle s, e_0 \rangle$.

Dovetail between a and b below until, if ever, the search in b succeeds.

    a.   **For** $x = 0$ to ∞ **do**

            enumerate $\langle x, e_j \rangle$ into W_{e_j} for each $j \leq n$.

       Endfor

    b.   Search for a τ extending σ such that

        (i) $content(\tau) \subseteq \{\, \langle x, e_i \rangle \mid i \leq n \,\}$ and

        (ii) $\mathrm{Last}_n(\mathbf{M}, \tau) \neq \mathrm{Last}_n(\mathbf{M}, \sigma)$.

If and when the search in b succeeds, then:

    Let $S = content(\tau) \cup \bigcup_{j \leq n}[W_{e_j}$ enumerated until now].

    For each $j \leq n$, enumerate S into W_{e_j}.

    Choose σ_{s+1} to be an extension of τ such that $content(\sigma_{s+1}) = S$.

    Go on to stage $s + 1$.

End *(Stage s)*

We have the following two cases.

Case 1: Each stage terminates. Then, $W_{e_0} = W_{e_1} = W_{e_2} = \cdots = W_{e_n}$. Let $L = W_{e_0}$. Let $T = \cup_s \sigma_s$. Clearly, T is a text for L and $L \in \mathcal{L}_{n+1}$, but $\mathbf{M}$ on T does not finitely converge to a set of cardinality at most n. Hence, $\mathbf{M}$ does not $\mathbf{TxtFex}_n^*$-identify $\mathcal{L}$.

Case 2: Some stage s starts but fails to terminate. For each $j \leq n$, let $L_j = W_{e_j}$. Clearly, for each $j \leq n$, $L_j \in \mathcal{L}_{n+1}$ and $content(\sigma_s \diamond \langle s, e_0 \rangle) \subseteq L_j$. Since the search in b fails in stage s, for every τ extending $\sigma_s \diamond \langle s, e_0 \rangle$ such that $content(\tau) \subseteq \{\langle x, e_i \rangle \mid i \leq n\}$, we have $\mathbf{M}(\tau) \in \text{Last}_n(\mathbf{M}, \sigma_s \diamond \langle s, e_0 \rangle)$. Moreover, for each $0 \leq j < j' \leq n$, $L_j \triangle L_{j'}$ is infinite. Thus, there is a $j \leq n$ such that, for all $i \in \text{Last}_n(\mathbf{M}, \sigma_s)$, $L_j \triangle W_i$ is infinite. Thus, $\mathbf{M}$ fails to $\mathbf{TxtFex}_n^*$-identify $L_j \in \mathcal{L}_{n+1}$.

The above two cases imply the proposition. ∎

In contrast to the above result, part (a) of the next proposition shows that there are collections of languages for which an $(m+1)$-error index can be identified in the limit, but for which m-error indexes cannot be learned even if the scientist is allowed to vacillate among a finite, but unbounded, number of conjectures.

6.28 Proposition

(a) *For $m \in N$, $\mathbf{TxtFex}_1^{m+1} - \mathbf{TxtFex}_*^m \neq \emptyset$.*

(b) *For all $b \in (N^+ \cup \{*\})$, $\mathbf{TxtFex}_1^* - \cup_{m \in N} \mathbf{TxtFex}_b^m \neq \emptyset$.*

Proof: We prove only part (a). The proof of part (b) is left to the reader.

Recall that $\mathcal{ASD}^{m+1} = \{ f \mid \varphi_{f(0)} =^{m+1} f \}$ and that, by Proposition 6.5, $\mathcal{ASD}^{m+1} \in \mathbf{Ex}^{m+1} - \mathbf{Ex}^m$. Let L_f and $\mathcal{L}_S$ be as in the proof of Proposition 6.19. Consider the collection of single-valued total languages $\mathcal{L} = \mathcal{L}_{\mathcal{ASD}^{m+1}}$.

It is easy to see that $\mathcal{L} \in \mathbf{TxtFex}_1^{m+1}$. We argue that $\mathcal{L} \notin \mathbf{TxtFex}_*^m$. Suppose by way of contradiction $\mathcal{L} \in \mathbf{TxtFex}_*^m$. Then, in a way similar to the proof of Proposition 6.19 it can shown that there exists a scientist that $\mathbf{Fex}^m$-identifies $\mathcal{ASD}^{m+1}$. But $\mathbf{Fex}^m = \mathbf{Ex}^m$ by Proposition 6.17. Hence, $\mathcal{ASD}^{m+1} \in \mathbf{Ex}^m$, a contradiction. ∎

Exercises 6-12 and 6-13 below contain additional results comparing $\mathbf{TxtFex}$ with $\mathbf{TxtBc}$.

§6.3 Bibliographic notes

Errors in the final hypothesis for function identification were first considered by Blum and Blum [18] and later investigated extensively by Case and Smith [35]. The terminology "errors of omission" and "errors of commission" is due to Daley. Behaviorally correct function identification appears in the work of Bārzdiņš [14] (see also Feldman [58]). Case and Smith [35] investigated behaviorally correct identification in its full generality, including errors in the hypotheses. The result $\mathcal{R} \in \mathbf{Bc}^*$ is due to Harrington (cited in Case and Smith [35]). The result that vacillatory function identification is the same as identification of functions is due to Bārzdiņš and Podnieks [16]. Later, Case and Smith [35] showed that this result holds even if errors are allowed in the final program.

In the context of languages, errors in the final hypotheses were considered by Osherson and Weinstein [143] and by Case and Lynes [33]. These two papers also considered behaviorally correct language identification and its variants. Vacillatory language identification was first considered by Osherson and Weinstein [143] and later investigated extensively by Case [26].

§6.4 Exercises

6-1 Suppose $a \in (N \cup \{*\})$. Show that there exists a recursively enumerable sequence of total computable scientists $\mathbf{M}_0, \mathbf{M}_1, \ldots$ such that, for each $\mathcal{C} \in \mathbf{Bc}^a$ there is an i such that $\mathcal{C} \subseteq \mathbf{Bc}^a(\mathbf{M}_i)$.

6-2 Consider the following criteria of function identification.

6.29 Definition Let $m \in N$.

(a) $\mathbf{M}$ $\mathbf{Ex}^{=m}$-*identifies* f (written: $f \in \mathbf{Ex}^{=m}(\mathbf{M})$) just in case $\mathbf{M}(f)\!\downarrow$ and $card(\{\, n \mid \varphi_{\mathbf{M}(f)}(n) \neq f(n) \,\}) = m$.

(b) $\mathbf{M}$ $\mathbf{Ex}^{=m}$-*identifies* $\mathcal{S}$ just in case $\mathcal{S} \subseteq \mathbf{Ex}^{=m}(\mathbf{M})$.

(c) $\mathbf{Ex}^{=m} = \{\, \mathcal{S} \mid \mathcal{S} \subseteq \mathbf{Ex}^{=m}(\mathbf{M})$ for some $\mathbf{M}\,\}$.

Show that for all $m \in N$, $\mathbf{Ex}^m = \mathbf{Ex}$.

6-3 Prove each of the following.

(a) $\mathcal{COFIN}$ is $\mathbf{TxtEx}^*$-identifiable, where $\mathcal{COFIN}$ is the collection of cofinite languages.

(b) For each $m \in N$, $\{\, L \mid L =^m N \,\} \in \mathbf{TxtEx}^m$.

(c) Let $a \in (N \cup \{*\})$. If scientist $\mathbf{M}$ $\mathbf{TxtEx}^a$-identifies L, then there exists a $\sigma \in \mathrm{SEQ}$ such that the following hold:

1. $content(\sigma) \subseteq L$;
2. $W_{\mathbf{M}(\sigma)} =^a L$;
3. $(\forall \tau \mid content(\tau) \subseteq L)[\mathbf{M}(\sigma \diamond \tau) = \mathbf{M}(\sigma)]$.

The sequence σ is referred to as $\mathbf{TxtEx}^a$-locking sequence for $\mathbf{M}$ on L. (This is an analog of Definition 3.24 for the $\mathbf{TxtEx}^a$ paradigm.)

(d) For all $m \in N$, $\{ L \mid L =^{m+1} N \} \notin \mathbf{TxtEx}^m$. (Use the above locking sequence result.) Further conclude that $\mathbf{TxtEx} \subset \mathbf{TxtEx}^1 \subset \mathbf{TxtEx}^2 \subset \cdots$.

6-4 (J. Steel cited in Case and Smith [35]) Show $\mathbf{Ex}^* \subseteq \mathbf{Bc}$.

6-5   Consider the following definition.

6.30 Definition Let $a \in (N \cup \{*\})$.

(a) $\mathbf{M}$ $\mathbf{Ext}^a$-*identifies* f (written: $f \in \mathbf{Ext}^a(\mathbf{M})$) just in case $(\exists g \in \mathcal{R} \mid g =^a f)$ $(\overset{\infty}{\forall} n)[\varphi_{\mathbf{M}(f[n])} = g]$.

(b) $\mathbf{Ext}^a = \{ \mathcal{S} \mid \mathcal{S} \subseteq \mathbf{Ext}^a(\mathbf{M}) \text{ for some } \mathbf{M} \}$.

Show that $\mathbf{Ext}^a = \mathbf{Ext}^0 = \mathbf{Bc}$.

6-6   Consider the following criteria of success on functions.

6.31 Definition (Case and Smith [35]) Let $a \in (N \cup \{*\})$.

(a) $\mathbf{M}$ $\mathbf{Oex}^a$-*identifies* f (written: $f \in \mathbf{Oex}^a(\mathbf{M})$) just in case there exists a nonempty finite set D such that the following hold:

1. for some $i \in D$, $\varphi_i =^a f$,
2. for all but finitely many n, $\mathbf{M}(f[n]) \in D$, and
3. for each $i \in D$, there are infinitely many n such that $\mathbf{M}(f[n]) = i$.

(b) $\mathbf{Oex}^a = \{ \mathcal{S} \mid \mathcal{S} \subseteq \mathbf{Oex}^a(\mathbf{M}) \text{ for some } \mathbf{M} \}$.

Thus, $\mathbf{M}$ $\mathbf{Oex}^a$ identifies a function f just in case $\mathbf{M}$, fed the graph of f, vacillates among a nonempty finite set D of indexes such that there is at least one a-error index for f in the set D and each index in D is conjectured infinitely often by $\mathbf{M}$. Show that for each $m \in N$ we have that $\mathbf{Oex}^m = \mathbf{Ex}^m$, but that $\mathbf{Oex}^* - \mathbf{Ex}^* \neq \emptyset$.

6-7 Motivated by the definition of **Oex** above, consider the following variation in the definition of scientists.

6.32 Definition Suppose $a \in (N \cup \{*\})$.

(a) A scientist is a mapping from SEG to finite sets of programs.

(b) A scientist **M** is said to **FOex**^{a}-identify f (written: $f \in$ **FOex**^{a}(**M**)) just in case there exists a nonempty finite set D such that the following hold:

    1. for some $i \in D$, $\varphi_i =^a f$, and

    2. for all but finitely many n, $\mathbf{M}(f[n]) = D$.

(c) **FOex**$^a = \{\, \mathcal{S} \mid \mathcal{S} \subseteq$ **FOex**^{a}(**M**) for some **M** $\}$.

Show that **Oex**$^a =$ **FOex**^{a}.

6-8 Let $\mathcal{C}_0 = \{\, f \in \mathcal{R} \mid \varphi_{f(0)} = f \}$ and $\mathcal{C}_1 = \{\, f \in \mathcal{R} \mid (\overset{\infty}{\forall} x)[f(x) = 0] \,\}$. Show that, for all n, $\mathcal{C}_0 \cup \mathcal{C}_1 \notin \mathbf{Bc}^n$. (This generalizes the Nonunion Theorem (Theorem 4.25.))

6-9 Prove each of the following.

(a) Let $a \in (N \cup \{*\})$. If **M TxtBc**^{a}-identifies L, then there exists $\sigma \in$ SEQ such that the following hold:

    1. $content(\sigma) \subseteq L$;

    2. $W_{\mathbf{M}(\sigma)} =^a L$;

    3. $(\forall \tau \mid content(\tau) \subseteq L)[W_{\mathbf{M}(\sigma \diamond \tau)} =^a L]$.

Such a σ is called a **TxtBc**^{a}-locking sequence for **M** on L. (This is an analog of the locking sequence lemma (Theorem 3.22) for **TxtBc**^{a}-identification.)

(b) For $m \in N$, $\{\, L \mid L =^{2m+1} N \,\} \notin \mathbf{TxtBc}^m$.

(c) $\{\, L \mid card(L) < \infty \,\} \cup \{\, N \,\} \notin \mathbf{TxtBc}^*$.

(d) $\mathcal{COFIN} \in (\mathbf{TxtEx}^* - \mathbf{TxtBc})$.

6-10 Consider the following variation on **TxtBc**^{a}-identification.

6.33 Definition Let $a \in (N \cup \{*\})$.

(a) $\mathbf{M}$ $\mathbf{TxtExt}^a$-*identifies* L (written: $L \in \mathbf{TxtExt}^a(\mathbf{M})$) just in case $(\exists L' \mid L =^a L')$ $(\forall$ texts T for $L)(\overset{\infty}{\forall} n)[W_{\mathbf{M}(T[n])} = L']$.

(b) $\mathbf{TxtExt}^a = \{\, \mathcal{L} \mid \mathcal{L} \subseteq \mathbf{TxtExt}^a(\mathbf{M})$ for some $\mathbf{M}\,\}$.

Intuitively, a scientist $\mathbf{M}$ $\mathbf{TxtExt}^a$-identifies L just in case $\mathbf{M}$, fed any text for L, semantically converges to indexes for some fixed a-variant of L. Clearly, $\mathbf{TxtBc} = \mathbf{TxtExt}^0$.

(a) Show that $\mathbf{TxtEx}^{i+1} - \mathbf{TxtExt}^i \neq \emptyset$.

(b) Show that $\mathbf{TxtBc}^1 - \mathbf{TxtExt}^* \neq \emptyset$.

(c) Is $\mathbf{TxtExt}^{2i} \subseteq \mathbf{TxtBc}^i$?

6-11   Consider the following variation on $\mathbf{TxtFex}_b^a$ identification in which b is the exact number of indexes to which a scientist is required to converge.

6.34 Definition Let $a \in (N \cup \{*\})$ and $b \in (N^+ \cup \{*\})$.

(a) $\mathbf{M}$ $\mathbf{TxtFex}_{=b}^a$-*identifies* L (written: $L \in \mathbf{TxtFex}_{=b}^a(\mathbf{M})$) just in case for each text T for L there exists a nonempty finite set D such that the following hold:

1. $card(D) = b$,

2. for each $i \in D$, $W_i =^a L$,

3. for all but finitely many n, $\mathbf{M}(T[n]) \in D$, and

4. for each $i \in D$, there are infinitely many n such that $\mathbf{M}(T[n]) = i$.

(b) $\mathbf{TxtFex}_{=b}^a = \{\, \mathcal{L} \mid \mathcal{L} \subseteq \mathbf{TxtFex}_{=b}^a(\mathbf{M})$ for some $\mathbf{M}\,\}$.

Answer the following questions.

(a) Show that for $a \in (N \cup \{*\})$ and $b \in N^+$, $\mathbf{TxtFex}_{=b}^a = \mathbf{TxtEx}^a$.

(b) Analogous to the above definition, define the criteria $\mathbf{TxtFex}_{=b}^{=a}$ in which the parameter a is now the exact number of errors made by each of the b indexes. Show that for $a \in N$ and $b \in N^+$, $\mathbf{TxtFex}_{=b}^{=a} = \mathbf{TxtEx}$.

6-12   Show that $\mathbf{TxtBc} - \mathbf{TxtFex}_*^* \neq \emptyset$. Then, observe as a corollary that for $a \in (N \cup \{*\})$, $\mathbf{TxtFex}_*^a \subset \mathbf{TxtBc}^a$.

Show the following.

(a) For each $i \in N$, $\mathbf{Ex}^{i+1} - \mathbf{LimEx}^i \neq \emptyset$.

(b) $\mathbf{Ex}^* - \bigcup_{i \in N} \mathbf{LimEx}^i \neq \emptyset$. Observe that this result together with part (a) implies $\mathbf{LimEx}^0 \subset \mathbf{LimEx}^1 \subset \cdots \subset \mathbf{LimEx}^*$.

(c) $\mathbf{Bc} - \mathbf{LimEx}^* \neq \emptyset$.

(d) For each $i \in N$, $\mathbf{LimEx} - \mathbf{Bc}^i \neq \emptyset$.

(e) For each $a \in (N \cup \{*\})$, $\mathbf{Ex}^a \subset \mathbf{LimEx}^a$.

A **Lim**-program for a function may be viewed as a higher-order program for the function. A three argument φ-program i is called a **Lim**^{2}-program for η just in case for all x, $\eta(x) = \lim_{t_1 \to \infty} \lim_{t_2 \to \infty} \varphi(x, t_1, t_2)$. This process can easily be iterated to define **Lim**^{n} programs. The reference [29] considers identification of such higher-order programs for functions.

6-13 Show the following refinements of the observation in Exercise 6-12.

(a) $\mathbf{TxtFex}_*^m \subseteq \mathbf{TxtBc}^{m'} \iff m \leq 2 \cdot m'$.

(b) $\{\, L \mid L =^{2m+1} N \,\} \in (\mathbf{TxtFex}_1^{2m+1} - \mathbf{TxtBc}^m)$.

6-14 (Advanced) Consider the following variation on $\mathbf{TxtFex}_b^a$-identification.

> **6.35 Definition (Osherson, Stob, and Weinstein [140])** Let $a \in (N \cup \{$
> and $b \in (N^+ \cup \{*\})$.
>
> (a) $\mathbf{M}$ $\mathbf{TxtFExt}_b^a$-*identifies* L (written: $L \in \mathbf{TxtFExt}_b^a(\mathbf{M})$) just in case for e
> text T for L there is a finite, nonempty set D of cardinality at most b such that
> $\mathbf{M}$ finitely converges to D, (ii) for each $i \in D$, $W_i =^a L$, and (iii) for all $i, j \in$
> $W_i = W_j$.
>
> (b) $\mathbf{TxtFExt}_b^a = \{\, \mathcal{L} \mid \mathcal{L} \subseteq \mathbf{TxtFExt}_b^a(\mathbf{M}) \text{ for some } \mathbf{M} \,\}$.

Show that for all $i \in N$, $\mathbf{TxtFex}_*^i \subseteq \mathbf{TxtFExt}_*^*$.

Open Question: Is $\mathbf{TxtFex}_*^* = \mathbf{TxtFExt}_*^*$?

6-15 Two approaches to relaxing the strict requirement of **Ex**-identification have
considered in this chapter, namely, allowing anomalies in the final program and weake
the notion of convergence. Here we consider a third approach. Instead requiring con
gence to a program for the function, we allow a scientist to converge to a "trial and er
procedure for the function. We formalize what we mean by a "trial and error" proced
for a function through programs for limiting approximations. A two argument φ-progi
i is referred to as **Lim**-*program* for η just in case for all x, $\eta(x) = \lim_{t\to\infty} \varphi_i(x, t)$, wh
$\eta(x)$ is undefined just in case the limit fails to exist. Intuitively, such a **Lim**-program,
a given input, is allowed finitely many mind changes about what output to produce. T
next definition introduces a paradigm in which the scientist converges to a **Lim**-progra
for a finite variant of the function to be identified.

> **6.36 Definition (Case, Jain, and Sharma [29])** Let $a \in (N \cup \{*\})$.
>
> (a) $\mathbf{M}$ $\mathbf{LimEx}^a$-*identifies* $f \in \mathcal{R}$ (written: $f \in \mathbf{LimEx}^a(\mathbf{M})$) just in case $\mathbf{M}(f)\downarrow$
> and $\mathbf{M}(f)$ is a **Lim**-program for an a-variant of f.
>
> (b) $\mathbf{LimEx}^a = \{\, \mathcal{S} \mid \mathcal{S} \subseteq \mathbf{LimEx}^a(\mathbf{M}) \text{ for some } \mathbf{M} \,\}$.

7   Inference of Approximations

§7.1   Approximations

Lakatos [117] claimed that most scientific theories are "born refuted." That is, the theories are put forth in the face of prima facie anomalies. To back this claim Lakatos sketched the history of a number of successful scientific theories that were nonetheless awash in an "ocean of anomalies." These theories, which are approximate explanations for the phenomenon in question, succeed in part because they were judged to be close enough approximations to be useful. Approximations arise in language learning also. To see this, have a conversation with a three-year-old child who, we will assume, speaks English. Now, the child's grammar almost certainly does not match "standard" English grammar. For example, irregular verbs may be regularized, adjectives and adverbs may appear in peculiar places in sentences, and whole grammatical categories may be missing. Yet despite this, you can probably carry out a successful conversation. So there are quite reasonable informal criteria under which a learner of a language can be judged to have learned a sufficiently good approximation to the target language, even though this approximation may have vast differences from the target.

We previously considered inference of approximations in Chapter 6 where the $\mathbf{Ex}^a$ and $\mathbf{TxtEx}^a$ ($a \in (N \cup \{*\})$) criteria were introduced and studied. It is questionable whether Lakatos' "oceans of anomalies" are properly reflected in, say, the setting of the $\mathbf{Ex}^*$ criterion which demands that final explanations be correct on a co-finite set. In defense of $\mathbf{Ex}^*$ one might argue that a clever coding of experiments could fence the anomalies into a finite set. (For instance, if a theory was known to be anomalous in the X-ray region of the EM-spectrum, then one could simply code all experiments on the X-ray region as a single "don't care" experiment.) But the cleverness seems only to mask Lakatos' insight. More is accomplished by attempting to frame success criteria that permit infinitely many anomalies in final explanations or grammars. Such is the topic of the present chapter.

Criteria permitting infinitely many anomalies in final explanations or grammars usually make some restriction on the allowed distribution of these anomalies. (Otherwise, the criteria are typically degenerate—see Exercise 7-1.) Most of this chapter concerns criteria that require that the "density" of anomalies be no more than a fixed amount, where the notion of "density" is formalized in various ways. We begin with a short excursion into elementary real analysis to introduce some tools that help in formalizing these density notions.

§7.2 Some background

Real numbers, supremums, and infimums

Here we review the small amount of real analysis required for this chapter. For more details on the following, see almost any book on real analysis, for example, Dudley [56] or Rudin [162].

Recall from Chapter 2 that $\mathbf{R}$ denotes the set of real numbers. In this chapter, let a, b, and c range over $\mathbf{R}$. Recall that:

$$[\![a,c]\!] \;=\; \{\, b \in \mathbf{R} \mid a \le b \le c \,\}. \qquad (\!(a,c)\!) \;=\; \{\, b \in \mathbf{R} \mid a < b < c \,\}.$$
$$[\![a,c)\!) \;=\; \{\, b \in \mathbf{R} \mid a \le b < c \,\}. \qquad (\!(a,c]\!] \;=\; \{\, b \in \mathbf{R} \mid a < b \le c \,\}.$$

Also recall that, for natural numbers x and z:

$$[x,z] \;=\; \{\, y \in N \mid x \le y \le z \,\}. \qquad (x,z) \;=\; \{\, y \in N \mid x < y < z \,\}.$$
$$[x,z) \;=\; \{\, y \in N \mid x \le y < z \,\}. \qquad (x,z] \;=\; \{\, y \in N \mid x < y \le z \,\}.$$

Let X be a nonempty set of real numbers. We define $\inf(X)$ as follows. If there is a w such that, for all $x \in X$, $w \le x$, then $\inf(X)$ is the largest such w; otherwise, $\inf(X) = -\infty$. For example, $\inf\left([\![0,1]\!]\right) = 0 = \inf\left((\!(0,1]\!]\right)$, but note that $0 \notin (\!(0,1]\!]$. For another example, $\inf(\{\, -x \mid x \in N \,\}) = -\infty$. We define $\sup(X)$ as $-\inf(\{\, -x \mid x \in X \,\})$. Equivalently, if there is a y such that, for all $x \in X$, $y \ge x$, then $\sup(X)$ is the smallest such y; otherwise, $\sup(X) = \infty$. Suppose that $a_0, a_1, \ldots$ is a sequence of real numbers. Define:

$$\liminf_{n \to \infty} a_n \;=\; \lim_{n \to \infty} \inf(\{\, a_n \mid n \ge m \,\}).$$
$$\limsup_{n \to \infty} a_n \;=\; \lim_{n \to \infty} \sup(\{\, a_n \mid n \ge m \,\}).$$

For example, for each n, let $a_{2n} = \frac{1}{n+1}$ and $a_{2n+1} = 1 - \frac{1}{n+1}$. Then $\lim_{n \to \infty} a_n$ is undefined, but $\liminf_{n \to \infty} a_n = 0$ and $\limsup_{n \to \infty} a_n = 1$. We note that, for any sequence $a_0, a_1, \ldots$,

$$\inf(\{\, a_0, a_1, \ldots \,\}) \le \liminf_{n \to \infty} a_n \le \limsup_{n \to \infty} a_n \le \sup(\{\, a_0, a_1, \ldots \,\}). \qquad (7.1)$$

Density

We make use of the above real analysis to define a notion of the density of a set of natural numbers.

7.1 Definition

(a) Suppose B is finite and nonempty. We say that the *density of A in B* (written: $den(A, B)$) is the number $|A \cap B|/|B|$.

(b) The *density* of A (written: $den(A)$) is $\liminf\limits_{x \to \infty} den(A, [0, x])$.

Clearly, the density of every subset of N is defined and in $[\![0, 1]\!]$. For instance, for each n we have, $den(\{\, 3x \mid x \in N \,\}, \{\, 0, 1, \ldots, n \,\}) = \frac{[(n+1)/3]}{n+1}$ and thus it follows that $den(\{\, 3x \mid x \in N \,\}) = \frac{1}{3}$. Here is a more involved example: Let

$$A_0 \;=\; \bigcup_{n \geq 0} [(2n)!, (2n+1)!)$$

and $A_1 = N - A_0$. Then $den(A_0) = 0$ because, for each n, $den(A_0, [0, (2n+2)!]) \leq (2n+1)!/(2n+2)! = 1/(2n+2)$; hence, $\liminf_{x \to \infty} den(A_0, [0, x]) = 0$. By a similar argument, $den(A_1) = 0$. But, since $A_0 \cup A_1 = N$, $den(A_0 \cup A_1) = 1$. In general, this notion of density is subadditive in the sense of part (a) of the following lemma.

7.2 Lemma

(a) If A and B are disjoint, then $den(A) + den(B) \leq den(A \cup B)$.

(b) If $B \subseteq A$, then $den(A - B) \leq den(A) - den(B)$.

Part (b) of the lemma is an easy consequence of part (a). The proof of part (a) is left for Exercise 7-2. The next lemma states a key fact that we need about r.e. sets and density. Its proof is outlined in Exercise 7-3.

7.3 Lemma *For each r.e. set A and each $\epsilon > 0$, there exists a recursive $B \subseteq A$ such that $den(B) \geq den(A) - \epsilon$.*

Lemma 7.3 is simply a density analog of the standard result in recursion theory that every infinite r.e. set has an infinite recursive subset. The existence of nonrecursive r.e. sets also has a density analog: there exists an r.e. set A such that each B, a recursive subset of A, has $den(B) < den(A)$. See Exercise 7-4 for details.

Our primary use of this density notion is to obtain measures of how closely different sets and functions approximate each other.

7.4 Definition Suppose $A, B \subseteq N$ and $\alpha, \beta \colon N \rightharpoonup N$.

(a) The *asymptotic agreement* between A and B (written: $aa(A, B)$) is $den(\overline{A \bigtriangleup B})$.

(b) The *asymptotic agreement* between α and β (written: $aa(\alpha, \beta)$) is $den(\{\, x \mid \alpha(x) = \beta(x) \,\})$.

(c) The *asymptotic disagreement* between A and B (written: $ad(A, B)$) is $1 - aa(A, B)$.

(d) The *asymptotic disagreement* between α and β (written: $ad(\alpha, \beta)$) is $1 - aa(\alpha, \beta)$.

Note that $ad(\alpha, \beta) = \limsup_{n \to \infty} den(\{\, x \mid \alpha(x) \neq \beta(x) \,\}, [0, n])$. So, $ad(\alpha, \beta)$ is an asymptotic upper bound on the amount of disagreement of α and β on sufficiently large initial segments of N. The next proposition says that there is no finite function β, partial recursive α, and $a \in [\![0, 1)\!)$ such that the "a-radius ball around α," i.e., $\{\, f \mid ad(\alpha, f) \leq a \,\}$ includes all recursive extensions of β.

7.5 Proposition *For each $a \in [\![0, 1)\!)$, finite function β, and partial recursive α, there is a recursive f such that $\beta \subseteq f$ and $ad(\alpha, f) > a$.*

Proof: Fix a, β, and α. Let $f_0 = \beta \cup \{\, (x, 0) \mid x \notin domain(\beta) \,\}$. If $ad(\alpha, f_0) > a$, we are done. Suppose $ad(\alpha, f_0) \leq a$. We construct from f_0 an f as required. Let $A = \{\, x \mid \alpha(x) = f_0(x) \,\}$. Since $ad(f, \alpha) \leq a < 1$, we have $den(A) \geq 1 - a > 0$. Choose some $b \in (\!(0, 1 - a)\!)$. So, $den(A) > b > 0$. As A is r.e., we have, by Lemma 7.3, that there is a recursive $B \subseteq A$ with $den(B) \geq den(A) - b$. Without loss of generality we assume $B \cap domain(\beta) = \emptyset$. Let $f = \lambda x.[1 - f_0(x), \text{if } x \in B; f_0(x), \text{if } x \notin B]$. By definitions of f and f_0 and our assumption that $B \cap domain(\beta) = \emptyset$, $\beta \subseteq f$. Since B is recursive and $f_0 \in \mathcal{R}$, $f \in \mathcal{R}$ also. Observe that $\{\, x \mid \alpha(x) = f(x) \,\} \subseteq (A - B)$. Therefore,

$$
\begin{aligned}
den(\{\, x \mid \alpha(x) = f(x) \,\}) \ &\leq \ den(A - B) \\
&\leq \ den(A) - den(B) \quad &\text{(by Lemma 7.2(b))} \\
&\leq \ b \quad &\text{(by the choice of } B) \\
&< \ 1 - a \quad &\text{(by the choice of } b).
\end{aligned}
$$

Therefore, by Definition 7.4(d), $ad(\alpha, f) > a$, as desired. ∎

§7.3 Approximate explanatory identification

We now make use of the density notions of the previous section to develop a series of identification criteria based on approximations. (We follow the pattern of Chapter 6 by first considering extensions of **Ex** followed by extensions of **TxtEx**.) The idea is that when a scientist **M** is presented with a function f, we would like the scientist to infer, in the limit, an explanation, p, such that the asymptotic disagreement between f and φ_p is no more that a prespecified amount. Here are the formal details.

7.6 Definition Suppose $a \in [0, 1]$.

(a) **M Aex^a**-identifies f (written: $f \in \mathbf{Aex}^a(\mathbf{M})$) if and only if $\mathbf{M}(f)\!\downarrow$ and $ad(f, \varphi_{\mathbf{M}(f)})$ $\leq a$.

(b) **M Aex^a**-*identifies* $\mathcal{S}$ just in case $\mathcal{S} \subseteq \mathbf{Aex}^a(\mathbf{M})$.

(c) $\mathbf{Aex}^a = \{\, \mathcal{S} \mid \text{for some } \mathbf{M}, \ \mathcal{S} \subseteq \mathbf{Aex}^a(\mathbf{M}) \,\}$.

Thus, for each $f \in \mathbf{Aex}^0(\mathbf{M})$, scientist **M**, fed f, converges to an explanation $p = \mathbf{M}(f)$ such that the asymptotic disagreement between f and φ_p is zero. At first glance, φ_p looks like an excellent approximation of f, but in reality the definition begs an important question. Suppose f is viewed as representing some physical phenomenon, say x represents a setting of a device and $f(x)$ represents the device's reading for this setting. Then the representations of settings and readings each involve some coding into the natural numbers and, in the case of the settings, their coding can have a huge impact on density concerns. For instance, suppose f' is defined so that, for each x, $f'(2x) = f(x)$ and $f'(2x+1) = 0$. Then, f' can be considered to represent the same phenomenon as f, but $ad(f', \lambda x\,.0) \leq 1/2$, so it is very easy to obtain "good" approximations of f' that are not very informative. More dramatic examples of this problem are simple to arrange—see Exercise 7-6. Exercise 7-7 develops a "coding invariant," density-based identification criteria, but the notion appears artificial. As there does not seem to be any easy way out of the difficulty, we will simply live with the dependency of density on codings, and proceed to explore success criteria like **Aex**.

The next proposition states the basic hierarchy result for the **Aex** criteria. Its proof follows the proofs of Lemmas 7.8 and 7.9 below.

7.7 Proposition *Suppose $0 \leq a < b \leq 1$. Then $\mathbf{Aex}^a \subset \mathbf{Aex}^b$.*

7.8 Lemma *For each rational $q \in [\![0, 1)\!)$, $\mathcal{R} \notin \mathbf{Aex}^q$.*

Proof: Fix a rational $q \in [\![0, 1)\!)$ and an **M**. We exhibit an $f \in (\mathcal{R} - \mathbf{Aex}^q(\mathbf{M}))$. Let $\sigma_0 = \emptyset$ and consider the following stages $s = 0, 1, 2, \cdots$.

Begin (*Stage s*)
  Search for the least τ such that
    (a) $[\tau \supseteq \sigma_s$ and $\hat{\tau}(s)\!\downarrow]$ and
    (b) $[\mathbf{M}(\tau) \neq \mathbf{M}(\sigma_s)]$.
  If such a τ is ever found, set σ_{s+1} to τ.
End (*Stage s*)

One of two things happen with this construction. Either (Case 1) it progresses through all the stages, or (Case 2) it progresses only up to some stage s_0 because the search for τ in that stage never terminates. The f we exhibit depends on which case holds.

Case 1: We have, for each s, that σ_{s+1} is defined and, by clause (a) in the search, that $domain(\hat{\sigma}_{s+1}) \supseteq \{0, \ldots, s\}$ and $\sigma_{s+1} \supseteq \sigma_s$. Hence, $\bigcup_{s \geq 0} \hat{\sigma}_s$ is a total recursive function which we call f. Since clause (b) in the search is satisfied for each s, we also have $\mathbf{M}(f)\!\uparrow$. Hence, $f \notin \mathbf{Aex}^q$, as required.

Case 2: Let $p_0 = \mathbf{M}(\sigma_{s_0})$. By Proposition 7.5 there is a recursive f such that $f \supset \sigma_{s_0}$ and $ad(\varphi_{p_0}, f) > q$. But, by this case $\mathbf{M}(f) = p_0$. Hence, $f \notin \mathbf{Aex}^q$, as required. ∎

7.9 Lemma *Suppose q and r are rationals with $0 \leq q < r \leq 1$. Then $\mathbf{Aex}^q \subset \mathbf{Aex}^r$.*

Proof: Let m and $n \in N$ be such that $r = m/n$. Let $B = \{x \mid (x \bmod n) < m\}$. B is thus a recursive set with $den(B) = r$ and $den(\overline{B}) = 1 - r$. Let $\mathcal{S} = \{f \in \mathcal{R} \mid f(x) = 0$ for each $x \in \overline{B}\}$. Clearly, $\mathcal{S} \in \mathbf{Aex}^r$.

Suppose by way of contradiction that, for some $\mathbf{M}$, $\mathcal{S} \subseteq \mathbf{Aex}^q(\mathbf{M})$. For each $f \in \mathcal{R}$, let $f' = \lambda x.[f(x)$, if $x \in B$; 0, if $x \notin B]$. Thus, for all $f \in \mathcal{R}$, $f' \in \mathcal{S}$; hence, $f' \in \mathbf{Aex}^q(\mathbf{M})$. Let $\mathbf{M}'$ be such that, for all f, $\mathbf{M}'(f) = \mathbf{M}(f')$. We show that $\mathcal{R} \subseteq \mathbf{Aex}^{1-(r-q)}(\mathbf{M}')$, contradicting Lemma 7.8.

Fix an arbitrary recursive f and let $p = \mathbf{M}(f')$ ($= \mathbf{M}'(f)$) and $A = \{x \mid \varphi_p(x) = f'(x)\}$. Since $f' \in \mathbf{Aex}^q(\mathbf{M})$, we have $den(A) \geq 1 - q$. Without loss of generality we assume that $A \supseteq \overline{B}$. *Claim:* $den(A \cap B) \geq r - q$. (See Exercise 7-5 for the proof.) Since $A \cap B \subseteq \{x \mid \varphi_p(x) = f(x)\}$, we have that $r - q \leq den(\{x \mid \varphi_p(x) = f(x)\}) = den(\{x \mid \varphi_{\mathbf{M}'(f)}(x) = f(x)\})$. Hence, $f \in \mathbf{Aex}^{1-(r-q)}(\mathbf{M}')$. Since f was arbitrary, we have that $\mathcal{R} \subseteq \mathbf{Aex}^{1-(r-q)}(\mathbf{M}')$, a contradiction. ∎

Proof (of Proposition 7.7): Fix reals a and b such that $0 \leq a < b \leq 1$. Since the rationals are dense in the reals (Dudley [56], Rudin [162]), there are rationals q and r

such that $a < q < r < b$. Since $\mathbf{Aex}^a \subseteq \mathbf{Aex}^q$, $\mathbf{Aex}^r \subseteq \mathbf{Aex}^b$, and, by Lemma 7.9, $\mathbf{Aex}^q \subset \mathbf{Aex}^r$, the proposition follows.   ∎

The next two propositions establish the relations between the $\mathbf{Aex}$ and the $\mathbf{Bc}$ hierarchies.

7.10 Proposition $(\mathbf{Aex}^0 - \bigcup_{n=0}^{\infty} \mathbf{Bc}^n) \neq \emptyset$.

For the proof, see Exercise 7-8.

7.11 Corollary $\mathbf{Ex}^* \subset \mathbf{Aex}^0$.

7.12 Proposition $(\mathbf{Bc} - \bigcup_{0 \leq a < 1} \mathbf{Aex}^a) \neq \emptyset$.

Proof: Let $\mathcal{S} = \{\, f \in \mathcal{R} \mid (\overset{\infty}{\forall} n)[\varphi_{f(n)} = f]\,\}$. The proof of Proposition 6.10 showed that $\mathcal{S} \in (\mathbf{Bc} - \mathbf{Ex}^*)$. Here we modify that proof to show that $\mathcal{S} \notin \bigcup_{0 \leq a < 1} \mathbf{Aex}^a$.

Choose arbitrary $\mathbf{M}$ and $a \in [\![0, 1)\!]$. By the operator recursion theorem (Theorem 2.6) there is a one-one, recursive function p such that the behavior of programs with indexes $p(0)$, $p(1)$, $p(2)$, ... is described in stages below. We arrange things so that one $\varphi_{p(0)}$, $\varphi_{p(1)}$, $\varphi_{p(2)}$, ... witnesses the failure of $\mathbf{M}$ to $\mathbf{Aex}^a$-identify $\mathcal{S}$.

The $\varphi_{p(i)}$'s are defined in stages $s = 0, 1, 2, \cdots$. For each i and s, $\varphi_{p(i)}^s$ denotes the finite segment of $\varphi_{p(i)}$ defined before stage s. We take $\varphi_{p(i)}^0 = \emptyset$. Let k be an integer such that $k \cdot (1 - a) > 1$. For each s, let x_s denote the least number not in the domain of $\varphi_{p(0)}^s$, let $q_s = \mathbf{M}(\varphi_{p(0)}[x_s])$, and let $I_s = [sk + 1, sk + k]$.

Begin (*Stage s*)

For each $i \in I_s$ and each $x < x_s$, make $\varphi_{p(i)}^{s+1}(x) = \varphi_{p(0)}^s(x)$.

For $x = x_s$, $x_s + 1$, $x_s + 2$, ... in turn, define $\varphi_{p(i)}^{s+1}(x) = p(i)$ for each $i \in I_s$ until, if ever, an x is discovered such that $\mathbf{M}(\varphi_{p(i)}[x + 1]) \neq q_s$ for some $i \in I_s$.

If such an x is discovered, then let i be the least element of I_s such that $\mathbf{M}(\varphi_{p(i)}[x + 1]) \neq q_s$. Set $\varphi_{p(0)}^{s+1} = \varphi_{p(i)}^{s+1}$ and from now on make $\varphi_{p(i)}$ follow $\varphi_{p(0)}$ so that $p(i)$ is an index for $\varphi_{p(0)}$.

End (*Stage s*)

We consider the following two cases.

Case 1: All stages terminate. By the construction, the range of $\varphi_{p(0)}$ contains only indexes for $\varphi_{p(0)}$, hence $\varphi_{p(0)} \in \mathcal{S}$. However, $\mathbf{M}$ on $\varphi_{p(0)}$ makes infinitely many mind changes.

Case 2: Some stage s starts but fails to terminate. For each $i \in I_s$ we have by the construction that $\varphi_{p(i)} =^* \lambda x . p(i)$ and is total; hence $\varphi_{p(i)} \in \mathcal{S}$. Note that $\mathbf{M}(\varphi_{p(i)})\!\downarrow = q_s$ for each $i \in I_s$. We show that $\mathbf{M}$ fails to $\mathbf{Aex}^a$-identify at least one of these $\varphi_{p(i)}$. For each $i \in I_s$, let $A_i = \{\, x \mid \varphi_{q_s}(x) = p(i) \,\}$. Clearly, the A_i's are disjoint. Hence, by Lemma 7.2(a), $den(A_{sk+1}) + \cdots + den(A_{sk+k}) \leq den(\cup_{i \in I_s} A_s)$, which is ≤ 1. Now, if it *were* the case that $\{\, \varphi_{p(i)} \mid i \in I_s \,\} \subseteq \mathbf{Aex}^a(\mathbf{M})$, then we would have $den(A_i) \geq (1-a)$ for each $i \in I_s$; but then $den(A_{sk+1}) + \cdots + den(A_{sk+k}) \geq k \cdot (1-a) > 1$, a contradiction. Therefore, for at least one $i \in I_s$, $\varphi_{p(i)} \in (\mathcal{S} - \mathbf{Aex}^a(\mathbf{M}))$.

From the above cases it follows that $\mathcal{S} \not\subseteq \mathbf{Aex}^a(\mathbf{M})$. ∎

The $\mathbf{Aex}$ criteria is thus seen to be a hierarchy that sits above the $\mathbf{Ex}^a$ criteria and which is incomparable to the $\mathbf{Bc}^a$ hierarchy, except for the obvious degenerative case of $\mathbf{Bc}^* = \mathbf{Aex}^1$.

We conclude this section by brief consideration of the text analogs of the $\mathbf{Aex}$ criteria.

7.13 Definition Suppose $a \in [\![0,1]\!]$. We say that $\mathbf{M}$ $\mathbf{TxtAex}^a$-*identifies* L (written: $L \in \mathbf{TxtAex}^a(\mathbf{M})$) if and only if, for each text T for L, $\mathbf{M}(L)\!\downarrow$ and $ad(L, W_{\mathbf{M}(T)}) \leq a$. Define "$\mathbf{M}$ $\mathbf{TxtAex}^a$-*identifies* $\mathcal{S}$" and "$\mathbf{TxtAex}^a$" in the usual way.

The results for the $\mathbf{Aex}$ criteria all carry over to this new setting. For example, we have:

7.14 Proposition *If* $0 \leq a < b \leq 1$, *then* $\mathbf{TxtAex}^a \subset \mathbf{TxtAex}^b$.

In proving these results one cannot employ the trick of Section 6.2 used to convert $\mathbf{Ex}$-based results to analogous $\mathbf{TxtEx}$-based results. The difficulty is that the conversion $f \mapsto L_f$ plays havoc with densities. On the other hand, Lemma 7.3—the foundation for the arguments of this section—works equally well in the text setting. Hence, one can fairly directly translate $\mathbf{Aex}$ arguments to $\mathbf{TxtAex}$ arguments. Exercise 7-9 illustrates this method by working through a proof of Proposition 7.14. Since these translations are all straightforward, we leave $\mathbf{TxtAex}$ versions of the other results of this section as exercises for the reader.

§7.4 Uniform approximate explanatory identification

The $\mathbf{Aex}$ criterion allows infinite many errors provided that the density of these errors is suitably bounded. Notice, however, that $\mathbf{Aex}$ permits approximations that — although globally good — are locally terrible. As an example, let $C = \cup_{n \in N}[2^n + n, 2^{n+1})$. Clearly, $den(C) = 1$ and, if p and f are such that $\{x \mid \varphi_p(x) = f(x)\} = C$, then $aa(\varphi_p, f) = 1$. Thus the asymptotic agreement between φ_p and f is as good as possible, but $\{x \mid \varphi_p(x) \neq f(x)\} = \cup_{n \in N}[2^n, 2^n+n)$ contains arbitrarily large gaps. The following definition addresses this defect in **Aex** by introducing a stricter notion of density.

7.15 Definition

(a) The *uniform density of A in intervals of length* $\geq m$ (written: $uden_m(A)$) is $\inf(\{den(A, [x, y]) \mid x, y \in N \text{ and } y - x \geq m\})$.

(b) The *uniform density of A* (written: $uden(A)$) is $\lim_{m \to \infty} udm_m(A)$.[1]

(c) The *asymptotic uniform agreement between A and B* (written: $aua(A, B)$) is $uden(\overline{A \bigtriangleup B})$. The *asymptotic uniform agreement between α and β* (written: $aua(\alpha, \beta)$) is $uden(\{x \mid \alpha(x) = \beta(x)\})$.

(d) The *asymptotic uniform disagreement between A and B* (written: $aud(A, B)$) is $1 - aua(A, B)$. The *asymptotic uniform disagreement between α and β* (written: $aud(\alpha, \beta)$) is $1 - aua(\alpha, \beta)$.

So, if $uden(A) \leq a$, then for each $\epsilon > 0$ there is an m_ϵ such that for *every* interval I of length at least m_ϵ, $den(A, I) > a - \epsilon$. In particular, if C is as above, then for each m, $udm_m(C) = 0$; hence $uden(C) = 0$.

7.16 Definition Suppose a is a real in $[\![0, 1]\!]$.

(a) An **M** **Uex**^{a}-*identifies* f (written: $f \in \textbf{Uex}^a(\textbf{M})$) if and only if $\textbf{M}(f){\downarrow}$ and $aud(f, \varphi_{\textbf{M}(f)}) \leq a$.

(b) $\textbf{Uex}^a = \{\mathcal{S} \mid \text{for some } \textbf{M}, \mathcal{S} \subseteq \textbf{Uex}^a(\textbf{M})\}$.

For example, if **M** **Uex**^{0}-identifies f with $p = \textbf{M}(f)$, then

$$\lim_{m \to \infty} \left(\sup\{den(\{z \mid \varphi_p(z) \neq f(z)\}, [x, y]) \mid y - x \geq m\} \right) = 0,$$

thus p is a uniformly good approximation to f. The relationship of the **Uex** criteria to the **Ex**, **Bc**, and **Aex** criteria is easy to establish.

---

[1] Note that for each A and m, $udm_m(A) \leq udm_{m+1}(A) \leq 1$, and hence by elementary real analysis, the limit $\lim_{m \to \infty} udm_m(A)$ always exists.

7.17 Proposition *Suppose a and b are reals in $[\![0, 1)\!)$.*

(a) $\mathbf{Uex}^a \subset \mathbf{Uex}^b$, *for $a < b$.*

(b) $(\mathbf{Uex}^0 - \bigcup_{n=0}^{\infty} \mathbf{Bc}^n) \neq \emptyset$.

(c) $\mathbf{Ex}^* \subset \mathbf{Uex}^0$.

(d) $(\mathbf{Bc} - \bigcup_{0 \leq a < 1} \mathbf{Uex}^a) \neq \emptyset$.

(e) $(\mathbf{Aex}^0 - \mathbf{Uex}^a) \neq \emptyset$.

(f) $\mathbf{Uex}^a \subset \mathbf{Aex}^b$, *for $a \leq b$.*

(g) $(\mathbf{Uex}^b - \mathbf{Aex}^a) \neq \emptyset$, *for $a < b$.*

Proof: For parts (a) through (d) adapt the proofs of the analogous results in the previous section.

For part (e), first let $C = \cup_{n \in N}[2^n + n, 2^{n+1})$ and $\mathcal{S} = \{ f \in \mathcal{R} \mid f(x) = 0 \text{ for each } x \in C \}$. It is straightforward that $\mathcal{S} \in \mathbf{Aex}^0$ but that, for each $a \in [\![0, 1)\!)$, $\mathcal{S} \notin \mathbf{Uex}^a$.

Part (f) follows from part (e).

To show part (g), first fix rationals q and r with $0 \leq q < r \leq 1$ and let $\mathcal{S}$ be as in Lemma 7.9. Clearly, $\mathcal{S} \in \mathbf{Uex}^r$. By the argument of Lemma 7.9, $\mathcal{S} \notin \mathbf{Aex}^q$. Therefore, $(\mathbf{Uex}^r - \mathbf{Aex}^q) \neq \emptyset$, and thus part (g) follows by the density of the rationals in the reals. ∎

Thus, as might have been expected, the **Uex** hierarchy turns out to be a stricter version of the **Aex** hierarchy. The formulation of the text version of the **Uex** criteria and the proof of the analog of Proposition 7.17 are both straightforward and left to the reader.

Uex is an improvement over **Aex**, but it fails to capture every aspect of uniform density. Consider the following example. For each $k \in N$, let

$$C_k \;=\; [0, 2^k) \cup \bigcup_{n \geq k} [2^n + k, 2^{n+1}),$$

let g_k be the characteristic function of $\overline{C_k}$, let $z = \lambda x.0$, and, finally, let $\mathbf{M}$ be such that on every input, $\mathbf{M}$ produces some fixed index for z. Clearly, for each k, $ud(C_k) = 1$ and $aud(z, g_k) = 0$. Hence, $\mathbf{M}$ $\mathbf{Uex}^0$-identifies every element of $\{ g_k \mid k \in N \}$. But, for each k_0, for all but finitely many k, the set $\{ x \mid z(x) \neq g_k(x) \}$ contains intervals of length k_0 or greater. Thus $\mathbf{M}$ fails to give *uniformly* good approximations across the class $\{ g_k \mid k \in N \}$. The **Huex** (for *h*omogeneous *u*niform approximate *ex*planatory identification) criteria, developed in the next definition, address this problem.

7.18 Definition Suppose $a \in [\![0, 1]\!]$ and $m \in N$.

(a) The *asymptotic uniform agreement between α and β on intervals of length $\geq m$* (written: $aua_m(\alpha, \beta)$) is $ud_m(\{\, x \mid \alpha(x) = \beta(x) \,\})$.

(b) The *asymptotic uniform disagreement between α and β on intervals of length $\geq m$* (written: $aud_m(\alpha, \beta)$) is $1 - aua_m(\alpha, \beta)$.

(c) An **M** **Huex**^{a,m}-*identifies* f (written: $f \in$ **Huex**$^{a,m}(\mathbf{M})$) if and only if $\mathbf{M}(f)\!\downarrow$ and $aud_m(f, \varphi_{\mathbf{M}(f)}) \leq a$.

(d) **Huex**$^{a,m} = \{\, \mathcal{S} \mid$ for some **M**, $\mathcal{S} \subseteq$ **Huex**$^{a,m}(\mathbf{M}) \,\}$.

(e) **Huex**$^{a} = \{\, \mathcal{S} \mid$ for some **M** and m, $\mathcal{S} \subseteq$ **Huex**$^{a,m}(\mathbf{M}) \,\}$.

If $aud_m(\alpha, \beta) \leq a$, then $den(\{\, x \mid \alpha(x) \neq \beta(x) \,\}, I) \leq a$ for all intervals I of length m or more. Note that there is no notion of an **M** **Huex**^{a}-identifying a particular f. If $\mathcal{S} \subseteq$ **Huex**^{a}, then for some m we have that for every interval I of length m or greater and for every $f \in \mathcal{S}$, $den(\{\, x \mid \varphi_{\mathbf{M}(f)}(x) \neq f(x) \,\}, I) \leq a$. The basic properties of the **Huex** criteria are easy to establish.

7.19 Proposition

(a) *For all $a, b \in [\![0, 1]\!]$ with $a < b$,* **Huex**$^a \subset$ **Huex**^{b}.

(b) $(\mathbf{Bc} - \bigcup_{0 \leq a < 1} \mathbf{Huex}^a) \neq \emptyset$.

(c) $(\mathbf{Huex}^0 - \mathbf{Ex}^*) \neq \emptyset$.

(d) $(\mathbf{Huex}^0 - \bigcup_{n=0}^{\infty} \mathbf{Bc}^n) \neq \emptyset$.

Proof: For parts (a), (b), (c), and (d), adapt the proofs of Proposition 7.7, Proposition 7.12, Corollary 7.11, and Proposition 7.10, respectively. ∎

The most interesting property of the **Huex**^{a} (for $a < 1$) criteria is that they fail to contain the **Ex*** criterion. That is,

7.20 Proposition $\mathcal{ASD}^* \in (\mathbf{Ex}^* - \bigcup_{0 \leq a < 1} \mathbf{Huex}^a)$.

Proving the proposition requires taking a closer look at the **Ex**^{n} criteria. This is accomplished in the propositions that follow, from which Proposition 7.20 is obtained as an immediate corollary.

A basic problem with the **Ex**^{n} criterion for large n is that it permits a scientist to converge to an explanation that is correct on all but n points, but these n points many include all the experiments for which one would like correct predictions. Proposition 7.21

162   *Inference of Approximations*

provides a particular example of this. Chen[36] proved the analogous result for the $\mathbf{Bc}^n$ criteria.

Terminology: We say that x is the *point of convergence of* $\mathbf{M}$ *on* f if and only if $\mathbf{M}(f){\downarrow}$ and x is the least number such that, for all $y > x$, $\mathbf{M}(f[x]) = \mathbf{M}(f[y])$.

7.21 Proposition *Suppose* $\mathbf{M}$ *is a scientist and* $m \in N$.

(a) *There is an* $f \in \mathcal{ASD}^{m+1}$ *such that either* $\mathbf{M}(f){\uparrow}$ *or else* $\mathbf{M}(f){\downarrow}$ *and, if* x *is the point of convergence of* $\mathbf{M}$ *on* f, *then for each* $y \in [x, x+m]$, $f(y) \neq \varphi_{\mathbf{M}(f)}(y)$.

(b) *There are infinitely many* $f \in \mathcal{ASD}^*$ *such that either* $\mathbf{M}(f){\uparrow}$ *or else* $\mathbf{M}(f){\downarrow}$ *and, if* x *is the point of convergence of* $\mathbf{M}$ *on* f, *then for each* $y \in [x, x+m]$, $f(y) \neq \varphi_{\mathbf{M}(f)}(y)$.

Part (a) of this proposition follows from the proof of Proposition 6.5. We leave it to the reader to check the details of this. Part (b) follows as an easy consequence of part (a). Using this proposition we can establish the relation of the **Huex** criteria to the $\mathbf{Ex}^n$ criteria and some final details of the relation of the **Huex** with the **Uex** and **Aex** criteria.

7.22 Proposition *Suppose* $a, b \in [\![0,1]\!]$ *and* $m, n \in N$.

(a) *If* $n \leq a \cdot (m+1)$, *then* $\mathbf{Ex}^n \subseteq \mathbf{Huex}^{a,m}$.

(b) *If* $n > a \cdot (m+1)$, *then* $\mathcal{ASD}^n \in (\mathbf{Ex}^n - \mathbf{Huex}^{a,m})$.

(c) *If* $a < 1$, *then* $(\mathbf{Uex}^0 - \mathbf{Huex}^a) \neq \emptyset$.

(d) *If* $a < 1$ *and* $a \leq b$, *then* $\mathbf{Huex}^a \subset \mathbf{Uex}^b$.

(e) *If* $a < b$, *then* $(\mathbf{Huex}^b - \mathbf{Aex}^a) \neq \emptyset$.

Proof: *Observation:* If $f \in \mathbf{Huex}^{a,m}(\mathbf{M})$, then $\{x \mid \varphi_{\mathbf{M}(f)}(x) \neq f(x)\}$ can have as many as $\lfloor a \cdot (m+1) \rfloor$ members in any interval of length m, but no more than that.

We have from the Observation that, if $n \leq a \cdot (m+1)$ and if $f \in \mathbf{Ex}^n(\mathbf{M})$, then $f \in \mathbf{Huex}^{a,m}(\mathbf{M})$; hence part (a) follows.

Part (b) follows from the Observation and Proposition 7.21(a).

Part (c) follows from Proposition 7.17(c) and Proposition 7.20.

By Definitions 7.16 and 7.18, if $a \leq b$, then $\mathbf{Huex}^a \subseteq \mathbf{Uex}^b$. By part (c), this containment is strict; hence part (d) follows.

Suppose $a < b$ and suppose q and r are rationals such that $a < q < r < b$. The $\mathcal{S}$ of the proof of Lemma 7.9 is clearly in $\mathbf{Huex}^r$, hence by the proof of Lemma 7.9,

$\mathcal{S} \in (\mathbf{Huex}^r - \mathbf{Aex}^q)$. Part (e) then follows by the density of the rationals in the reals. ∎

Finally we note that Proposition 7.20 follows from Proposition 7.22(b). We thus see that by making our notion of density sufficiently uniform we obtain a hierarchy of criteria, each of which allows infinitely many anomalies but fails to include the $\mathbf{Ex}^*$ criterion because $\mathbf{Ex}^*$ is too liberal in the way it permits anomalies to be distributed.

We do not consider the relationships between the $\mathbf{Huex}^{a,m}$ criteria here. We also leave to the reader the details of the formalization and proofs of the text variants of the above notions and results.

§7.5 Bibliographic notes

Podnieks [152] and, in improving Podnieks' results, Chen [36, Theorem 5.9] employed what amounts to a learning theoretic density notion, but they did not use density notions to define identification criteria. The criteria considered above were introduced by Royer in [159]. This chapter is largely based on that paper. Independently, Smith defined something similar, but less general, to the $\mathbf{Aex}$ criteria. Smith and Velauthapillai study the $\mathbf{Aex}$ criteria and mind-change bounds in [179, 180]. The reader can find other applications of this chapter's density notions in Chapters 8 and 10 below.

Another approach to learning approximations, due to Fulk and Jain [73], is treated in Exercise 7-10.

§7.6 Exercises

7-1 We say that $\mathbf{M}$ $\mathbf{Ex}^\infty$-*identifies* f if and only if $\mathbf{M}(f){\downarrow} = p$ and $\{\, x \mid \varphi_p(x) = f(x) \,\}$ is infinite. Define $\mathbf{Ex}^\infty(\mathbf{M})$ and $\mathbf{Ex}^\infty$ as usual. Show that $\mathcal{R} \in \mathbf{Ex}^\infty$. *Hint:* Show there is a p_0 such that, for every $f \in \mathcal{R}$, $\{\, x \mid \varphi_p(x) = f(x) \,\}$ is infinite.

7-2 Here we develop a proof of Lemma 7.2(a).

(a) Fix a sequence $a_0, a_1, \cdots$. Show: $a \leq \liminf_{n\to\infty} a_n$ if and only if, for each $\epsilon > 0$, there exists n' such that for all $n \geq n'$, $a - \epsilon \leq a_n$.

(b) Suppose $\liminf_{n\to\infty} b_n = b > -\infty$ and $\liminf_{n\to\infty} c_n = c > -\infty$. Use part (a) to show that $b + c \leq \liminf_{n\to\infty} b_n + c_n$.

(c) Use part (b) to show Lemma 7.2(a).

7-3   Here we work through the proof of Lemma 7.3. Fix an r.e. set A with index i and an $\epsilon > 0$. We shall construct B, a recursive subset of A with $den(B) \geq den(A) - \epsilon$.

Choose a rational number q and integer n such that $den(A) - \epsilon \leq q - \frac{1}{n} < q \leq den(A)$. Let $x_0 = 0$; let x_1 be the least number > 0 such that, for all $x \geq x_1$, $den(A, [0, x]) > q - \frac{1}{2n}$, and for each $s > 0$, let $x_{s+1} = 2nx_s$. Let $B_0 = \emptyset$; for each $s > 0$, let t_s be the least number such that, for each $x \in [x_1, x_{s+1}]$, $den(W_{i,t_s}, [0, x]) > q - \frac{1}{2n}$; and let $B_s = B_{s-1} \cup (W_{i,t_s} \cap [x_{s-1}, x_s])$. Finally, set $B = \cup_{s \geq 0} B_s$.

(a) Show that there exists an x_1 as claimed.

(b) Show that, for each $s > 0$, there exists a t_s as claimed. Use this to show that B is a recursive subset of W_i.

(c) Fix an $s > 0$. Show that $B \supset (W_{i,t_s} \cap [x_{s-1}, \infty))$ and thus, for each $x \geq x_s$, $den(B, [0, x]) \geq den(W_{i,t_s}, [0, x]) - den([0, x_{s-1}], [0, x]) \geq den(W_{i,t_s}, [0, x]) - 1/2n$.

(d) Fix an $s > 0$. Use part (c) and our choice of t_s to show that, for all $x \in [x_s, x_{s+1}]$, $den(B, [0, x]) \geq q - 1/n$.

(e) Use part (d) to conclude that $den(B) \geq den(W_i) - \epsilon$.

7-4   (**Advanced**) Show the following.

(a) $\{\, i \mid den(W_i) = 1 \,\}$ is Π_4-complete.

(b) $\{\, i \mid W_i$ has a density 1 recursive subset $\}$ is a Δ_4 set. Conclude that not every density 1 r.e. set has a density 1 recursive subset.

7-5   We prove the claim in the proof of Lemma 7.9. Let $r = m/n$; let q be a rational number in $[\![0, r)\!]$; let $B = \{\, x \mid (x \bmod n) < m \,\}$; and let $A \supseteq \overline{B}$ with $den(A) \geq 1 - q$.

(a) Show that, for all x, $den(\overline{B}, [0, x]) \leq 1 - r$.

(b) Show that for each $\epsilon > 0$ there is an x_0 such that, for all $x \geq x_0$, $den(A) - \epsilon \leq den(A \cap B, [0, x]) + 1 - r$.

(c) Show that $den(A \cap B) \geq r - q$.

7-6   Construct π, a recursive isomorphism (i.e., a recursive permutation of N) and a set A such that $den(A) = 1$ and $den(\overline{A}) = 0$, but $den(\pi(A)) = 0$ and $den(\pi(\overline{A})) = 1$.

7-7   We say that a set A is *scattered* if and only if, for all recursive, one-one f, $\limsup_{n \to \infty} den(f^{-1}(A), [0, n]) = 0$.

(a) Show that infinite scattered sets exist and that each scattered set is either finite or immune.

(b) Show that there are hyperimmune sets which are not scattered and that there are infinite scattered sets which are not hyperimmune.

(c) Show that if S is a scattered set and π is a recursive isomorphism, then $\pi(S)$ is also a scattered set.

(d) We say $\mathbf{M}$ $\mathbf{Ex}^{\text{scat}}$-*identifies* f if and only if $\mathbf{M}(f)\!\downarrow$ and $\{\, x \mid f(x) \neq \varphi_{\mathbf{M}(f)}(x) \,\}$ is scattered. We also define $\mathbf{Ex}^{\text{scat}}(\mathbf{M})$ and $\mathbf{Ex}^{\text{scat}}$ in the usual way. Show that $\mathbf{Ex}^* \subset \mathbf{Ex}^{\text{scat}} \subset \mathbf{Aex}^0$.

7-8 Here we show Proposition 7.10: $(\mathbf{Aex}^0 - \bigcup_{n=0}^{\infty} \mathbf{Bc}^n) \neq \emptyset$. Let $B = \overline{\{\, 2^n \mid n \in N \,\}}$ and $\mathcal{S} = \{\, f \in \mathcal{R} \mid f(x) = 0 \text{ for each } x \in B \,\}$. Clearly, $\mathcal{S} \in \mathbf{Aex}^0$. Fix n. Show that if $\mathcal{S} \in \mathbf{Bc}^n$, then $\mathcal{R} \in \mathbf{Bc}^n$, a contradiction.

7-9 Here we develop a proof of Proposition 7.14.

(a) Show that for each $a \in [\![0, 1)\!)$, τ, and $L \in \mathcal{E}$, there is a recursive set R such that $R \supseteq content(\tau)$ and $ad(L, R) > a$. *Hint:* Consider the two cases of $ad(L, N) > a$ and $ad(L, N) \leq a$.

(b) Show that for each rational $q \in [\![0, 1)\!)$, $\mathcal{E} \notin \mathbf{TxtAex}^q$.

(c) Show that for rationals q and r with $0 \leq q < r \leq 1$, $\mathbf{TxtAex}^q \subset \mathbf{TxtAex}^r$.

(d) Prove Proposition 7.14.

7-10 C.S. Peirce [147] held that one should not expect science to converge on a final theory of a phenomenon X; instead, the expectation should be that science will produce a series of better and better approximations to X. Fulk and Jain [73] define the following identification criteria intended to model Peirce's theory of inference. $\mathbf{M}$ $\mathbf{Ap}$-identifies f (written: $f \in \mathbf{Ap}(\mathbf{M})$) if and only if there is a sequence $\langle S_n^f \rangle_{n \in N}$ of subsets of N such that (i) for each n, $S_n^f \subseteq \{\, x \mid \varphi_{\mathbf{M}(f[n])}(x) = f(x) \,\}$; (ii) $S_0^f \subseteq S_1^f \subseteq S_2^f \subseteq \cdots$; (iii) $N = \bigcup_n S_n^f$; and (iv) for infinitely many n, $(S_{n+1}^f - S_n^f)$ is infinite. This turns out to be an extremely powerful criteria, as there is an $\mathbf{M}$ that $\mathbf{Ap}$-identifies every element of $\mathcal{R}$ [73, Theorem 1]. We work through a proof of this below.

(a) For each $f \in \mathcal{R}$, let p_f denote the least p such that $\varphi_p = f$. Show that there is an $\mathbf{M}'$ that takes a function argument f *and* a numeric argument m and which is such that, for each f in $\mathcal{R}$ and each $m \geq p_f$, $\mathbf{M}'(f, m)\!\downarrow = p'$ and $\varphi_{p'} = f$.

(b) Consider an **M** such that for each σ, $\mathbf{M}(\sigma) = p_\sigma$ where, for all x,

$$\varphi_{p_\sigma}(x) \;=\; \begin{cases} \sigma(x), & \text{if } x \in domain(\hat{\sigma}); \\ \varphi_{\mathbf{M}'(\sigma,i)}(x), & \text{otherwise, where } x = \langle i, y\rangle. \end{cases}$$

Show that **M Ap**-identifies each member of $\mathcal{R}$.

7-11   Fulk and Jain [73] define the following density-restricted version of the **Ap** criterion (see Exercise 7-10). For each $a \in [\![0,1]\!]$, we say that **M Dap**^{a}-identifies f (written: $f \in \mathbf{Dap}^a(\mathbf{M})$) if and only if there is a sequence $\langle S_n^f \rangle_{n \in N}$ of subsets of N that satisfy (i) through (iv) as in Exercise 7-10 and (v) $\lim_{n \to \infty} den(S_n^f) \geq a$. For each $a \in [\![0,1]\!]$, define $\mathbf{Dap}^a(\mathbf{M})$ and $\mathbf{Dap}^a$ as usual.

(a) Show that for each $a \in (\!(0,1]\!]$, $\mathcal{R} \notin \mathbf{Dap}^a$. (*Hint::* Use an operator recursion theorem argument.) Thus, while the **Ap** criterion is independent of encodings of experiments (unlike the **Aex** criteria), the **Ap** criterion has serious difficulties with density.

(b) Show that for each a and b with $0 \leq a < b \leq 1$, $\mathbf{Dap}^a \not\subseteq \mathbf{Dap}^b$.

8 Environments

Recall the component concepts of a learning paradigm:

(a) *a theoretically possible reality*

(b) *intelligible hypotheses*

(c) *the data available about any given reality, were it actual*

(d) *a scientist*

(e) *successful behavior by a scientist working in a given, possible reality*

Recursively enumerable languages and total recursive functions are the theoretically possible realities proper to the paradigms discussed so far. For both languages and functions, computer programs have been conceived as intelligible hypotheses.

In Chapter 5 we examined alternative interpretations of item (d) by restricting the concept "scientist" to subsets of the computable functions. Chapters 6 and 7 were devoted to a range of success criteria, in the sense of item (e). The present chapter concerns alternative construals of available data, item (c). Until now, the potential environments for a language or function have been equated with the class of all its texts. This equation embodies three assumptions about the character of the scientist's data, namely, that: (i) none are missing, (ii) those that reach the scientist are free of error, and (iii) they may arrive in any order. All three assumptions obviously misrepresent the circumstances of language acquisition. Thus, it is clear that children need not hear every sentence of their language in order to stabilize to an accurate grammar. They are also likely to face at least some ungrammatical intrusions (although perhaps not many; see [182]). There is also no doubt that children face a constrained order of sentences inasmuch as the speech addressed to them starts off simply. The same considerations apply to adult scientists conducting empirical inquiry. Their data are neither complete nor error-free, and the order of their arrival is constrained by such factors as cost. (Cheaper data arrive first!)

In what follows, erroneous data will be conceived as intrusions into the interface between a language and a scientist. Error thus expands the class of texts for a given language. Allowing data to be omitted has a similar effect whereas constraints on order shrink the class of texts a scientist might face. These ideas are defined precisely in Sections 8.1 and 8.2. We subsequently discuss how scientists can exploit multiple sources of data about the same reality.

§8.1 Inaccurate data

A text for a language L may suffer omissions from L, erroneous intrusions from $\bar{L}$, or both omissions and intrusions. Three kinds of inaccurate texts may thus be distinguished, to be called "incomplete," "noisy," and "imperfect" in what follows. We also distinguish different, finite numbers of the two defects (intrusion and omission). Infinite error is not considered here, but pointers to the relevant literature are provided later.

§8.1.1 Texts with finite number of inaccuracies

Pursuant to our classification of inaccuracies, we define three kinds of inaccurate texts for languages.

8.1 Definition Let $L \in \mathcal{E}$ and $a \in (N \cup \{*\})$ be given. A text T is *a-noisy* for L just in case $L \subseteq content(T)$ and $card(content(T) - L) \leq a$.

An a-noisy text for a language L can be viewed as a text for L into which any number of intrusions from a set of cardinality at most a have been inserted. Note that any single such intrusion may occur infinitely often in T.

8.2 Definition Let $L \in \mathcal{E}$ and let $a \in (N \cup \{*\})$ be given. A text T is *a-incomplete* for L just in case $content(T) \subseteq L$ and $card(L - content(T)) \leq a$.

An a-incomplete text for L can be viewed as a text for L from which all occurrences of a given set of cardinality at most a have been removed.

8.3 Definition Let $L \in \mathcal{E}$ and $a \in (N \cup \{*\})$ be given. A text T is *a-imperfect* for L just in case $card(L \bigtriangleup content(T)) \leq a$.

Thus, an a-imperfect text for L omits some finite $S_1 \subseteq L$ and includes some finite $S_2 \subseteq \bar{L}$; moreover the cardinality of $S_1 \cup S_2$ is bounded by a.

Note that in the above three definitions, the case in which $a = *$ implies that the number of inaccuracies is any finite number. The other cases model situations in which a scientist may be aware, *a priori*, of an upper bound on the number of inaccuracies infecting her environment. We now consider inaccurate texts for functions. Recall that we identify functions with their graphs and that SEG is the collection of all finite initial segments of (nonnoisy!) texts for functions. Thus, $\langle (0,0), (0,1) \rangle \notin$ SEG and we have no convenient way to denote the data available to scientists from noisy texts. The following definition remedies this.

8.4 Definition The set of all finite sequences over N^2 is denoted SEGI. By a *scientist for identifying functions using imperfect data* is meant any computable function (partial or total) from SEGI to N.

For brevity in this chapter, we drop the qualifier "for identifying functions using imperfect data" when referring to scientists.

8.5 Definition Let $f \in \mathcal{R}$ and $a \in (N \cup \{*\})$ be given. Let G be a text.

(a) G is *a-noisy* for f just in case $f \subseteq content(G)$ and $card(content(G) - f) \leq a$.

(b) G is *a-incomplete* for f just in case $content(G) \subseteq f$ and $card(f - content(G)) \leq a$.

(c) G is *a-imperfect* for f just in case $card(f \,\triangle\, content(G)) \leq a$.

Note that two incorrect values for $f(n)$ count as distinct, noisy points. To understand this idea, suppose that G is an inaccurate text for $f \in \mathcal{R}$, that $f(n) = x$, that $(n, y), (n, z) \in content(G)$, and that x, y, z are all distinct. Then, provided there are no other intrusions, G is a 2-noisy text for f. Further, if we suppress the correct pair (n, x) from the foregoing text G, then it becomes a 3-imperfect text for f.

Our task is now to embed the foregoing conceptions of inaccurate data within an associated learning paradigm. One means of achieving this is to require scientists to converge to an accurate index for the target object (language or function), even on texts that harbor inaccuracies. The next definition formalizes this idea for the language case.

8.6 Definition Let $a, b \in (N \cup \{*\})$ and scientist **M** be given.

(a.1) **M** $\mathbf{N}^a\mathbf{TxtEx}^b$-*identifies* $L \in \mathcal{E}$ (written: $L \in \mathbf{N}^a\mathbf{TxtEx}^b(\mathbf{M})$) just in case for all a-noisy texts T for L, $\mathbf{M}(T){\downarrow}$ and $W_{\mathbf{M}(T)} =^b L$.

(a.2) $\mathbf{N}^a\mathbf{TxtEx}^b = \{ \mathcal{L} \mid \mathcal{L} \subseteq \mathbf{N}^a\mathbf{TxtEx}^b(\mathbf{M})$ for some $\mathbf{M} \}$.

(b.1) **M** $\mathbf{In}^a\mathbf{TxtEx}^b$-*identifies* L (written: $L \in \mathbf{In}^a\mathbf{TxtEx}^b(\mathbf{M})$) just in case for all a-incomplete texts T for L, $\mathbf{M}(T){\downarrow}$ and $W_{\mathbf{M}(T)} =^b L$.

(b.2) $\mathbf{In}^a\mathbf{TxtEx}^b = \{ \mathcal{L} \mid \mathcal{L} \subseteq \mathbf{In}^a\mathbf{TxtEx}^b(\mathbf{M})$ for some $\mathbf{M} \}$.

(c.1) **M** $\mathbf{Im}^a\mathbf{TxtEx}^b$-*identifies* L (written: $L \in \mathbf{Im}^a\mathbf{TxtEx}^b(\mathbf{M})$) just in case for all a-imperfect texts T for L, $\mathbf{M}(T){\downarrow}$ and $W_{\mathbf{M}(T)} =^b L$.

(c.2) $\mathbf{Im}^a\mathbf{TxtEx}^b = \{\,\mathcal{L}\mid \mathcal{L}\subseteq \mathbf{Im}^a\mathbf{TxtEx}^b(\mathbf{M})$ for some $\mathbf{M}\,\}$.

We illustrate the above definitions with a few examples. Let $\mathcal{L} = \{\,E, O\,\}$, where E denotes the set of even numbers and O denotes the set of odd numbers. Let e and o be indexes for E and O, respectively. Let scientist $\mathbf{M}$, fed σ, emit e if the majority of $content(\sigma)$ are even; o otherwise. It is easy to see that $\mathbf{M}$ identifies $\mathcal{L}$ on $*$-noisy texts, $*$-incomplete texts, and $*$-imperfect texts. In contrast, there are two-element classes of languages that are not identifiable on 1-noisy texts. For example, let $L \in (\mathcal{E} - \{\,N\,\})$, $L' = L \cup \{\,x\,\}$, where $x \notin L$, and let T be some text for L'. Then T is also a 1-noisy text for both L and L'. Since $L \neq L'$, no scientist $\mathbf{M}$ converges on T to an index for both languages. It is also easy to verify that $\{\,L, L'\,\} \notin \mathbf{In}^1\mathbf{TxtEx}$.

The above example demonstrates that inaccuracies in texts affect identifiability. The next proposition highlights the disruptive effects of 1-noisy texts. The reader is referred to the exercises for a discussion of identification from noisy texts without the computability restriction on scientists.

8.7 Proposition *There is a collection of infinite, pairwise disjoint r.e. languages in* $\mathbf{TxtEx} - \mathbf{N}^1\mathbf{TxtEx}$.

Proof: For each $m, n \in N$, define $L_{n,m} = \{\,\langle n, x\rangle \mid x \neq m\,\}$. It is easy to verify that no scientist $\mathbf{N}^1\mathbf{TxtEx}$-identifies both $L_{n,m}$ and $L_{n,m'}$ for $m \neq m'$. Now let h be any permutation of N, and define $\mathcal{L}_h = \{\,L_{n,h(n)} \mid n \in N\,\}$. It is easy to see that for any permutation h, $\mathcal{L}_h \in \mathbf{TxtEx}$. But if $h \neq h'$, and if $\mathbf{M}$ $\mathbf{N}^1\mathbf{TxtEx}$-identifies $\mathcal{L}_h$, then $\mathbf{M}$ fails to $\mathbf{N}^1\mathbf{TxtEx}$-identifies $\mathcal{L}_{h'}$. Since there are only $\aleph_0$ many scientists and $2^{\aleph_0}$ many permutations of N, there must be a permutation h such that no scientist $\mathbf{N}^1\mathbf{TxtEx}$-identifies $\mathcal{L}_h$. ∎

The next proposition parallels Proposition 8.7 and highlights the disruptive effects of identification from 1-incomplete texts. A proof analogous to the above suffices; details are left to the reader.

8.8 Proposition *There is a collection, $\mathcal{L}$, of infinite, pairwise disjoint r.e. languages, such that $\mathcal{L} \in (\mathbf{TxtEx} - \mathbf{In}^1\mathbf{TxtEx})$.*

Paradigms for function learning may be defined analogously to the language case.

8.9 Definition Let $a, b \in (N \cup \{*\})$ and scientist $\mathbf{M}$ be given.

(a.1) **M** $\mathbf{N}^a\mathbf{Ex}^b$*-identifies* f (written: $f \in \mathbf{N}^a\mathbf{Ex}^b(\mathbf{M})$) just in case for all a-noisy texts G for f, $\mathbf{M}(G)\!\downarrow$ and $\varphi_{\mathbf{M}(G)} =^b f$.

(a.2) $\mathbf{N}^a\mathbf{Ex}^b = \{\, \mathcal{C} \mid \mathcal{C} \subseteq \mathbf{N}^a\mathbf{Ex}^b(\mathbf{M})$ for some **M** $\}$.

(b.1) **M** $\mathbf{In}^a\mathbf{Ex}^b$*-identifies* f (written: $f \in \mathbf{In}^a\mathbf{Ex}^b(\mathbf{M})$) just in case for all a-incomplete texts G for f, $\mathbf{M}(G)\!\downarrow$ and $\varphi_{\mathbf{M}(G)} =^b f$.

(b.2) $\mathbf{In}^a\mathbf{Ex}^b = \{\, \mathcal{C} \mid \mathcal{C} \subseteq \mathbf{In}^a\mathbf{Ex}^b(\mathbf{M})$ for some **M** $\}$.

(c.1) **M** $\mathbf{Im}^a\mathbf{Ex}^b$*-identifies* f (written: $f \in \mathbf{Im}^a\mathbf{Ex}^b(\mathbf{M})$) just in case for all a-imperfect texts G for f, $\mathbf{M}(G)\!\downarrow$ and $\varphi_{\mathbf{M}(G)} =^b f$.

(c.2) $\mathbf{Im}^a\mathbf{Ex}^b = \{\, \mathcal{C} \mid \mathcal{C} \subseteq \mathbf{Im}^a\mathbf{Ex}^b(\mathbf{M})$ for some **M** $\}$.

As an example of a collection of functions whose identifiability is not affected by the presence of a finite number of inaccuracies in texts, consider the class $\mathcal{C}$ of constant functions, i.e., $\mathcal{C} = \{\, f \mid (\exists c)(\forall x)[f(x) = c]\,\}$. It is easy to construct a scientist that identifies $\mathcal{C}$ on $*$-noisy texts, $*$-incomplete texts, and $*$-imperfect texts. On the other hand, no scientist identifies $\mathcal{SD}$, the collection of self-describing functions[1], from 1-incomplete texts.

The basic idea of the foregoing Definitions 8.6 and 8.9 is easily extended to other criteria of learning introduced in Chapter 6. For example, consider the language learning criterion $\mathbf{TxtFex}_c^b$, according to which a scientist **M** is successful on a language L just in case, given any text for L, **M** converges to a finite set of indexes D such that $card(D) \leq c$ and each index in D is for some b-variant of L. An a-noisy-text version of $\mathbf{TxtFex}_c^b$ is defined by requiring the scientist to $\mathbf{TxtFex}_c^b$-identify a language on any a-noisy text. The resulting paradigm is named $\mathbf{N}^a\mathbf{TxtFex}_c^b$. With this background, the reader may easily formulate the exact definitions of the following paradigms for language identification: $\mathbf{N}^a\mathbf{TxtFex}_c^b$, $\mathbf{In}^a\mathbf{TxtFex}_c^b$, $\mathbf{Im}^a\mathbf{TxtFex}_c^b$, $\mathbf{N}^a\mathbf{TxtBc}^b$, $\mathbf{In}^a\mathbf{TxtBc}^b$, and $\mathbf{Im}^a\mathbf{TxtBc}^b$.

Several criteria of function identification studied in Chapter 6 may also be adapted to the present context. In particular, we shall focus on $\mathbf{N}^a\mathbf{Bc}^b$, $\mathbf{In}^a\mathbf{Bc}^b$, and $\mathbf{Im}^a\mathbf{Bc}^b$ in what follows.

§8.1.2 Hierarchy results

The present section considers the tradeoff between inaccuracy in the available data versus leniency in the learning criterion. In particular, we investigate the effect of allowing

---

[1] Recall from Chapter 4 (Definition 4.24) that $\mathcal{SD} = \{\, f \mid \varphi_{f(0)} = f\,\}$.

additional errors in the output theory, in the sense discussed in Section 6.1.1. To what extent does such leniency compensate for additional noisy or missing points in the input data? The proposition stated below shows that the tradeoff is not straightforward. To see this, consider $\mathbf{Im}^n\mathbf{Ex}^n$. $\mathcal{S} \in \mathbf{Im}^n\mathbf{Ex}^n$ just in case there is some scientist $\mathbf{M}$ that behaves as follows. Given an n-imperfect text G for any $f \in \mathcal{S}$, $\mathbf{M}$ converges on G to an index for a (partial) function η that differs from f on no more than n arguments. It might be thought that $\mathbf{Im}^n\mathbf{Ex}^n$ defines the same family of collections as $\mathbf{Im}^m\mathbf{Ex}^m$ for distinct n and m. However, this is not true. Indeed, Part (a) of the next proposition shows that allowing one additional error in the output theory, in some cases, more than compensates for additional imperfection in the input data. Specifically, there are classes of functions for which an $(i+1)$-error program can be identified from texts with an arbitrarily large finite number of imperfections, but for which an i-error program cannot be synthesized, even from completely accurate texts. Part (c) of the proposition is a similar result about $\mathbf{Bc}$-identification. It is also interesting to note that by part (e) there is a scientist that can $\mathbf{Bc}^*$-identify every computable function, even from texts with an unbounded, finite number of imperfections.

8.10 Proposition *For all $i \in N$:*

(a) $\mathbf{Im}^*\mathbf{Ex}^{i+1} - \mathbf{Ex}^i \neq \emptyset$.

(b) $\mathbf{Im}^*\mathbf{Ex}^* - \bigcup_i \mathbf{Ex}^i \neq \emptyset$.

(c) $\mathbf{Im}^*\mathbf{Bc} - \mathbf{Ex}^* \neq \emptyset$.

(d) $\mathbf{Im}^*\mathbf{Bc}^{i+1} - \mathbf{Bc}^i \neq \emptyset$.

(e) $\mathcal{R} \in \mathbf{Im}^*\mathbf{Bc}^*$.

Proof: *Part (a).* Let $\mathcal{C} = \{\, f \in \mathcal{R} \mid \varphi_{f(0)} =^{i+1} f \text{ and } (\forall x)[f(2x) = f(0)] \,\}$. It is easy to see that $\mathcal{C} \in \mathbf{Im}^*\mathbf{Ex}^{i+1}$. An easy extension of the proof of Proposition 6.5 shows that $\mathcal{C} \notin \mathbf{Ex}^i$.

Parts (b), (c), and (d) can be shown by similar extensions of the proofs of Corollary 6.6 and Propositions 6.10 and 6.13 in Chapter 6. The proof of part (e) is left to the reader. ∎

Proposition 8.10 yields a hierarchy of paradigms that may be summarized as follows.

8.11 Corollary *Let $a \in (N \cup \{*\})$. Then:*

(a) $\mathbf{Im}^a\mathbf{Ex}^0 \subset \mathbf{Im}^a\mathbf{Ex}^1 \subset \mathbf{Im}^a\mathbf{Ex}^2 \subset \cdots \subset \mathbf{Im}^a\mathbf{Ex}^*$.

(b) $\mathbf{Im}^a\mathbf{Bc}^0 \subset \mathbf{Im}^a\mathbf{Bc}^1 \subset \mathbf{Im}^a\mathbf{Bc}^2 \subset \cdots \subset \mathbf{Im}^a\mathbf{Bc}^* = 2^{\mathcal{R}}$.

We leave it to the reader to work out counterparts of Proposition 8.10 and Corollary 8.11 for noisy and incomplete texts.

It is worth examining in more detail the impact on function identification of just a single noisy input. The next proposition shows that there are collections of functions for which programs can be identified from accurate texts, but for which programs for arbitrary finite variants cannot be identified from texts with at most one spurious datum.

8.12 Proposition $\mathbf{Ex} - \mathbf{N}^1\mathbf{Ex}^* \neq \emptyset$.

Proof: For each $f \in \mathcal{R}$, define f' and f'' as follows, for each j and $x \in N$:

$f'(\langle 0, 0 \rangle) = 0.$
$f''(\langle 0, 0 \rangle) = 1.$
$f'(\langle 0, x + 1 \rangle) = f''(\langle 0, x + 1 \rangle) = 0.$
$f'(\langle j + 1, x \rangle) = f''(\langle j + 1, x \rangle) = f(x).$

Consider the following collections of functions:

$$
\begin{aligned}
\mathcal{S}_a &= \{\, f \in \mathcal{R} \mid (\overset{\infty}{\forall} x)[f(x) = 0] \,\}. & \mathcal{S}'_a &= \{\, f' \mid f \in \mathcal{S}_a \,\}. \\
\mathcal{S}_b &= \{\, f \in \mathcal{SD} \mid (\overset{\infty}{\exists} x)[f(x) \neq 0] \,\}. & \mathcal{S}'_b &= \{\, f'' \mid f \in \mathcal{S}_b \,\}. \\
\mathcal{C} &= \mathcal{S}_a \cup \mathcal{S}_b. & \mathcal{C}' &= \mathcal{S}'_a \cup \mathcal{S}'_b.
\end{aligned}
$$

It is easy to verify that $\mathcal{S}_a \in \mathbf{Ex}$ and $\mathcal{S}_b \in \mathbf{Ex}$ (and hence $\mathcal{S}'_a, \mathcal{S}'_b \in \mathbf{Ex}$). However, according to Theorem 4.25, $\mathcal{C} = \mathcal{S}_a \cup \mathcal{S}_b \notin \mathbf{Ex}^*$. It is easy to see that for any $f \in \mathcal{C}'$, $f(\langle 0, 0 \rangle)$ can be used to determine whether $f \in \mathcal{S}'_a$ or $f \in \mathcal{S}'_b$. Thus, a scientist which $\mathbf{Ex}$-identifies $\mathcal{C}'$ can be constructed.

Suppose by way of contradiction that scientist $\mathbf{M}$ $\mathbf{N}^1\mathbf{Ex}$-identifies $\mathcal{C}'$. Then, using $\mathbf{M}$, we show how to construct $\mathbf{M}'$ which $\mathbf{Ex}^*$-identifies $\mathcal{S}_a \cup \mathcal{S}_b$, contradicting Theorem 4.25.

We first define two recursive functions twit and untwit. Let twit: SEGI $\rightarrow$ SEGI be a recursive function such that, for all σ and τ:

$$
\begin{aligned}
\mathit{content}(\mathrm{twit}(\sigma)) = \ & \{\, (\langle r, x \rangle, y) \mid (x, y) \in \mathit{content}(\sigma) \wedge 1 \leq r \leq |\sigma| \,\} \\
& \cup \ \{\, (\langle 0, 0 \rangle, 0), (\langle 0, 0 \rangle, 1) \,\} \\
& \cup \ \{\, (\langle 0, r \rangle, 0) \mid 1 \leq r \leq |\sigma| \,\}.
\end{aligned}
$$

$$\sigma \subseteq \tau \ \Rightarrow \ \mathrm{twit}(\sigma) \subseteq \mathrm{twit}(\tau).$$

Let untwit be a recursive function such that, for any φ-program i, for all x, $\varphi_{\text{untwit}(i)}(x) = \varphi_i(\langle 1, x \rangle)$.

Now, let $\mathbf{M}'(\sigma) = \text{untwit}(\mathbf{M}(\text{twit}(\sigma)))$. It is easy to see that if $\mathbf{M}$ $\mathbf{N}^1\mathbf{Ex}^*$-identifies $\mathcal{C}'$, then $\mathbf{M}'$ $\mathbf{Ex}^*$-identifies $\mathcal{S}_a \cup \mathcal{S}_b$. But this yields a contradiction; hence $\mathcal{C}' \notin \mathbf{N}^1\mathbf{Ex}^*$. ∎

Consider the following generalization of collection $\mathcal{C}'$ defined in the proof of Proposition 8.12 above. For each $k \in N$ and $f \in \mathcal{R}$, define f'_k and f''_k as follows.

For $x \leq k$, let $f'_k(\langle 0, x \rangle) = 0$, and $f''_k(\langle 0, x \rangle) = 1$.
For $x > k$, let $f'_k(\langle 0, x \rangle) = f''_k(\langle 0, x \rangle) = 0$.
For $j, x \in N$, $f'_k(\langle j+1, x \rangle) = f''_k(\langle j+1, x \rangle) = f(x)$.

Consider also the following collections of functions (where $\mathcal{S}_a, \mathcal{S}_b$ are defined in the proof of Proposition 8.12).

$$
\begin{aligned}
\mathcal{S}_{a,k} &= \{\, f'_k \mid f \in \mathcal{S}_a \,\}. \\
\mathcal{S}_{b,k} &= \{\, f''_k \mid f \in \mathcal{S}_b \,\}. \\
\mathcal{C}_k &= \mathcal{S}_{a,k} \cup \mathcal{S}_{b,k}.
\end{aligned}
$$

Using the proof of Proposition 8.12 as a model, it is easy to show that $\mathcal{C}_k \in \mathbf{Im}^k\mathbf{Ex}$, but $\mathcal{C}_k$ is in neither $\mathbf{N}^{k+1}\mathbf{Ex}^*$ nor $\mathbf{In}^{k+1}\mathbf{Ex}^*$. As a straightforward consequence (details are left for the reader), we have the following proposition.

8.13 Proposition *For all $k \in N$:*

(a) $\mathbf{Im}^k\mathbf{Ex} - \mathbf{N}^{k+1}\mathbf{Ex}^* \neq \emptyset$.

(b) $\mathbf{Im}^k\mathbf{Ex} - \mathbf{In}^{k+1}\mathbf{Ex}^* \neq \emptyset$.

Proposition 8.13 yields several corollaries that clarify the relationship between the number of inaccuracies allowed in a text and the ability of scientists to learn on those texts. The following corollary, for example, provides information about $\mathbf{Ex}$-identification from noisy texts.

8.14 Corollary *Let $a \in (N \cup \{*\})$. Then $\mathbf{N}^0\mathbf{Ex}^a \supset \mathbf{N}^1\mathbf{Ex}^a \supset \mathbf{N}^2\mathbf{Ex}^a \supset \cdots$.*

Let us now turn our attention to the identification of languages from inaccurate texts. The following Proposition is the language counterpart to Proposition 8.10 and can be shown using techniques similar to those used in Proposition 8.10. We leave the details as an exercise.

8.15 Proposition *For all $i \in N$:*

(a) $\mathbf{Im}^* \mathbf{TxtEx}^{i+1} - \mathbf{TxtFex}_*^i \neq \emptyset$.

(b) $\mathbf{Im}^* \mathbf{TxtEx}^* - \bigcup_{j \in N} \mathbf{TxtFex}_*^j \neq \emptyset$.

(c) $\mathbf{Im}^* \mathbf{TxtFex}_{i+1} - \mathbf{TxtFex}_i^* \neq \emptyset$.

(d) $\mathbf{Im}^* \mathbf{TxtEx}^{2i+1} - \mathbf{TxtBc}^i \neq \emptyset$.

(e) $\mathbf{Im}^* \mathbf{TxtBc} - \mathbf{TxtFex}_*^* \neq \emptyset$.

(f) $\mathbf{Im}^* \mathbf{TxtBc}^{i+1} - \mathbf{TxtBc}^i \neq \emptyset$.

The foregoing result yields a collection of hierarchies that are the subject of Exercise 8-16. Some other hierarchies are implied by the following result:

8.16 Proposition *For each $i \in N$,* $\mathbf{Im}^i \mathbf{TxtEx} - (\mathbf{N}^{i+1} \mathbf{TxtBc}^* \cup \mathbf{In}^{i+1} \mathbf{TxtBc}^*) \neq \emptyset$.

Proof: For each finite $L \in \mathcal{E}$, define:

$$
\begin{aligned}
L' &= \{\, \langle j, x \rangle \mid j \geq 1 \wedge x \in L \,\} \cup \{\, \langle 0, i+j+1 \rangle \mid j \leq i \,\}. \\
N' &= \{\, \langle j, x \rangle \mid j \geq 1, x \in N \,\} \cup \{\, \langle 0, j \rangle \mid j \leq i \,\}. \\
\mathcal{L} &= \{\, L' \mid L \text{ is finite } \,\} \cup \{\, N' \,\}.
\end{aligned}
$$

It is easy to verify that $\mathcal{L} \in \mathbf{Im}^i \mathbf{TxtEx}$. Also, $[\mathcal{L} \in \mathbf{N}^{i+1} \mathbf{TxtBc}^* \vee \mathcal{L} \in \mathbf{In}^{i+1} \mathbf{TxtBc}^*] \Rightarrow \{\, L \mid L \text{ is finite or } L = N \,\} \in \mathbf{TxtBc}^*$. But, $\{\, L \mid L \text{ is finite or } L = N \,\} \notin \mathbf{TxtBc}^*$ (see Exercise 6-9); thus $\mathcal{L} \notin (\mathbf{N}^{i+1} \mathbf{TxtBc}^* \cup \mathbf{In}^{i+1} \mathbf{TxtBc}^*)$. ∎

§8.1.3 Comparison of different kinds of inaccuracies

The last section revealed the extent to which inaccurate data can impede learning. However, no information was provided about the relative impact of different kinds of inaccuracies. For example, which is worse—noise or missing data? In the case of function learning we will see that missing data is strictly more disruptive than noise. To begin, the next proposition shows that there are collections of functions for which programs can be synthesized despite an arbitrary, finite number of noisy points, but for which even finite-variant programs cannot be synthesized if just one datum is missing. The language-identification counterpart of this result follows as an easy corollary.

8.17 Proposition $\mathbf{N}^* \mathbf{Ex} - \mathbf{In}^1 \mathbf{Ex}^* \neq \emptyset$.

Proof: For each $f \in \mathcal{R}$, define:

$$
\begin{aligned}
p_f &= min(\{\, j \mid \varphi_j = f \,\}). \\
\text{err}_j &= min(\{\, x \mid \varphi_j(x) \neq f(x) \,\}), \quad \text{for each } j < p_f \\
f'(0) &= \langle p_f, \langle \text{err}_0, \text{err}_1, \text{err}_2, \dots, \text{err}_{p_f - 1} \rangle \rangle. \\
f'(1 + \langle k, x \rangle) &= f(x), \quad \text{for all } x \text{ and } k.
\end{aligned}
$$

Consider the collection of functions $\mathcal{C} = \{\, f' \mid f \in \mathcal{R} \,\}$. We first show that $\mathcal{C} \notin \mathbf{In}^1 \mathbf{Ex}^*$. Suppose, by way of contradiction, that some scientist $\mathbf{M}\ \mathbf{In}^1 \mathbf{Ex}^*$-identifies $\mathcal{C}$. We describe a scientist $\mathbf{M}'$ which $\mathbf{Ex}^*$-identifies $\mathcal{R}$—yielding a contradiction. For each f, let G_f denote a text such that for all k, x, $G_f(\langle k, x \rangle) = (1 + \langle k, x \rangle, f(x))$. Note that G_f is a 1-incomplete text for f'. Also, note that $G_f[n]$ can be effectively computed from $f[n]$. Let g be a recursive function such that for all p, x, $\varphi_{g(p)}(x) = \varphi_p(\langle 1 + \langle 0, x \rangle \rangle)$. Define $\mathbf{M}'$ such that $\mathbf{M}'(f[n]) = g(\mathbf{M}(G_f[n]))$. Note that $\mathbf{M}'$ can easily be constructed from a description of $\mathbf{M}$. Clearly, for each $f \in \mathcal{R}$, if $\varphi_p =^* f'$, then $\varphi_{g(p)} =^* f$. Since $\mathbf{M}\ \mathbf{In}^1 \mathbf{Ex}^*$-identifies $\mathcal{C}$, it follows that $\mathbf{M}'\ \mathbf{Ex}^*$-identifies $\mathcal{R}$. However, $\mathcal{R} \notin \mathbf{Ex}^*$ (Corollary 6.11); thus $\mathcal{C} \notin \mathbf{In}^1 \mathbf{Ex}^*$.

We now show that $\mathcal{C} \in \mathbf{N}^* \mathbf{Ex}$. Let F be a mapping from SEGI to SEGI such that for each $n < |\sigma|$,

$$
(F(\sigma))(n) = \begin{cases}
(1 + \langle i, x \rangle, y) & \text{if } \sigma(n) = (1 + \langle i, x \rangle, y) \text{ and, for each} \\
& (1 + \langle j, x \rangle, z) \in content(\sigma), \text{ there is a } j' \geq j \\
& \text{such that } (1 + \langle j', x \rangle, y) \in content(\sigma); \\
(0, y) & \text{if } \sigma(n) = (0, y); \\
\# & \text{otherwise.}
\end{cases}
$$

Also, for each text G, define the text G' such that for all n,

$$
G'(n) = \begin{cases}
(1 + \langle i, x \rangle, y) & \text{if } G(n) = (1 + \langle i, x \rangle, y) \text{ and, for each} \\
& (1 + \langle j, x \rangle, z) \in content(G), \text{ there is a } j' \geq j \\
& \text{such that } (1 + \langle j', x \rangle, y) \in content(G); \\
(0, y) & \text{if } G(n) = (0, y); \\
\# & \text{otherwise.}
\end{cases}
$$

Now let G be a $*$-noisy text for $f' \in \mathcal{C}$. It is easy to see that for all but finitely many n, $G'[n] = F(G[n])$. Also, for all i, x, and y, we have $(1 + \langle i, x \rangle, y) \in content(G') \iff f'(1 + \langle i, x \rangle) = y$. Moreover, from the finitely many candidates for $f'(0)$ (at least one of which is correct), the actual value of $f'(0)$ can be determined in the limit. This is possible because

$$\pi_1(f'(0)) \;=\; max \left(\left\{ \; j \; \left| \; \begin{array}{l} \text{there are } e_0,\; e_1,\; \ldots,\; e_{j-1} \text{ such that} \\ (0,\; \langle j,\; \langle e_0, e_1, \ldots, e_{j-1} \rangle \rangle) \;\in\; content(G) \\ \text{and, for each } i < j, \;\; \varphi_i(e_i) \neq f'(1 + \langle 0, e_i \rangle) \end{array} \right. \right\} \right).$$

Thus $\pi_1(f'(0))$ can be obtained from G' (and hence G) in the limit. Also, it is easy to determine $f'(0)$, in the limit, from $\pi_1(f'(0))$, and from $f'(0)$, a φ-program for f' can easily be found. ∎

8.18 Corollary $\mathbf{N^* TxtEx} - \mathbf{In^1 TxtEx^*} \neq \emptyset$.

We leave it to the reader to modify the above proof to show the following result.

8.19 Proposition *For each* $i \in N$, $\mathbf{N^* Ex} - \mathbf{In^1 Bc^i} \neq \emptyset$.

8.20 Corollary *For each* $i \in N$, $\mathbf{N^* TxtEx} - \mathbf{In^1 TxtBc^i} \neq \emptyset$.

Propositions 8.17 and 8.19 may be paraphrased this way: there are collections of functions that can be learned from the most offensive noisy texts (*-noisy texts), but not from the least offensive incomplete texts (1-incomplete texts). It is natural to ask whether the reverse is true, i.e., whether there are collections of functions that can be learned from the most offensive incomplete texts (*-incomplete texts), but not from the least offensive noisy texts (1-noisy texts). Proposition 8.21 below answers this question negatively, thereby implying that—in the context of function identification—missing data are strictly more harmful than noisy data.

8.21 Proposition *Let* $a, b \in (N \cup \{*\})$. *Then:*

(a) $\mathbf{In^a Ex^b} \subseteq \mathbf{N^a Ex^b}$.

(b) $\mathbf{In^a Bc^b} \subseteq \mathbf{N^a Bc^b}$.

Proof: Let scientist $\mathbf{M}$ be given. We construct a scientist $\mathbf{M'}$ such that $\mathbf{In^a Ex^b(M)} \subseteq \mathbf{N^a Ex^b(M')}$ and $\mathbf{In^a Bc^b(M)} \subseteq \mathbf{N^a Bc^b(M')}$.

Let $F \colon \mathrm{SEGI} \to \mathrm{SEGI}$ be such that, for all σ, all $n < |\sigma|$, and all $x, y \in N$,

$$(F(\sigma))(n) \;=\; \begin{cases} (x, y), & \text{if } \sigma(n) = (x, y) \text{ and } (\forall(x, z) \in content(\sigma))[\, z = y\,]; \\ \#, & \text{otherwise.} \end{cases}$$

For each text G, let the text G' be such that, for all $n, x, y \in N$,

$$G'(n) = \begin{cases} (x,y), & \text{if } G(n) = (x,y) \text{ and } (\forall(x,z) \in content(G))[\, z = y \,]; \\ \#, & \text{otherwise.} \end{cases}$$

Now, if G is an a-noisy text for $f \in \mathcal{R}$, then G' is an a-incomplete text for f. Moreover, for all but finitely many n, $G'[n] = F(G[n])$.

For each σ, let $\mathbf{M}'(\sigma) = \mathbf{M}(F(\sigma))$. It is easy to see that both $\mathbf{In}^a\mathbf{Ex}^b(\mathbf{M}) \subseteq \mathbf{N}^a\mathbf{Ex}^b(\mathbf{M}')$ and $\mathbf{In}^a\mathbf{Bc}^b(\mathbf{M}) \subseteq \mathbf{N}^a\mathbf{Bc}^b(\mathbf{M}')$. ∎

The foregoing propositions show that missing data perturb function identification more than noisy data do. In the context of language identification, however, the matter is more subtle. The following proposition, for example, shows that there are collections of languages that can be identified despite one missing datum but cannot be identified in the presence of one noisy datum.

8.22 Proposition *For each $i > 0$, $\mathbf{In}^{2i-1}\mathbf{TxtEx}^i - \mathbf{N}^i\mathbf{TxtEx}^* \neq \emptyset$.*

Proof: Let $\mathcal{L}$ denote the collection of all such $L \in \mathcal{E}$ for which there are at least two distinct $x \leq 2$ such that $\mathrm{col}_x(L)$ is nonempty, finite, and $W_{max(\mathrm{col}_x(L))} = L$.

We show below, in Lemma 8.23, that $\mathcal{L} \notin \mathbf{TxtEx}^*$. Using $\mathcal{L}$, for each $i \in N$ we define $\mathcal{L}_i$ to be the collection of languages $L \in \mathcal{E}$ such that for some $L' \in \mathcal{L}$ the following hold for all j and x:

1. $\langle j+1, x \rangle \in L \iff x \in L'$.
2. $\langle 0, x \rangle \in L \Rightarrow x \leq 3i$.
3. $\langle 0, j \rangle \in L \iff \langle 0, j \bmod 3 \rangle \in L$.
4. At least two of $\langle 0,0 \rangle$, $\langle 0,1 \rangle$, and $\langle 0,2 \rangle$ are in L.
5. If $\langle 0, x \rangle \in L$ and $x \leq 2$, then $\mathrm{col}_x(L')$ is nonempty and finite and $W_{max(\mathrm{col}_x(L'))} = L'$.

We leave it to the reader to show that, for each i, $\mathcal{L}_i \in \mathbf{In}^{2i-1}\mathbf{TxtEx}^i$.

Let $\mathrm{Noisy}_i(L) = L \cup \{ \langle 0, k \rangle \mid k < 3i \}$. Clearly, for each $L \in \mathcal{L}_i$, any text T for $\mathrm{Noisy}_i(L)$ is also an i-noisy text for L. Lemma 8.23 thus implies that $\mathcal{L}_i \notin \mathbf{N}^i\mathbf{TxtEx}^*$. ∎

8.23 Lemma *Let $\mathcal{L}$ be as defined in the proof of Proposition 8.22. Then, $\mathcal{L} \notin \mathbf{TxtEx}^*$.*

Proof: Suppose by way of contradiction that **M TxtEx***-identifies $\mathcal{L}$. Then by the operator recursion theorem, there exists a recursive, 1–1, increasing p such that $W_{p(\cdot)}$ may be defined in stages as described below.

In the following construction, $W_{p(i)}^s$ denotes the part of $W_{p(i)}$ enumerated before stage s. (Note that there is no stage 0.) Let $W_{p(0)}^1 = W_{p(1)}^1 = \{\langle 0, p(0)\rangle, \langle 1, p(1)\rangle\}$ and, for each $i > 1$, let $W_{p(i)}^1 = \emptyset$. Also let $\sigma_1 = (\langle 0, p(0)\rangle, \langle 1, p(1)\rangle)$. Go to stage 1.

Begin (*Stage s*)

1. Enumerate $W_{p(0)}^s \cup W_{p(1)}^s$ into each of $W_{p(0)}, W_{p(1)}, W_{p(2s)}$ and $W_{p(2s+1)}$.

    Enumerate $\langle 2, p(2s)\rangle$ into both $W_{p(0)}$ and $W_{p(2s)}$.

    Enumerate $\langle 2, p(2s+1)\rangle$ into both $W_{p(1)}$ and $W_{p(2s+1)}$.

    Let τ_0 be an extension of σ_s such that $content(\tau_0) = [W_{p(0)}$ enumerated until now].

    Let τ_1 be an extension of σ_s such that $content(\tau_1) = [W_{p(1)}$ enumerated until now].

2. Dovetail between 2a and 2b until, if ever, step 2b succeeds. If and when step 2b succeeds, go to step 3.

    2a. **For $x = 0$ to ∞ do**
         enumerate $\langle 4, x\rangle$ into both $W_{p(0)}$ and $W_{p(2s)}$ and
         enumerate $\langle 5, x\rangle$ into both $W_{p(1)}$ and $W_{p(2s+1)}$.

    2b. Search for $i \in \{0, 1\}$, $n \in N$ such that
         $\mathbf{M}(\tau_i \diamond \langle 4+i, 0\rangle \diamond \langle 4+i, 1\rangle \diamond \ldots \diamond \langle 4+i, n\rangle)) \neq \mathbf{M}(\sigma_s)$.

3. If and when 2b succeeds, let i and n be as found in 2b and set
$$S = \{\langle 4+i, 0\rangle, \langle 4+i, 1\rangle, \ldots, \langle 4+i, n\rangle\}$$
$$\cup\; [W_{p(1)}\text{ enumerated until now}]$$
$$\cup\; [W_{p(0)}\text{ enumerated until now}].$$

    Let $\sigma_{s+1} = $ an extension of $\tau_i \diamond \langle 4+i, 0\rangle \diamond \langle 4+i, 1\rangle \diamond \ldots \diamond \langle 4+i, n\rangle)$ such that $content(\sigma_{s+1}) = S$.

    Enumerate S in both $W_{p(0)}$ and $W_{p(1)}$.

    Go to stage $s+1$.

End (*Stage s.*)

Consider the following two cases.

Case 1: Infinitely many stages are executed. In this case, let $L = W_{p(0)} = W_{p(1)} \in \mathcal{L}$. But **M** on $\bigcup_{s \in N} \sigma_s$, a text for L, makes infinitely many mind changes—since the only way in which infinitely many stages can exist is by the success of step (2b) infinitely often.

Case 2: Some stage s is started but never left. In this case, let $L_0 = W_{p(0)} = W_{p(2s)} \in \mathcal{L}$ and $L_1 = W_{p(1)} = W_{p(2s+1)} \in \mathcal{L}$. Note that L_0 and L_1 are infinitely different from each other. Let $T_0 = \tau_0 \diamond \langle 4, 0 \rangle \diamond \langle 4, 1 \rangle \diamond \cdots$, and $T_1 = \tau_1 \diamond \langle 5, 0 \rangle \diamond \langle 5, 1 \rangle \diamond \cdots$, where τ_0 and τ_1 are as defined in step 1 of stage s. Now, T_0 is a text for L_0 and T_1 is a text for L_1. However, **M** converges to the same grammar for both T_0 and T_1, thus **M** does not **TxtEx***-identify $\mathcal{L}$.

The above cases imply that $\mathcal{L} \notin \textbf{TxtEx}^*$. ∎

Having investigated noisy versus incomplete data, it is natural to consider next the relationship between incomplete and imperfect texts. How much more damage to learning results from adding noise to an environment already missing data? In this matter only approximate results are known; the exact relationship is still open. We provide a list of some sample results. Proofs for some of them are developed in the exercises.

8.24 Proposition *For all $i > 0$,* $\textbf{In}^{3i-1}\textbf{Ex} - \textbf{Im}^{2i}\textbf{Ex}^* \neq \emptyset$.

8.25 Proposition *For all $i > 0$ and $j \in N$,* $\textbf{In}^{3i-1}\textbf{Ex} - \textbf{Im}^{2i}\textbf{Bc}^j \neq \emptyset$.

8.26 Proposition *For all $i, j \in N$,* $\textbf{In}^{4i}\textbf{Ex}^j \subseteq \textbf{Im}^{2i}\textbf{Ex}^{2j}$.

§8.2 Texts with additional structure

The paradigms discussed until now suppose that an input text can be ordered arbitrary, and thus require scientists to succeed regardless of the manner in which their data are presented. This is, however, a questionable representation of many natural environments. It seems unlikely, for example, that children face an entirely arbitrary order of linguistic input, since simpler sentences usually arrive earlier than complex ones. The present section briefly discusses some paradigms that begin to respond to this consideration.

§8.2.1 Ascending texts

It is often claimed that children encounter simple sentences first and difficult ones later. Complexity may be measured by the length of the sentence, degree of embedding, inflection etc. For our purposes we assume that a sentence whose code is smaller is simpler.

Thus presenting simple sentences first and difficult ones later amounts to presenting the text in increasing order. We call such texts "ascending." By convention, we order $N \cup \{\#\}$ thus: $\# < 0 < 1 < 2 < \cdots$.

8.27 Definition A text T over natural numbers is *ascending* just in case T is nondecreasing as a function from N to $N \cup \{\#\}$. A text G over pairs of natural numbers is *ascending* just in case $\pi_1 \circ G$ is nondecreasing where, for all x and y, $\pi_1((x, y)) = x$.

Consider the identification of functions on perfect text (i.e., containing no noise or omissions). It is important to see that presenting such texts in ascending order does not augment the family of identifiable collections of functions. This is because any perfect text for a function can be gradually and effectively converted into an ascending text for the same function (see Exercise 8-36 for details). The present section will therefore limit itself to language learning.

8.28 Definition Let $a \in N$.

(a) We say that **M AscTxtEx**^{a}-*identifies* L (written: $L \in \mathbf{AscTxtEx}^a(\mathbf{M})$) just in case for all ascending texts T for L, $\mathbf{M}(T)\!\downarrow$ and $W_{\mathbf{M}(T)} =^a L$.

(b) $\mathbf{AscTxtEx}^a = \{ \mathcal{L} \mid \mathcal{L} \subseteq \mathbf{AscTxtEx}^a(\mathbf{M}) \text{ for some } \mathbf{M} \}$.

(c) $\mathbf{AscTxtBc}^a$ is defined similarly.

8.29 Proposition AscTxtEx $-$ **TxtBc**$^* \neq \emptyset$.

Proof: Consider the following collection of languages:

$$\mathcal{L} \;\; = \;\; \{\, N \,\} \;\cup\; \{\, L \mid L \text{ is finite and } not \text{ an initial segment of } N \,\}.$$

We leave it to the reader to show that $\mathcal{L} \notin \mathbf{TxtBc}^*$. We argue that $\mathcal{L} \in \mathbf{AscTxtEx}$. Let **Gram** be a recursive function such that for all finite sets D, $W_{\mathbf{Gram}(D)} = D$. Let i_N be an index for N. Now, for each σ, define:

$$\mathbf{M}(\sigma) \;\; = \;\; \begin{cases} i_N, & \text{if } content(\sigma) \text{ is an initial segment of } N; \\ \mathbf{Gram}(content(\sigma)), & \text{otherwise.} \end{cases}$$

It is easy to verify that **M AscTxtEx**-identifies $\mathcal{L}$. ∎

§8.2.2 Informant presentation

It is often assumed that children do not receive direct information about the non-sentences of their language (see the discussion in Chapters 1 and 3). Let us consider, however, what happens when texts contain both positive and negative information.

8.30 Definition We say that a text G for a 0–1 valued function is an *informant* for L just in case $content(G) = \{\,(x,1) \mid x \in L\,\} \cup \{\,(x,0) \mid x \notin L\,\}$.

8.31 Definition Let $a \in (N \cup \{*\})$.

(a) A scientist $\mathbf{M}$ $\mathbf{InfTxtEx}^a$-identifies L (written: $L \in \mathbf{InfTxtEx}^a(\mathbf{M})$) just in case on all informants G for L, $\mathbf{M}(G)\!\downarrow$ and $W_{\mathbf{M}(G)} =^a L$.

(b) $\mathbf{InfTxtEx}^a = \{\,\mathcal{L} \mid \mathcal{L} \subseteq \mathbf{InfTxtEx}^a(\mathbf{M}) \text{ for some } \mathbf{M}\,\}$.

We can similarly define $\mathbf{InfTxtBc}^a$, etc. It is easy to see that $\mathbf{AscTxtEx}^a \subseteq \mathbf{InfTxtEx}^a$ and $\mathbf{AscTxtBc}^a \subseteq \mathbf{InfTxtBc}^a$. We now prove the following Proposition which shows the distinction between the two.

8.32 Proposition $\mathbf{InfTxtEx} - \mathbf{AscTxtBc}^* \neq \emptyset$.

Proof: Let $\mathcal{L} = \{\,N\,\} \cup \{\,[0, n] \mid n \in N\,\}$. It is easy to see that $\mathcal{L} \in \mathbf{InfTxtEx}$, but not in $\mathbf{AscTxtBc}^*$. $\blacksquare$

§8.2.3 Recursive texts and nonrecursive texts

A text, T, is said to be recursive just in case there exists a recursive function f such that for all n, $f(n) = T(n)$.

If children's caretakers are machine simulable and are sheltered from random environmental influence, they might be limited to the production of recursive texts. Similarly, if natural phenomena are computable processes devoid of any random behavior, a scientist may be restricted to operating on recursive texts. Would such a limitation affect in principle the class of learnable languages? We first incorporate the notion of recursive texts into our learning paradigm.

8.33 Definition Let $a \in (N \cup \{*\})$.

(a) $\mathbf{M}$ $\mathbf{RecTxtEx}^a$-*identifies* L (written : $L \in \mathbf{RecTxtEx}^a(\mathbf{M})$) just in case for all recursive texts T for L, $\mathbf{M}(T)\!\downarrow$ and $W_{\mathbf{M}(T)} =^a L$.

(b) $\mathbf{RecTxtEx}^a = \{\, \mathcal{L} \mid \mathcal{L} \subseteq \mathbf{RecTxtEx}^a(\mathbf{M})$ for some $\mathbf{M}\,\}$.

The following proposition shows that identification from recursive texts fails to yield any advantage over identification from arbitrary texts.

8.34 Proposition *For all* $a \in (N \cup \{*\})$, $\mathbf{TxtEx}^a = \mathbf{RecTxtEx}^a$.

Proof: Follows from the stabilizing sequence construction given in Chapter 5.   ▌

However, the story is completely different if the scientists are not required to be computable. The following definition introduces the notion of identification from recursive texts by scientists that may not be computable. *Convention:* $\mathbf{F}$ in the following ranges over possibly noncomputable scientists.

8.35 Definition

(a) $\mathbf{F}$ $\mathbf{RecLang}$-*identifies* L (written : $L \in \mathbf{RecLang}(\mathbf{F})$) just in case for all recursive texts T for L, $\mathbf{F}(T){\downarrow}$ and $W_{\mathbf{F}(T)} = L$.

(b) $\mathbf{RecLang} = \{\, \mathcal{L} \mid \mathcal{L} \subseteq \mathbf{RecLang}(\mathbf{F})$ for some $\mathbf{F}\,\}$.

The next proposition says that there is a single noncomputable scientist that identifies each recursively enumerable language from recursive texts.

8.36 Proposition $\mathcal{E} \in \mathbf{RecLang}$.

Proof: Consider the following $\mathbf{F}$:

Begin *(* $\mathbf{F}$ *on* σ *)*
    Let i be the least number such that for all $n < |\sigma|$, $\varphi_i(n) = \sigma(n)$.
    Output the least grammar for $range(\varphi_i) - \{\,\#\,\}$.
End *(* $\mathbf{F}$ *on* σ *)*

It is easy to see that $\mathcal{E} \subseteq \mathbf{RecLang}(\mathbf{F})$.   ▌

It should be noted that if caretakers and natural phenomena are assumed to be computer simulable, then there is no reason to consider, as in the above case, noncomputable scientists and children. But, since the computable nature of children and their environments is only a hypothesis, it is worth considering identification on nonrecursive texts by both computable and noncomputable scientists. We have yet to isolate the nonrecursive texts for separate study. The following definition fills this gap.

8.37 Definition

(a) **F NonrecLang**-*identifies* L (written : $L \in$ **NonrecLang**(**F**)) just in case for any nonrecursive text T for L, $\mathbf{F}(T)\!\downarrow$ and $W_{\mathbf{F}(T)} = L$.

(b) **NonrecLang** $= \{\, \mathcal{L} \mid \mathcal{L} \subseteq$ **NonrecLang**(**F**) for some **F** $\}$.

8.38 Definition

(a) **M NonrecTxtEx**^{a}-*identifies* L (written : $L \in$ **NonrecTxtEx**^{a}(**M**)) just in case for any nonrecursive text T for L, $\mathbf{M}(T)\!\downarrow$ and $W_{\mathbf{M}(T)} =^a L$.

(b) **NonrecTxtEx**$^a = \{\, \mathcal{L} \mid \mathcal{L} \subseteq$ **NonrecTxtEx**^{a}(**M**) for some **M** $\}$.

It is natural to inquire whether the limitation to nonrecursive texts facilitates identification. The next proposition provides a negative answer to this question for both computable and noncomputable scientists. We omit the proof.

8.39 Proposition

(a) **NonrecLang** = **Lang**.

(b) (**Wiehagen [195]**) **NonrecTxtEx** = **TxtEx**.

§8.3 Multiple texts

The paradigms discussed so far assume that scientists receive data about a given reality from a single source. The source is represented by the single text delivered to a scientist in the course of a single "run." Provided all data are accurate, this model embraces multiple sources of data as well, since a scientist can easily construct a single accurate text by consulting her different sources in some cyclical order. Matters become more complicated if one or more sources are faulty. Consider, for example, a scientist receiving data from multiple sources, some of which produce 1-imperfect text. It is not obvious that she can convert such data into a single 1-imperfect text.

This kind of consideration is important to modeling both language acquisition and scientific practice. In the former case it is clear that children are confronted with several sources of linguistic data (in the form of different caretakers, older children, etc.), none of which is 100% grammatically reliable. Similarly, it is common for scientists to base their theories on data collected by different teams working at different places using different instruments, with each team subject to particular forms of error.

The present section begins to deal with these issues by extending our paradigms to model multiple sources of data, some of which are inaccurate. For this purpose scientists will be conceived as receiving a finite number of texts, announcing hypotheses after examining some initial segment of each of them. To keep the present discussion manageable, we confine ourselves to the identification of functions.

To begin, we need to enrich our definition of scientist.

8.40 Definition Let $k \in N^+$. A *scientist with k streams* is a computable mapping from SEGI^k into N.

8.41 Definition Let $k \in N^+$. Fix a k stream scientist $\mathbf{M}$, texts $G_1, G_2, \ldots, G_k$, and $i \in N$. We say $\mathbf{M}$ *converges* on $G_1, G_2, \ldots, G_k$ to i (written: $\mathbf{M}(G_1, G_2, \ldots, G_k)\!\downarrow = i$) just in case there exists an n such that $\mathbf{M}(G_1[n_1], G_2[n_2], \ldots, G_k[n_k]) = i$ whenever $n_1, \ldots, n_k > n$.

Next, we define the identification of functions from multiple texts, some of which could be inaccurate.

8.42 Definition Let $j, k \in N^+$ with $j \leq k$. Let $a, b \in N \cup \{*\}$.

(a) $\mathbf{M}$ $\mathbf{Mul}_k^j \mathbf{N}^a \mathbf{Ex}^b$-*identifies* f (written: $f \in \mathbf{Mul}_k^j \mathbf{N}^a \mathbf{Ex}^b(\mathbf{M})$) just in case for any collection of k texts, $G_1, G_2, \ldots, G_k$, at least j of which are a-noisy for f, $\mathbf{M}(G_1, G_2, \ldots, G_k)\!\downarrow$ and $\varphi_{\mathbf{M}(G_1, G_2, \ldots, G_k)} =^b f$.

(b) $\mathbf{Mul}_k^j \mathbf{N}^a \mathbf{Ex}^b = \{\mathcal{S} \mid \mathcal{S} \subseteq \mathbf{Mul}_k^j \mathbf{N}^a \mathbf{Ex}^b(\mathbf{M}) \text{ for some } \mathbf{M}\}$.

(c) $\mathbf{Mul}_k^j \mathbf{In}^a \mathbf{Ex}^b$ and $\mathbf{Mul}_k^j \mathbf{Im}^a \mathbf{Ex}^b$ are defined similarly to $\mathbf{Mul}_k^j \mathbf{N}^a \mathbf{Ex}^b$.

8.43 Definition When discussing identification criteria involving multiple data sources, those texts for which the number of inaccuracies is within the bound required by the criteria will be referred to as *good* texts.

The next three propositions describe situations in which learning from multiple inaccurate texts is no more difficult than learning from a single inaccurate text.

8.44 Proposition *Let j and $k \in N$ be such that $j > \lfloor \frac{k}{2} \rfloor$ and let $a \in (N \cup \{*\})$. Then:*

(a) $\mathbf{Mul}_k^j \mathbf{N}^* \mathbf{Ex}^a = \mathbf{N}^* \mathbf{Ex}^a$.

(b) $\mathbf{Mul}_k^j \mathbf{In}^* \mathbf{Ex}^a = \mathbf{In}^* \mathbf{Ex}^a$.

(c) $\mathbf{Mul}_k^j \mathbf{Im}^* \mathbf{Ex}^a = \mathbf{Im}^* \mathbf{Ex}^a$.

(d) $\mathbf{Mul}_k^j \mathbf{N}^0 \mathbf{Ex}^a = \mathbf{Mul}_k^j \mathbf{In}^0 \mathbf{Ex}^a = \mathbf{Mul}_k^j \mathbf{Im}^0 \mathbf{Ex}^a = \mathbf{Ex}^a$.

Proof: Given k texts $G_1, G_2, \ldots, G_k$, form a text G such that $(x, y) \in content(G) \Longleftrightarrow card(\{\, i \mid (x, y) \in content(G_i)\,\}) \geq \lfloor \frac{k}{2} \rfloor + 1$. It is easy to see that, if at least $\lfloor \frac{k}{2} \rfloor + 1$ of the k texts are $*$-noisy ($*$-incomplete, $*$-imperfect, accurate) for f, then so is G. The proposition follows. ∎

8.45 Proposition *Let j and $k \in N$ be such that $j > \lfloor \frac{k}{2} \rfloor$ and let $a \in (N \cup \{*\})$. Then:*

(a) $\mathbf{Mul}_k^j \mathbf{N}^a \mathbf{Ex} = \mathbf{N}^a \mathbf{Ex}$.

(b) $\mathbf{Mul}_k^j \mathbf{In}^a \mathbf{Ex} = \mathbf{In}^a \mathbf{Ex}$.

(c) $\mathbf{Mul}_k^j \mathbf{Im}^a \mathbf{Ex} = \mathbf{Im}^a \mathbf{Ex}$.

Proof: We first introduce a technical notion. Let P be a finite set of programs. Define program $Unify(P)$ as follows.

Begin ($\varphi_{Unify(P)}$)
  On input x:
    Search for an $i \in P$ such that $\varphi_i(x)\downarrow$.
    If and when such an i is found, output $\varphi_i(x)$ for the first such i found.
End ($\varphi_{Unify(P)}$)

Proof of Part (a). Let $\mathbf{M}$ $\mathbf{N}^a \mathbf{Ex}$-identify $\mathcal{C}$. We show how to $\mathbf{Ex}$-identify $f \in \mathcal{C}$ from k texts, $G_1, G_2, \ldots, G_k$, at least j of which are a-noisy for f.

So suppose $f \in \mathcal{C}$, and $G_1, G_2, \ldots, G_k$ are k texts such that at least j of them are a-noisy for f.

First we claim that there are distinct $i_1, i_2, \ldots, i_j$ such that,
  (A) for $1 \leq l \leq j$, $\mathbf{M}(G_{i_l})\downarrow$ and
  (B) for each $l, m \in \{1, \ldots, j\}$, there is no x such that $\varphi_{\mathbf{M}(G_{i_l})}(x)\downarrow \neq \varphi_{\mathbf{M}(G_{i_m})}(x)\downarrow$.
This is so, since if we choose $i_1, i_2, \ldots, i_j$ to be such that $G_{i_1}, \ldots, G_{i_j}$ are good, then (A) and (B) above are satisfied.

Note that, given texts $G_1, G_2, \ldots, G_k$, one can find, in the limit, distinct $i_1, i_2, \ldots, i_j$ satisfying (A) and (B) above. So let $\mathbf{M}'$ be a scientist that, in the limit, finds such $i_1, i_2, \ldots, i_j$ and outputs $Unify(P)$, where $P = \{\,\mathbf{M}(G_{i_1}), \ldots, \mathbf{M}(G_{i_j})\,\}$.

Since $j > \lfloor \frac{k}{2} \rfloor$ and $f \in \mathbf{N}^a \mathbf{Ex}(\mathbf{M})$, there is a $p \in P$ such that $\varphi_p = f$. This, along with (B) above, implies that $Unify(P)$ is a program for f; hence part (a) follows.

Parts (b) and (c) can be proved similarly. ∎

By Exercise 8-25 we also have:

8.46 Proposition *Let j and $k \in N$ be such that $\lfloor \frac{k}{2} \rfloor < j \leq k$ and let $a \in (N \cup \{*\})$. Then:*

(a) $\mathbf{Mul}_k^j \mathbf{N}^a \mathbf{Ex}^* = \mathbf{N}^a \mathbf{Ex}^*$.

(b) $\mathbf{Mul}_k^j \mathbf{In}^a \mathbf{Ex}^* = \mathbf{In}^a \mathbf{Ex}^*$.

(c) $\mathbf{Mul}_k^j \mathbf{Im}^a \mathbf{Ex}^* = \mathbf{Im}^a \mathbf{Ex}^*$.

The last three results inform us that if the number of inaccuracies is finite without any preassigned bound, or if the final program witnessing the identification is required to be either accurate or make a finite number of mistakes without any preassigned bound, then learning from multiple texts does no harm so long as a majority of the input texts are good.

The next two propositions follow from Propositions 8.45, 8.44, 8.13, and 8.10.

8.47 Proposition *Let $b, j, k \in N$, $j > \lfloor \frac{k}{2} \rfloor$. Then:*

(a) $\mathbf{Mul}_k^j \mathbf{Im}^* \mathbf{Ex}^{b+1} - \mathbf{Ex}^b \neq \emptyset$.

(b) $\mathbf{Mul}_k^j \mathbf{Im}^* \mathbf{Ex}^* - \bigcup_{b \in N} \mathbf{Ex}^b \neq \emptyset$.

8.48 Proposition *Let $b, j, k \in N$ be such that $j > \lfloor \frac{k}{2} \rfloor$. Then,*
$\mathbf{Mul}_k^j \mathbf{Im}^b \mathbf{Ex} - (\mathbf{N}^{b+1} \mathbf{Ex}^* \cup \mathbf{In}^{b+1} \mathbf{Ex}^*) \neq \emptyset$.

Proposition 8.47(a), for example, says that there are collections of functions for which a program that makes up to $(b+1)$ errors can be identified from multiple texts, a majority of which are *-imperfect, but for which a program that makes only up to b errors *cannot* be identified from a single accurate text. Propositions 8.47 and 8.48 yield a number of hierarchies. We note one of them in the next corollary, which implies that strictly larger classes of functions can be identified from multiple inaccurate texts, a majority of which are *-imperfect, by allowing extra anomalies in the final program.

8.49 Corollary *Let $j, k \in N$ be such that $j > \lfloor \frac{k}{2} \rfloor$. Then,*
$\mathbf{Mul}_k^j \mathbf{Im}^* \mathbf{Ex}^0 \subset \mathbf{Mul}_k^j \mathbf{Im}^* \mathbf{Ex}^1 \subset \cdots \subset \mathbf{Mul}_k^j \mathbf{Im}^* \mathbf{Ex}^*$.

We now consider situations in which a scientist pays a price for learning from multiple inaccurate texts instead of learning from a single inaccurate text. We restrict ourselves to the case of noisy data delivered on three inaccurate texts, at least two of which are good. The reader is directed to the exercises and Baliga, Jain, and Sharma [12] for more results.

The following lemma gives information about the parameters a, b, c, and d, for which $\mathbf{N}^a\mathbf{Ex}^b - \mathbf{Mul}_3^2\mathbf{N}^c\mathbf{Ex}^d \neq \emptyset$.

8.50 Lemma *Let $a, b, c, d \in N$ be given. Suppose $r, \alpha \in N$ are such that the following hold: (i) $r - b \leq \alpha \leq min(\{\, b, r\,\})$, (ii) $a/2 < r \leq c$, and (iii) $d < max(\{\, b + \alpha - \frac{r}{2}, b + \frac{\alpha}{3}\,\})$. Then, $\mathbf{N}^a\mathbf{Ex}^b - \mathbf{Mul}_3^2\mathbf{N}^c\mathbf{Ex}^d \neq \emptyset$.*

Proof: Let $A = \{\langle 0, x \rangle \mid 0 \leq x < r\}$. Let $\mathcal{C}$ be the collection of functions $f \in \mathcal{R}$ that satisfy the following three conditions.

1. $f(A) = \{\, f(\langle 0, 0 \rangle)\,\} \subset \{\, 1, 2, 3\,\}$.
2. For each $i \in (\{\, 1, 2, 3\,\} - \{\, f(\langle 0, 0 \rangle)\,\})$, the set $\{\, f(\langle i, \langle x, 0 \rangle \rangle) \mid x \in N\,\}$ is finite and $\varphi_{max(\{\, f(\langle i, \langle x, 0 \rangle \rangle) \mid x \in N\,\})} =^b f$.
3. For each $i \in \{\, 1, 2, 3\,\}$ and $x, y, z \in N$, $f(\langle i, \langle x, y \rangle \rangle) = f(\langle i, \langle x, z \rangle \rangle)$.

For any a-noisy text G for $f \in \mathcal{C}$, since $2r > a$, there exist an $x < r$ and an $i \in \{\, 1, 2, 3\,\}$ such that $(\langle 0, x \rangle, i) \notin content(G)$. Thus, using clauses 2 and 3 in the definition of $\mathcal{C}$, it is easy to see that $\mathcal{C} \in \mathbf{N}^a\mathbf{Ex}^b$. The proof of $\mathcal{C} \notin \mathbf{Mul}_3^2\mathbf{N}^c\mathbf{Ex}^d$ is fairly complex and we direct the reader to Baliga, Jain, and Sharma [12] for the proof. ∎

Among other corollaries to this lemma we have the following.

8.51 Corollary *Let $a, b, c \in N$ be such that $c \leq a \leq 2c - 1$ and $\frac{c}{2} \leq b \leq \frac{3}{4}\lceil\frac{a+1}{2}\rceil$. Then, $\mathbf{N}^a\mathbf{Ex}^b - \mathbf{Mul}_3^2\mathbf{N}^c\mathbf{Ex}^{\lceil\frac{4b}{3}\rceil - 1} \neq \emptyset$.*

Proof: Take $r = c$ and $\alpha = b$ in the above lemma. ∎

8.52 Corollary *Let $a, b, c \in N$ be such that $c \leq a \leq 2c - 1$ and $c \leq b$. Then, $\mathbf{N}^a\mathbf{Ex}^b - \mathbf{Mul}_3^2\mathbf{N}^c\mathbf{Ex}^{b + \lceil\frac{c}{2}\rceil - 1} \neq \emptyset$.*

Proof: Take $r = \alpha = c$ in the above lemma. ∎

8.53 Corollary *Let $a, b, c \in N$ be such that $c \leq a \leq 2c - 1$ and $\frac{a}{2} < b \leq c$. Then, $\mathbf{N}^a\mathbf{Ex}^b - \mathbf{Mul}_3^2\mathbf{N}^c\mathbf{Ex}^{\lceil\frac{3b}{2}\rceil - 1} \neq \emptyset$.*

Proof: Take $r = \alpha = b$ in the above lemma. ∎

8.54 Corollary *Let $a, b, c \in N$ be such that $c \leq a \leq 2c-1$ and $max(\frac{c}{2}, \frac{3}{4}\lceil\frac{a+1}{2}\rceil) \leq b \leq \frac{a}{2}$. Then, $\mathbf{N}^a\mathbf{Ex}^b - \mathbf{Mul}_3^2\mathbf{N}^c\mathbf{Ex}^{\lceil 2b - \frac{a+2}{4}\rceil - 1} \neq \emptyset$.*

Proof: Take $r = \lceil\frac{a+1}{2}\rceil$, $\alpha = b$ in the above lemma. ∎

The above results show that there are collections of functions for which a program that makes up to d errors can be identified from a single c-noisy text, but for which a program with up to d errors *cannot* be identified from three texts, at least two of which are c-noisy. Clearly, a price is being paid for distinguishing good texts from "bad" ones. An obvious question is whether this decrease in competence due to learning from multiple texts can be overcome by either decreasing the noise in good texts or by allowing the final inferred program to make extra errors. Some of these questions are treated in the exercises.

§8.4 Bibliographic notes

The first study of inaccuracies is due to Schäfer-Richter [167]. This subject was also treated by Osherson, Stob, and Weinstein [140], Fulk and Jain [74], and Fulk, Jain, and Osherson [75]. The subject of infinite inaccuracies is treated by Jain [83]. An interesting approach to modeling noise in data is due to Stephan [186]. The study of learning from multiple sources of inaccuracies is due to Baliga, Jain, and Sharma [12].

The study of informants was first considered by Gold [80]. The subject of recursive and nonrecursive texts has been investigated by Wiehagen [195] and Freivalds [64].

§8.5 Exercises

8-1 For each $f \in \mathcal{R}$, let f' be such that $(\forall i, x)[f'(\langle i, x\rangle) = f(x)]$. Suppose $\mathcal{C} \subseteq \mathcal{R}$ is given. Show that $\{ f' \mid f \in \mathcal{C} \} \in \mathbf{Im}^*\mathbf{Ex} \Leftrightarrow \mathcal{C} \in \mathbf{Ex}$.

8-2 Prove the following. Recall that $A \otimes B = \{ \langle a, b\rangle \mid a \in A \text{ and } b \in B \}$.

(a) Let $L \in \mathcal{E}$ be recursive. Then, $\{ (L \cup \{ x \}) \otimes N \mid x \notin L \} \in \mathbf{N}^*\mathbf{TxtEx}$.

(b) $\{ (N - \{ x \}) \otimes N \mid x \in N \} \in \mathbf{N}^*\mathbf{TxtEx}$.

8-3 Consider the notion of identification from ∗-noisy texts by scientists that need not be computable. Recall that $\mathbf{F}$ ranges over any kind of scientists, possibly noncomputable.

F is said to **N*Lang**-identify $L \in \mathcal{E}$ (written: $L \in \mathbf{N^*Lang(F)}$) just in case given any *-noisy text for L, **F** converges to an index for L. The class **N*Lang** is $\{\, \mathcal{L} \subseteq \mathcal{E} \mid (\exists \mathbf{F})[\mathcal{L} \subseteq \mathbf{N^*Lang}]\,\}$. Prove the following generalization of Theorem 3.22 from Chapter 3.

(a) Let **F N*Lang**-identify $L \in \mathcal{E}$. Then, for every finite $D \subset N$, there is $\sigma \in \mathrm{SEQ}$ such that $content(\sigma) \subseteq L \cup D$, $W_{\mathbf{F}(\sigma)} = L$, and for all $\tau \in \mathrm{SEQ}$, if $content(\tau) \subseteq L \cup D$, then $\mathbf{F}(\sigma \diamond \tau) = \mathbf{F}(\sigma)$.

(b) Let **F N*Lang**-identify $L \in \mathcal{E}$. Show that for every $\sigma \in \mathrm{SEQ}$ there is some $\tau \in \mathrm{SEQ}$ such that $content(\tau) \subseteq L$, $W_{\mathbf{F}(\sigma \diamond \tau)} = L$ and for every $\sigma' \in \mathrm{SEQ}$, if $content(\sigma') \subseteq L$, then $\mathbf{F}(\sigma \diamond \tau \diamond \sigma') = \mathbf{F}(\sigma \diamond \tau)$.

8-4   Let $L \in (\mathcal{E} - \{\, N \,\})$. Show that $\{\, (L \cup D) \otimes N \mid D$ is finite $\} \notin \mathbf{N^*Lang}$.

8-5   Prove the following.

(a) Let $L, L' \in \mathcal{E}$ be such that $L \neq L'$ and $\{\, L, L' \,\} \in \mathbf{N^*Lang}$. Then, both $L - L'$ and $L' - L$ are infinite.

(b) Let $\mathcal{L} \subseteq \mathcal{E}$ be such that whenever $L, L' \in \mathcal{L}$ and $L \neq L'$, then both $L - L'$ and $L' - L$ are infinite. Then, $\mathcal{L} \in \mathbf{N^*Lang}$.

8-6   Define **In*Lang** and **Im*Lang** analogously to the definition of **N*Lang** in Exercise 8-3. Prove the following generalizations of Theorem 3.22 from Chapter 3.

(a) Let **F In*Lang**-identify $L \in \mathcal{E}$. Then, for every finite $D \subset N$ there is $\sigma \in \mathrm{SEQ}$ such that $content(\sigma) \subseteq L - D$, $W_{\mathbf{F}(\sigma)} = L$, and for all $\tau \in \mathrm{SEQ}$, if $content(\sigma) \subseteq L - D$, then $\mathbf{F}(\sigma \diamond \tau) = \mathbf{F}(\sigma)$.

(b) Let **F Im*Lang**-identify $L \in \mathcal{E}$. Then, for every finite variant L' of L there is $\sigma \in \mathrm{SEQ}$ such that $content(\sigma) \subseteq L'$, $W_{\mathbf{F}(\sigma)} = L$, and for all $\tau \in \mathrm{SEQ}$, if $content(\tau) \subseteq L'$, then $\mathbf{F}(\sigma \diamond \tau) = \mathbf{F}(\sigma)$.

8-7   Prove **N*Lang** $\subset$ **In*Lang**.

8-8   Define **N*Func** and **In*Func** analogously to **N*Lang** and **In*Lang**. Prove **N*Func** = **In*Func**.

8-9   Prove the following.

(a) $\{\,(N - \{\,x\,\}) \otimes N \mid x \in N\,\} \in \mathbf{In^*Lang}$.

(b) Let L be recursive. Then, $\{\,(L \cup D) \otimes N \mid D$ is finite $\} \in \mathbf{In^*TxtEx}$. Compare this result to Exercise 8-4.

8-10 Prove: $\mathbf{N^*Lang} = \mathbf{Im^*Lang}$.

8-11 Prove: $\mathcal{R} \in \mathbf{Im^*Bc^*}$.

8-12 Prove: $\mathbf{Ex} - [\bigcup_i \mathbf{In^1Bc}^i \cup \bigcup_i \mathbf{N^1Bc}^i] \neq \emptyset$.

Hint: Note that $\mathcal{C}'$ from the proof of Proposition 8.12 can be used to show that $\mathcal{C}' \notin \mathbf{In^1Ex^*}$. A similar argument works here.

8-13 Prove, for all $j \in N$, that $\mathbf{Im^jEx} - [\mathbf{N^{j+1}Ex^*} \cup \mathbf{In^{j+1}Ex^*} \cup (\bigcup_i \mathbf{In^{j+1}Bc}^i) \cup (\bigcup_i \mathbf{N^{j+1}Bc}^i)] \neq \emptyset$. This is an extension of Proposition 8.13.

8-14 In the context of identification from inaccurate texts with a finite number of inaccuracies, this exercise compares situations in which a bound on the number of inaccuracies is available to situations in which there is no such bound. Show that $(\bigcup_{i \in N} \mathbf{N^iEx}) - \mathbf{N^*Ex^*}$ is nonempty. *Hint:* The positive part of this has to be non-constructive in i.

8-15 Prove Proposition 8.15.

8-16 Obtain the following hierarchies as corollaries to Proposition 8.15.

(a) $(\forall a, b)[\mathbf{N^aTxtFex}_b^0 \subset \mathbf{N^aTxtFex}_b^1 \subset \cdots \subset \mathbf{N^aTxtFex}_b^*]$.

(b) $(\forall a, b)[\mathbf{N^aTxtFex}_1^b \subset \mathbf{N^aTxtFex}_2^b \subset \cdots \subset \mathbf{N^aTxtFex}_*^b]$.

(c) $(\forall a)[\mathbf{N^aTxtBc}^0 \subset \mathbf{N^aTxtBc}^1 \subset \cdots \subset \mathbf{N^aTxtBc}^*]$.

8-17 Prove Proposition 8.19.

8-18 Since $\mathcal{E} \notin \mathbf{TxtBc^*}$, there is scope for further fine-tuning of Corollary 8.20. As an example of such a refinement, show that for each $j \in N$, $\mathbf{N^jTxtEx} - \mathbf{In^1TxtBc^*} \neq \emptyset$.

Open Question: $\mathbf{N^*TxtEx} - \mathbf{In^1TxtBc^*} \neq \emptyset$?

8-19 Prove: $\mathbf{In^*TxtEx} - \mathbf{N^*TxtBc^*} \neq \emptyset$.

8-20   Prove Proposition 8.24

Hint: First consider the case $i = 1$. For a function f, define $S_f = \{ f(x) \mid card(\{ y \mid f(y) \geq f(x) \}) \leq 3 \}$. Let

$$\mathcal{C} = \{ f \mid (\forall j \in S_f)[W_j \text{ is finite and } \varphi_{max(W_j)} = f] \}.$$

Show that $\mathcal{C} \in \mathbf{In^2 Ex} - \mathbf{Im^2 Ex}$. For $i > 1$, modify the definition of S_f appropriately.

8-21   Prove Proposition 8.25

8-22   Prove Proposition 8.26

Hint: First consider the case $j = 0$. Suppose a rearrangement-independent scientist $\mathbf{M}$ is given. For $f \in \mathbf{In^{4i} Ex(M)}$, consider any text G that is $2i$ imperfect for f. For each x, y, z such that $y \neq z$, assume without loss of generality that $\{ (x, y), (x, z) \} \not\subseteq content(G)$. Note that this implies there are at most i noisy elements in G. First show that if for some D of cardinality i and for some n_1 and n_2 with $n_1 < n_2$ we have

> for each $D' \subseteq content(G[n_1])$ with cardinality i, there is a $\tau_{D'}$ with $content(\tau_{D'}) = content(G[n_2]) - D - D'$ such that $\tau_{D'}$ is a locking sequence for $\mathbf{M}$ on $content(G) - D - D'$;

then, either

(i)   there exists a noisy element in $content(G[n_2]) - content(G[n_1])$, or

(ii)   for some $D' \subseteq content(T_{n_1})$ with cardinality i, $\mathbf{M}(\tau_{D'})$, where $\tau_{D'}$ is as above, is a program for f.

Next, use the above facts to obtain, in the limit, a finite set of programs, one of which is a program for f.

8-23   Prove: $\mathbf{In^* Ex} - \mathbf{Im^* Ex^*} \neq \emptyset$.

8-24   Prove: $(\forall j \in N) [\mathbf{In^* Ex} - \mathbf{Im^* Bc^j} \neq \emptyset]$.

8-25   Prove Proposition 8.46.

8-26 Prove: $(\forall b, c \in N)[\mathbf{N}^{2c}\mathbf{Ex}^b \subseteq \mathbf{Mul}_3^2\mathbf{N}^c\mathbf{Ex}^b]$.

Hint: First show how to obtain a 2c-noisy text from 3 texts, at least 2 of which are c-noisy.

8-27 Prove: $(\forall b, c \in N)[\mathbf{In}^{c+\lfloor \frac{c}{2} \rfloor}\mathbf{Ex}^b \subseteq \mathbf{Mul}_3^2\mathbf{In}^c\mathbf{Ex}^b]$.

8-28 Prove: $(\forall b, c \in N \mid b < \lceil \frac{c}{2} \rceil)[\mathbf{N}^{2c-1}\mathbf{Ex}^b \subseteq \mathbf{Mul}_3^2\mathbf{N}^c\mathbf{Ex}^b]$.

Hint: Consider the case in which 3 texts, at least 2 of which are c-noisy, do not suffice to give a $2c - 1$ noisy text for f. Then use the fact that $b < \lceil \frac{c}{2} \rceil$.

8-29 Prove: $(\forall b, c \in N)[\mathbf{N}^{\frac{3c+2b}{2}}\mathbf{Ex}^b \subseteq \mathbf{Mul}_3^2\mathbf{N}^c\mathbf{Ex}^b]$.

8-30 Prove: $(\forall b, c \in N \mid b \geq c)[\mathbf{In}^c\mathbf{Ex}^b \subseteq \mathbf{Mul}_3^2\mathbf{In}^c\mathbf{Ex}^{b+\lceil \frac{c}{2} \rceil}]$.

8-31 Let $b, c \in N$. Prove the following:

(a) $\mathbf{N}^c\mathbf{Ex}^b \subseteq \mathbf{Mul}_3^2\mathbf{N}^c\mathbf{Ex}^{2b}$,

(b) $\mathbf{In}^c\mathbf{Ex}^b \subseteq \mathbf{Mul}_3^2\mathbf{In}^c\mathbf{Ex}^{2b}$,

(c) $\mathbf{Im}^c\mathbf{Ex}^b \subseteq \mathbf{Mul}_3^2\mathbf{Im}^c\mathbf{Ex}^{2b}$.

8-32 Prove the following, which is an analog of Lemma 8.50 for incomplete texts.
$(\forall b, c \in N \mid b \geq c > 1)[\mathbf{In}^{\lfloor \frac{3c}{2} \rfloor - 1}\mathbf{Ex}^b - \mathbf{Mul}_3^2\mathbf{In}^c\mathbf{Ex}^{b+\lceil \frac{c}{2} \rceil - 1} \neq \emptyset]$.

8-33 Prove: $(\forall a \in N)[\mathbf{In}^a\mathbf{Ex}^1 = \mathbf{Mul}_3^2\mathbf{In}^a\mathbf{Ex}^1]$.

8-34 Let $i \in N$. Prove the following:

(a) $\mathbf{TxtEx}^{i+1} - \mathbf{AscTxtEx}^i \neq \emptyset$,

(b) $\mathbf{TxtBc}^{i+1} - \mathbf{AscTxtBc}^i \neq \emptyset$,

(c) $\mathbf{TxtBc} - \mathbf{AscTxtEx}^* \neq \emptyset$,

(d) $\mathbf{AscTxtEx}^* \subseteq \mathbf{AscTxtBc}$,

(e) $\mathcal{E} \notin \mathbf{AscTxtBc}^*$.

8-35 Let $i \in N$. Prove the following:

(a) $\mathbf{TxtEx}^{i+1} - \mathbf{InfTxtEx}^i \neq \emptyset$,

(b) $\mathbf{TxtBc}^{i+1} - \mathbf{InfTxtBc}^i \neq \emptyset$,

(c) $\mathbf{TxtBc} - \mathbf{InfTxtEx}^* \neq \emptyset$,

(d) $\mathbf{InfTxtEx}^* \subseteq \mathbf{InfTxtBc}$,

(e) $\mathcal{E} \in \mathbf{InfTxtBc}^*$.

8-36   Using the definition of **AscTxtEx** as a model, define **AscEx**. Show that **Ex** = **AscEx**. Thus, in the context of function learning, requiring data to be presented in ascending order does not yield any extra learning power.

Part III

Part III: Additional Topics

9   Team and Probabilistic Learning

§9.1 Introduction

The paradigms presented so far have modeled empirical inquiry by a single, deterministic, computable scientist. In the present chapter, we consider paradigms that permit more liberal conceptions.

Empirical inquiry in the scientific domain is seldom an individual enterprise. Many scientific breakthroughs result from the efforts of several scientists investigating a problem; scientific success is achieved if one or more of the scientists are successful. This observation about the practice of science can be partially incorporated into our model of empirical inquiry by a "team" of computable scientists. The team is said to be successful just in case one or more members in the team are successful.

Another variation on the notion of "scientist" is obtained by considering those machines which, in addition to their algorithmic nature, have the added ability to base their actions on the outcomes of random events. Such scientists can be modeled using probabilistic Turing machines (in the sense of Gill [78]).

The present chapter considers identification of functions and languages by teams of computable scientists and by probabilistic scientists.

§9.2 Motivation for identification by teams

The next two propositions are commonly referred to as "nonunion theorems." They respectively establish that the classes **Ex** and **TxtEx** are not closed under union. That is, the union of two identifiable collections of functions (respectively, languages) is not necessarily identifiable. (Proposition 9.1 is a restatement of Theorem 4.25 due to L. Blum and M. Blum, and Proposition 9.2 restates a fact established in Chapter 4.)

9.1 Proposition Let $\mathcal{S}_1 = \{\, f \in \mathcal{R} \mid \varphi_{f(0)} = f \,\}$ and $\mathcal{S}_2 = \{\, f \in \mathcal{R} \mid (\overset{\infty}{\forall} n)[f(n) = 0] \,\}$. Then, both $\mathcal{S}_1$ and $\mathcal{S}_2$ are in **Ex**, but $\mathcal{S}_1 \cup \mathcal{S}_2 \notin$ **Ex**.

9.2 Proposition Let $\mathcal{L}_1 = \{\, L \in \mathcal{E} \mid L$ is finite $\}$ and $\mathcal{L}_2 = \{\, N \,\}$. Then, both $\mathcal{L}_1$ and $\mathcal{L}_2$ are in **TxtEx**, but $\mathcal{L}_1 \cup \mathcal{L}_2 \notin$ **TxtEx**.

These results may be viewed as a fundamental limitation on our ability to build general purpose devices for empirical inquiry and motivate the use of heuristic methods in Artificial Intelligence. However, they also suggest a weaker criterion of identification in which a team of scientists is employed and success of the team is equated with the success of any member in the team. Let us illustrate this idea in the context of functions.

Consider the collections of functions $\mathcal{S}_1$ and $\mathcal{S}_2$ in Proposition 9.1. Let $\mathbf{M}_1$ Ex-identify $\mathcal{S}_1$ and $\mathbf{M}_2$ Ex-identify $\mathcal{S}_2$. Now, if we employed the team of $\mathbf{M}_1$ and $\mathbf{M}_2$ to identify $\mathcal{S}_1 \cup \mathcal{S}_2$ and weakened the criterion of success to the requirement that success is achieved just in case at least one member in the team is successful, then under this changed criterion, the collection $\mathcal{S}_1 \cup \mathcal{S}_2$ is identifiable by the team of $\mathbf{M}_1$ and $\mathbf{M}_2$. This idea can be extended to teams of n scientists, at least m of which are required to be successful.

We now formalize function and language identification by teams. Anomalies in the hypothesized programs are also incorporated in the definitions.

9.3 Definition (Smith [178]) Let m, $n \in N^+$ and $a \in (N \cup \{*\})$.

(a) A team of n scientists $\mathbf{M}_1, \mathbf{M}_2, \ldots, \mathbf{M}_n$ is said to $\mathbf{Team}_n^m \mathbf{Ex}^a$-*identify* $f \in \mathcal{R}$ (written: $f \in \mathbf{Team}_n^m \mathbf{Ex}^a(\mathbf{M}_1, \mathbf{M}_2, \ldots, \mathbf{M}_n)$) just in case f is $\mathbf{Ex}^a$-identified by at least m of the $\mathbf{M}_i$'s.

(b) $\mathbf{Team}_n^m \mathbf{Ex}^a$ is the collection of $\mathcal{S} \subseteq \mathcal{R}$ such that some team of n scientists $\mathbf{Team}_n^m \mathbf{Ex}^a$-identifies each function in $\mathcal{S}$.

9.4 Definition (Osherson, Stob, and Weinstein [140]) Let m, $n \in N^+$ and $a \in (N \cup \{*\})$.

(a) A team of n scientists $\mathbf{M}_1, \mathbf{M}_2, \ldots, \mathbf{M}_n$ is said to $\mathbf{Team}_n^m \mathbf{TxtEx}^a$-*identify* $L \in \mathcal{E}$ (written: $L \in \mathbf{Team}_n^m \mathbf{TxtEx}^a(\mathbf{M}_1, \mathbf{M}_2, \ldots, \mathbf{M}_n)$) just in case L is $\mathbf{TxtEx}^a$-identified by at least m of the $\mathbf{M}_i$'s.

(b) $\mathbf{Team}_n^m \mathbf{TxtEx}^a$ is the collection of $\mathcal{L} \subseteq \mathcal{E}$ such that some team of n scientists $\mathbf{Team}_n^m \mathbf{TxtEx}^a$-identifies each language in $\mathcal{L}$.

For both $\mathbf{Team}_n^m \mathbf{Ex}^a$ and $\mathbf{Team}_n^m \mathbf{TxtEx}^a$, the fraction $\frac{m}{n}$ is referred to as the *success ratio* of the paradigm. As has been the practice, the cases $a = 0$ are simply referred to as $\mathbf{Team}_n^m \mathbf{Ex}$ and $\mathbf{Team}_n^m \mathbf{TxtEx}$. Most of the results presented in the present chapter are for the case $a = 0$; other cases are considered in the exercises. Let us note that Definitions 9.3 and 9.4 fail to formalize one aspect of scientific practice that is central to the informal idea of teamwork. When different scientists work separately on the same problem it is often the case that individual progress is recognizable by all concerned. The hypotheses of the individual scientists thus influence each other in a way that is not captured by the paradigms discussed in the present chapter.

§9.3 Team identification of functions

We first consider team identification of functions when the success of the team requires any one member in the team to be successful.

The following result says that there are collections of functions for which a correct program can be synthesized by a team of $(n+1)$ scientists, at least one of which is successful, but for which even a finite variant program cannot be synthesized by a team of n scientists with the requirement that at least one of them be successful.

9.5 Proposition (Smith [178]) *For each $n \geq 1$, $\mathbf{Team}^1_{n+1}\mathbf{Ex} - \mathbf{Team}^1_n\mathbf{Ex}^* \neq \emptyset$.*

Proof: For each $n \in N^+$, let

$$\mathcal{C}_n = \{ f \in \mathcal{R} \mid (\exists x \leq n)[W_{f(x)} \text{ is finite, nonempty, and } \varphi_{max(W_{f(x)})} = f]\}.$$

It is easy to verify that $\mathcal{C}_n \in \mathbf{Team}^1_{n+1}\mathbf{Ex}$. We argue, using a diagonalization argument, that $\mathcal{C}_2 \notin \mathbf{Team}^1_2\mathbf{Ex}^*$. This argument can easily be generalized to show that $\mathcal{C}_n \notin \mathbf{Team}^1_n\mathbf{Ex}^*$.

Suppose, by way of contradiction, there exists a team of two scientists, $\mathbf{M}_0$ and $\mathbf{M}_1$, that witnesses $\mathcal{C}_2 \in \mathbf{Team}^1_2\mathbf{Ex}^*$. Then, by the implicit use of the operator recursion theorem, there exists a 1-1, monotonically increasing, recursive function p such that $\varphi_{p(\cdot)}$ (and, hence, $W_{p(\cdot)}$) is as described in stages below.

We initialize $\varphi_{p(3)}(0) = p(0)$, $\varphi_{p(3)}(1) = p(1)$, and $\varphi_{p(3)}(2) = p(2)$. Enumerate $p(3)$ into $W_{p(0)}$. Set avail = 3. Intuitively, avail denotes the least number such that, for all $i > $ avail, $p(i)$ has not yet been used in the diagonalization. Let x_s denote the least x such that $\varphi_{p(3)}(x)$ has not been defined before stage s. Go to stage 0.

Begin *(Stage s)*
1. Set avail = avail + 1.

    Set cur = avail.

    Enumerate $p(\text{cur})$ into $W_{p(1)}$.

    For each $x < x_s$, set $\varphi_{p(\text{cur})}(x) = \varphi_{p(3)}(x)$.

Set $r = s \bmod 2$.

2. Dovetail steps 3 and 4 until, if ever, step 3 succeeds. If and when step 3 succeeds go to step 5.

    (*Intuitively, if step 3 succeeds in each stage, then $\varphi_{p(3)} \in \mathcal{C}_2$ and neither $\mathbf{M}_0$ nor $\mathbf{M}_1$ $\mathbf{Ex}^*$-identifies $\varphi_{p(3)}$.*)

3. Search for an extension $\sigma \in \text{INIT}$ of $\varphi_{p(3)}[x_s]$ such that $\varphi_{\mathbf{M}_r(\sigma)}(|\sigma|)\downarrow$.

4. Let $x_{s,s'}$ denote the least x such that $\varphi_{p(\text{cur})}(x)$ has not been defined before sub-stage s' of stage s.

    Go to substage 0.

    Begin (*Substage s'*)

    4.1. Set avail = avail + 1.

    Enumerate $p(\text{avail})$ into $W_{p(2)}$.

    For each $x < x_{s,s'}$, set $\varphi_{p(\text{avail})}(x) = \varphi_{p(\text{cur})}(x)$.

    4.2. Dovetail steps 4.3 and 4.4 until, if ever, step 4.3 succeeds. If and when step 4.3 succeeds, go to step 4.5.

    4.3. Search for an extension $\tau \in \text{INIT}$ of $\varphi_{p(\text{cur})}[x_{s,s'}]$ such that $\varphi_{\mathbf{M}_{1-r}(\tau)}(|\tau|)\downarrow$.

    4.4. **For** $x = x_{s,s'}$ **to** ∞ **do** set $\varphi_{p(\text{avail})}(x) = 0$.

    4.5   Let τ be as found in step 4.3.

    For each $(x, y) \in content(\tau)$, set $\varphi_{p(\text{cur})}(x) = y$ if $\varphi_{p(\text{cur})}(x)$ is not already defined.

    Set $\varphi_{p(\text{cur})}(|\tau|) = \varphi_{\mathbf{M}_{1-r}(\tau)}(|\tau|) + 1$. *(Note the diagonalization.)*

    Go to substage $s' + 1$.

    End (*Substage s'*)

5. Let σ be as found in step 3.

    For each $(x, y) \in content(\sigma)$, set $\varphi_{p(3)}(x) = y$ if $\varphi_{p(3)}(x)$ is not already defined.

    Set $\varphi_{p(3)}(|\sigma|) = \varphi_{\mathbf{M}_r(\sigma)}(|\sigma| + 1)$. *(Note the diagonalization.)*

    Go to stage $s + 1$.

End (*Stage s*)

Now, consider the following cases.

Case 1: Each stage terminates. Let $f = \varphi_{p(3)}$. Clearly, f is computable and a member of $\mathcal{C}_2$ (since $f(0) = p(0)$ and $W_{p(0)} = \{ p(3) \}$). Also, because of the success of step 3 and the diagonalization at step 5 in each even (respectively, odd) stage, we have that either $\mathbf{M}_0$ (respectively, $\mathbf{M}_1$) diverges on f or else the last program output by $\mathbf{M}_0$ (respectively, $\mathbf{M}_1$) on f commits infinitely many convergent errors.

Case 2: Some stage s starts but does not terminate. Let r and cur be as defined in step 1 of stage s. Since step 3 does not succeed, $\mathbf{M}_r$ does not $\mathbf{Ex}^*$-identify any extension of $\varphi_{p(3)}$, and thus $\mathbf{M}_r$ does not $\mathbf{Ex}^*$-identify any extension of $\varphi_{p(\text{cur})}$. We have two subcases.

Subcase 2.1: Each substage in stage s terminates. Let $f = \varphi_{p(\text{cur})}$. Clearly, f is computable and a member of $\mathcal{C}_2$, since $f(1) = p(1)$ and $max(W_{p(1)}) = p(\text{cur})$. Also, by the success of step 4.3 and the diagonalization in step 4.5 in each substage, $\mathbf{M}_{1-r}$ either diverges on f, or the last program output by $\mathbf{M}_{1-r}$ on f commits infinitely many convergent errors.

Subcase 2.2: Some substage s' in stage s starts but does not terminate. In this case, let avail be as of the end of step 4.1 in substage s' of stage s. Let $f = \varphi_{p(\text{avail})}$. Clearly, f is recursive and an extension of $\varphi_{p(\text{cur})}$. Also, f is a member of $\mathcal{C}_2$, since $f(2) = p(2)$ and $max(W_{p(2)}) = p(\text{avail})$. However, since step 4.3 does not succeed, $\mathbf{M}_{1-r}$, does not $\mathbf{Ex}^*$-identify any extension of $\varphi_{p(\text{cur})}$ and thus does not $\mathbf{Ex}^*$-identify f.

From the above cases it follows that $\mathcal{C}_2 \notin \mathbf{Team}_2^1 \mathbf{Ex}^*$. ∎

We leave it to the reader to show that the above proposition implies the following corollary which says that increasing the size of team results in identifiability of larger collections of functions.

9.6 Corollary *Let* $a \in (N \cup \{*\})$. $\mathbf{Ex}^a = \mathbf{Team}_1^1 \mathbf{Ex}^a \subset \mathbf{Team}_2^1 \mathbf{Ex}^a \subset \cdots \subset \mathbf{Team}_n^1 \mathbf{Ex}^a \subset \mathbf{Team}_{n+1}^1 \mathbf{Ex}^a \subset \cdots$.

The study of the general case, $\mathbf{Team}_n^m \mathbf{Ex}$, to which we will return in Section 9.5, is aided by results on identification of functions by probabilistic scientists—our next topic.

§9.4 Identification by probabilistic scientists

Computable scientists have played a central role in the paradigms studied thus far. In this section we consider probabilistic scientists that behave like computable scientists except that every now and then they have the ability to base their actions on the outcome of a random event such as the flip of a fair coin.

More formally, a *probabilistic scientist* $\mathbf{P}$ may be construed as an algorithmic machine that is equipped with a fair t-sided coin (or die), where t is an integer greater than 1. $\mathbf{P}$'s response to an evidential state σ depends, in general, not only on σ but also on the outcomes of the coin flips that $\mathbf{P}$ performed up to that point. We formalize coin flips and coin flip sequences in the following definition.

9.7 Definition Suppose $t > 1$.

(a) N_t denotes $\{0, 1, 2, \ldots, t - 1\}$, the set of possible outcomes of a flip of a t-sided coin.

(b) For each $k \in N$, N_t^k denotes the collection of all length k sequences of possible flips of a t-sided coin. N_t^* denotes $\bigcup_{k=0}^{\infty} N_t^k$, the collection of all finite t-ary sequences. (A typical variable for elements of N_t^* is ρ).

(c) N_t^{∞} denotes the collection of infinite sequences of flips of a t-sided coin. Elements of N_t^{∞} are called *oracles for a t-sided coin* or *t-ary oracles*. O will range over oracles.

We treat a t-ary oracle somewhat like a text for the finite language N_t and carry over notation for texts to oracles as follows.

9.8 Definition Let $t > 1$.

(a) Let $\rho \in N_t^*$. The length of ρ is denoted by $|\rho|$. For $n < |\rho|$, the nth member of ρ is denoted by $\rho(n)$, and the initial sequence of length n in ρ is denoted by $\rho[n]$.

(b) Let O be a t-ary oracle. Then, the nth member of O is denoted $O(n)$. The initial finite sequence of O of length n is denoted $O[n]$.

Let $\mathbf{P}$ be a probabilistic scientist equipped with a t-sided coin, $\rho \in N_t^*$, and let $\sigma \in \mathrm{SEG}$ be given. Then $\mathbf{P}^\rho(\sigma)$ denotes the output (if any) of $\mathbf{P}$ on σ after $|\rho|$ or fewer coin flips are read from ρ. That is, the outcome of $\mathbf{P}$'s first coin flip (if it occurs) is $\rho(0)$, the outcome of the second flip is $\rho(1)$, and so on. If $\mathbf{P}$ tries to perform more coin flips than $|\rho|$ in responding to the evidential state σ, then $\mathbf{P}^\rho(\sigma)$ is undefined. Let O be an oracle. Then $\mathbf{P}^O(\sigma)$ denotes $\mathbf{P}^{O[n]}(\sigma)$, where n is the least number, if any, such that $\mathbf{P}^{O[n]}(\sigma)$ is defined; if no such n exists, then $\mathbf{P}^O(\sigma)$ is undefined. Finally, $\mathbf{P}^O(f)$ is the limit of $\mathbf{P}^O(f[m])$ (as $m \to \infty$) as usual. If $\mathbf{P}^O(f)\downarrow$ to an index for f, we say that $\mathbf{P}^O$ **Ex**-identifies f. Intuitively, the probability of $\mathbf{P}$ **Ex**-identifying f will be the same as the probability of $\{O \mid \mathbf{P}^O$ **Ex**-identifies $f\}$. We formalize this notion in Section 9.4.2 after reviewing some basic probability theory in the next subsection.

Convention: For the rest of this chapter we shall assume that probabilistic scientists are total in the sense that, for each $\mathbf{P}$, O, and σ, there is an n such that $\mathbf{P}^{O[n]}(\sigma)$ is defined. It can be easily verified that this assumption does not affect the generality of the results discussed below.

The subject of identification by probabilistic scientists was first studied by Freivalds [63] and by Pitt [149, 150]. Our presentation closely follows that of Pitt.

§9.4.1 Background probability theory

A *probability space* consists of

- Ω, a set of possible outcomes of experiments;
- $\mathcal{B}$, a collection of subsets of Ω (satisfying conditions of Definition 9.9 below), called *events* or *measurable sets*; and
- pr, a function from $\mathcal{B}$ to the real interval $[\![0, 1]\!]$ (satisfying the conditions of Definition 9.10 below), called a *probability measure*.

Before discussing the conditions on $\mathcal{B}$ and pr, we consider the familiar example of the uniform probability measure on a finite, nonempty set Ω. In this case $\mathcal{B} =$ the collection of all subsets of Ω and $pr(E) = card(E)/card(\Omega)$ for $E \subseteq \Omega$. So if $\Omega = N_2$, then the probability of 0 (heads) $= pr(\{\,0\,\}) = 1/2 = pr(\{\,1\,\}) =$ the probability of 1 (tails) and $pr(\Omega) = 1$. If $\Omega = N_2^3$, then the probability of an even number of 0's in three flips $= pr(E)$ (where $E = \{\,(0,0,1),(0,1,0),(0,0,1),(1,1,1)\,\})) = card(E)/card(N_2^3) = 4/8 = 1/2$. If Ω is a finite or countable set, then one can usually take every subset of Ω to be an event. If Ω is uncountable (such as N_t^∞), then set-theoretic difficulties typically force one to take $\mathcal{B}$ to be a proper subset of the powerset of Ω that satisfies the properties given in the following definition.

9.9 Definition $\mathcal{B} \subseteq 2^\Omega$ is a *Borel field* (or *σ-algebra*) if and only if

(a) $\Omega \in \mathcal{B}$,

(b) $A \in \mathcal{B} \Rightarrow \Omega - A \in \mathcal{B}$, and

(c) $\mathcal{B}$ is closed under countable unions, i.e., if $\mathcal{A} \subseteq \mathcal{B}$ is countable, then $\cup\mathcal{A} \in \mathcal{B}$.

The smallest Borel field that contains a particular collection, $\mathcal{A}$, of subsets of Ω is called the *Borel field generated by $\mathcal{A}$*.

As $\cap_i A_i = N - \cup_i(N - A_i)$, Borel fields are also closed under countable intersections.

9.10 Definition A *probability measure* on a Borel field $\mathcal{B}$ of subsets of Ω is a real-valued function $pr\colon \mathcal{B} \to [\![0, 1]\!]$ such that

(a) $pr(\Omega) = 1$, and

(b) pr is *countably additive*, i.e., if $\mathcal{A} \subseteq \mathcal{B}$ is a countable collection of pairwise disjoint sets, then $pr(\cup\mathcal{A}) = \sum_{A \in \mathcal{A}} pr(A)$.

For each $k \geq 1$ and $t > 1$, let $\mathcal{B}_t^k =$ the collection of all subsets of N_t^k and, for each $A \subseteq N_t^k$, define $\mathrm{pr}_t^k(A) = card(A)/t^k$. So $(N_t^k, \mathcal{B}_t^k, \mathrm{pr}_t^k)$ is just the uniform probability space on N_t^k. *Easy exercise:* Show that, for each k and t, $\mathcal{B}_t^k$ and pr_t^k satisfy the conditions for a Borel field and probability measure, respectively.

Now let us consider the problem of constructing for N_t^∞ an appropriate probability space $(N_t^\infty, \mathcal{B}_t^\infty, \mathrm{pr}_t^\infty)$, where, as usual, t is an integer greater that 1. Somehow, this space should be the "limit" of the $(N_t^k, \mathcal{B}_t^k, \mathrm{pr}_t^k)$'s. Moreover, we want the probability that an infinite sequence of coin flips starts with a 0 (respectively, $1, \ldots, t-1$) to be $1/t$, and, in general, we want the probability that an infinite sequence of coin flips has ρ (a particular finite t-ary sequence) as an initial subsequence to be $1/t^{|\rho|}$. So, defining, for each $\rho \in N_t^*$,

$$\langle\!\langle \rho \rangle\!\rangle \;\; = \;\; \{\, O \mid O \text{ extends } \rho \,\},$$

we know that all of the $\langle\!\langle \rho \rangle\!\rangle$'s should be in $\mathcal{B}_t^\infty$ with $\mathrm{pr}_t^\infty(\langle\!\langle \rho \rangle\!\rangle) = 1/t^{|\rho|}$. Thus, we take $\mathcal{B}_t^\infty$ to be the Borel field generated by $\{\, \langle\!\langle \rho \rangle\!\rangle \mid \rho \in N_t^* \,\}$, and, less obviously, for each $A \in \mathcal{B}_t^\infty$, define

$$\mathrm{pr}_t^\infty(A) \;\; = \;\; \inf\left(\left\{ \sum_{\rho \in \mathcal{C}} \mathrm{pr}_t^\infty(\langle\!\langle \rho \rangle\!\rangle) \;\middle|\; \mathcal{C} \subseteq N_t^* \text{ and } A \subseteq \bigcup_{\rho \in \mathcal{C}} \langle\!\langle \rho \rangle\!\rangle \right\} \right).$$

It can be shown (see Dudley [56]) that this pr_t^∞ is a probability measure for $\mathcal{B}_t^\infty$. This probability space on N_t^∞ will suffice for our purposes. Henceforth, we will say that an $A \subseteq N_t^\infty$ is *measurable* if and only if $A \in \mathcal{B}_t^\infty$. Many natural sets turn out to be measurable, as shown by the next lemma. First, we introduce a bit of terminology. For $t \geq 2$ and $k \in N$, we say a relation $P \subseteq \{\, O \mid O \text{ is a } t\text{-ary oracle} \,\} \times N^k$ is *arithmetic* if and only if P can be expressed in the language of first-order arithmetic augmented by a 1-ary function variable $\mathbf{O}$. So for example, the relation "there are infinitely many n such that $O(n) = 0$" is expressible by: $(\forall m)(\exists n)[\, n > m \wedge \mathbf{O}(n) = 0 \,]$. (Rogers discusses and characterizes such arithmetic relations in Section 15.2 of [158].)

9.11 Lemma *Suppose $k \geq 0$, $t \geq 2$, and $P \subseteq \{\, O \mid O \text{ is a } t\text{-ary oracle} \,\} \times N^k$ is arithmetic. Then, for each $x_1, \ldots, x_k$, the set $\mathcal{P} = \{\, O \subseteq N \mid P(O, x_1, \ldots, x_k) \,\}$ is measurable.*

Proof: Without loss of generality, suppose that for all $O, x_1, \ldots x_k$,

$$P(O, x_1, \ldots, x_k) \;\; \Longleftrightarrow \;\; (Q_1 y_1) \ldots (Q_n y_n) R(O, x_1, \ldots, x_k, y_1, \ldots, y_n),$$

where $n \geq 0$, each Q_i is either the quantifier $\exists$ or $\forall$, and R can be expressed without quantifiers. We proceed by induction on n. Suppose $n = 0$. Then, there is a number m such that in the quantifier free statement that expresses P, all references to elements of O involve elements $\leq m$. Hence it follows that $\mathcal{P}$ can be expressed as a finite union of particular $\langle\!\langle \rho \rangle\!\rangle$ with $|\rho| \leq m$. Thus the base case follows. Suppose $n > 0$ and the lemma holds for $n - 1$. Then for each y_1, the collection,

$$\mathcal{S}_{y_1} = \{ O \mid (Q_2 y_2) \ldots (Q_n y_n) R(O, x_1, \ldots, x_k, y_1, \ldots, y_n) \},$$

is measurable. Moreover, if $Q_1 = \exists$, then $\mathcal{P} = \cup_{y_1=0}^{\infty} \mathcal{S}_{y_1}$ and if $Q_1 = \forall$, then $\mathcal{P} = \cap_{y_1=0}^{\infty} \mathcal{S}_{y_1}$. In either case it follows that $\mathcal{P}$ is measurable. Hence, the induction step follows. ∎

Fix a probabilistic scientist $\mathbf{P}$ and $f \in \mathcal{R}$ and let i_f be an index for f. Then we have that $[\mathbf{P}^O \ \mathbf{Ex}\text{-identifies } f]$ is equivalent to

$$(\exists j)[\, \varphi_j = \varphi_{i_f} \text{ and } (\overset{\infty}{\forall} m)(\exists n)[\mathbf{P}^{O[n]}(\varphi_{i_f}[m]) = j]\,]]$$

which, by standard tricks (see Section 14.8 of Rogers [158]), is seen to be arithmetical. Hence, as desired, we have

9.12 Lemma (Pitt [149, 150]) *For each probabilistic scientist $\mathbf{P}$ and $f \in \mathcal{R}$, $\{ O \mid \mathbf{P}^O$ $\mathbf{Ex}$-identifies $f \}$ is measurable.*

§9.4.2 Probability of function identification

The work of the last subsection justifies the following definition.

9.13 Definition (Pitt [149, 150]) Let $\mathbf{P}$ be a probabilistic scientist equipped with a t-sided coin $(t \geq 2)$ and $f \in \mathcal{R}$. Then, $\mathrm{pr}_t^{\infty}(\mathbf{P} \ \mathbf{Ex}\text{-identifies } f) = \mathrm{pr}_t^{\infty}(\{ O \mid \mathbf{P}^O \ \mathbf{Ex}\text{-identifies } f \})$.

The next lemma says that the notion of probabilistic $\mathbf{Ex}$-identifiability does not depend on the value of t.

9.14 Lemma (Pitt [149, 150]) *Let $t > 2$. Let $\mathbf{P}$ be a probabilistic scientist with a t-sided coin. Then, there exists a probabilistic scientist $\mathbf{P}'$ with a two-sided coin such that for each $f \in \mathcal{R}$, $\mathrm{pr}_2^{\infty}(\mathbf{P}' \ \mathbf{Ex}\text{-identifies } f) = \mathrm{pr}_t^{\infty}(\mathbf{P} \ \mathbf{Ex}\text{-identifies } f)$.*

The proof of this lemma involves more technical probability theory than we want to discuss here. We refer the reader to Pitt [150] for its proof. The lemma frees us from specifying the number of sides of the coin, thereby allowing us to talk about probability function pr_t^∞ without specifying t. For this reason, we will refer to pr_t^∞ as simply pr in the sequel. Also, we are at liberty to use whatever number of sides of a coin that is convenient for the presentation at hand.

9.15 Definition (Pitt [149, 150]) Let $p \in [\![0, 1]\!]$.

(a) We say that **P** **Prob**^{p}**Ex**-*identifies* f (written: $f \in$ **Prob**^{p}**Ex(P)**) just in case $\mathrm{pr}(\mathbf{P}\ \mathbf{Ex}\text{-identifies } f) \geq p$.

(b) **Prob**^{p}**Ex** $= \{\, \mathcal{S} \subseteq \mathcal{R} \mid \mathcal{S} \subseteq \mathbf{Prob}^p\mathbf{Ex(P)}$ for some **P** $\}$.

The next proposition establishes a link between team and probabilistic inference. It says that any class of functions team-identifiable by a team of scientists of size n can also be identified by a single probabilistic scientist with probability $\geq 1/n$.

9.16 Proposition (Pitt [149, 150]) *Let* $n \geq 1$. *Then,* **Team**$_n^1$**Ex** $\subseteq$ **Prob**$^{\frac{1}{n}}$**Ex**.

Proof: Let $\mathcal{S} \in \mathbf{Team}_n^1\mathbf{Ex}$, as witnessed by the team of scientists $\mathbf{M}_1, \mathbf{M}_2, \ldots, \mathbf{M}_n$. Let **P** be a probabilistic scientist, equipped with an n-sided coin, that behaves as follows. **P** on $f \in \mathcal{R}$ first flips its coin once and obtains a number $i \in N_n$ and henceforth simulates scientist $\mathbf{M}_{i+1}$ on f. Clearly, for each $f \in \mathcal{S}$, $\mathrm{pr}(\mathbf{P}\ \mathbf{Ex}\text{-identifies } f) \geq 1/n$.   ■

Pitt [149, 150] also established the converse of the above result: for each $n \geq 1$, **Prob**$^{\frac{1}{n}}$**Ex** $\subseteq$ **Team**$_n^1$**Ex** and thus showed that probabilistic identification and team identification are successful on essentially the same collections on functions. This result will be an immediate corollary of Proposition 9.24 below. In order to prove this result, Pitt used a technique of calculating probabilities on "infinite computation trees" described in the next subsection. To facilitate the description, it is helpful to standardize the way probabilistic machines make use of their coin flips—see the next definition. The lemma following this definition shows that we may, without loss of generality, assume all probabilistic scientists are so standardized.

9.17 Definition (Pitt [149, 150]) Suppose **P** is a probabilistic scientist. **P** is *nice* just in case **P** is equipped with a two-sided coin and the behavior of **P** on a function f is an infinite sequence of *rounds* each of which consists of the following three phases carried out in the order indicated.

Phase a: Receive an element of the graph of f.

Phase b: Issue an hypothesis.

Phase c: Flip the coin.

9.18 Lemma (Pitt [149, 150]) *Let* **P** *be a probabilistic scientist. Then there exists a nice* **P'** *such that, for each* $f \in \mathcal{R}$, $pr(\mathbf{P}$ Ex-*identifies* $f) \leq pr(\mathbf{P'}$ Ex-*identifies* $f)$.

§9.4.3 Infinite computation trees

Let **P** be a nice probabilistic scientist and let $f \in \mathcal{R}$ be given. The infinite computation tree for **P** on f, denoted $\mathcal{T}_{\mathbf{P},f}$, is a record of **P**'s behavior on all possible 2-ary oracles when **P** is fed the graph of f in canonical order. We describe $\mathcal{T}_{\mathbf{P},f}$ and its relation to probabilistic **Ex**-identification in this subsection.

Convention: Throughout this subsection we will keep **P** and f fixed. All terminology and notation will be understood to be relative to the choice of particular **P** and f. When we use these terms and notation in later sections, the particular **P** and f we have in mind will always be understood.

$\mathcal{T}_{\mathbf{P},f}$ is an infinite complete binary tree. Each node of $\mathcal{T}_{\mathbf{P},f}$ is labeled with an element of N_2^*. The root of $\mathcal{T}_{\mathbf{P},f}$ is labeled with ϵ (the empty sequence) and, if a node of $\mathcal{T}_{\mathbf{P},f}$ is labeled with ρ, then the node's left child is labeled $\rho \diamond 0$ and its right child is labeled $\rho \diamond 1$. A node with label ρ represents the state of **P** just after phase b of round $|\rho|$ when **P** is fed the graph of f in canonical order and receives ρ as the result of its first $|\rho|$ coin flips; guess(ρ) denotes the hypothesis issued by **P** in phase b of this round. We identify nodes with their labels so that when we speak of node ρ we mean the node in $\mathcal{T}_{\mathbf{P},f}$ with label ρ. The *depth* of node ρ is simply $|\rho|$. Hence, the depth of the root is 0.

A *path* ϱ in $\mathcal{T}_{\mathbf{P},f}$ is an infinite sequence of nodes $\varrho_0, \varrho_1, \varrho_2, \ldots$, such that, for each i, $|\varrho_i| = i$ and ϱ_{i+1} extends ϱ_i. (That is, ϱ_0 is the root and ϱ_i occurs at depth i in the tree and is the parent of node ϱ_{i+1}.) ϱ will range over paths in $\mathcal{T}_{\mathbf{P},f}$. There is an obvious one-to-one correspondence between paths and 2-ary oracles. By convention, when we speak of the measure of a set of paths, we will mean the measure of the corresponding set of oracles. The next definition introduces the path analog of the $\langle\!\langle \rho \rangle\!\rangle$'s.

9.19 Definition For each node ρ of $\mathcal{T}_{\mathbf{P},f}$, $P\langle \rho \rangle$ denotes $\{\, \varrho \mid \varrho_{|\rho|} = \rho \,\}$.

It is obvious that $P\langle \rho \rangle$ corresponds to $\langle\!\langle \rho \rangle\!\rangle$, and, hence, $pr(P\langle \rho \rangle) = 2^{-|\rho|}$. The measurable sets $P\langle \rho \rangle$ will be used in computing probabilities of more interesting collections of paths. To help talk about these more interesting collections, the next definition describes what it means for a path in $\mathcal{T}_{\mathbf{P},f}$ to converge and introduces some terminology about convergence of paths.

9.20 Definition

(a) We say that ϱ *converges* to j just in case, for all but finitely many i, $\operatorname{guess}(\varrho_i) = j$.

(b) We say that ϱ *converges at node* ρ just in case, for $k = |\rho|$, $\varrho_k = \rho$ and k is the least number such that for all $i \geq k$, $\operatorname{guess}(\varrho_i) = \operatorname{guess}(\varrho_k)$.

(c) For each ρ, C_ρ denotes $\{\,\varrho \mid \varrho \text{ converges at } \rho\,\}$.

(d) We say that a path ϱ *k-agrees with* C_ρ just in case:

    (i) $\varrho_{|\rho|} = \rho$ and $k \geq |\rho|$,

    (ii) for $i = |\rho|, \ldots, k$, $\operatorname{guess}(\varrho_i) = \operatorname{guess}(\rho)$, and

    (iii) either $\rho = \epsilon$ or $\operatorname{guess}(\varrho_{|\rho|-1}) \neq \operatorname{guess}(\rho)$.

(e) For each ρ and each $k \geq |\rho|$, $C_{\rho,k}$ denotes $\{\,\varrho \mid \varrho \text{ } k\text{-agrees with } C_\rho\,\}$.

(f) For each $A \subseteq N$, $C(A)$ denotes $\{\,\varrho \mid \varrho \text{ converges to some } a \in A\,\}$.

It follows from Lemma 9.11 that all of the C_ρ's, $C_{\rho,k}$'s, and $C(A)$'s are measurable. We shall be interested in computing $\operatorname{pr}(C(A))$ for particular sets A, and the C_ρ's and $C_{\rho,k}$'s will be our avenue for doing this. The next lemma summarizes the relationship between the $C(A)$'s and C_ρ's and states some elementary properties of the C_ρ's and $C_{\rho,k}$'s. We leave its proof to the reader.

9.21 Lemma (Pitt [149, 150]) *Fix ρ and k with $k \geq |\rho|$. Then:*

(a) *For each $A \subseteq N$, $C(A) = \cup\{\, C_\rho \mid \operatorname{guess}(\rho) \in A\,\}$.*

(b) *For each ρ and $k \geq |\rho|$, $C_{\rho,k} \supseteq C_{\rho,k+1}$ and $\operatorname{pr}(C_{\rho,k}) \geq \operatorname{pr}(C_\rho)$.*

(c) *For each ρ, $C_\rho = \bigcap_{k=|\rho|}^{\infty} C_{\rho,k}$ and $\operatorname{pr}(C_\rho) = \lim_{i \to \infty} \operatorname{pr}(C_{\rho,|\rho|+i})$.*

(d) *For distinct ρ and ρ', $C_\rho \cap C_{\rho'} = \emptyset$.*

Fix an A and let $\mathcal{C} = \{\, C_\rho \mid \operatorname{guess}(\rho) \in A\,\}$. It follows from the above lemma that $C(A)$ is the disjoint union of the members of $\mathcal{C}$, and hence $\operatorname{pr}(C(A)) = \sum_{C_\rho \in \mathcal{C}_A} \operatorname{pr}(C_\rho)$. The probability of C_ρ, in turn, is the monotone decreasing limit of $\operatorname{pr}(C_{\rho,k})$ as $k \to \infty$. The next lemma shows how to compute the probabilities of the $C_{\rho,k}$'s.

9.22 Lemma (Pitt [149, 150]) *Suppose $k \geq |\rho|$ and $N_{\rho,k}$ denotes $\{\, \varrho_k \mid \varrho \in C_{\rho,k} \,\}$. Then,*

(a) $pr(C_{\rho,k}) = card(N_{\rho,k})/2^k$, *and*

(b) $pr(C_{\rho,k})$ *can be computed by looking at only the first $k+1$ levels of $\mathcal{T}_{\mathbf{P},f}$.*

Proof: We first argue

Claim: $C_{\rho,k}$ is the disjoint union of members of $\{\, P\langle\rho'\rangle \mid \rho' \in N_{\rho,k} \,\}$.

Proof of the Claim: For distinct ρ_0 and ρ_1 in $N_{\rho,k}$, $P\langle\rho_0\rangle$ and $P\langle\rho_1\rangle$ are disjoint because both nodes ρ_0 and ρ_1 are at depth k and, since they are distinct, no path can pass through both.

Suppose $\varrho \in C_{\rho,k}$. Then, ϱ passes through some $\rho' \in N_{\rho,k}$, and hence $\varrho \in P\langle\rho'\rangle \subseteq \cup\{\, P\langle\rho'\rangle \mid \rho' \in N_{\rho,k} \,\}$.

Suppose $\varrho \in \cup\{\, P\langle\rho'\rangle \mid \rho' \in N_{\rho,k} \,\}$. Since the definition of $N_{\rho,k}$ does not depend on nodes deeper than level $k+1$, all paths passing through ϱ_k must be in $C_{\rho,k}$. Hence, $\varrho \in C_{\rho,k}$.

The claim thus follows.

Therefore, by the claim and the countable additivity of pr we have

$$pr(C_{\rho,k}) = \sum_{\rho' \in N_{\rho,k}} pr(P\langle\rho'\rangle) = \sum_{\rho' \in N_{\rho,k}} 2^{-|\rho'|} = \sum_{\rho' \in N_{\rho,k}} 2^{-k} = card(N_{\rho,k})/2^k,$$

and so, part (a) follows.

It is easy to see that $N_{\rho,k}$ can be effectively determined by observing only the first $k+1$ levels of $\mathcal{T}_{\mathbf{P},f}$. Thus, part (b) follows from part (a).   ∎

We now present a lemma that is crucial to the proof of the main result of this section.

9.23 Lemma (Pitt [149, 150]) *Suppose $A \subseteq N$ and $pr(C(A)) > p \geq 0$. Then, there is a finite collection of nodes $\{\, \rho_0, \ldots, \rho_k \,\}$ such that $guess(\rho_i) \in A$, for each $i \leq k$, and $\sum_{i \leq k} pr(C_{\rho_i}) = pr(\cup_{i \leq k} C_{\rho_i}) > p$.*

Proof: Let $\mathcal{C}_A = \{\, C_\rho \mid guess(\rho) \in A \,\}$. By Lemma 9.21 we have, for all $\delta > 0$,

$$\sum_{C_\rho \in \mathcal{C}_A} pr(C_\rho) = pr(\cup_{C_\rho \in \mathcal{C}_A} C_\rho) = pr(C(A)) > pr(C(A)) - \delta.$$

Now, if the sum of infinitely many nonnegative quantities is $> p$, then there is a finite subcollection of these that sum up to some number $> p$. Therefore, there is a finite $\{\, C_{\rho_0}, \ldots, C_{\rho_k} \,\} \subseteq \mathcal{C}_A$ such that $\{\, \rho_0, \ldots, \rho_k \,\}$ are as required.   ∎

§9.4.4 The Key Correspondence

We are now in a position to prove

9.24 Proposition (Pitt [149, 150]) *For each* $n \geq 1$ *and* $p \in (\frac{1}{n+1}, 1]$, $\mathbf{Prob}^p\mathbf{Ex} \subseteq \mathbf{Team}^1_n\mathbf{Ex}$.

This proposition immediately follows from the next proposition and the fact that **FOex = Ex** (see Exercise 6-7 in Chapter 6).

9.25 Proposition (Pitt [149, 150]) *Let* $p > 1/(n+1)$ *and* $\mathcal{S} \in \mathbf{Prob}^p\mathbf{Ex}$. *Then, there are* $\mathbf{M}_1, \mathbf{M}_2, \ldots, \mathbf{M}_n$ *such that* $\mathcal{S} \subseteq \bigcup_{i=1}^n \mathbf{FOex}(\mathbf{M}_i)$.

Proof: Let **P** be a probabilistic scientist such that $\mathcal{S} \subseteq \mathbf{Prob}^p\mathbf{Ex}(\mathbf{P})$.

We construct from **P** a team of n deterministic scientists $\mathbf{M}_1, \mathbf{M}_2, \ldots, \mathbf{M}_n$ as follows. (*Note:* We use the usual ordering on N_2^* below.)

Begin ($\mathbf{M}_i(\sigma)$, *with* $k = |\sigma|$)

    Construct $\mathcal{T}_k$, the first $k+1$ levels of $\mathcal{T}_{\mathbf{P},f}$, by simulating **P** with input σ and all 2-ary sequences of length k.

    For each node ρ in $\mathcal{T}_k$, compute $\mathrm{pr}(C_{\rho,k})$.

    Let ρ_k be the least node in $\mathcal{T}_k$, if any, such that $\sum_{\rho \leq \rho_k} \mathrm{pr}(C_{\rho,k}) > i/(n+1)$.

    If ρ_k is found,

        then output the canonical index of $\{ \text{guess}(\rho) \mid \rho \leq \rho_k \}$

        else output 0

End ($\mathbf{M}_i(\sigma)$)

Notation: Let good_f denote the collection of all φ-indices for f, i.e., $\text{good}_f = \{ i \mid \varphi_i = f \}$. Then, $C(\text{good}_f)$ is the collection of all paths (oracles) that result in successful **Ex**-identification of f by **P**. Hence, $\mathrm{pr}(\mathbf{P} \text{ } \mathbf{Ex}\text{-identifies } f) = \mathrm{pr}(C(\text{good}_f))$.

Now, $f \in \mathbf{Prob}^p\mathbf{Ex}(\mathbf{P})$ implies that $\mathrm{pr}(C(\text{good}_f)) \geq p$. Recall that $C(N)$ is the collection of all converging paths in $\mathcal{T}_{\mathbf{P},f}$. Hence, $C(\text{good}_f) \subseteq C(N)$ and $\mathrm{pr}(C(N)) \geq \mathrm{pr}(C(\text{good}_f)) > 1/(n+1)$. Since $1/(n+1) < \mathrm{pr}(C(N)) \leq 1$, there exists an $m \in \{1, \ldots, n\}$ such that $m = \max(\{ i \mid i/(n+1) < \mathrm{pr}(C(N)) \})$.

We argue that the scientist $\mathbf{M}_m$ **FOex**-identifies f. Let us focus on the behavior of $\mathbf{M}_m$ on $f[k]$. $\mathbf{M}_m$ correctly assumes that the probability of converging paths in $\mathcal{T}_{\mathbf{P},f}$ is greater than $m/(n+1)$ and attempts to find, in the limit, a finite collection of nodes where most paths converge. To this end, $\mathbf{M}_m$ first finds the smallest ρ_k such that $\sum_{\rho \leq \rho_k} \text{pr}(C_{\rho,k}) > m/(n+1)$ and then outputs the canonical index for the finite set $\{\, \text{guess}(\rho) \mid \rho \leq \rho_k \,\}$.

Now, by Lemma 9.23, there exists a collection of nodes $\{\, \rho_0, \ldots, \rho_v \,\}$ in $\mathcal{T}_{\mathbf{P},f}$ such that $\sum_{i=0}^{v} \text{pr}(C_{\rho_i}) > m/(n+1)$. This implies that there exists a smallest numbered node ρ_* such that $\sum_{\rho \leq \rho_*} \text{pr}(C_{\rho,k}) > m/(n+1)$, for all $k > \text{depth}(j)$. (Choosing any $\rho_* \geq max(\{\, \rho_0, \ldots, \rho_v \,\})$ satisfies the inequality.)

The result follows from the following claim.

9.26 Claim

(a) *For all but finitely many* k, $\rho_k = \rho_*$.

(b) $\{\, \text{guess}(\rho) \mid \rho \leq \rho_* \,\}$ *contains a* φ*-index for* f.

We can deduce the proposition from the claim as follows. Since $\mathbf{M}_m$, fed $f[k]$, outputs the canonical index for the finite set $\{\, \text{guess}(\rho) \mid \rho \leq \rho_k \,\}$, (a) implies that $\mathbf{M}_m$ converges to the canonical index for $\{\, \text{guess}(\rho) \mid \rho \leq \rho_* \,\}$. Moreover, according to (b), $\{\, \text{guess}(\rho) \mid \rho \leq \rho_k \,\}$ contains a φ-index for f, thereby implying that $\mathbf{M}_m$ **FOex**-identifies f. We now prove the claim.

Part (a). It is easy to verify that part (a) follows from the choice of ρ_*.

Part (b). Since good_f is the set of all φ-indexes for f, $(N - \text{good}_f)$ is the collection of all such φ-indexes that are not for f. Now, observe that since $C(\text{good}_f)$ and $C(N - \text{good}_f)$ are disjoint, $\text{pr}(C(N)) = \text{pr}(C(\text{good}_f)) + \text{pr}(C(N - \text{good}_f))$. We also know by the hypothesis of the proposition and the choice of m that $\text{pr}(C(N)) \leq (m+1)/(n+1)$ and $\text{pr}(C(\text{good}_f)) > 1/(n+1)$. Thus, $\text{pr}(C(N - \text{good}_f)) < m/(n+1)$.

Let I denote the set $\{\, \text{guess}(\rho) \mid \rho \leq \rho_* \,\}$. Observe that $\text{pr}(C(I)) \geq m/(n+1)$. Therefore, at least one element in I must be a correct φ-index for f, because otherwise $I \subseteq N - \text{good}_f$, $C(I) \subseteq C(N - \text{good}_f)$, and $\text{pr}(C(N - \text{good}_f)) \geq m/(n+1)$, a contradiction. Hence, I contains a φ-index for f.

This completes the proof of the proposition. ∎

As an immediate corollary to Propositions 9.16 and 9.24, we have the following:

9.27 Corollary (Pitt [149, 150]) *For each* $n \geq 1$, $\mathbf{Prob}^{\frac{1}{n}}\mathbf{Ex} = \mathbf{Team}_n^1\mathbf{Ex}$.

The above corollary, together with Corollary 9.6 implies the following:

9.28 Corollary (Pitt [149, 150]) *For each* $n \geq 1$, $\mathbf{Prob}^{\frac{1}{n}}\mathbf{Ex} \subset \mathbf{Prob}^{\frac{1}{n+1}}\mathbf{Ex}$.

Thus, the team hierarchy is contained in the probabilistic hierarchy. However, it turns out that the probabilistic hierarchy is no finer than the team hierarchy. To see this, let $1/(n+1) < p \leq 1/n$. Clearly, $\mathbf{Prob}^{\frac{1}{n}}\mathbf{Ex} \subseteq \mathbf{Prob}^p\mathbf{Ex}$. Now, by Theorem 9.24, $\mathbf{Prob}^p\mathbf{Ex} \subseteq \mathbf{Team}_n^1\mathbf{Ex}$. But, Corollary 9.27 implies that $\mathbf{Team}_n^1\mathbf{Ex} = \mathbf{Prob}^{\frac{1}{n}}\mathbf{Ex}$. Thus, $\mathbf{Prob}^{\frac{1}{n}}\mathbf{Ex} = \mathbf{Prob}^p\mathbf{Ex}$. We have essentially shown the following corollary, which says that the probabilistic hierarchy is exactly the same as the team hierarchy.

9.29 Corollary (Pitt [149, 150]) *For each $n \geq 1$ and each $p \in (\!(1/(n+1), 1/n]\!]$, $\mathbf{Prob}^p\mathbf{Ex} = \mathbf{Team}_n^1\mathbf{Ex}$.*

§9.5 $\mathbf{Team}_n^m\mathbf{Ex}$-identification

Corollary 9.29 can be used to characterize generalized team identification paradigms in which more than one member of the team is required to be successful. To make this clear we rely on the following definition.

9.30 Definition For each $p \in (\!(0, 1]\!]$, let $\mathrm{IN}(p) = 1/n$, where $n \in N$ is such that $1/(n+1) < p \leq 1/n$.

It is easy to verify that for $p \in (\!(0, 1]\!]$, $\mathrm{IN}(p) = 1/\lfloor \frac{1}{p} \rfloor$. The next result is simply a restatement of Corollary 9.29 using this notion.

9.31 Corollary (Pitt and Smith [151]) *For each $p \in (\!(0, 1]\!]$, we have $\mathbf{Prob}^p\mathbf{Ex} = \mathbf{Team}_{\frac{1}{\mathrm{IN}(p)}}^1\mathbf{Ex}$.*

The following result says that all collections of functions that can be identified by a team of n scientists with the requirement that at least m out of n are successful can also be identified by a single probabilistic scientist with probability $\frac{m}{n}$.

9.32 Proposition (Pitt and Smith [151]) *Suppose $n \geq m > 0$ and $p \in (\!(0, 1]\!]$. Then, $\mathbf{Team}_n^m\mathbf{Ex} \subseteq \mathbf{Prob}^{\frac{m}{n}}\mathbf{Ex}$.*

Proof: Let $\mathcal{S} \subseteq \mathcal{R}$. Let $\mathbf{M}_1, \mathbf{M}_2, \ldots, \mathbf{M}_n$ be (deterministic) scientists witnessing $\mathcal{S} \in \mathbf{Team}_n^m\mathbf{Ex}$. Let $\mathbf{P}$ be a probabilistic scientist equipped with an n-sided coin. The behavior of $\mathbf{P}$ can be described thus: $\mathbf{P}$, before receiving any input, flips its n-sided coin and obtains a number $i \in N_n$. $\mathbf{P}$ then simulates the deterministic scientist $\mathbf{M}_{i+1}$. Clearly, for each $f \in \mathcal{S}$, $\mathrm{pr}(\mathbf{P}\ \mathbf{Ex}\text{-identifies} f) \geq m/n$. Hence, $\mathcal{S} \in \mathbf{Prob}^{\frac{m}{n}}\mathbf{Ex}$.   ∎

The next result completely characterizes $\mathbf{Team}_n^m \mathbf{Ex}$-identification in terms of probabilistic identification.

9.33 Proposition (Pitt and Smith [151]) *Suppose $n \geq m > 0$.*
Then, $\mathbf{Team}_n^m \mathbf{Ex} = \mathbf{Team}_{\lfloor \frac{n}{m} \rfloor}^1 \mathbf{Ex} = \mathbf{Prob}^{\mathrm{IN}(\frac{m}{n})} \mathbf{Ex}$.

Proof: We first show that $\mathbf{Team}_{\lfloor \frac{n}{m} \rfloor}^1 \mathbf{Ex} = \mathbf{Prob}^{\mathrm{IN}(\frac{m}{n})} \mathbf{Ex}$. The definition of IN implies that for all $p \in (\!(0,1]\!]$, $\mathrm{IN}(\mathrm{IN}(p)) = \mathrm{IN}(p)$. Now, by Corollary 9.31, we have $\mathbf{Prob}^{\mathrm{IN}(\frac{m}{n})} \mathbf{Ex} = \mathbf{Team}_{\frac{1}{\mathrm{IN}(\mathrm{IN}(\frac{m}{n}))}}^1 \mathbf{Ex} = \mathbf{Team}_{\frac{1}{\mathrm{IN}(\frac{m}{n})}}^1 \mathbf{Ex} = \mathbf{Team}_{1/\lfloor \frac{n}{m} \rfloor}^1 \mathbf{Ex} = \mathbf{Team}_{\lfloor \frac{n}{m} \rfloor}^1 \mathbf{Ex}$.

We now show that $\mathbf{Team}_n^m \mathbf{Ex} = \mathbf{Team}_{\lfloor \frac{n}{m} \rfloor}^1 \mathbf{Ex}$. Since $m \leq n$, Proposition 9.32 implies that $\mathbf{Team}_n^m \mathbf{Ex} \subseteq \mathbf{Prob}^{\frac{m}{n}} \mathbf{Ex}$. Observe that $1/(\lfloor \frac{n}{m} \rfloor + 1) < \frac{m}{n} \leq 1/\lfloor \frac{n}{m} \rfloor$. Thus, by Corollary 9.29, we have $\mathbf{Prob}^{\frac{m}{n}} \mathbf{Ex} = \mathbf{Team}_{\lfloor \frac{n}{m} \rfloor}^1 \mathbf{Ex}$. Hence, $\mathbf{Team}_n^m \mathbf{Ex} \subseteq \mathbf{Team}_{\lfloor \frac{n}{m} \rfloor}^1 \mathbf{Ex}$. We need now only show that $\mathbf{Team}_{\lfloor \frac{n}{m} \rfloor}^1 \mathbf{Ex} \subseteq \mathbf{Team}_n^m \mathbf{Ex}$. Observe that for any $c \in N^+$, $\mathbf{Team}_k^1 \mathbf{Ex} \subseteq \mathbf{Team}_{c \cdot k}^c \mathbf{Ex}$. Thus, $\mathbf{Team}_{\lfloor \frac{n}{m} \rfloor}^1 \mathbf{Ex} \subseteq \mathbf{Team}_{m \cdot \lfloor \frac{n}{m} \rfloor}^m \mathbf{Ex}$. Since $m \cdot \lfloor n/m \rfloor \leq n$, we have $\mathbf{Team}_{m \cdot \lfloor \frac{n}{m} \rfloor}^m \mathbf{Ex} \subseteq \mathbf{Team}_n^m \mathbf{Ex}$. Therefore, $\mathbf{Team}_{\lfloor \frac{n}{m} \rfloor}^1 \mathbf{Ex} \subseteq \mathbf{Team}_n^m \mathbf{Ex}$. ∎

§9.6 Team and probabilistic identification of languages

Team identification of languages was introduced in Definition 9.4. We now adapt the machinery of probabilistic scientists introduced in Section 9.4 to language identification.

Let $\mathbf{P}$ be a probabilistic scientist equipped with a t-sided coin and let T be a text for some language $L \in \mathcal{E}$. Then, the probability of $\mathbf{P}$ $\mathbf{TxtEx}$-identifying T is taken to be $\mathrm{pr}_t^\infty(\{O \mid \mathbf{P}^O \mathbf{TxtEx}\text{-identifies } T\})$. It follows from Lemma 9.11 that $\{O \mid \mathbf{P}^O \mathbf{TxtEx}\text{-identifies } T\}$ is measurable.

The following definition, motivated by the above discussion, introduces the probability of identification of a text.

9.34 Definition (Pitt [149]) Let T be a text and $\mathbf{P}$ be a probabilistic scientist equipped with a t-sided coin ($t \geq 2$). Then, $\mathrm{pr}_t^\infty(\mathbf{P} \ \mathbf{TxtEx}\text{-identifies } T)$ denotes $\mathrm{pr}_t^\infty(\{O \mid \mathbf{P}^O \ \mathbf{TxtEx}\text{-identifies } T\})$.

The next definition describes language identification by probabilistic scientists. As in the case of function identification, there is no loss of generality in assuming a two-sided coin, since the analog of Lemma 9.14 can easily be shown to hold in this new context.

We are thus freed from specifying the number of sides of the coin, and can write the probability function without its subscript t. In the sequel, we shall in fact refer to pr_t^∞ by pr.

9.35 Definition (Pitt [149]) Let $0 \leq p \leq 1$.

(a) **P** **Prob**^{p}**TxtEx**-*identifies* L (written: $L \in \mathbf{Prob}^p\mathbf{TxtEx(P)}$) just in case for each text T for L pr(**P** **TxtEx**-identifies T) $\geq p$.

(b) $\mathbf{Prob}^p\mathbf{TxtEx} = \{\, \mathcal{L} \subseteq \mathcal{E} \mid \mathcal{L} \subseteq \mathbf{Prob}^p\mathbf{TxtEx(P)}$ for some **P** $\}$.

We now discuss some results about team and probabilistic identification of languages. In the context of functions, it is a simple consequence of the equivalence of team and probabilistic identification that if the success ratio of a team is greater than $\frac{1}{2}$, then the team can be simulated by a single scientist without any loss in learning power. Such a cut-off ratio is referred to as the *aggregation ratio* of the team learning paradigm. It is also clear that in the context of functions the only success ratios of interest are of the form $\frac{1}{k}$ with $k > 1$.

The story is different for language identification. First, the aggregation ratio for language identification turns out to be $\frac{2}{3}$. Second, the notions of team and probabilistic identification fail to coincide in the language case. Probabilistic identification turns out to be strictly more powerful than team identification. Finally, the results for languages are more difficult to obtain and only a partial picture is known. In what follows, we first present results for team identification of languages with success ratios $\geq \frac{2}{3}$. This is followed by the presentation of some results for success ratios of the form $\frac{1}{k}$ with $k > 2$.

Team language identification with success ratio $\geq \frac{2}{3}$

We first consider when a team of scientists can be simulated by a single scientist without loss of learning ability. The next proposition below says that the collections of languages that can be identified by teams with success ratio greater than $\frac{2}{3}$ (that is, more than two-thirds of the members in the team are required to be successful) are the same as those collections of languages that can be identified by a single scientist.

9.36 Proposition *Suppose j and k are such that $\frac{j}{k} > \frac{2}{3}$. Then* $\mathbf{Team}_k^j\mathbf{TxtEx} = \mathbf{TxtEx}$.

To facilitate the proof of the above proposition and other results in this chapter, we define the following technical notion.

9.37 Definition Let $\widehat{A}$ be a *nonempty finite* multiset of grammars. Then the grammar majority($\widehat{A}$) is defined to be a grammar such that $W_{\text{majority}(\widehat{A})} = \{\, x \in N \mid \text{for majority}$ of $g \in \widehat{A},\, x \in W_g \,\}$.

Clearly, majority($\widehat{A}$) can be defined using the *s-m-n* theorem (Theorem 2.1). Intuitively, majority($\widehat{A}$) is a grammar for a language that consists of all such elements that are enumerated by a majority of grammars in $\widehat{A}$. Below, whenever we use a set as an argument to majority we assume the argument to be a multiset.

Proof (of Proposition 9.36): Let j and k be as given in the hypothesis of the proposition. Let $\mathcal{L}$ be $\textbf{Team}_k^j\textbf{TxtEx}$-identified by a team consisting of scientists $\mathbf{M}_1$, $\mathbf{M}_2$, ..., $\mathbf{M}_k$. We then describe a scientist $\mathbf{M}$ that $\textbf{TxtEx}$-identifies $\mathcal{L}$.

For a finite sequence σ and a scientist $\mathbf{M}'$, define

$$\text{conv}(\mathbf{M}', \sigma) = max\left(\{\, |\tau| \mid \tau \subseteq \sigma \text{ and } \mathbf{M}'(\tau) \neq \mathbf{M}'(\sigma) \,\}\right). \qquad (9.1)$$

Intuitively, $\text{conv}(\mathbf{M}', \sigma)$ is the length of the longest subsequence of σ where $\mathbf{M}'$ conjectures a hypothesis distinct from the one it conjectures on σ.

Let $m_1^\sigma, m_2^\sigma, \ldots, m_k^\sigma$ be a permutation of $1, 2, \ldots, k$, such that, for $1 \leq r < k$,

$$(\text{conv}(\mathbf{M}_{m_r^\sigma}, \sigma), m_r^\sigma) < (\text{conv}(\mathbf{M}_{m_{r+1}^\sigma}, \sigma), m_{r+1}^\sigma).$$

Note: "$<$" here refers to ordering on pairs: $(k_0, l_0) < (k_1, l_1)$ just in case either $k_0 < k_1$ or else $k_0 = k_1$ and $l_0 < l_1$.

For each σ, define $\mathbf{M}(\sigma) = \text{majority}(\{\, \mathbf{M}_{m_1^\sigma}(\sigma), \mathbf{M}_{m_2^\sigma}(\sigma), \ldots, \mathbf{M}_{m_j^\sigma}(\sigma) \,\})$.

To complete the proof it must be shown that if the team consisting of scientists $\mathbf{M}_1$, $\mathbf{M}_2$, ..., $\mathbf{M}_k$ $\textbf{Team}_k^j\textbf{TxtEx}$-identifies $L \in \mathcal{L}$, then $\mathbf{M}$ $\textbf{TxtEx}$-identifies L. This is the subject of Exercise 9-8. ∎

Proposition 9.38 below says that the collections of languages that can be identified by a team with success ratio $\frac{2}{3}$ (that is, at least two-thirds of the members in the team are required to be successful) are the same as those collections of languages that can be identified by a team of 3 scientists, at least 2 of which are required to be successful.

9.38 Proposition *For each $j > 0$,* $\textbf{Team}_{3j}^{2j}\textbf{TxtEx} = \textbf{Team}_3^2\textbf{TxtEx}$.

Proof: Let j be as given in the hypothesis of the proposition. Suppose a team consisting of scientists $\mathbf{M}_1$, ..., $\mathbf{M}_{3j}$ $\textbf{Team}_{3j}^{2j}\textbf{TxtEx}$-identifies $\mathcal{L}$. We then describe scientists $\mathbf{M}_1'$, $\mathbf{M}_2'$, and $\mathbf{M}_3'$ such that the team consisting of $\mathbf{M}_1'$, $\mathbf{M}_2'$, and $\mathbf{M}_3'$ witnesses $\mathcal{L} \in \textbf{Team}_3^2\textbf{TxtEx}$.

Let conv be as defined in Equation 9.1. Let m_1^σ, m_2^σ, ..., m_{3j}^σ be a permutation of $1, 2, \ldots, 3j$, such that, for each $r = 1, \ldots, 3j - 1$,

$$(\text{conv}(\mathbf{M}_{m_r^\sigma}, \sigma), m_r^\sigma) \quad < \quad (\text{conv}(\mathbf{M}_{m_{r+1}^\sigma}, \sigma), m_{r+1}^\sigma).$$

Define scientists $\mathbf{M}_1'$, $\mathbf{M}_2'$, and $\mathbf{M}_3'$ so that for each σ:

$$\mathbf{M}_1'(\sigma) \;=\; \mathbf{M}_{m_1^\sigma}(\sigma).$$
$$\mathbf{M}_2'(\sigma) \;=\; \text{majority}(\{\, \mathbf{M}_{m_2^\sigma}(\sigma), \mathbf{M}_{m_3^\sigma}(\sigma), \ldots, \mathbf{M}_{m_{2j}^\sigma}(\sigma) \,\}).$$
$$\mathbf{M}_3'(\sigma) \;=\; \text{majority}(\{\, \mathbf{M}_{m_1^\sigma}(\sigma), \mathbf{M}_{m_2^\sigma}(\sigma), \ldots, \mathbf{M}_{m_{2j+1}^\sigma}(\sigma) \,\}).$$

Now suppose T is a text for $L \in \mathcal{L}$. Consider the following two cases.

Case 1: At least $2j + 1$ of the scientists in the team consisting of scientists $\mathbf{M}_1, \mathbf{M}_2, \ldots, \mathbf{M}_{3j}$ converge on T. In this case, it is easy to verify that $\mathbf{M}_3'$ **TxtEx**-identifies T. Moreover, $\mathbf{M}_1'$ (respectively, $\mathbf{M}_2'$) **TxtEx**-identifies T if $\mathbf{M}_{\lim_{s \to \infty} m_1^{T[s]}}$ **TxtEx**-identifies T (respectively, does not **TxtEx**-identify T).

Case 2: Not case 1. In this case, $\mathbf{M}_1'$ and $\mathbf{M}_2'$ **TxtEx**-identify T.   ∎

We leave it to the reader to modify the above proof to show the following result, which says that probabilistic identification of languages with probability of success at least $\frac{2}{3}$ is the same as team identification of languages with success ratio $\frac{2}{3}$.

9.39 Proposition $\mathbf{Prob}^{2/3}\mathbf{TxtEx} = \mathbf{Team}_3^2\mathbf{TxtEx}$.

Proposition 9.40 below establishes that $\frac{2}{3}$ is indeed the cut-off point at which team identification of languages becomes more powerful than identification by a single scientist.

9.40 Proposition $\mathbf{Team}_3^2\mathbf{TxtEx} - \mathbf{TxtEx}^* \neq \emptyset$.

Proof: Let $\mathcal{L}$ be as in the proof of Proposition 8.22. By Lemma 8.23, $\mathcal{L} \notin \mathbf{TxtEx}^*$. So we need only show that $\mathcal{L} \in \mathbf{Team}_3^2\mathbf{TxtEx}$. Consider a team consisting of three scientists $\mathbf{M}_0$, $\mathbf{M}_1$, and $\mathbf{M}_2$. For each $i \leq 2$, scientist $\mathbf{M}_i$ behaves as follows: On $T[n]$, $\mathbf{M}_i$ outputs the maximum y, if any, such that $\langle i, y \rangle \in content(T[n])$. It is easy to verify that if T is a text for some language in $\mathcal{L}$, then at least two of the scientists will converge in the limit to a grammar for $content(T)$. Thus, $\mathcal{L} \in \mathbf{Team}_3^2\mathbf{TxtEx}$.   ∎

Team Language Identification for Success Ratios $\frac{1}{k}$

We first discuss results for success ratio $\frac{1}{2}$. In the context of functions, the following result immediately follows from Proposition 9.33.

9.41 Corollary (Pitt [149], Pitt and Smith [151]) *For all $j > 0$,* $\mathbf{Team}^{j}_{2j}\mathbf{Ex} = \mathbf{Team}^{1}_{2}\mathbf{Ex}$.

This result says that the collections of functions that can be identified by a team with success ratio $1/2$ are the same as those collections of functions that can be identified by a team employing two scientists and requiring at least one to be successful. Consequently, $\mathbf{Team}^{1}_{2}\mathbf{Ex} = \mathbf{Team}^{2}_{4}\mathbf{Ex} = \mathbf{Team}^{3}_{6}\mathbf{Ex} = \cdots$. In other words, there is nothing to be gained by introducing redundancy into a team learning functions.

Surprisingly, in the context of language identification, Proposition 9.42 below implies that for success ratio $\frac{1}{2}$ there is something to be gained by introducing redundancy. As a consequence of this result, a direct analog of Pitt's connection for function inference does *not* lift to language learning.

A proof of this result can be obtained by a somewhat complex version of the proof of Proposition 9.40. We direct the reader to Jain and Sharma [92] for the details.

9.42 Theorem $\mathbf{Team}^{2}_{4}\mathbf{TxtEx} - \mathbf{Team}^{1}_{2}\mathbf{TxtEx} \neq \emptyset$.

Even more surprising is the next proposition, which implies that the collections of languages that can be identified by teams employing six scientists and requiring at least three to be successful are exactly the same as those collections of languages that can be identified by teams employing two scientists and requiring at least one to be successful!

9.43 Proposition *For all j,* $\mathbf{Team}^{2j+1}_{4j+2}\mathbf{TxtEx} = \mathbf{Team}^{1}_{2}\mathbf{TxtEx}$.

Proof: Let j be as given in the hypothesis of the proposition. Suppose a team consisting of scientists $\mathbf{M}_1, \mathbf{M}_2, \ldots, \mathbf{M}_{4j+2}$ $\mathbf{Team}^{2j+1}_{4j+2}\mathbf{TxtEx}$-identifies $\mathcal{L}$. We describe two scientists, $\mathbf{M}'_1$ and $\mathbf{M}'_2$, that $\mathbf{Team}^{1}_{2}\mathbf{TxtEx}$-identify $\mathcal{L}$.

Let conv be as defined in the proof of Proposition 9.36. Let m^{σ}_1, m^{σ}_2, $\ldots$, m^{σ}_{4j+2} be a permutation of $1, 2, \ldots, 4j + 2$ such that, for each $r = 1, \ldots, 4j + 1$,

$$(\mathrm{conv}(\mathbf{M}_{m^{\sigma}_r}, \sigma), m^{\sigma}_r) < (\mathrm{conv}(\mathbf{M}_{m^{\sigma}_{r+1}}, \sigma), m^{\sigma}_{r+1}).$$

For each r and σ, define $\mathrm{match}(r, \sigma) =$

$$max\left(\left\{ n \leq |\sigma| \,\Big|\, card\left((content(\sigma[n]) - W_{r,|\sigma|}) \cup (W_{r,n} - content(\sigma))\right) \leq i \right\}\right).$$

Let $S_\sigma \subseteq \{i \mid 1 \leq i \leq 2j+1\}$ be the (lexicographically least) set of cardinality j such that, for $1 \leq r, k \leq 2j+1$ with $r \in S_\sigma$ and $k \notin S_\sigma$, we have $\text{match}(\mathbf{M}_{m_r^\sigma}(\sigma), \sigma) \geq \text{match}(\mathbf{M}_{m_k^\sigma}(\sigma), \sigma)$.

For each σ, let $\mathbf{M}_1'$ and $\mathbf{M}_2'$ be such that:

$$\mathbf{M}_1'(\sigma) \quad = \quad \text{majority}(\{\, \mathbf{M}_{m_1^\sigma}(\sigma), \mathbf{M}_{m_2^\sigma}(\sigma), \ldots, \mathbf{M}_{m_{2j+1}^\sigma}(\sigma) \,\}).$$

$$\mathbf{M}_2'(\sigma) \quad = \quad \text{majority}(\{\, \mathbf{M}_{m_{2j+2}^\sigma}(\sigma), \ldots, \mathbf{M}_{m_{3j+2}^\sigma}(\sigma) \,\} \cup \{\, \mathbf{M}_{m_r^\sigma}(\sigma) \mid r \in S_\sigma \,\}).$$

Claim: The team consisting of $\mathbf{M}_1'$ and $\mathbf{M}_2'$ witnesses that $\mathcal{L} \in \textbf{Team}_2^1\textbf{TxtEx}$.

Proof: Let T be a text. If $j+1$ of the first $2j+1$ converging scientists on T converge to a correct grammar, then clearly $\mathbf{M}_1'$ converges to a correct grammar. Otherwise, $\mathbf{M}_2'$ in its selection of S_σ, removes $j+1$ incorrect scientists from the first $2j+1$ converging scientists, ensuring that at least $j+1$ of the scientists captured in S_σ and the next $j+1$ converging scientists (that is, scientists converging in order $2j+2, \ldots, 3j+2$) converge to a correct grammar. This will guarantee that $\mathbf{M}_2'$ converges to a correct grammar. Thus, the claim and the proposition follow. ∎

The picture for team success ratio $\frac{1}{2}$ is completed by Proposition 9.44 below. The proof is complicated; the reader is directed to Jain and Sharma [92] for the details. We leave it to the reader to verify the corollary following the proposition.

9.44 Proposition *For all m and $n \in N^+$ such that $2n$ does not divide m, we have that* $\textbf{Team}_{4n}^{2n}\textbf{TxtEx} - \textbf{Team}_{2m}^m\textbf{TxtEx} \neq \emptyset$.

9.45 Corollary *For all m and $n \in N^+$,* $\textbf{Team}_{2m}^m\textbf{TxtEx} \subseteq \textbf{Team}_{2n}^n\textbf{TxtEx} \iff m$ *divides n or m is odd.*

Proposition 9.44 can also be used to show the next result that shows that probabilistic identification of languages with probability of success at least $\frac{1}{2}$ is strictly more powerful than team identification of languages with success ratio $\frac{1}{2}$ (see Jain and Sharma [92]).

9.46 Proposition $\textbf{Prob}^{1/2}\textbf{TxtEx} - \bigcup_m \textbf{Team}_{2m}^m\textbf{TxtEx} \neq \emptyset$.

The next proposition notes a similar fact about the power of probability over teams. Again, we direct the reader to Jain and Sharma [92] for the details.

9.47 Proposition *For all $k \geq 2$,* $\textbf{Prob}^{1/k}\textbf{TxtEx} - \bigcup_j \textbf{Team}_{j \cdot k}^j\textbf{TxtEx} \neq \emptyset$.

§9.7 Bibliographic notes

Team identification of functions ($\mathbf{Team}_n^1\mathbf{Ex}$) was first defined by Case, motivated by the nonunion theorem of Blum and Blum [18]. It was studied extensively by Smith [178]. The general case of team identification (m out of n) is due to Osherson, Stob, and Weinstein [139]. Probabilistic scientists in the context of learning were first considered by Freivalds [60]. Pitt [149] was the first to notice the connection between team identification and probabilistic identification of functions.

Jain and Sharma [92] investigated team identification of languages. Proposition 9.36 also appears in Osherson, Stob, and Weinstein [139], and may also be shown using an argument from Pitt [149] about probabilistic language learning.

Recently there has been lively interest in the interaction between probability, teams, and the number of allowable mind changes (see Wiehagen, Freivalds, and Kinber [201] and Daley and Kalyanasundaram [48]). Considerable work has been devoted to the special case of 0 mind changes (i.e., finite identification). We direct the reader to Freivalds [63], Jain, Sharma, and Velauthapillai [97], Daley, Pitt, Velauthapillai, and Will [53], Daley, Kalyanasundaram, and Velauthapillai [50]. The problem of teams for Popperian finite identification of functions is addressed by Daley, Kalyanasundaram, and Velauthapillai [51] and Daley and Kalyanasundaram [49].

Allowing teams of finite learners to make up to a finite number of errors in the conjectured hypothesis has been addressed by Daley, Kalyanasundaram, and Velauthapillai[52]. Behaviorally correct function identification by teams has been studied by Daley [46, 47]. In the context of language identification, work has hardly begun on other criteria. We direct the reader to Jain and Sharma [90] for results on finite, vacillatory, and behaviorally correct identification of languages by teams. Meyer [130] has investigated probabilistic identification of indexed families of computable languages (see Meyer [131] for interaction between monotonicity constraints and probabilistic identification of indexed families of computable languages).

An attempt at investigating some general properties of teams has been made by Ambainis [2]. The notion of asymmetric teams has been introduced and studied by Apsītis, Freivalds, and Smith [7].

§9.8 Exercises

9-1 This exercise investigates whether, in the context of functions, anomalies in the final program can be traded for extra team members. Show: For all $i, j \in N$ and $m \in N^+$, $\mathbf{Team}_m^1\mathbf{Ex}^i \subseteq \mathbf{Team}_n^1\mathbf{Ex}^j$, where $n = m(1 + \lfloor\frac{i}{j+1}\rfloor)$.

9-2   This exercise establishes that the tradeoff established in Exercise 9-1 is optimal. For each $r, l \geq 1$, define

$$\mathcal{C}_{r,l} \;=\; \{\, f \in \mathcal{R} \mid \varphi_{f(0)} =^{r \cdot l} f \text{ and } (\exists i \leq r)[\, card(\{\, x \mid \varphi_{f(0)}(x) \neq f(x) \,\}) = i \cdot l \,] \,\}.$$

Show the following:

(a) For all k, $\mathcal{C}_{r,l} \in \mathbf{Team}_m^1 \mathbf{Ex}^{k \cdot l}$, where $m = 1 + \lfloor \frac{r}{k+1} \rfloor$.

(b) $\mathcal{C}_{r,l} \notin \mathbf{Team}_r^1 \mathbf{Ex}^{l-1}$. *Hint:* Use a priority construction.

9-3   Show that $\mathbf{Team}_m^1 \mathbf{Ex}^a \subseteq \mathbf{Team}_n^1 \mathbf{Ex}^b$ if and only if (i) $n \geq m$ and (ii) $b = *$ or $n \geq m \cdot (1 + \lfloor a/(b+1) \rfloor)$.

9-4   Show that: $\bigcup_i \bigcup_m \mathbf{Team}_m^1 \mathbf{Ex}^i = \bigcup_m \mathbf{Team}_m^1 \mathbf{Ex}$.

9-5   (**Pitt [149, 150]**) Adapt the definition of $\mathbf{Prob}^p \mathbf{Ex}$ to incorporate anomalies in the final program. Then establish the following analog of Corollary 9.29: For all $a \in (N \cup \{*\})$, $n \geq 1$, and $p \in (\!(1/(n+1), 1/n]\!]$, $\mathbf{Prob}^p \mathbf{Ex}^a = \mathbf{Team}_n^1 \mathbf{Ex}^a$.

9-6   (**Pitt and Smith [151]**) Establish the following analog of Proposition 9.33: For all $a \in (N \cup \{*\})$ and all $m, n \in N^+$ with $m \leq n$, $\mathbf{Team}_n^m \mathbf{Ex}^a = \mathbf{Team}_{\lfloor \frac{n}{m} \rfloor}^1 \mathbf{Ex}^a = \mathbf{Prob}^{\mathrm{IN}(\frac{m}{n})} \mathbf{Ex}^a$.

9-7   Prove: For all $j, k \in N$ with $\frac{2}{3} < \frac{j}{k} \leq 1$ and $a \in (N \cup \{*\})$, $\mathbf{Team}_k^j \mathbf{TxtEx}^a \subseteq \mathbf{TxtEx}^{\lceil (j+1)/2 \rceil \cdot a}$. Observe that this result implies that, for all $j, k \in N$ with $\frac{2}{3} < \frac{j}{k} \leq 1$, $\mathbf{Team}_k^j \mathbf{TxtEx}^* = \mathbf{TxtEx}^*$.

9-8   Complete the proof of Proposition 9.36.

9-9   Prove: For all $j > 0$ and $a \in N$, $\mathbf{Team}_{3j}^{2j} \mathbf{TxtEx}^a \subseteq \mathbf{Team}_3^2 \mathbf{TxtEx}^{(j+1) \cdot a}$. Observe that this result implies that, for all $j > 0$, $\mathbf{Team}_{3j}^{2j} \mathbf{TxtEx}^* = \mathbf{Team}_3^2 \mathbf{TxtEx}^*$.

9-10   Prove: For all $i, j \in N$, $\mathbf{Team}_{4j+2}^{2j+1} \mathbf{TxtEx}^i \subseteq \mathbf{Team}_2^1 \mathbf{TxtEx}^{i \cdot (j+1)}$. Observe that this result implies that, for j, $\mathbf{Team}_{4j+2}^{2j+1} \mathbf{TxtEx}^* = \mathbf{Team}_2^1 \mathbf{TxtEx}^*$.

10   Learning with Additional Information

§10.1 Introduction

Scientific inquiry almost never starts from scratch. Previous inquiry, common sense, or mere intuition cut back the range of potential realities that scientists are willing or able to consider. In the favorable case, reducing the search space leaves reality among the possibilities still under consideration. (Otherwise, the door is wide open for frustration.) In the case of linguistic development, there is broad agreement that successful language acquisition depends upon limitations in the class of potential languages that the child is willing to impute to her caretakers. Indeed, if all r.e. sets were genuine candidates for natural languages, the child might get stuck conjecturing the finite set of sentences heard to date!

It is clear that our models of inquiry (either scientific or developmental) should represent such *a priori* restrictions on the class of possible hypotheses. To the present point in our discussion, however, such restrictions have been handled in the crudest possible way. We have simply declared a particular collection of functions or languages to be relevant to scientific success, and allowed the scientist to fail with impunity on the others. For example, to say that $\mathcal{L} = \{ N - \{ x \} \mid x \in N \}$ is identifiable means that if the class of possible realities is limited to $\mathcal{L}$, then some scientist can reliably determine which member of these potentialities is actual. The curtailment of possible reality to $\mathcal{L}$ is modeled by including no more than $\mathcal{L}$ in the criterion of successful inquiry. In this way it is possible to ask whether success can be guaranteed if reality is pinned down *a priori* to $\mathcal{L}$. For $\mathcal{L}$ the answer is Yes; the answer is negative for many other collections of functions and languages — which is what makes the subject interesting. Nevertheless, much is missing from our account of the scientist's starting point. Not every collection of functions or languages need constitute a feasible or meaningful restriction on hypotheses, yet our theory provides no natural means for enforcing such a distinction.

The issue of scientific starting points is so fundamental and complex that we cannot hope to provide much insight at the present stage of theory construction. (Perhaps the reader will consent to visit us again when the book is in its fourth or fifth edition?) We would nonetheless like to discuss one aspect of the topic for which some results have been obtained. The class of plausible hypotheses that come to the mind of a scientist might interact with the character of the true hypothesis. In other words, since the scientist is part of (or at least connected to) the reality she is trying to discover, she might have a certain set of ideas if the world is one way, and a different set if the world is another. To take the starkest example, if DNA had different chemical properties than it does then geneticists (whose minds are partly determined by their own stock of DNA) might have started off with a different set of potential hypotheses about enzyme production and cell regulation. This kind of interaction suggests a richer representation of scientists, to be pursued in the present chapter. Specifically, scientists will be fitted out with a numerical parameter that communicates partial information about the reality inscribed in the text they are examining. In this way, the correct hypothesis impacts the class of potential realities for which the scientist is suited. We shall consider two such parameterization schemes, as follows.

Upper bounds on hypotheses.   First, we shall assume that scientists have prior information about the size of a correct explanation for the phenomenon under investigation. Specifically, they are given an upper bound on the minimum size program for the function they are facing. Section 10.2 considers the extent to which this kind of information facilitates inquiry.

Approximate hypotheses.   Second, we assume that scientists have approximately true theories about the language or function with which Nature confronts them. The utility of different kinds of approximations will be examined in Section 10.3.

§10.2   Upper bound on the size of hypothesis

We begin by considering the impact on function identification of advance information about the size of the smallest, explanatory hypothesis for the incoming data. Then we consider the analogous issue for language learning.

§10.2.1   Function identification with program size upper bound

Recall from the discussion on page 23 that our standard program size measure is $\lambda p.p$. That is, the size of program index p is simply p itself. This measure, while not completely natural, is mathematically convenient and, as discussed in Chapter 2, recursion theoretically equivalent to any other program size measure (Definition 2.8). Thus, in the following, "an upper bound on the size of the minimal sized hypothesis for $f \in \mathcal{R}$" shall mean "an upper bound on the minimal index for f." Such additional information can be incorporated into the identification paradigm by viewing a scientist as computing a mapping from $N \times \mathrm{SEG}$ into N, where the first argument is the size bound. We let $\mathbf{M}$, with or without decorations, range over such scientists; it will be clear from context if we mean a scientist with or without additional information. Thus, $\mathbf{M}(x, \sigma)$ denotes the hypothesis conjectured by scientist $\mathbf{M}$ on evidential state σ and additional information x. The following definition formalizes the notion of convergence of a scientist on a function in the presence of additional information.

10.1 Definition $\mathbf{M}(x, f)\!\downarrow$ (read: $\mathbf{M}$ on f with additional information x converges) just in case there exists an i such that for all but finitely many n, $\mathbf{M}(x, f[n]) = i$. If $\mathbf{M}(x, f)\!\downarrow$, then $\mathbf{M}(x, f)$ is defined $=$ the unique i such that for all but finitely many n, $\mathbf{M}(x, f[n]) = i$; otherwise, $\mathbf{M}(x, f)$ is said to be undefined.

The next definition extends the $\mathbf{Ex}$ paradigm to model situations where a scientist, in addition to being fed a graph of the function, is also presented with an upper bound on the minimal program index for the function. The definition below also models cases in which an upper bound may only be available for the minimal program index for a finite variant of the function being identified. To this end, for $c \in (N \cup \{*\})$, we let $MinProg_c(f)$ denote the minimal program index in the φ-programming system that computes f with at most c errors, i.e., $MinProg_c(f) = \mu i.[\varphi_i =^c f]$.

10.2 Definition Let $a, c \in (N \cup \{*\})$.

(a) $\mathbf{M}$ $\mathbf{Bex}^{a,c}$*-identifies* f (written: $f \in \mathbf{Bex}^{a,c}(\mathbf{M})$) just in case, for all $x \geq MinProg_c(f)$, $\mathbf{M}(x, f)\!\downarrow$ and $\varphi_{\mathbf{M}(x,f)} =^a f$.

(b) $\mathbf{Bex}^{a,c} = \{\, \mathcal{S} \mid \mathcal{S} \subseteq \mathbf{Bex}^{a,c}(\mathbf{M}) \text{ for some } \mathbf{M} \,\}$.

Thus a scientist $\mathbf{M}$ $\mathbf{Bex}^{a,c}$-identifies f just in case $\mathbf{M}$, fed the graph of f and an upper bound on $MinProg_c(f)$, converges to an index for a program that computes f with at most a errors. The notion of $\mathbf{Bex}^{0,0}$-identification was first studied by Freivalds and Wiehagen [67]. In the $\mathbf{Bex}^{a,c}$ paradigm, a is the bound on the number of errors allowed in the converged program and c is the bound on the number of errors allowed in the additional information. The reader should note that in this paradigm a scientist may converge to different indexes for different upper bounds. However, if we further require that the final converged index be the same for any upper bound, we get a new identification paradigm defined below.

10.3 Definition Let $a, c \in (N \cup \{*\})$.

(a) **M UniBex^{a,c}-identifies** f (written: $f \in \mathbf{UniBex}^{a,c}(\mathbf{M})$) just in case, for some i with $\varphi_i =^a f$, we have that for every $x \geq MinProg_c(f)$, $\mathbf{M}(x, f)\!\downarrow = i$.

(b) $\mathbf{UniBex}^{a,c} = \{ \mathcal{S} \mid \mathcal{S} \subseteq \mathbf{UniBex}^{a,c}(\mathbf{M})$ for some $\mathbf{M} \}$.

The **UniBex^{0,0}**-identification criterion was first introduced by Freivalds and Wiehagen [67]. The following proposition is immediate.

10.4 Proposition Let $a, a_1, a_2 \in (N \cup \{*\})$ such that $a_1 \leq a_2$. Let $c, c_1, c_2 \in (N \cup \{*\})$ such that $c_1 \leq c_2$. Then,

(a) $\mathbf{Bex}^{a_1,c} \subseteq \mathbf{Bex}^{a_2,c}$.

(b) $\mathbf{Bex}^{a,c_1} \supseteq \mathbf{Bex}^{a,c_2}$.

(c) $\mathbf{UniBex}^{a_1,c} \subseteq \mathbf{UniBex}^{a_2,c}$.

(d) $\mathbf{UniBex}^{a,c_1} \supseteq \mathbf{UniBex}^{a,c_2}$.

Proposition 10.4 suggests that the highest quality additional information is an upper bound on the minimal 0-error program and the worst quality is an upper bound on the minimal $*$-error program. The natural question is: upon replacing the $\leq$'s in the hypothesis of the above proposition with $<$'s, do the containments become strict? Another immediate observation is that for $a, c \in (N \cup \{*\})$, $\mathbf{UniBex}^{a,c} \subseteq \mathbf{Bex}^{a,c}$. Again, we would like to know whether this containment is strict. The results below, together with the exercises, answer these questions.

The next proposition shows that even the best quality **UniBex** type of additional information does not always compensate for allowing an extra error in the final program. That is, there are collections of functions for which an $(a + 1)$-error program can be identified, but for which an a-error program cannot be **UniBex**-identified even if the scientist has knowledge of an upper bound on the minimal 0-error program index of the function.

10.5 Proposition For all $a \in N$, $\mathbf{Ex}^{a+1} - \mathbf{UniBex}^{a,0} \neq \emptyset$.

Proof: Let $\mathcal{S} = \{f \mid \varphi_{f(0)} =^{a+1} f\}$, which clearly is in $\mathbf{Ex}^{a+1}$. Fix an arbitrary scientist $\mathbf{M}$. We shall exhibit a function $f \in \mathcal{S}$ that $\mathbf{M}$ fails to $\mathbf{UniBex}^{a,0}$-identify. The f in question will be computed by one of a repetition-free, r.e. sequence of programs, $p(0), p(1), p(2), \ldots$ constructed through implicit use of the operator recursion theorem (Theorem 2.6).

We give an informal effective construction of the $\varphi_{p(i)}$'s in successive stages $s = 1$, $2, 3, \cdots$. At the beginning of stage $s > 0$, $\varphi_{p(s)}$ will be completely undefined and $\varphi_{p(0)}$ will be defined only on the initial segment $\{0, \ldots, n_s - 1\}$, where n_s denotes the least number not yet in $domain(\varphi_{p(0)})$. We initialize $\varphi_{p(0)}(0)$ to $p(0)$ and go to stage 1.

Begin (*Stage s*)

Set $\varphi_{p(0)}(n_s) = 1$, and for each $x \leq n_s$, set $\varphi_{p(s)}(x) = \varphi_{p(0)}(x)$.

Let $j = \mathbf{M}(p(0), \varphi_{p(0)}[n_s + 1])$.

If $\mathbf{M}(p(s), \varphi_{p(s)}[n_s + 1]) = j$, then go to step 1, else go to step 2.

Step 1.

Let n'_s be the least x not yet in $domain(\varphi_{p(0)})$.

For $l = 0, \ldots, a$, set $\varphi_{p(s)}(n'_s + l) = 0$.

Set $y = n'_s + a + 1$.

Repeat

Set $\varphi_{p(s)}(y) = \varphi_{p(0)}(y) = 0$ and reset $y = y + 1$.

until, if ever, at least one of the following two conditions holds.

Condition 1A: $\mathbf{M}(p(s), \varphi_{p(s)}[y]) \neq j$.

Condition 1B: $(\exists l \mid 0 \leq l \leq a)[\Phi_j(n'_s + l) \leq y]$.

Step 1a. If Condition 1A holds then go to step 2.

Step 1b. If Condition 1B, but not $1A$, holds then:

Let l be the least convergence point discovered in Condition 1B.

Set $\varphi_{p(0)}(n'_s + l) = \varphi_j(n'_s + l) + 1$.

For each $r \leq a$, set $\varphi_{p(0)}(n'_s + r) = 0$ if $r \neq l$.

Go to stage $s + 1$.

Step 2.

Let n''_s be the least x not yet in $domain(\varphi_{p(s)})$.

For each $x < n''_s$ not yet in $domain(\varphi_{p(0)})$, set $\varphi_{p(0)}(x) = \varphi_{p(s)}(x)$.

Repeat

Set $\varphi_{p(0)}(n''_s) = \varphi_{p(s)}(n''_s) = 0$ and reset $n''_s = n''_s + 1$.

until, if ever, at least one of the following two conditions holds.

Condition 2A: $\mathbf{M}(p(0), \varphi_{p(0)}[n''_s]) \neq j$.

Condition 2B: $\mathbf{M}(p(s), \varphi_{p(s)}[n''_s]) = j$.

Step 2a. If Condition 2A holds then go to stage $s + 1$.

Step 2b. If Condition 2B, but not 2A, holds then go to Step 1.

End (*Stage s*)

Now consider the following two cases.

Case 1: All stages halt. In this case, let $p(0)$ be the additional information and $f = \varphi_{p(0)}$. Clearly, $\varphi_{p(0)}$ is total and is in $\mathcal{S}$. We then have two subcases.

Subcase 1a: $\mathbf{M}(p(0), f)$ diverges. In this case, $\mathbf{M}$ fails to $\mathbf{UniBex}^{a,0}$-identify f.

Subcase 1b: $\mathbf{M}(p(0), f)$ converges to j at stage s. In this case, the only way in which all stages halt is by the execution of step 1b infinitely often. But, $\varphi_{\mathbf{M}(p(0),f)}$ is then infinitely different from f.

Case 2: Some stage s begins but does not halt. We then have three subcases.

Subcase 2a: Steps 1 and 2 are both executed infinitely often. In this case, let $f = \varphi_{p(0)} = \varphi_{p(s)}$, which is clearly in $\mathcal{S}$. Now, the only way that steps 1 and 2 can be executed infinitely often without leaving stage s is by the repeated execution of steps 1a and 2b. Thus, $\mathbf{M}$ with additional information $p(s)$ infinitely often outputs j without converging to j. Therefore, $\mathbf{M}$ on f with additional information $p(s)$ fails to converge.

Subcase 2b: In stage s, the algorithm eventually enters and never leaves step 1. In this case, let $f = \varphi_{p(s)}$. Since $\varphi_{p(0)} =^{a+1} \varphi_{p(s)}$, we have $f \in \mathcal{S}$. Observe that $\mathbf{M}$ on f with additional information $p(s)$ converges to j because, otherwise, Condition 1A would succeed. Also observe that φ_j does not converge on at least $a + 1$ values because, otherwise, Condition 1B would succeed. Thus, $\mathbf{M}$ fails to $\mathbf{UniBex}^{a,0}$-identify f.

Subcase 2c: In stage s, the algorithm eventually enters and never leaves step 2. In this case, let $f = \varphi_{p(0)} = \varphi_{p(s)}$, which is clearly in $\mathcal{S}$. Observe that $\mathbf{M}$ on f with additional information $p(s)$ does not converge to j because, otherwise, Condition 2B would succeed. Also observe that $\mathbf{M}$ on f with additional information $p(0)$ converges to j because, otherwise, Condition 2A would succeed. Thus, $\mathbf{M}$ fails to $\mathbf{UniBex}^{a,0}$-identify f.

As the above cases and subcases are exhaustive, we have that $\mathbf{M}$ fails to $\mathbf{UniBex}^{a,0}$-identify $\mathcal{S}$. ∎

10.6 Corollary *Suppose* $c \in (N \cup \{*\})$. *Then,* $\mathbf{UniBex}^{0,c} \subset \mathbf{UniBex}^{1,c} \subset \cdots \subset \mathbf{UniBex}^{i,c} \subset \mathbf{UniBex}^{i+1,c} \subset \cdots \subset \mathbf{UniBex}^{*,c}$.

The corollary implies that if one keeps fixed the bound on the number of errors allowed in the additional information, then larger collections of functions can be $\mathbf{UniBex}$-identified by allowing extra errors in the final inferred program. The proof of the corollary is left to the reader.

A natural question to ask at this point is whether a similar hierarchy also holds for **Bex**-identification. The next proposition shows that only a weak analog of Proposition 10.5 for **Bex**-identification is possible.

10.7 Proposition *For all $n \in N$, $\mathcal{R} \in \mathbf{Bex}^{n,n}$.*

Proof: Fix n. We construct a scientist **M** that $\mathbf{Bex}^{n,n}$-identifies all of $\mathcal{R}$. Recall from Chapter 2 that, for each i, s, and x, we define $\varphi_{i,s}(x) = \varphi_i(x)$, if both $x < s$ and $\Phi_i(x) < s$; and $\varphi_{i,s}(x)$ is undefined otherwise. For each j, σ, and x, define:

$$
\begin{aligned}
errors(\sigma, j) &= \{\, y < |\sigma| \mid \varphi_{j,|\sigma|}(y)\!\downarrow \neq \hat{\sigma}(y) \,\}. \\
S_{\sigma,x} &= \{\, j \leq x \mid card(errors(\sigma, j)) \leq n \,\}.
\end{aligned}
$$

Intuitively, $S_{\sigma,x}$ is a set of programs that appear correct for the given additional information x and the finite initial segment σ. For each j and σ, let $patch(\sigma, j)$ be a program that computes

$$
\lambda y. \begin{cases} \hat{\sigma}(y), & \text{if } y \in errors(\sigma, j); \\ \varphi_j(y), & \text{otherwise.} \end{cases}
$$

Thus, if j is a program that computes f with at most n errors, then, for sufficiently large s, program $patch(f[s], j)$ will not make any convergent errors. For each finite set A, let $Unify(A)$ be a program that computes

$$
\lambda y. \begin{cases} \varphi_i(y), & \text{if } \langle i, t \rangle \text{ is the least number such that } i \in A \text{ and } \varphi_{i,t}(y)\!\downarrow; \\ \uparrow, & \text{if no such } \langle i, t \rangle \text{ exists.} \end{cases}
$$

Clearly, we can take *errors*, *patch*, and *Unify* to be recursive. Finally, for each σ and x, we define

$$
\mathbf{M}(x, \sigma) = Unify(\{\, patch(\sigma, j) \mid j \in S_{\sigma,x} \,\}).
$$

Fix an $f \in \mathcal{R}$ and an $x \geq MinProg_n(f)$. Then for sufficiently large s, the only errors program $Unify(\{\, patch(\sigma, j) \mid j \in S_{\sigma,x} \,\})$ makes are divergent errors whose total count is bounded by n. Therefore, **M** $\mathbf{Bex}^{n,n}$-identifies f as required. ∎

Let us contrast the result above with the following proposition which shows that the $n = *$ analog of Proposition 10.7 fails.

10.8 Proposition $\mathcal{R} \notin \mathbf{Bex}^{*,*}$.

Proof: Consider the following collections of functions:

$$\mathcal{S}_1 = \{ f \mid \varphi_{f(0)} = f \}.$$
$$\mathcal{S}_2 = \{ f \mid (\overset{\infty}{\forall} x)[f(x) = 0] \}.$$
$$\mathcal{S} = \mathcal{S}_1 \cup \mathcal{S}_2.$$

We argue that $\mathcal{S} \notin \mathbf{Bex}^{*,*}$. Suppose by way of contradiction that a scientist $\mathbf{M}$ $\mathbf{Bex}^{*,*}$-identifies $\mathcal{S}$. Let i_0 be a program for $\lambda x.0$, the everywhere 0 function. Let $\mathbf{M}'$ be a scientist (which uses no additional information) such that, for each σ,

$$\mathbf{M}'(\sigma) = \begin{cases} 0, & \text{if } \sigma = \epsilon; \\ \mathbf{M}(max(\widehat{\sigma}(0), i_0), \sigma), & \text{otherwise.} \end{cases}$$

For any $f \in \mathcal{S}$, $max(f(0), i_0)$ is clearly an upper bound on the minimal program for a finite variant of f, hence $\mathbf{M}'$ $\mathbf{Ex}^*$-identifies every $f \in \mathcal{S}$. This is a contradiction, since it was shown in Theorem 4.25 that $\mathcal{S} \notin \mathbf{Ex}^*$. Therefore, $\mathcal{S} \notin \mathbf{Bex}^{*,*}$. ∎

Proposition 10.7 limits us to the following weak analog of Proposition 10.5 for **Bex**-identification.

10.9 Proposition *Suppose* $a \in N$. *Then,* $\mathbf{Ex}^{a+1} - \mathbf{Bex}^{a,a+1} \neq \emptyset$.

Proof: Let $\mathcal{S} = \{ f \in \mathcal{R} \mid \varphi_{f(0)} =^{a+1} f \}$, which is clearly in $\mathbf{Ex}^{a+1}$. Suppose by way of contradiction that there is a scientist $\mathbf{M}$ that $\mathbf{Bex}^{a,a+1}$-identifies $\mathcal{S}$. Let $\mathbf{M}'$ be a scientist (without any additional information) such that, for all σ,

$$\mathbf{M}'(\sigma) = \begin{cases} 0, & \text{if } \sigma = \epsilon; \\ \mathbf{M}(\widehat{\sigma}(0), \sigma), & \text{otherwise.} \end{cases}$$

Since for any $f \in \mathcal{S}$, $f(0)$ is an upper bound on $MinProg_{a+1}(f)$, it follows that for each $f \in \mathcal{S}$, $\varphi_{\mathbf{M}'(f)} =^a f$. Thus, $\mathbf{M}'$ $\mathbf{Ex}^a$-identifies $\mathcal{S}$. This is a contradiction, since it was shown in Proposition 6.5 that $\mathcal{S} \notin \mathbf{Ex}^a$. ∎

Propositions 10.9, 10.7, and 10.8 yield the following two corollaries.

10.10 Corollary *For each* $c \in N$, $\mathbf{Bex}^{0,c} \subset \mathbf{Bex}^{1,c} \subset \cdots \subset \mathbf{Bex}^{c,c} = \mathbf{Bex}^{c+1,c} = \cdots =$ *the powerset of* $\mathcal{R}$.

10.11 Corollary $\mathbf{Bex}^{0,*} \subset \mathbf{Bex}^{1,*} \subset \mathbf{Bex}^{2,*} \subset \cdots \subset \mathbf{Bex}^{n,*} \subset \mathbf{Bex}^{n+1,*} \subset \cdots \subset \mathbf{Bex}^{*,*} \subset$ *the powerset of* $\mathcal{R}$.

The first corollary says that if we fix the number of errors allowed in the additional information, then larger collections of functions can be **Bex**-identified by allowing extra errors in the final inferred program. This gain is achieved, however, only so far as the bound on the number of errors in the final inferred program does not exceed the bound on the number of errors allowed in the additional information. When these two bounds become equal, there is nothing to be gained by allowing extra errors in the final program. The second corollary says that, on the other hand, if a finite but unbounded number of errors is allowed in the additional information, allowing extra errors in the final program always yields a gain.

Thus far we have concentrated on showing the advantage of allowing extra errors in the final inferred program. We now consider the effects of allowing extra errors in the additional information. The next result shows that there are collections of functions for which an accurate program can be **UniBex**-identified in the presence of an upper bound on the minimal size c-error program, but for which even a $*$-error program cannot be **UniBex**-identified in the presence of an upper bound on the minimal size $(c+1)$-error program.

10.12 Proposition *For each $c \in N$,* $\mathbf{UniBex}^{0,c} - \mathbf{UniBex}^{*,c+1} \neq \emptyset$.

Proof: Consider the following collections of functions:

$$\begin{aligned}
\mathcal{S}_1 &= \{\, f \mid \varphi_{f(0)} = f \text{ and } (\overset{\infty}{\exists} x)[\, f(x) > 0\,]\,\}. \\
\mathcal{S}_2 &= \{\, f \mid card(\{x \mid f(x) \neq 0\}) \leq MinProg_c(f)\,\}. \\
\mathcal{S} &= \mathcal{S}_1 \cup \mathcal{S}_2.
\end{aligned}$$

We exhibit a scientist $\mathbf{M}_0$ that $\mathbf{UniBex}^{0,c}$-identifies $\mathcal{S}$. First we define an auxiliary function F such that, for any finite set D,

$$\varphi_{F(D)} \;=\; \lambda y. \begin{cases} min(\{\, z \mid \langle y, z \rangle \in D\,\}), & \text{if } \{\, z \mid \langle y, z \rangle \in D\,\} \text{ is nonempty;} \\ 0, & \text{otherwise.} \end{cases}$$

Now, for each x and σ, define

$$\mathbf{M}_0(x, \sigma) =$$

$$\begin{cases} \widehat{\sigma}(0), & \text{if (i) } card(\{\, y < |\sigma| \mid \widehat{\sigma}(y) > 0\,\}) > x; \\[2ex] F\left(\left\{\, \langle y, \widehat{\sigma}(y)\rangle \;\middle|\; \begin{array}{l} y < |\sigma| \ \& \\ \widehat{\sigma}(y) > 0 \end{array} \,\right\}\right), & \text{(ii) otherwise.} \end{cases}$$

Fix an $f \in \mathcal{S}_1$ and an $x \in N$. Clearly, condition (i) in definition of $\mathbf{M}_0$ will succeed for sufficiently large initial segments of f. Thus, $\mathbf{M}_0(x, f){\downarrow} = f(0)$, which by definition of $\mathcal{S}_1$, is a program for f.

Fix an $f \in \mathcal{S}_2$ and an $x \geq MinProg_c(f)$. Then, for any initial segment of f and this x, condition (i) will fail. Thus, for any sufficiently large n, $\mathbf{M}_0(x, f[n])$ will stabilize to $F(\{\, x \mid f(x) \neq 0 \,\})$, a program for f.

Therefore, $\mathcal{S} \in \mathbf{UniBex}^{0,c}$.

The proof of $\mathcal{S} \notin \mathbf{UniBex}^{*,c+1}$ is a diagonalization employing the operator recursion theorem (Theorem 2.6). We refer the reader to Jain and Sharma [86] for the proof. ∎

The next proposition illustrates the power of even a small amount of additional information. The proposition says that there are collections of functions that can be **UniBex**-identified in the presence of an upper bound on the minimal size $*$-error program, but which cannot be **Bc**-identified even if the scientist is allowed to output programs that commit no more than a predetermined number of errors.

10.13 Proposition *For each* $a \in N$, $\mathbf{UniBex}^{0,*} - \mathbf{Bc}^a \neq \emptyset$.

The proof of this result is the subject of Exercise 10-3. Propositions 10.12 and 10.13 have the following corollary on **UniBex**-identification.

10.14 Corollary *Suppose* $a \in (N \cup \{*\})$. *Then:*

(a) $\mathbf{UniBex}^{a,*} \supset \mathbf{Ex}^a$.

(b) $\mathbf{UniBex}^{a,0} \supset \mathbf{UniBex}^{a,1} \supset \cdots \supset \mathbf{UniBex}^{a,i} \supset \mathbf{UniBex}^{a,i+1} \supset \cdots \supset \mathbf{UniBex}^{a,*}$.

Part (a) of the corollary says that even the worst quality of additional information (an upper bound on a minimal $*$-error program) yields extra learning power over $\mathbf{Ex}^a$-identification. Part (b) says that if the bound on the number of errors allowed in the final inferred program is fixed in advance, then decreasing the quality of the additional information results in a reduction in learning power with respect to **UniBex**-identification. The proof of the above corollary is left to the reader. A related result about **Bex**-identification is the subject of Exercise 10-4.

We end this section by presenting a result that implies the advantages of **Bex**-identification over **UniBex**-identification.

10.15 Proposition *Suppose* $c \in N$. *Then,* $\mathbf{Bex}^{0,c} - \mathbf{UniBex}^{*,0} \neq \emptyset$.

10.16 Corollary *For all $a \in (N \cup \{*\})$ and all $c \in N$,* $\mathbf{UniBex}^{a,c} \subset \mathbf{Bex}^{a,c}$.

Thus, if the bound on the number of errors allowed in both the additional information and the final program are fixed, then requiring a scientist to converge to the same program for any upper bound is restrictive.

Proof (of Proposition 10.15): Let $\mathcal{S} = \{ f \mid (\forall y, z)[f(\langle y, 0 \rangle) = f(\langle y, z \rangle)] \}$.

Fix an $f \in \mathcal{S}$ and an $x \geq MinProg_c(f)$. Since $\mathcal{R} \in \mathbf{Bex}^{c,c}$, given f and x, one can infer in the limit a program p such that $\varphi_p =^c f$. For each y, let w_y be the unique number such that $card(\{z < 2c + 1 \mid \varphi_p(\langle y, z \rangle) = w_y\}) \geq c + 1$. (The uniqueness of w_y follows from the definition of $\mathcal{S}$ and the fact that $\varphi_p =^c f$.) Let $modify(p)$ be a program obtained from p such that, for all y and z, $\varphi_{modify(p)}(\langle y, z \rangle) = w_y$, where w_y is as defined above. It follows immediately that $modify(p)$ is a program for f.

It thus follows that $\mathcal{S} \in \mathbf{Bex}^{0,c}$.

Suppose $\mathbf{M}$ $\mathbf{UniBex}^{*,0}$-identifies $\mathcal{S}$. Then it is easy to modify $\mathbf{M}$ to $\mathbf{UniBex}^{*,0}$-identify $\mathcal{R}$. But as $\mathcal{R} \notin \mathbf{UniBex}^{*,0}$ (see the remark in Exercise 10-7), this is a contradiction. Hence, $\mathcal{S} \notin \mathbf{UniBex}^{*,0}$. ∎

It is open at present whether Proposition 10.15 can be extended to show $\mathbf{Bex}^{0,*} - \mathbf{UniBex}^{*,0} \neq \emptyset$. Similar notions of additional information for the $\mathbf{Bc}$ paradigm are treated in the exercises.

§10.2.2 Language identification with an upper bound on grammar size

Additional information for a language-learning scientist can be modeled as an upper bound on the minimal index grammar for the language to be learned. We view scientists that learn languages in the presence of such additional information as computing a mapping $N \times \mathrm{SEQ} \to N$. Our treatment of languages is thus analogous to that of functions. For this reason we highlight only basic definitions and results that turn out differently from the functional context.

For each $c \in (N \cup \{*\})$ and language L, $MinGram_c(L)$ denotes the minimal grammar in the φ-system that accepts L with at most c errors. That is, $MinGram_c(L) = \mu i.[W_i =^c L]$.

10.17 Definition $\mathbf{M}(x, T){\downarrow}$ (read: $\mathbf{M}$ *on text T with additional information x converges*) just in case there is an i such that for all but finitely many n, $\mathbf{M}(x, T[n]) = i$, in which case $\mathbf{M}(x, T)$ is defined to be this i. If no such i exists, then $\mathbf{M}(x, T)$ is said to be undefined.

The following two definitions state the text analogs of the **Bex** and **UniBex** paradigms.

10.18 Definition Let $a, c \in (N \cup \{*\})$.

(a) **M TxtBex**^{a,c}-*identifies* L (written: $L \in \mathbf{TxtBex}^{a,c}(\mathbf{M})$) just in case, for all $x \geq MinGram_c(L)$, there is an i with $W_i =^a L$ such that, for each text T for L, we have $\mathbf{M}(x, T)\downarrow = i$.

(b) $\mathbf{TxtBex}^{a,c} = \{ \mathcal{L} \mid \mathcal{L} \subseteq \mathbf{TxtBex}^{a,c}(\mathbf{M}) \text{ for some } \mathbf{M} \}$.

10.19 Definition Let $a, c \in (N \cup \{*\})$.

(a) **M TxtUniBex**^{a,c}-*identifies* L (written: $L \in \mathbf{TxtUniBex}^{a,c}(\mathbf{M})$) just in case there is an i with $W_i =^a L$ such that, for each $x \geq MinGram_c(L)$ and each text T for L, we have $\mathbf{M}(x, T)\downarrow = i$.

(b) $\mathbf{TxtUniBex}^{a,c} = \{ \mathcal{L} \mid \mathcal{L} \subseteq \mathbf{TxtUniBex}^{a,c}(\mathbf{M}) \text{ for some } \mathbf{M} \}$.

Thus, **M TxtBex**^{a,c}-identifies L just in case **M**, fed a text for L and an upper bound on $MinGram_c(L)$, converges to a grammar that accepts L with at most a errors. As in the case of functions, the reader should note that in the $\mathbf{TxtBex}^{a,c}$ paradigms, the scientist may converge to different grammars for different upper bounds.

Using the technique demonstrated in Chapter 6 (see, for example, the proof of Proposition 6.19), it is easy to see that the diagonalization results about **Bex**-identification and **UniBex**-identification yield analogous results for **TxtBex**-identification and **TxtUniBex**-identification. For example, the following result immediately follows from Proposition 10.5.

10.20 Proposition *For each* $a \in N$, $\mathbf{TxtEx}^{a+1} - \mathbf{TxtUniBex}^{a,0} \neq \emptyset$.

10.21 Corollary *For each* $c \in (N \cup \{*\})$, $\mathbf{TxtUniBex}^{0,c} \subset \mathbf{TxtUniBex}^{1,c} \subset \cdots \subset \mathbf{TxtUniBex}^{i,c} \subset \mathbf{TxtUniBex}^{i+1,c} \subset \cdots \subset \mathbf{TxtUniBex}^{*,c}$.

The corollary says that by keeping the number of errors in the additional information fixed, larger collections of languages can be **TxtUniBex**-identified by increasing the bound on the number of errors in the final inferred grammar. (We note that Corollary 10.21 may be directly argued from Corollary 10.6.)

One might attempt to use Corollary 10.10 in a similar fashion in order to obtain an analogous hierarchy result about **TxtBex**-identification. However, this strategy yields only the partial hierarchy:

for all $c \in N$, $\mathbf{TxtBex}^{0,c} \subset \mathbf{TxtBex}^{1,c} \subset \cdots \subset \mathbf{TxtBex}^{c,c}$.

Corollary 10.10 provides no information about whether $\mathbf{TxtBex}^{c,c} = \mathbf{TxtBex}^{c+1,c}$ or $\mathbf{TxtBex}^{c,c} \subset \mathbf{TxtBex}^{c+1,c}$. This is because only diagonalization results can be translated from functions to languages. To obtain the full hierarchy we establish the following proposition which says that there is a collection of languages such that, for each member language L, an $(a+1)$-error grammar can be identified, but an a-error grammar cannot always be **TxtBex**-identified even if the scientist is given the best possible additional information—an upper bound on $MinGram_0(L)$.

10.22 Proposition *Suppose $a \in N$. Then, $\mathbf{TxtEx}^{a+1} - \mathbf{TxtBex}^{a,0} \neq \emptyset$.*

Proof: Let $\mathcal{L} = \{L \mid L =^{a+1} N\}$, which is clearly in $\mathbf{TxtEx}^{a+1}$. Suppose by way of contradiction that some scientist **M** $\mathbf{TxtBex}^{a,0}$-identifies $\mathcal{L}$. Then, by Kleene's recursion theorem (Theorem 2.3), there exists a grammar e informally described in stages below.

Let i_N be a grammar for N. Let W_e^s denote the finite subset of W_e enumerated before stage s. Let $\sigma_0 = \emptyset$ and $w = max(\{e, i_N\})$. Go to stage 0.

Begin *(Stage s)*

   Step 1.

      Search for a σ extending σ_s until at least one of

         Condition 1A. $\mathbf{M}(w, \sigma) \neq \mathbf{M}(w, \sigma_s)$.

         Condition 1B. A set $D \subseteq (W_{\mathbf{M}(w,\sigma_s)} - W_e^s)$ of cardinality $a+1$ is found.

      holds.

      If Condition 1A held, go to Step 2, otherwise go to Step 3.

   Step 2. *(The mind change case.)*

      Set $m = max(content(\sigma)) + 1$.

      Enumerate all of $\{0, \ldots, m\}$ into W_e.

      Let σ_{s+1} be an extension of σ with $content(\sigma_{s+1}) = \{0, \ldots, m\}$.

      Go to stage $s+1$.

   Step 3. *(A suitable D was found in Condition 1B.)*

Set $m = max(W_e^s \cup D)$.

Enumerate all of $(\{0, \ldots, m\} - D)$ into W_e.

Let σ' be an extension of σ_s such that $content(\sigma') = (\{0, \ldots, m\} - D)$.

Repeat

Set $m = m + 1$.

Enumerate m into W_e.

Set $\sigma' = \sigma' \diamond m$.

until $\mathbf{M}(w, \sigma_s) \neq \mathbf{M}(w, \sigma')$.

Enumerate all of D into W_e.

Let σ_{s+1} be an extension of σ' with $content(\sigma_{s+1}) = [W_e$ enumerated until now$]$.

Go to stage $s + 1$.

End (*Stage s*)

Now consider the following cases:

Case 1: Infinitely many stages halt. In this case, let $L = W_e = N \in \mathcal{L}$. But, $\mathbf{M}$ on text $T = \bigcup_{s \in N} \sigma_s$ for L with additional information $w = max(\{e, i_N\})$ fails to converge.

Case 2: Some stage, s, begins but does not halt.

Subcase 2a: The construction never leaves Step 1 in stage s. In this case, let $L = N \in \mathcal{L}$. Note that $\mathbf{M}$ on all extensions of σ_s converges to $\mathbf{M}(w, \sigma_s)$, and $W_{\mathbf{M}(w, \sigma_s)}$ is finite. Thus, $\mathbf{M}$ fails to $\mathbf{TxtBex}^{a,0}$-identify N.

Subcase 2b: The construction enters, but never leaves Step 3 in stage s. In this case, let $L = N - D = W_e \in \mathcal{L}$. $\mathbf{M}$ on a text for L converges to $\mathbf{M}(w, \sigma_s)$. But, $W_{\mathbf{M}(w, \sigma_s)} - W_e = D$. Thus, $W_{\mathbf{M}(w, \sigma_s)}$ is not an a-variant of L.

From the above cases, it follows that $\mathbf{M}$ fails to $\mathbf{TxtBex}^{a,0}$-identify $\mathcal{L}$. ■

The above result has the following corollary that summarizes the advantages of allowing extra errors in the final converged grammar for $\mathbf{TxtBex}$-identification.

10.23 Corollary *For each $c \in (N \cup \{*\})$, we have* $\mathbf{TxtBex}^{0,c} \subset \mathbf{TxtBex}^{1,c} \subset \mathbf{TxtBex}^{2,c} \subset \cdots \subset \mathbf{TxtBex}^{i,c} \subset \mathbf{TxtBex}^{i+1,c} \subset \cdots \subset \mathbf{TxtBex}^{*,c}$.

The advantage of a better quality of additional information, for both $\mathbf{TxtBex}$-identification and $\mathbf{TxtUniBex}$-identification, is summarized in Corollaries 10.25 and 10.26. These corollaries follow from the next proposition, whose proof is left to Exercise 10-9.

10.24 Proposition *For each $c \in N$,* $\mathbf{TxtUniBex}^{0,c} - \mathbf{TxtBex}^{*,c+1} \neq \emptyset$.

10.25 Corollary *For all* $a \in (N \cup \{*\})$,
$$\mathbf{TxtUniBex}^{a,0} \supset \cdots \supset \mathbf{TxtUniBex}^{a,i} \supset \mathbf{TxtUniBex}^{a,i+1} \supset \cdots \supset \mathbf{TxtUniBex}^{a,*}.$$

10.26 Corollary *For all* $a \in (N \cup \{*\})$,
$$\mathbf{TxtBex}^{a,0} \supset \cdots \supset \mathbf{TxtBex}^{a,i} \supset \mathbf{TxtBex}^{a,i+1} \supset \cdots \supset \mathbf{TxtBex}^{a,*}.$$

We have the next corollary as an immediate consequence of Proposition 10.15.

10.27 Corollary *For each* $c \in N$, $\mathbf{TxtBex}^{0,c} - \mathbf{TxtUniBex}^{*,0} \neq \emptyset$.

This last corollary yields Corollary 10.28, which is the language counterpart of Corollary 10.16. Corollary 10.28 says that if the bound on the number of errors allowed in both the additional information and the converged grammar are fixed, then requiring a scientist to converge to the same grammar for any upper bound is restrictive.

10.28 Corollary *For each* $a \in (N \cup \{*\})$ *and all* $c \in N$, $\mathbf{TxtUniBex}^{a,c} \subset \mathbf{TxtBex}^{a,c}$.

It is tempting to be somewhat metaphoric about the above result and read into it an observation about human language learning—we yield to the temptation. Children tend to learn a language effortlessly, compared to adults in a class room setting. A possible explanation may be that the learning criteria used by children allows them to converge to any grammar for the language, whereas adults are constrained to learn some unique grammar prescribed by the teacher!

As in the case of functions, it is still open whether the above result holds for $c = *$. Similar notions of additional information for other language learning paradigms (**TxtFex** and **TxtBc**) are treated in the exercises.

§10.3 Approximate hypotheses as additional information

Pursuant to our introductory discussion, we now explore a second conception of *a priori* information about the environment, and again allow this information to depend on which potential environment is "actual." This time we provide the scientist with an approximately true theory about the language or function with which they are confronted. To model the approximate character of the information provided, we rely on the "density of agreement" concepts defined in Chapter 7.

Convention: For the remainder of the present chapter, d, d_0, d_1, $d_2 \ldots$ range over real numbers in the unit interval.

§10.3.1 Function identification in the presence of approximations

In the following *an approximation to a function f* will be taken as a partial recursive function η that agrees with f to some extent. The following definition introduces two different formalizations of "extent of agreement."

10.29 Definition Let $d \in [\![0,1]\!]$, $\eta \in \mathcal{P}$, and $f \in \mathcal{R}$.

(a) We say that η is *d-conforming with f* just in case:

    (1) $\eta \subseteq f$, i.e., η does not contradict f; and

    (2) $den(domain(\eta)) \geq d$.

(b) We say that η is *uniformly d-conforming with f* just in case:

    (1) $\eta \subseteq f$, i.e., η does not contradict f; and

    (2) $uden(domain(\eta)) \geq d$.

Let us recall from Chapter 7 the motivation for uniform d-conformity. It is this: even if η is 1-conforming with f, η may be a bad approximation locally for many large intervals; uniform conformity renders the approximation more homogeneous.

In the paradigms defined below, a scientist learning f is fitted out with a program for an approximation η to f, along with access to the graph of f. The approximation η will be either d-conforming or uniformly d-conforming. Thus, our scientists again compute mappings from $N \times$ SEG to N, and $\mathbf{M}(p, \sigma)$ denotes the conjecture of $\mathbf{M}$ on prior information p plus evidential state σ. A definition similar to Definition 10.1 can be stated to describe the convergence of a scientist on information p and graph f.

The next definition makes things official. It extends the **Ex** paradigm to situations in which the scientist has access to a program for a partial function that is d- conforming with the function to be learned.

10.30 Definition Let $a \in (N \cup \{*\})$ and $d \in [\![0,1]\!]$.

(a) A scientist $\mathbf{M}$ $\mathbf{Ap}^d\mathbf{Ex}^a$-*identifies* f (written: $f \in \mathbf{Ap}^d\mathbf{Ex}^a(\mathbf{M})$) just in case, for all p such that φ_p is d-conforming with f, $\mathbf{M}(p, f)\!\downarrow$ and $\varphi_{\mathbf{M}(p,f)} =^a f$.

(b) $\mathbf{Ap}^d\mathbf{Ex}^a = \{\, \mathcal{S} \mid \mathcal{S} \subseteq \mathbf{Ap}^d\mathbf{Ex}^a(\mathbf{M}) \text{ for some } \mathbf{M} \,\}$.

Replacing d-conformity by uniform d-conformity in Definition 10.30 produces the following paradigm.

10.31 Definition Let $a \in (N \cup \{*\})$ and $d \in [\![0, 1]\!]$.

(a) A scientist **M** $\mathbf{Uap}^d\mathbf{Ex}^a$-*identifies* f (written: $f \in \mathbf{Uap}^d\mathbf{Ex}^a(\mathbf{M})$) just in case, for all p such that φ_p is uniformly d-conforming with f, $\mathbf{M}(p, f)\!\downarrow$ and $\varphi_{\mathbf{M}(p,f)} =^a f$.

(b) $\mathbf{Uap}^d\mathbf{Ex}^a = \{\, \mathcal{S} \mid \mathcal{S} \subseteq \mathbf{Uap}^d\mathbf{Ex}^a(\mathbf{M}) \text{ for some } \mathbf{M} \,\}$.

Ap and **Uap** are abbreviations for '**A**pproximate **p**artial additional information' and '**U**niform **a**pproximate **p**artial additional information,' respectively. The **Uap**-type additional information is intuitively better than the **Ap** type, and indeed the results to follow will confirm this. Since any $\mathbf{Uap}^d$-type additional information is also an $\mathbf{Ap}^d$-type additional information, we have the following.

10.32 Proposition *For all* $a \in (N \cup \{*\})$ *and all* $d \in [\![0, 1]\!]$, $\mathbf{Ap}^d\mathbf{Ex}^a \subseteq \mathbf{Uap}^d\mathbf{Ex}^a$.

We next establish that there are collections of functions that can be identified with some **Uap**-type additional information of nonzero density, but cannot be identified in the presence of the best possible **Ap**-type additional information even if the the scientist is allowed to converge to a finite variant program.

10.33 Proposition *Suppose* $0 < d \le 1$. *Then* $\mathbf{Uap}^d\mathbf{Ex} - \mathbf{Ap}^1\mathbf{Ex}^* \neq \emptyset$.

Proof: Let $n_0 = 0$ and, for each $i \ge 0$, let $n_{2i+1} = n_{2i} + i + 1$ and $n_{2i+2} = n_{2i+1} \cdot 2^i$. For each j, define

$$S_j \;=\; \bigcup_{k \in N} [n_{2 \cdot \langle j, k \rangle}, n_{2 \cdot \langle j, k \rangle + 1}).$$

Also, define

$$S_* \;=\; \bigcup_{i \in N} [n_{2i+1}, n_{2i+2}).$$

Finally, let

$$\mathcal{C} \;=\; \{\, f \in \mathcal{R} \mid f(S_*) = \{\, 0 \,\} \text{ and, for each } j,\; card(f(S_j)) = 1 \,\}.$$

We show that $\mathcal{C} \in (\mathbf{Uap}^d\mathbf{Ex} - \mathbf{Ap}^1\mathbf{Ex}^*)$ in the next two claims and thus establish the proposition.

10.34 Claim $\mathcal{C} \notin \mathbf{Ap}^1\mathbf{Ex}^*$.

Proof: Suppose by way of contradiction that some scientist $\mathbf{M}$ $\mathbf{Ap}^a\mathbf{Ex}^*$-identifies $\mathcal{C}$. We show that the existence of such an $\mathbf{M}$ implies that $\mathcal{R}$ is $\mathbf{Ex}^*$-identifiable, contradicting Corollary 6.11. First, let p_* be a program such that

$$\varphi_{p_*} = \lambda x . \begin{cases} 0, & x \in S_*; \\ \uparrow, & \text{otherwise.} \end{cases}$$

Clearly, for each $f \in \mathcal{C}$, we have that $\varphi_{p_*} \subseteq f$ and $den(\{x \mid \varphi_{p_*}(x) = f(x)\}) = 1$. Hence, φ_{p_*} is 1-conforming with each member of $\mathcal{C}$. Next, for each f, define

$$f' = \lambda x . \begin{cases} 0, & \text{if } x \in S_*; \\ f(j), & \text{if } x \in S_j. \end{cases}$$

So, if $f \in \mathcal{R}$, then $f' \in \mathcal{C}$. Also let r be a recursive function such that, for all i and j, $\varphi_{r(i)}(j) = \varphi_i(min(S_j))$. So if $\varphi_i = f'$, for some $f \in \mathcal{R}$, then $\varphi_{r(i)} = f$. Finally, let $\mathbf{M}'$ be a scientist such that, for each f,

$$\mathbf{M}'(f) = r(\mathbf{M}(p_*, f')).$$

As the reader may check, it follows from our assumption on $\mathbf{M}$ and the above definitions that $\mathbf{M}'$ must $\mathbf{Ex}^*$-identify $\mathcal{R}$. Thus we have the desired contradiction. $\square$

10.35 Claim *Suppose* $d \in (\!(0, 1]\!]$. *Then* $\mathcal{C} \in \mathbf{Uap}^d\mathbf{Ex}$.

Proof: Let p be a recursive function such that, for each s and x,

$$\varphi_{p(s)}(x) = \begin{cases} 0, & \text{if (i) } x \in S_*; \\ \varphi_s(y), & \text{if (ii) } x \in S_j \text{ and } \langle y, t \rangle \text{ is the least number such} \\ & \quad \text{that } y \in S_j \text{ and } \Phi_s(y) = t; \\ \uparrow, & \text{if (iii) } x \in S_j, \text{ but there is no such } \langle y, t \rangle \text{ as in (ii).} \end{cases}$$

Also, let $\mathbf{M}$ be a scientist such that, for all s and σ, $\mathbf{M}(s, \sigma) = p(s)$.

Fix some $f \in \mathcal{C}$ and suppose that s is such that φ_s is uniformly d-conforming to f. Then it easily follows that, for each j, $S_j \cap domain(\varphi_s) \neq \emptyset$, and hence, $\varphi_{p(s)} = f$. Therefore, $\mathbf{M}$ $\mathbf{Uap}^d\mathbf{Ex}$-identifies f. $\square$ ∎

Let us contrast the preceding result with the following proposition, showing that $\mathbf{Uap}$-type additional information cannot, in general, compensate for a higher density $\mathbf{Ap}$-type additional information. The proof of this proposition is left to Exercise 10-18.

10.36 Proposition *Suppose* $0 \leq d_1 < d_2 \leq 1$. *Then* $\mathbf{Ap}^{d_2}\mathbf{Ex} - \mathbf{Uap}^{d_1}\mathbf{Ex}^* \neq \emptyset$.

We next show that allowing an extra error in the final inferred program cannot, in general, be compensated by the best **Uap**-type additional information.

10.37 Proposition

(a) *For all* $i \in N$, $\mathbf{Ex}^{i+1} - \mathbf{Uap}^1\mathbf{Ex}^i \neq \emptyset$.

(b) $\mathbf{Ex}^* - \bigcup_{i \in N} \mathbf{Uap}^1\mathbf{Ex}^i \neq \emptyset$.

Proof: For each $f \in \mathcal{R}$, define

$$f' = \lambda x . \begin{cases} f(y), & \text{if } x \text{ is a power of 2 and } 2^y = x; \\ 0, & \text{otherwise.} \end{cases}$$

Also, for each $\mathcal{C} \subseteq \mathcal{R}$, define $\mathcal{C}' = \{\, f' \mid f \in \mathcal{C} \,\}$. Observe that for all $a \in (N \cup \{*\})$,

$$\mathcal{C} \in \mathbf{Ex}^a \iff \mathcal{C}' \in \mathbf{Ex}^a \iff \mathcal{C}' \in \mathbf{Uap}^1\mathbf{Ex}^a.$$

We leave it as exercise to show that the proposition follows from the above observation together with results from Section 6.1.1. ∎

The previous three results imply the following corollary, which reveals the complete relationship between $\mathbf{Uap}^d\mathbf{Ex}^a$ and $\mathbf{Ap}^d\mathbf{Ex}^a$ for various values of a and d. The proof of the corollary is left to the reader.

10.38 Corollary *Let* $a, b \in (N \cup \{*\})$ *and* $d_1, d_2 \in [\![0, 1]\!]$.

(a) $\mathbf{Ap}^{d_1}\mathbf{Ex}^a \subseteq \mathbf{Ap}^{d_2}\mathbf{Ex}^b \iff [d_1 \leq d_2 \text{ and } a \leq b]$.

(b) $\mathbf{Uap}^{d_1}\mathbf{Ex}^a \subseteq \mathbf{Uap}^{d_2}\mathbf{Ex}^b \iff [d_1 \leq d_2 \text{ and } a \leq b]$.

(c) *For all* $d \in (\!(0, 1]\!]$, $\mathbf{Ap}^d\mathbf{Ex}^a \subset \mathbf{Uap}^d\mathbf{Ex}^a$.

In the paradigms considered above, partial explanations do not contradict the function being learned. There is no reason to believe, however, that the state-of-the-art explanation available to a scientist is necessarily free of errors of commission. A natural, and currently open, line of further investigation is to consider approximations that are correct on a set of certain density and either undefined or incorrect off that set.

§10.3.2 Language identification with approximations

In the following *an approximation to a language L* will be taken to be another language L' such that $L' \subseteq L$ and L' "conforms" to L. We will consider two different formalizations of conformity. We first introduce the notions of *relative density of L' in L* and of *uniform relative density of L' in L*. These notions are then used in Definition 10.40 to present the two formalizations of conformity.

10.39 Definition Let $L = \{\, x_0 < x_1 < x_2 < \cdots \,\}$ and L' be members of $\mathcal{E}$.

(a) The *relative density* of L' in L (written: $rd(L', L)$) is defined as:

$$rd(L', L) \;=\; \begin{cases} den(\{\, i \mid x_i \in L' \,\}), & \text{if } L \text{ is infinite;} \\ den(L', L), & \text{otherwise.} \end{cases}$$

(b) The *uniform relative density* of L' in L (written: $urd(L', L)$) is defined as:

$$urd(L', L) \;=\; \begin{cases} uden(\{\, i \mid x_i \in L' \,\}), & \text{if } L \text{ is infinite;} \\ uden(L', L), & \text{otherwise.} \end{cases}$$

10.40 Definition Let $d \in [\![0, 1]\!]$. Let L and $L' \in \mathcal{E}$.

(a) We say that L' is *language d-conforming* with L just in case we have

    (1) $L' \subseteq L$; and

    (2) $rd(L', L) \geq d$.

(b) We say L' is *language uniformly d-conforming* with L just in case we have

    (1) $L' \subseteq L$; and

    (2) $urd(L', L) \geq d$.

The paradigms now to be discussed are analogous to the function paradigms introduced in Definitions 10.30 and 10.31. A scientist attempting to learn a language L is provided with a grammar for a language $L' \subseteq L$, in addition to access to a text for L. In the first paradigm, L' is a language that d-conforms with L; in the second paradigm, L' uniformly d-conforms with L. Thus (just as before), we conceive our scientists as computing mappings from $N \times$ SEQ to N. Once again, a definition similar to Definition 10.17 can be formulated to describe convergence on advance information x and text T. Officially, we proceed as follows.

10.41 Definition Let $a \in (N \cup \{*\})$ and $d \in [\![0,1]\!]$.

(a) A scientist **M** $\mathbf{TxtAp}^d\mathbf{Ex}^a$-*identifies* L (written: $L \in \mathbf{TxtAp}^d\mathbf{Ex}^a(\mathbf{M})$) just in case, for all texts T for L and all p such that W_p is language d-conforming with L, we have $\mathbf{M}(p,T)\!\downarrow$ and $W_{\mathbf{M}(p,T)} =^a L$.

(b) $\mathbf{TxtAp}^d\mathbf{Ex}^a = \{\, \mathcal{L} \mid \mathcal{L} \subseteq \mathbf{TxtAp}^d\mathbf{Ex}^a(\mathbf{M}) \text{ for some } \mathbf{M} \,\}$.

Replacing d-conformity in the above definition by uniform d-conformity yields the paradigm $\mathbf{TxtUap}^d\mathbf{Ex}^a$.

Before presenting results about $\mathbf{TxtAp}^d\mathbf{Ex}^a$ and $\mathbf{TxtUap}^d\mathbf{Ex}^a$, let us take another step in the elaboration of paradigms. In both of the foregoing models, the advance information about the incoming language L is "positive" in the sense that it describes a subset of L rather than its complement. It can also be imagined that the child receives advance, negative information in the form of an index for a subset of $N - L$. (This possibility does not bear on the debate about the existence of negative information in texts; textual information is provided by caretakers whereas advance information is lodged in the child's mind through the genome.) We rely on the following definition to formulate the possibility of advance, negative information.

10.42 Definition Let $a \in (N \cup \{*\})$ and $d \in [\![0,1]\!]$.

(a) A scientist **M** $\mathbf{TxtAcp}^d\mathbf{Ex}^a$-*identifies* L (written: $L \in \mathbf{TxtAcp}^d\mathbf{Ex}^a(\mathbf{M})$) just in case, for all texts T for L and all p such that W_p is language d-conforming with $(N-L)$, we have $\mathbf{M}(p,T)\!\downarrow$ and $W_{\mathbf{M}(p,T)} =^a L$.

(b) $\mathbf{TxtAcp}^d\mathbf{Ex}^a = \{\, \mathcal{L} \mid \mathcal{L} \subseteq \mathbf{TxtAcp}^d\mathbf{Ex}^a(\mathbf{M}) \text{ for some } \mathbf{M} \,\}$.

Acp is an abbreviation for "**A**pproximate **c**omplement **p**artial additional information." Replacing d-conformity in the above definition by uniform d-conformity yields the paradigm $\mathbf{TxtUacp}^d\mathbf{Ex}^a$.

Finally, we introduce paradigms in which the learner receives advance information about both L and $N - L$, where L is the language being presented. Within these paradigms, scientists compute mappings from $N \times N \times \mathrm{SEQ}$ to N. The first argument provides advance information about a subset of L and the second about a subset of $N - L$. Thus, $\mathbf{M}(x, y, \sigma)$ denotes the conjecture of scientist **M** on a grammar x for a language L, plus a grammar y for an (r.e.) subset of $N - L$, plus an initial segment σ of a text for L. Setting things down in an official way yields the following definitions.

10.43 Definition $\mathbf{M}(x, y, T)\!\downarrow$ (read: $\mathbf{M}$ *on text T with positive additional information x and negative additional information y converges*) just in case there is an i such that for all but finitely many n, $\mathbf{M}(x, y, T[n]) = i$, in which case $\mathbf{M}(x, y, T)$ is defined to be this i. If $\mathbf{M}(x, y, T)$ fails to converge, then $\mathbf{M}(x, y, T)$ is undefined.

10.44 Definition Let $a \in (N \cup \{*\})$ and $d_1, d_2 \in [\![0, 1]\!]$.

(a) We say that a scientist $\mathbf{M}$ $\mathbf{TxtAp}^{d_1}\mathbf{Acp}^{d_2}\mathbf{Ex}^a$-*identifies* a language L (written: $L \in \mathbf{TxtAp}^{d_1}\mathbf{Acp}^{d_2}\mathbf{Ex}^a(\mathbf{M})$) just in case, for all texts T for L, all p_1 with W_{p_1} is d_1-language conforming with L, and all p_2 with W_{p_2} is d_2-language conforming with $(N - L)$, we have $\mathbf{M}(p_1, p_2, T)\!\downarrow$ and $W_{\mathbf{M}(p_1, p_2, T)} =^a L$.

(b) $\mathbf{TxtAp}^{d_1}\mathbf{Acp}^{d_2}\mathbf{Ex}^a = \{\, \mathcal{L} \mid \mathcal{L} \subseteq \mathbf{TxtAp}^{d_1}\mathbf{Acp}^{d_2}\mathbf{Ex}^a(\mathbf{M}) \text{ for some } \mathbf{M} \,\}$.

In $\mathbf{TxtAp}^{d_1}\mathbf{Acp}^{d_2}\mathbf{Ex}$, the positive additional information is of type $\mathbf{Ap}$ and negative additional information is of type $\mathbf{Acp}$. The reader can similarly provide definitions for the following paradigms that arise by taking all combinations of the $\mathbf{Ap}$ and $\mathbf{Uap}$ types of positive additional information and the $\mathbf{Acp}$ and $\mathbf{Uacp}$ types of negative additional information:

(a) $\mathbf{TxtAp}^{d_1}\mathbf{Uacp}^{d_2}\mathbf{Ex}^a$.

(b) $\mathbf{TxtUap}^{d_1}\mathbf{Acp}^{d_2}\mathbf{Ex}^a$.

(c) $\mathbf{TxtUap}^{d_1}\mathbf{Uacp}^{d_2}\mathbf{Ex}^a$.

Having defined these paradigms, we now are in a position to present some representative results. The reader may easily check that all of the results in Section 10.3.1 about the paradigms $\mathbf{Ap}^d\mathbf{Ex}^a$ and $\mathbf{Uap}^d\mathbf{Ex}^a$ have corresponding counterparts for the $\mathbf{TxtAp}^d\mathbf{Ex}^a$ and $\mathbf{TxtUap}^d\mathbf{Ex}^a$ paradigms.

We first prove that extra errors in the final inferred grammar cannot be compensated for by any amount of additional information. More precisely, we prove that there are collections of languages that can be identified by allowing up to $k + 1$ errors in the final grammar, but which cannot be identified by allowing up to k errors in the final grammar, even if the scientist is given the best possible additional positive information ($\mathbf{Uap}$-type density 1) and the best possible additional negative information ($\mathbf{Uacp}$-type density 1).

10.45 Proposition $\mathbf{TxtEx}^{k+1} - \mathbf{TxtUap}^1\mathbf{Uacp}^1\mathbf{Ex}^k \neq \emptyset$.

Proof: Fix some $m > 1$. Let $n_0 = 0$. For each $i \in N$, let $n_{3i+1} = n_{3i} + m^i$, $n_{3i+2} = n_{3i+1} + m^i$, and $n_{3i+3} = n_{3i+2} + 1$. Let $L_1 = \bigcup_{i \in N}[n_{3i}, n_{3i+1})$, $L_2 = \bigcup_{i \in N}[n_{3i+1}, n_{3i+2})$, and $L_3 = \{\, n_{3i+2} \mid i \in N \,\}$. Finally, let

$$\mathcal{L} \;=\; \{\, L \in \mathcal{E} \mid L_1 \subseteq L \subseteq \overline{L_2} \text{ and } card(\overline{L} \cap L_3) \le k+1 \,\}.$$

Clearly, $\mathcal{L} \in \mathbf{TxtEx}^{k+1}$. Also, since grammars for L_1 and L_2 are valid additional information of types $\mathbf{Uap}^1$ and $\mathbf{Uacp}^1$, respectively, we have that $\mathcal{L} \in \mathbf{TxtUap}^1\mathbf{Uacp}^1\mathbf{Ex}^k \iff \mathcal{L} \in \mathbf{TxtEx}^k$. Suppose by way of contradiction that $\mathbf{M}$ $\mathbf{TxtEx}^k$-identifies $\mathcal{L}$. It is, then, easy to convert $\mathbf{M}$ to $\mathbf{M}'$ such that $\mathbf{M}'$ $\mathbf{TxtEx}^k$-identifies $\{L \mid L =^{k+1} N\}$. But this is not true as implied by Exercise 6-3. Thus, no such $\mathbf{M}$ can exist. ∎

We leave the proof of the following as an exercise.

10.46 Proposition $\mathbf{TxtEx}^* - \bigcup_{k \in N} \mathbf{TxtUap}^1\mathbf{Uacp}^1\mathbf{Ex}^k \ne \emptyset$.

The next proposition illustrates the power of $\mathbf{Uacp}$-type negative additional information over $\mathbf{Acp}$-type negative additional information. More precisely, there are collections of languages that can be identified in the presence of some $\mathbf{Uacp}$-type additional information of nonzero density, but cannot be identified in the presence of the best possible $\mathbf{Acp}$-type negative additional information, even if the scientist is also given the best possible positive additional information ($\mathbf{Uap}$-type density 1) and is only required to converge to a grammar for a finite variant of the language. The proof of the proposition is treated in Exercise 10-19.

10.47 Proposition *For all* $d > 0$, $\mathbf{TxtUacp}^d\mathbf{Ex} - \mathbf{TxtUap}^1\mathbf{Acp}^1\mathbf{Ex}^* \ne \emptyset$.

A similar result below illustrates the power of $\mathbf{Uap}$-type positive additional information over $\mathbf{Ap}$-type positive additional information. That is, there are collections of languages that can be identified in the presence of some $\mathbf{Uap}$-type additional information of nonzero density, but cannot be identified in the presence of the best possible $\mathbf{Ap}$-type positive additional information, even if the scientist is also given the best possible negative additional information ($\mathbf{Uacp}$-type density 1) and is only required to converge to a grammar for a finite variant of the language. See Jain and Sharma [85] for the proof.

10.48 Proposition *For all* $d > 0$, $\mathbf{TxtUap}^d\mathbf{Ex} - \mathbf{TxtAp}^1\mathbf{Uacp}^1\mathbf{Ex}^* \ne \emptyset$.

The next result illustrates the power of $\mathbf{Ap}$-type positive additional information over lower density $\mathbf{Uap}$-type positive additional information. More precisely, if $d_2 > d_1$, then there are collections of languages that can be identified in the presence of $\mathbf{Ap}$-type positive additional information of density d_2, but that cannot be identified in the presence of **Uap**-type positive additional information of density d_1, even if the scientist is also given the best possible negative additional information (**Uacp**-type density 1) and is only required to output a grammar for a finite variant of the language.

10.49 Proposition *Suppose* $0 \leq d_1 < d_2 \leq 1$. *Then,* $\mathbf{TxtAp}^{d_2}\mathbf{Ex} - \mathbf{TxtUap}^{d_1}\mathbf{Uacp}^1\mathbf{Ex}^* \neq \emptyset$.

The proof of the proposition can be found in Jain and Sharma [85].

We next present a negative additional information counterpart of the previous proposition, and illustrate the power of **Acp**-type negative additional information over lower density **Uacp**-type negative additional information. Again, the reader is referred to Jain and Sharma [85] for a proof.

10.50 Proposition *Suppose* $0 \leq d_1 < d_2 \leq 1$. *Then,* $\mathbf{TxtAcp}^{d_2}\mathbf{Ex} - \mathbf{TxtUap}^1\mathbf{Uacp}^{d_1}\mathbf{Ex}^* \neq \emptyset$.

The following corollary summarizes the complete relationship between all the paradigms introduced in this subsection. It follows from the results presented above, as the reader may check.

10.51 Corollary *Let* $a, b \in (N \cup \{*\})$ *and* $d, d_1, d_2, d_3, d_4 \in [\![0,1]\!]$, $d_+ \in (\!(0,1]\!]$.

(a) $\mathbf{TxtAp}^{d_1}\mathbf{Acp}^{d_2}\mathbf{Ex}^a \subseteq \mathbf{TxtAp}^{d_3}\mathbf{Acp}^{d_4}\mathbf{Ex}^b \iff [d_1 \leq d_3 \text{ and } d_2 \leq d_4 \text{ and } a \leq b]$.

(b) $\mathbf{TxtUap}^{d_1}\mathbf{Uacp}^{d_2}\mathbf{Ex}^a \subseteq \mathbf{TxtUap}^{d_3}\mathbf{Uacp}^{d_4}\mathbf{Ex}^b \iff [d_1 \leq d_3 \text{ and } d_2 \leq d_4 \text{ and } a \leq b]$.

(c) $\mathbf{TxtAp}^{d_+}\mathbf{Acp}^d\mathbf{Ex}^a \subset \mathbf{TxtUap}^{d_+}\mathbf{Acp}^d\mathbf{Ex}^a$.

(d) $\mathbf{TxtAp}^{d_+}\mathbf{Uacp}^d\mathbf{Ex}^a \subset \mathbf{TxtUap}^{d_+}\mathbf{Uacp}^d\mathbf{Ex}^a$.

(e) $\mathbf{TxtAp}^d\mathbf{Acp}^{d_+}\mathbf{Ex}^a \subset \mathbf{TxtAp}^d\mathbf{Uacp}^{d_+}\mathbf{Ex}^a$.

(f) $\mathbf{TxtUap}^d\mathbf{Acp}^{d_+}\mathbf{Ex}^a \subset \mathbf{TxtUap}^d\mathbf{Uacp}^{d_+}\mathbf{Ex}^a$.

§10.4 Bibliographic notes

The subject of upper bound on program size as additional information for function identification was first considered by Freivalds and Wiehagen [67] and generalized by Jain and Sharma [86]. The latter paper also investigated analogs of these paradigms for **Bc**, **TxtEx**, **TxtFex**, and **TxtBc** paradigms.

The subject of **Ap** and **Uap** types of additional information for **Bc**, **TxtFex**, and **TxtBc** is covered in Jain and Sharma [85].

Other approaches to additional information have been considered by Fulk [68], by Case, Kaufmann, Kinber, and Kummer [32], by Baliga and Case[11], and by Kaufmann and Stephan [104].

§10.5 Exercises

10-1 Consider a variant of **Bex**^{a,c}-identification in which the additional information about a function f is provided as a sequence whose limiting value is an upper bound on $MinProg_c(f)$. More formally, let $\mathcal{X}$ range over infinite sequences of natural numbers $x_0, x_1, x_2, \ldots$ and let $\lim_{n \to \infty} \mathcal{X}$ denote the limit of the sequence, if the sequence converges.

> **10.52 Definition** Let $a, c \in (N \cup \{*\})$.
>
> (a) **M** **BEX**^{a,c}-*identifies* f (written: $f \in$ **BEX**$^{a,c}(\mathbf{M})$) just in case, for all $\mathcal{X}$ such that $\lim_{n \to \infty} \mathcal{X}\!\downarrow \geq MinProg_c(f))$, we have $\lim_{n \to \infty} \mathbf{M}(x_n, f[n])\!\downarrow$ and, for $i = \lim_{n \to \infty} \mathbf{M}(x_n, f[n])$, $\varphi_i =^a f$.
>
> (b) **BEX**$^{a,c} = \{\, \mathcal{S} \mid \mathcal{S} \subseteq$ **BEX**$^{a,c}(\mathbf{M})$ for some **M** $\}$.

Show that for each $a, c \in (N \cup \{*\})$, **Bex**$^{a,c} =$ **BEX**^{a,c}. Does a similar result hold for other paradigms in Section 10.2?

10-2 Complete the proof of Proposition 10.12.

10-3 Give a proof for Proposition 10.13.

Hint: Consider:

$$
\begin{aligned}
\mathcal{S}_0 &= \{\, f \in \mathcal{R} \mid \varphi_{f(0)} = f \text{ and } (\overset{\infty}{\exists} y)[\, f(y+1) \neq f(y)\,]\,\}. \\
\mathcal{S}_1 &= \{\, f \in \mathcal{R} \mid card(\{\, y \mid f(y+1) \neq f(y)\,\}) \leq \mu k.[\varphi_k =^* f\,]\,\}. \\
\mathcal{S} &= \mathcal{S}_0 \cup \mathcal{S}_1.
\end{aligned}
$$

It is easy to verify that $\mathcal{S} \in$ **UniBex**^{0,*}. Use Kleene's recursion theorem (Theorem 2.3) to show that $\mathcal{S} \notin$ **Bc**^{a}.

10-4   The aim of this exercise is to establish a hierarchy for **Bex**-identification which shows that decreasing the quality of additional information results in a reduction in learning power. Towards this goal, first prove that, for all $c \in N$, $\mathbf{UniBex}^{0,c} - \mathbf{Bex}^{c,c+1} \neq \emptyset$. Then, verify that this result implies that for all $c \in N$, $2^{\mathcal{R}} = \mathbf{Bex}^{c,c} \supset \mathbf{Bex}^{c,c+1} \supset \cdots \supset \mathbf{Bex}^{c,c+j} \supset \mathbf{Bex}^{c,c+j+1} \supset \cdots \supset \mathbf{Bex}^{c,*}$.

10-5   Show that, for each $c \in N$, $\mathbf{UniBex}^{0,c} - \mathbf{Bex}^{*,*} \neq \emptyset$.

Hint: Use the union of the following classes of functions:

$$\mathcal{S}_1 \;=\; \{\, f \mid \varphi_{f(0)} = f \text{ and } (\overset{\infty}{\exists} y)[\, f(y) \neq 0\,]\,\}.$$

$$\mathcal{S}_2 \;=\; \{\, f \mid card(\{\, y \mid f(y) \neq 0\,\}) \leq \mu k \cdot [\varphi_k =^c f]\,\}.$$

10-6   Show that $\mathbf{Bc} - \mathbf{Bex}^{*,*} \neq \emptyset$.

Hint: Consider $\mathcal{S}$, the class of functions $f \in \mathcal{R}$ each of which satisfies:

1. $\varphi_{f(0)} = f$ or $(\overset{\infty}{\forall} y)[\, f(y) = 0\,]$.
2. $(\overset{\infty}{\forall} y)[\, f(y) \neq 0 \implies \varphi_{f(y)} = f\,]$.
3. $card(\{ y \mid f(y) \neq 0\})$ is finite $\implies \varphi_{f(max(\{y|f(y)\neq 0\}))} = f$.

10-7   Show that $\mathbf{Bc}^1 - \mathbf{UniBex}^{*,0} \neq \emptyset$. Observe that this result implies that $\mathcal{R} \notin \mathbf{UniBex}^{*,0}$. This latter observation says that there is no scientist that can **UniBex**-identify every recursive function, even if the scientist is given the best quality additional information and is only required to output a finite variant program.

Hint: Use the class of functions $\mathcal{S} = \{\, f \mid (\overset{\infty}{\forall} n)[\varphi_{f(n)} =^1 f\,]\,\}$.

10-8   Use an argument similar to the one for Exercise 10-7 to argue $\mathbf{Bc} - \mathbf{UniBex}^{*,1} \neq \emptyset$. *Note:* It is currently open whether this result or the one in Exercise 10-7 can be extended to $\mathbf{Bc}^0 - \mathbf{UniBex}^{*,0} \neq \emptyset$.

10-9   Give a proof of Proposition 10.24.

Hint: For each $c \in N$, consider the class of languages $\mathcal{L}_c =$

$$\{\, L \mid L \text{ is infinite and } L = W_{min(L)}\,\} \;\cup\; \{\, L \mid card(L) < min(\{\, j \mid W_j =^c L\})\,\}.$$

It is easy to check that $\mathcal{L}_c \in \textbf{TxtUniBex}^{0,c}$. Using the n-ary recursion theorem (Theorem 2.5), show that $\mathcal{L}_0 \notin \textbf{TxtBex}^{*,1}$. Then generalize this argument to show that $\mathcal{L}_c \notin \textbf{TxtBex}^{*,c+1}$.

10-10 The purpose of this exercise is to extend **Aex** and **Uaex** paradigms from Chapter 7 to incorporate both **Ap** and **Uap** types of additional information. We illustrate this extension by defining $\textbf{Ap}^{d_1}\textbf{Aex}^{d_2}$ paradigm below. First recall from Chapter 7 that the asymptotic agreement between two partial functions η and θ (denoted: $aa(\eta,\theta)$) is $den(\{x \mid \eta(x) = \theta(x)\})$ and the asymptotic disagreement between η and θ (denoted: $ad(\eta,\theta)$) is $1 - aa(\eta,\theta)$.

10.53 Definition Let $d_1, d_2 \in [\![0,1]\!]$.

(a) A scientist $\textbf{M}$ $\textbf{Ap}^{d_1}\textbf{Aex}^{d_2}$-*identifies* f (written: $f \in \textbf{Ap}^{d_1}\textbf{Aex}^{d_2}(\textbf{M})$) just in case, for each p with φ_p that is d_1-conforming with f, we have that $\textbf{M}(p,f)\!\downarrow$ and $ad(f,\varphi_{\textbf{M}(p,f)}) \leq d_2$.

(b) $\textbf{Ap}^{d_1}\textbf{Aex}^{d_2} = \{\, \mathcal{S} \mid \mathcal{S} \subseteq \textbf{Ap}^{d_1}\textbf{Aex}^{d_2}(\textbf{M}) \text{ for some } \textbf{M} \,\}$.

Similarly to the above, define $\textbf{Uap}^{d_1}\textbf{Aex}^{d_2}$, $\textbf{Uap}^{d_1}\textbf{Uaex}^{d_2}$, and $\textbf{Ap}^{d_1}\textbf{Uaex}^{d_2}$ paradigms. Give simple arguments for the following.

(a) For all $d \in [\![0,1]\!]$, $\mathcal{R} \in \textbf{Ap}^{d}\textbf{Aex}^{1-d}$.

(b) For all $d \in [\![0,1]\!]$, $\mathcal{R} \in \textbf{Uap}^{d}\textbf{Uaex}^{1-d}$.

10-11 Show that, for all $d_1 > 0$ and all d_2, d_3 with $d_2 + d_3 < 1$, $\textbf{Uap}^{d_1}\textbf{Ex} - \textbf{Ap}^{d_2}\textbf{Aex}^{d_3} \neq \emptyset$.

Hint: Without loss of generality, assume that $d_1 = 2/m$, $d_2 = l/m$, $d_3 = (m-l-1)/m$ for integers $l \geq 1$ and $m \geq 2$. Let $n_0 = 0$. For each $i \in N$, let $n_{2i+1} = m^{i+1} + n_{2i}$, and $n_{2i+2} = n_{2i+1} + (i+1)\cdot m$. Let $S_j = \bigcup_{k\in N}[n_{2\cdot\langle j,k\rangle+1}, n_{2\cdot\langle j,k\rangle+2})$. Then, use $\mathcal{C}$, the class of functions $f \in \mathcal{R}$, each of which satisfy:

1. For all $x \in (\bigcup_{i\in N}[n_{2i}, n_{2i+1}))\bigcap\{ x \mid (x \bmod m) < l \})$, $f(x) = 0$.

2. For all j and all $x \in S_j$, $f(x) = f(j)$.

10-12 Suppose d_1, d_2, and d_3 are real numbers such that $0 \leq d_3 < d_1 \leq 1$ and $d_2 + d_3 < 1$. Use a technique similar to the one of Exercise 10-11 to show that $\textbf{Uaex}^{d_1} - \textbf{Uap}^{d_2}\textbf{Aex}^{d_3} \neq \emptyset$. Also, verify that this result implies $\textbf{Uaex}^{d_1} - \textbf{Uap}^{d_2}\textbf{Uaex}^{d_3} \neq \emptyset$.

10-13   Use a technique similar to the one for Exercise 10-11 to show that, for all d_1 and d_2 with $d_1 + d_2 < 1$, $\mathbf{Aex}^0 - \mathbf{Uap}^{d_1}\mathbf{Uaex}^{d_2} \neq \emptyset$. Also, verify that this result implies that, for all $d < 1$, $\mathbf{Aex}^0 - \mathbf{Ap}^1\mathbf{Uaex}^d \neq \emptyset$.

10-14   Show that, for all $d_1 > 0$ and all $d_2 < 1$, $\mathbf{Uap}^{d_1}\mathbf{Ex} - \mathbf{Ap}^1\mathbf{Uaex}^{d_2} \neq \emptyset$.

Hint: Without loss of generality, assume that $d_1 = 2/m$ and $d_2 = (m-2)/m$ for an integer $m \geq 3$. Let $n_0 = 0$, $n_{2i+1} = m^{i+1} + n_{2i}$, and $n_{2i+2} = n_{2i+1} + (i+1) \cdot m$. Let $S_* = \bigcup_{i \in N}[n_{2i}, n_{2i+1})$ and, for each j, $S_j = \bigcup_{k \in N+}[n_{2 \cdot \langle j,k \rangle +1}, n_{2 \cdot \langle j,k \rangle +2})$. Then, use $\mathcal{C}$, the class of functions $f \in \mathcal{R}$, each of which satisfies:

1. For all $x \in S_*$, $f(x) = 0$.

2. For all j and all $x \in S_j$, $f(x) = f(j)$.

10-15   Suppose d_1, d_2, and d_3 are such that $d_2 < d_1$ and $d_3 < 1$. Show $\mathbf{Ap}^{d_1}\mathbf{Ex} - \mathbf{Ap}^{d_2}\mathbf{Uaex}^{d_3} \neq \emptyset$.

Hint: Without loss of generality, assume that $d_2 = l/m$, $d_1 = (l+2)/m$, and $d_3 = (m-2)/m$ for integers $l \geq 1$ and $m \geq 4$. Let $n_0 = 0$, $n_{2i+1} = m^{i+1} + n_{2i}$, and $n_{2i+2} = n_{2i+1} + (i+1) \cdot m$. Let $S_* = \bigcup_{i \in N}[n_{2i}, n_{2i+1})$ and, for each j, let $S_j = \bigcup_{k \in N}[n_{2 \cdot \langle j,k \rangle}, n_{2 \cdot \langle j,k \rangle +1})$. Then, use $\mathcal{C}$, the class of functions $f \in \mathcal{R}$ each of which satisfies:

1. For each $x \in (S_* \cap \{\, x \mid (x \bmod m) < l \,\})$, $f(x) = 0$

2. For all j and all $x \in (S_j \cap \{\, x \mid (x \bmod m) \geq l \,\})$, $f(x) = f(j)$.

10-16   Use a technique similar to the one in the hint for Exercise 10-15 to show that, for all d_1 and d_2 with $d_1 > d_2$, $\mathbf{Uaex}^{d_1} - \mathbf{Ap}^1\mathbf{Uaex}^{d_2} \neq \emptyset$.

10-17   Use a technique similar to the one in the hint for Exercise 10-15 to show that, for all d_1, d_2, and d_3 with $d_2 > d_1$ and $d_1 + d_3 < 1$, $\mathbf{Ap}^{d_2}\mathbf{Ex} - \mathbf{Uap}^{d_1}\mathbf{Aex}^{d_3} \neq \emptyset$.

10-18   Give a proof of Proposition 10.36.

Hint: Without loss of generality, assume that $d_2 = (k+3)/m$ and $d_1 = k/m$ for integers k and m with $k + 3 \leq m$. Let $n_0 = -1$ and $n_i = m^i$. Let S_j denote the set $\bigcup_{l \in N}(n_{\langle j,l \rangle}, n_{\langle j,l \rangle +1}]$. Let $S'_j = S_j \cap \{\, x \mid (x \bmod m) \geq k \,\}$. Consider the class $\mathcal{C}$ of functions $f \in \mathcal{R}$, each of which satisfies:

1. $f(\{\, x \mid (x \bmod m) < k \,\}) = \{\, 0 \,\}$.

2. For each j, $card(f(S'_j)) = 1$.

Now show that $\mathcal{C} \notin \mathbf{Uap}^{d_1}\mathbf{Ex}^*$ and $\mathcal{C} \in \mathbf{Ap}^{d_2}\mathbf{Ex}$.

10-19 Give a proof of Proposition 10.47.

Hint: Fix some integer $m > 1$. Let $n_0 = 0$, and for each i and each $j < i$, let

$$n_{i(i+1)+1} = n_{i(i+1)} + m^i.$$
$$n_{i(i+1)+2} = n_{i(i+1)+1} + m^i.$$
$$n_{i(i+1)+2+2j+1} = n_{i(i+1)+2+(2j)} + 1.$$
$$n_{i(i+1)+2+2j+2} = n_{i(i+1)+2+(2j)+1} + m^i.$$

For each j, let $S_j = \{\, n_{\langle j,k \rangle \cdot (\langle j,k \rangle + 1) + 2 + 2l} \mid k \in N \text{ and } l < \langle j, k \rangle \,\}$. Consider $\mathcal{L}$, the class of languages $L \in \mathcal{E}$, each of which satisfies:

1. $\bigcup_{i \in N} [n_{i(i+1)}, n_{i(i+1)+1}) \subseteq L$.
2. $\bigcup_{i \in N} [n_{i(i+1)+1}, n_{i(i+1)+2}) \subseteq \overline{L}$.
3. $\bigcup_{i \in N} \bigcup_{j < i} [n_{i(i+1)+2+2j+1}, n_{i(i+1)+2+2j+2}) \subseteq L$.
4. $(\forall j)[S_j \subseteq L \text{ or } S_j \cap L = \emptyset]$.
5. $\{j \mid S_j \subseteq L\}$ is finite or co-finite.

Show that $\mathcal{L} \in \mathbf{TxtUacp}^d\mathbf{Ex}$ (first, use the additional information to construct a text for the complement of the input language; then use the identification method used to identify finite (respectively, co-finite) languages on characteristic function input). Also, observe that $\mathcal{L} \in \mathbf{TxtUap}^1\mathbf{Acp}^1\mathbf{Ex}^* \iff \mathcal{L} \in \mathbf{TxtEx}^*$, and $\mathcal{L} \in \mathbf{TxtEx}^* \implies \{\, L \mid L \text{ is finite or co-finite} \,\} \in \mathbf{TxtEx}^*$. Use this observation to argue that $\mathcal{L} \notin \mathbf{TxtUap}^1\mathbf{Acp}^1\mathbf{Ex}^*$.

11   Learning with Oracles

§11.1 Introduction

In Chapters 3 and 4 we observed that unidentifiability can arise for two distinct reasons:

1. there may be some information theoretic limitation inherent in the collection of underlying realities being identified; or

2. the collection of underlying realities is in some way too complex for a *computable* scientist to identify.

In this chapter we explore the second of these barriers. We do this by considering scientists that are allowed access to knowledge not obtainable through any computable process. We illustrate the key issues in the context of both functions and languages.

In the case of function identification, we know that $\mathcal{R}$, the collection of computable functions, is identifiable by a noncomputable scientist (Proposition 3.43), but cannot be identified by any computable scientist (Theorem 4.28). This suggests that if some additional information of noncomputable nature were available to computable scientists, the collection $\mathcal{R}$ might become identifiable. In this chapter such information is modeled as membership oracles for noncomputable sets, and through this we are able to classify the hardness of the problem of identifying $\mathcal{R}$.

In the context of languages we have seen that any collection of r.e. languages that contains all the finite languages and an infinite language cannot be identified by *any* scientist, computable or noncomputable (Corollary 3.28). So a scientist will not be able to overcome such a barrier simply by having access to information about noncomputable processes. However, it is still interesting to investigate whether larger collections of languages become identifiable if a scientist is provided information about processes that are increasingly noncomputable.

The results on these topics are primarily of technical interest, and this chapter provides only a brief survey, with proofs of some sample findings.

§11.2 Oracle scientists

Consider a machine that, in addition to performing algorithmic computation, is allowed to ask membership queries about some $A \subseteq N$ that may not be recursive. Such machines are referred to as *oracle machines*. In this section we consider identification by scientists that have access to such a membership oracle. A membership oracle for $A \subseteq N$ may be thought of as an infinite sequence of 0's and 1's whose bits appear in the sequence

$$\chi_A(0), \chi_A(1), \chi_A(2), \ldots,$$

where χ_A denotes the characteristic function of A. We use A to denote both the set and its membership oracle.

An oracle scientist may be construed as a computable scientist with the added ability to consult an oracle for membership queries. More concretely, an oracle scientist may be viewed as a Turing machine with an extra read-only tape, called the *oracle tape*, upon which the membership oracle for some set A is written. This oracle Turing machine behaves like a usual Turing machine except that its actions may also depend on the content of the oracle tape. In this chapter we let **M**, with or without decorations, range over oracle, as well as ordinary, scientists. It will always be clear from context whether **M** is intended as an ordinary or oracle scientist. We denote a scientist **M** equipped with an oracle A as $\mathbf{M}^A$, and $\mathbf{M}^A(\sigma)$ denotes the conjecture of **M** with access to a membership oracle for A on evidential state σ.

The next section concerns function identification by oracle scientists. Section 11.4 discusses language identification in this context.

§11.3 Function identification by oracle scientists

Suppose **M** is an oracle scientist and $A \subseteq N$. If the sequence of hypotheses issued by $\mathbf{M}^A$ on $f \in \mathcal{R}$ corresponds to an **Ex**-identification of f, then $\mathbf{M}^A$ is said to **Ex**-*identify* f, or alternatively, as defined below, **M** is said to $\mathbf{O}^A\mathbf{Ex}$-*identify* f (Gasarch and Pleszkoch [76]). We formalize this paradigm in the following definition, and leave it to the reader to check that the notion of convergence of a computable scientist on a function can be easily adapted for convergence of an oracle scientist on a function.

11.1 Definition (Gasarch and Pleszkoch [76]) Let $A \subseteq N$.

(a) **M**, $\mathbf{O}^A\mathbf{Ex}$-*identifies* f (written $f \in \mathbf{O}^A\mathbf{Ex}(\mathbf{M})$) just in case $\mathbf{M}^A(f){\downarrow}$ and $\varphi_{\mathbf{M}^A(f)} = f$.

(b) $\mathbf{O}^A\mathbf{Ex} = \{\, \mathcal{S} \mid \mathcal{S} \subseteq \mathbf{O}^A\mathbf{Ex}(\mathbf{M}) \text{ for some } \mathbf{M} \,\}$.

§11.3.1 Omniscient oracles

Recall that $\mathcal{R} \notin \mathbf{Ex}$ (Theorem 4.28). A natural question is: How much additional information (in the form of an oracle) need one supply to a scientist in order for $\mathcal{R}$ to be identifiable? Let us call A *omniscient* if and only if $\mathcal{R} \in \mathbf{O}^A\mathbf{Ex}$. The next proposition shows that K (the halting set) is omniscient.

11.2 Proposition (Adleman and Blum [1]) $\mathcal{R} \in \mathbf{O}^K\mathbf{Ex}$.

Proof: Let g be a relativized recursive function such that, for all x,

$$g^K(x) \;=\; 1 + max(\{\, \Phi_i(y) \mid i, y \leq x \text{ and } \Phi_i(y)\!\downarrow \,\}).$$

Recall that, for each $\sigma \in \mathrm{SEG}$, $\widehat{\sigma}$ is the finite function whose graph is $content(\sigma)$. For each X and σ, define

$$
\mathbf{M}^X(\sigma) \;=\;
\begin{cases}
i, & \text{if } i \text{ is the least number } \leq |\sigma|, \text{ if any, such that, for} \\
 & \quad s = g^X(max(domain(\widehat{\sigma}))) \text{ and for all } x \in domain(\widehat{\sigma}), \\
 & \quad \varphi_{i,s}(x) = \widehat{\sigma}(x); \\
0, & \text{otherwise.}
\end{cases}
$$

Clearly, $\mathbf{M}^K$ $\mathbf{Ex}$-identifies $\mathcal{R}$.   ∎

Adleman and Blum [1] completely characterize the omniscient sets as follows. Let A' denote the halting problem relative to oracle A. We say that A is *high* if and only if $K' \leq_T A'$. (See Soare [183] for a detailed discussion of high sets.)

11.3 Proposition (Adleman and Blum [1]) *For all A, $\mathcal{R} \in \mathbf{O}^A\mathbf{Ex}$ if and only if A is high.*

The *if* direction of this result is left for Exercise 11-1. The *only if* direction is quite involved and is omitted here.

§11.3.2 Trivial oracles

Let us call A *trivial* if and only if $\mathbf{O}^A\mathbf{Ex} = \mathbf{Ex}$. Clearly, every recursive A is trivial. There turn out to be nonrecursive trivial sets, and the class of all trivial sets has an attractive characterization which we give below. Before stating this characterization we first need to explain *1-generic sets*.

Let $\mathrm{STR} = \{\, \chi_A[n] \mid A \subseteq N \text{ and } n \in N \,\}$. We let γ, with or without decorations, range over STR. We write $\gamma_0 \preceq \gamma_1$ just in case γ_0 is a prefix of γ_1, and we write $\gamma \preceq A$

just in case γ is a prefix of χ_A. Clearly, $\preceq$ is a partial order on STR. We identify the elements of STR with those of N.[1]

11.4 Definition (Jockusch [101]) *A is 1-generic just in case, for every r.e. set L, there is an n such that either (a)* $\chi_A[n] \in L$, *or (b) for all* $\gamma \in L$, $\chi_A[n] \not\preceq \gamma$.

Jockusch [101] shows that 1-generic sets exist and are, in a reasonable sense, plentiful. Here then is the promised characterization of trivial sets.

11.5 Proposition *For all A,* $\mathbf{O}^A \mathbf{Ex} = \mathbf{Ex}$ *if and only if $A \leq_T K$ and A is Turing reducible to a 1-generic set.*

The *if* direction of the proposition is due to Fortnow, Gasarch, Jain, Kinber, Kummer, Kurtz, Pleszkoch, Slaman, Solovay, and Stephan [59], and the *only if* direction is due to Slaman and Solovay [177]. Slaman and Solovay's [177] proof of the *only if* direction is quite difficult. Kummer and Stephan [114] have an easier proof of this direction. Here we show Proposition 11.6 below, a weak version of the *if* direction. The full argument of the *if* direction is left to Exercise 11-4.

11.6 Proposition *Suppose A is a 1-generic set that is $\leq_T K$. Then* $\mathbf{O}^A \mathbf{Ex} = \mathbf{Ex}$.

The following two lemmas imply the proposition.

11.7 Lemma *Suppose A is 1-generic and $\mathcal{C} \subseteq \mathbf{O}^A \mathbf{Ex}$. Then there is an $\mathbf{M}$ such that, for each $f \in \mathcal{C}$, $\mathbf{M}^A$ $\mathbf{Ex}$-identifies f, making only finitely many queries to A.*

11.8 Lemma *Suppose $A \leq_T K$ and $\mathcal{C}$ and $\mathbf{M}$ are such that, for each $f \in \mathcal{C}$, $\mathbf{M}^A$ $\mathbf{Ex}$-identifies f, making only finitely many queries to A. Then $\mathcal{C} \in \mathbf{Ex}$.*

We prove Lemma 11.7 below. The proof of Lemma 11.8 is left to Exercise 11-3. Before proving Lemma 11.7, we introduce one more bit of notation. For each oracle scientist $\mathbf{M}$, $\sigma \in \mathrm{SEG}$, and $\gamma \in \mathrm{STR}$, we define

$$\mathbf{M}^\gamma(\sigma) = \begin{cases} \mathbf{M}^A(\sigma), & \text{if } A = \{\, x \mid \gamma(x) = 1 \,\} \text{ and all of the} \\ & \quad \text{queries to } A \text{ are in } domain(\gamma); \\ \uparrow, & \text{otherwise.} \end{cases}$$

---

[1] Via the isomorphism $\gamma \mapsto (2^{|\gamma|} - 1) + \sum_{i < |\gamma|} \gamma(i) \cdot 2^i$. *Exercise:* Show that this really is an isomorphism.

Proof (of Lemma 11.7): Let $\mathbf{M}_0$ be an oracle scientist such that $\mathbf{M}_0^A$ **Ex**-identifies $\mathcal{C}$. For each oracle X and each $\sigma \in \text{SEG}$, define $\text{use}^X(\sigma)$ to be the smallest prefix of X, if any, such that $\mathbf{M}_0^X(\sigma)\!\downarrow$. Clearly, use^X is partial recursive in X. We also define, for each oracle X and $\sigma \in \text{SEG}$,

$$
G^X(\sigma) \;=\;
\begin{cases}
0, & \text{if } |\sigma| = 0; \\[4pt]
G^X(\sigma^-) + 1, & \text{if } |\sigma| > 0 \text{ and, for } \sigma_0 = \sigma[G^X(\sigma^-)] \text{ and } \gamma_0 = \\
& \text{use}^X(\sigma_0), \text{ there are } \sigma_1 \text{ and } \gamma_1 \text{ such that } \sigma_0 \preceq \\
& \sigma_1 \preceq \sigma, \; |\gamma_1| \le |\sigma|, \; \gamma_0 \preceq \gamma_1, \text{ and, in } \le |\sigma| \\
& \text{steps}, \; \mathbf{M}_0^{\gamma_1}(\sigma_1)\!\downarrow \ne \mathbf{M}_0^{\gamma_0}(\sigma_0)\!\downarrow; \\[4pt]
G^X(\sigma^-), & \text{otherwise.}
\end{cases}
$$

11.9 Claim

(a) G^A *is recursive in A, monotone nondecreasing, and for each σ, $G^A(\sigma) \le |\sigma|$, and one can compute $G^A(\sigma)$ using only $\text{use}^A(\sigma[G^A(\sigma^-)])$ much of A.*

(b) *For each $f \in \mathcal{C}$, there is an n_f such that $\lim_{n\to\infty} G^A(f[n])\!\downarrow = n_f$ and $\mathbf{M}_0^A(f) = \mathbf{M}_0^A(f[n_f])$.*

Proof: Part (a) follows directly from the definition of G. For part (b), fix an $f \in \mathcal{C}$. It is clear from the definition of G that, if $\lim_{n\to\infty} G^A(f[n])\!\downarrow$ to say n_f, then $\mathbf{M}_0^A(f[n_f]) = \mathbf{M}_0^A(f)$. Moreover, since G^A is monotone increasing, if $n \mapsto G^A(f[n])$ is bounded, then $\lim_{n\to\infty} G^A(f[n])\!\downarrow$. So, for part (b) it suffices to simply show that $n \mapsto G^A(f[n])$ is bounded. For each n, let $\widehat{\gamma}_n = \text{use}^A(f[n])$. If $\lim_{n\to\infty} |\widehat{\gamma}_n|\!\downarrow < \infty$, then we are done by the definition of G. So, suppose $\lim_{n\to\infty} |\widehat{\gamma}_n| = \infty$. Since $\mathbf{M}_0^A$ **Ex**^{A}-identifies f, there are i_0 and n_0 such that, for all $n \ge n_0$, $\mathbf{M}_0^A(f[n]) = i_0$. Let

$$
L \;=\; \{\gamma \mid \widehat{\gamma}_{n_0} \preceq \gamma \text{ and, for some } j \in \{n_0, n_0+1, \ldots, |\gamma|\}, \; \mathbf{M}_0^\gamma(f[j])\!\downarrow \ne i_0 \}.
$$

Clearly, L is r.e. By our choice of n_0 we have that, for each m, $\chi_A[m] \notin L$. Therefore, by the 1-genericity of A, there must be an m_0 such that, for all $\gamma \in L$, $\chi_A[m_0] \not\preceq \gamma$. Let n_1 be the least number such that $|\widehat{\gamma}_{n_1}| \ge m_0$ (and, hence, $\chi_A[m_0] \preceq \widehat{\gamma}_{n_1}$). It thus follows from our choice of m_0 and the definition of G that, for all n, $G^A(f[n]) \le |\widehat{\gamma}_{n_1}|$. $\square$

For each X and σ, define $\mathbf{M}^X(\sigma) = \mathbf{M}_0^X(\sigma[G^X(\sigma)])$. It follows from Claim 11.9 that $\mathbf{M}$ is as required. ∎

§11.3.3 Bounded queries

An oracle scientist $\mathbf{M}$ in the process of $\mathbf{O}^A\mathbf{Ex}$-identifying a function f may ask infinitely many questions of the oracle A. A natural refinement on the $\mathbf{O}^A\mathbf{Ex}$ paradigm is to bound the number of questions a scientist is allowed to ask. This refinement is the subject of the next definition. First, we formalize the concept of "set of questions asked of an oracle by a scientist examining the graph of a function."

Let $Queries(\mathbf{M}, A, \sigma)$ denote the set $\{\, x \in N \mid \mathbf{M}$ asks a question of the form '$x \in A$?' of A in conjecturing a hypothesis on $\sigma\,\}$. Then the set of queries to A by $\mathbf{M}$ on a function f, denoted $Queries(\mathbf{M}, A, f)$, is $\bigcup_{n \in N} Queries(\mathbf{M}, A, f[n])$.

11.10 Definition (Gasarch and Pleszkoch [76]) Suppose $b \in (N \cup \{*\})$ and $\mathbf{M}$ is an oracle scientist.

(a) $\mathbf{M}$ $\mathbf{O}^{A,b}\mathbf{Ex}$-*identifies* f (written: $f \in \mathbf{O}^{A,b}\mathbf{Ex}(\mathbf{M})$) just in case $f \in \mathbf{O}^A\mathbf{Ex}(\mathbf{M})$ and $card(Queries(\mathbf{M}, A, f)) \leq b$.

(b) $\mathbf{O}^{A,b}\mathbf{Ex} = \{\, \mathcal{S} \mid \mathcal{S} \subseteq \mathbf{O}^{A,b}\mathbf{Ex}(\mathbf{M})$ for some $\mathbf{M}\,\}$.

Intuitively, an oracle scientist $\mathbf{M}$ is said to $\mathbf{O}^{A,b}\mathbf{Ex}$-identify a function f if and only if $\mathbf{M}$ $\mathbf{O}^A\mathbf{Ex}$-identifies f by asking only up to b distinct queries of A. As an immediate corollary of Lemma 11.8 we have

11.11 Corollary *If $A \leq_T K$, then $\mathbf{O}^{A,*}\mathbf{Ex} = \mathbf{Ex}$.*

Fortnow, Gasarch, Jain, *et al.* [59] show the converse to this.

A natural question is whether there is anything to gain from allowing oracle scientists to ask additional queries. The next proposition shows that this is indeed the case—provided the oracle involved is powerful enough.

11.12 Proposition (Fortnow, Gasarch, Jain, et al. [59]) *For all A, the following are equivalent.*

(a) *$A \not\leq_T K$.*

(b) *For all n, $\mathbf{O}^{A,n}\mathbf{Ex} \subset \mathbf{O}^{A,n+1}\mathbf{Ex}$.*

§11.4 Language identification by oracle scientists

We now consider the identification of languages by oracle scientists. The next definition extends the **TxtEx** paradigm to identification by oracle scientists. We again let the reader verify that notation about computable scientists converging on a text carries over to oracle scientists.

11.13 Definition Let $A \subseteq N$.

(a) An oracle scientist **M** $\mathbf{O}^A\mathbf{TxtEx}$-*identifies* L (written: $L \in \mathbf{O}^A\mathbf{TxtEx}(\mathbf{M})$) just in case, for each text T for L, we have $\mathbf{M}^A(T){\downarrow}$ and $W_{\mathbf{M}^A(T)} = L$.

(b) $\mathbf{O}^A\mathbf{TxtEx} = \{\, \mathcal{L} \subseteq \mathcal{E} \mid \mathcal{L} \subseteq \mathbf{O}^A\mathbf{TxtEx}(\mathbf{M})$ for some $\mathbf{M} \,\}$.

As was the case with functions, the first natural question is whether there are omniscient oracles, that is, whether there is an A such that $\mathcal{E} \in \mathbf{O}^A\mathbf{TxtEx}$. In contrast to the function case, in this setting we obtain a negative answer to this question.

11.14 Proposition *For all* A, $\mathcal{E} \notin \mathbf{O}^A\mathbf{TxtEx}$.

Proof: As the reader can check, Proposition 3.22 extends to oracle scientists. Hence, Corollary 3.28 implies the present proposition. ∎

Since no oracle suffices to make $\mathcal{E}$ identifiable, an interesting question is whether employing a more powerful oracle in the arithmetic hierarchy yields extra learning power. The following result provides a sufficient condition for an oracle B allowing the identification of at least one collection of languages that cannot be identified using oracle C. Recall that $A \otimes B = \{\, \langle a, b \rangle \mid a \in A \text{ and } b \in B \,\}$.

11.15 Proposition *Suppose* A_0, A_1, A_2, … *is a sequence of subsets of* N *such that* $\{\, i \mid A_i \text{ is finite} \,\} \notin \Sigma_2$. *Let* $B = \bigcup_{i \in N}(\{i\} \otimes A_i)$ *and let* C *be any set such that* $\{\, i \mid A_i \text{ is finite} \,\} \notin \Sigma_2^C$. *Then, there is an* $\mathcal{L} \in (\mathbf{O}^B\mathbf{TxtEx} - \mathbf{O}^C\mathbf{TxtEx})$.

For an example of a sequence of sets A_0, A_1, A_2, … satisfying the proposition's hypothesis, take $A_i = \overline{W_i}$ for each $i \in N$. Our proof of the above result relies on the following lemma, which is a relativization of the locking sequence lemma (Theorem 3.22). The proof of the lemma is left to the reader.

11.16 Lemma *Suppose* **M** $\mathbf{O}^A\mathbf{TxtEx}$-*identifies* L. *Then there is a* σ *such that:*

(a) *content*$(\sigma) \subseteq L$,

(b) $W_{\mathbf{M}^A(\sigma)} = L$, and

(c) for all τ with $\sigma \subseteq \tau$ and $content(\tau) \subseteq L$, we have that $\mathbf{M}^A(\sigma) = \mathbf{M}^A(\tau)$.

We refer to σ as an $\mathbf{O}^A\mathbf{TxtEx}$-*locking sequence for* $\mathbf{M}$ *on* L.

Proof (of Proposition 11.15): Define

$$
\begin{aligned}
\mathcal{L}_{\text{fin}} &= \{\{i\} \otimes N \mid A_i \text{ is finite}\}, \\
\mathcal{L}_{\text{inf}} &= \{\{i\} \otimes D \mid A_i \text{ is infinite and } D \text{ is finite and nonempty}\}, \text{ and} \\
\mathcal{L} &= \mathcal{L}_{\text{fin}} \cup \mathcal{L}_{\text{inf}}.
\end{aligned}
$$

11.17 Claim $\mathcal{L} \in \mathbf{O}^B\mathbf{TxtEx}$.

Proof: We first note that by the s-m-n theorem (Theorem 2.1) there are recursive functions g_0 and g_1 such that for all i and j:

$$
W_{g_0(i)} = \{i\} \otimes N. \qquad W_{g_1(i,j)} = \{i\} \otimes D_j.
$$

Consider the following oracle scientist (with oracle X).

Program for $\mathbf{M}^X$ on σ

If $content(\sigma) \neq \{i\} \otimes D$ for some $i \in N$ and some nonempty $D \subset N$,
  then output 0 and halt.

Otherwise:

  Let i and D be such that $content(\sigma) = \{i\} \otimes D$.
  If $card(D) > card(\{\langle i, x \rangle \in X \mid x < |\sigma|\})$
    then output $g_0(i)$
    else output $g_1(i,j)$, where j is the canonical index of D.

End Program

We leave it as an exercise to show that $\mathbf{M}^B$ $\mathbf{TxtEx}$-identifies $\mathcal{L}$. $\square$

11.18 Claim $\mathcal{L} \notin \mathbf{O}^C\mathbf{TxtEx}$.

Proof: Suppose by way of contradiction that there is an $\mathbf{M}$ that $\mathbf{O}^C\mathbf{TxtEx}$-identifies $\mathcal{L}$. We show that $\{i \mid A_i \text{ is finite}\} \in \Sigma_2^C$.

Suppose i is such that A_i is finite. Then by our definition of $\mathcal{L}$, $\{i\} \otimes N \in \mathcal{L}$. Thus, by Lemma 11.16 there is an $\mathbf{O}^C\mathbf{TxtEx}$-locking sequence for $\mathbf{M}$ on $\{i\} \otimes N$.

Suppose i is such that A_i is infinite. Then, for every σ with $content(\sigma) \subseteq \{i\} \otimes N$ there are infinitely many $L \in \mathcal{L}$ such that $content(\sigma) \subseteq L \neq W_{\mathbf{M}(\sigma)}$.

Therefore, we have that

$$A_i \text{ is finite } \iff$$
$$(\exists \sigma \mid content(\sigma) \subseteq \{i\} \otimes N)$$
$$(\forall \tau \mid \sigma \subseteq \tau \text{ and } content(\tau) \subseteq \{i\} \otimes N)$$
$$[\mathbf{M}^C(\sigma) = \mathbf{M}^C(\tau)].$$

So, $\{i \mid A_i \text{ is finite}\} \in \Sigma_2^C$, a contradiction. $\square$ ∎

§11.5 Bibliographic notes

The study of function identification in the presence of membership oracles was initiated by Gasarch and Pleszkoch [76]. An earlier work in this direction is due to Adleman and Blum [1]. The reader is referred to a comprehensive paper by Fortnow, Gasarch, Jain, Kinber, Kummer, Kurtz, Pleszkoch, Slaman, Solovay, and Stephan [59] for numerous results on this topic.

The investigation of language identification in the presence of membership oracles was first considered by Jain and Sharma [87], and extended by Kummer and Stephan [114]. Ott and Stephan [146] demonstrate the use of oracles in the context of a model for learning infinite recursive branches of recursive trees due to Kummer and Ott [113].

A related model studied by Gasarch and Smith [77] allows a scientist to ask a teacher questions, phrased in a prespecified first-order language, about the function being identified.

§11.6 Exercises

11-1 (Adleman and Blum [1]) Suppose A is high (see page 253). Show that $\mathcal{R} \in \mathbf{O}^A\mathbf{Ex}$.

11-2 (Gasarch and Pleszkoch [76]) A set A is said to be *low* if $A' \leq_T K$. Show that $\mathbf{O}^A\mathbf{Ex} = \mathbf{Ex} \Rightarrow [A \text{ low}]$.

11-3   Let $A \subseteq N$ be limiting recursive. Suppose that $\mathcal{C} \in \mathbf{O}^A \mathbf{Ex}(\mathbf{M})$. Further suppose that for each $f \in \mathcal{C}$, $\mathbf{M}$ on input f, makes at most finitely many queries to A, that is, $\mathcal{C} \in \mathbf{O}^{A,*} \mathbf{Ex}$. Show that $\mathcal{C} \in \mathbf{Ex}$.

11-4   (**Fortnow, Gasarch, Jain, et al. [59]**) Suppose A is Turing reducible to both K and some 1-generic set. Show that $\mathbf{O}^A \mathbf{Ex} = \mathbf{Ex}$.

11-5   Extend Definition 11.13 in the obvious way to allow oracle scientists to converge to finite variant grammars for the language being identified. That is, for $a \in (N \cup \{*\})$ and $A \subseteq N$, define paradigms $\mathbf{O}^A \mathbf{TxtEx}^a$. Then establish the following stronger version of Proposition 11.15:

Let A_0, A_1, $A_2, \ldots$ be a sequence of sets such that $\{\, i \mid A_i \text{ is finite}\,\} \notin \Sigma_2$ and let $B = \{\langle i, x \rangle \mid x \in A_i \wedge i \in N\}$. Choose C so that $\{\, i \mid A_i \text{ is finite}\,\} \notin \Sigma_2^C$. Then there is an $\mathcal{L} \in \mathbf{O}^B \mathbf{TxtEx} - \mathbf{O}^C \mathbf{TxtEx}^*$.

Hint: Consider a cylindrification of the class used in the proof of Proposition 11.15.

12   Complexity Issues in Identification

§12.1 Introduction

Our study has thus far concentrated on the question of what is learnable in principle when there are no constraints on either

(a) the computational resources required by the scientist, or

(b) the complexity of final hypotheses.

The present chapter discusses the prospects for learnability when resources are bounded, or when final hypotheses are required to be simple.

The complexity of the identification process.   Unlike the case for complexity of computable functions, there are no standard notions of "feasible" identification or even agreement about how to measure the computation costs of identification. Worse yet, the study of the computational complexity of functionals and operators is still in its infancy, with knotty questions surrounding even the most basic definitions — see Cook [44], Kapron and Cook [102], Seth [169, 170], and Royer [160].

In the light of the above difficulties, only partial attempts have been made to model the complexity of the identification process. Some of these are:

1. bounding the number of mind changes made by a scientist before convergence (discussed in Section 12.2);

2. bounding the number of examples required before the onset of convergence (discussed in Section 12.3);

3. measuring the amount of computation done by the scientist before the onset of convergence (discussed in Exercise 12-6).

Additionally, in Section 12.4 we discuss an axiomatic treatment of the complexity of convergence.

The complexity of the final hypothesis.   It is easy to motivate the desire for succinct final hypotheses. Numerous formulations of succinctness have been advanced for both functions and languages. Sections 12.5 and 12.6 examine a number of such proposals for languages. The analogous cases for functions can be found in the exercises.

§12.2 Mind change complexity

We refer to the abandonment of a scientific conjecture as a *mind change*. The definition of identification places no restriction on the number of mind changes that precede convergence. In the present section we examine the impact on identifiability of bounding this number. To proceed, it will be convenient to slight modify the definition of scientist.

We pick a nonnumerical entity "?" and append it to the range of scientists. Thus, in the functional context, scientists become mappings from SEG to $N \cup \{\,?\,\}$. Moreover, we restrict the term "scientist" to mappings $\mathbf{M}$ of this kind that meet the following, additional constraint: For all $\sigma \in$ SEG, and $x, y \in N$, if $\mathbf{M}(\sigma) \neq ?$ then $\mathbf{M}(\sigma \diamond (x, y)) \neq ?$. In other words, scientists (in our new sense) can issue ? only on some initial segment of the incoming graph; once they respond numerically (or are undefined), they do not issue ? again. Intuitively, "$\mathbf{M}(f[n]) = ?$" represents a situation in which $\mathbf{M}$ has not seen enough data to issue any sensible hypothesis and so instead issues a "?", which means 'no hypothesis yet.' For scientist $\mathbf{M}$ on function f, we say that $\mathbf{M}$ on f has a *mind change at* m if and only if we have: $m > 0$, $\mathbf{M}(f[m-1]) \in N$, and $\mathbf{M}(f[m-1]) \neq \mathbf{M}(f[m])$. Thus the case in which $\mathbf{M}(f[m-1]) = ?$ and $\mathbf{M}(f[m]) \in N$ does *not* count as a mind change.

We are now in a position to formalize identification with a bounded number of mind changes. The following definition also handles errors in final hypothesis. Recall that "$x \leq *$" means that x is finite.

12.1 Definition (Bārzdiņš and Freivalds [15], Case and Smith [35]) Let a and b be elements of $(N \cup \{*\})$.

(a) $\mathbf{M}$ $\mathbf{Ex}_b^a$-*identifies* f (written: $f \in \mathbf{Ex}_b^a(\mathbf{M})$) just in case

  1. $\mathbf{M}(f){\downarrow}$ and $\varphi_{\mathbf{M}(f)} =^a f$, and

  2. $card(\{\, n \mid \mathbf{M} \text{ on } f \text{ has a mind change at } n\,\}) \leq b$.

(b) $\mathbf{Ex}_b^a = \{\, \mathcal{S} \mid \mathcal{S} \subseteq \mathbf{Ex}_b^a(\mathbf{M}) \text{ for some } \mathbf{M}\,\}$.

So, $\mathbf{Ex}_*^a$ is simply the $\mathbf{Ex}^a$ paradigm defined in Chapter 6. The special case of $\mathbf{Ex}_0^0$ is variously referred to in the literature as: the **Fin** paradigm, *finite identification*, and *one shot learning*. The **Fin** paradigm, in which a scientist's first conjecture has to be correct, first appears in the work of Gold [80] and Trakhtenbrot and Bārzdiņš [188].

The following proposition says that there is a collection of functions $\mathcal{S}$ such that: there is some scientist that infers, with no mind changes, an $(n+1)$-error program for each element of $\mathcal{S}$, *but* there is no scientist that infers an n-error program for each element of $\mathcal{S}$—even if we allow the scientist to make an arbitrary number of mind changes. The proof of this proposition follows from the argument given for Proposition 6.5.

12.2 Proposition (Case and Smith [35]) *For each* $n \in N$, $\mathbf{Ex}_0^{n+1} - \mathbf{Ex}^n \neq \emptyset$.

Similarly, as an immediate consequence Corollary 6.6, we have the following.

12.3 Corollary (Case and Smith [35]) $\mathbf{Ex}_0^* - \bigcup_{n \in N} \mathbf{Ex}^n \neq \emptyset$.

The next result shows the advantages of allowing an extra number of mind changes. The first part says that there is a collection of functions $\mathcal{S}$ for which there is a scientist that for each function in $\mathcal{S}$ infers a program via only $n + 1$ mind changes, but for which even a $\star$-error program cannot be identified if only n mind changes are allowed

12.4 Proposition (Case and Smith [35])

(a) *Suppose* $n \in N$. *Then*, $\mathbf{Ex}_{n+1}^0 - \mathbf{Ex}_n^* \neq \emptyset$.

(b) $\mathbf{Ex}^0 - \bigcup_{n \in N} \mathbf{Ex}_n^* \neq \emptyset$.

Proof: We argue only the special case of part (a): $\mathbf{Ex}_{n+1}^0 - \mathbf{Ex}_n^0 \neq \emptyset$. Part (b) and the general case of part (a) are handled in Exercise 12-1.

Let $\mathcal{C}_n = \{\, f \mid card(\{\, x \mid f(x) \neq 0 \,\}) \leq n + 1 \,\}$, which is clearly in $\mathbf{Ex}_{n+1}$. Suppose by way of contradiction that there is an $\mathbf{M}$ that $\mathbf{Ex}_0^n$-identifies $\mathcal{C}_n$. Let $f_0 = \lambda x.0$, which is obviously in $\mathcal{C}_n$. Hence, by our assumption on $\mathbf{M}$, there is an

$$m_0 \;=\; \mu m. [\, (\forall k \geq m)[\, M(f_0[m]) = M(f_0[k]) \text{ and } \varphi_{\mathbf{M}(f_0[m])} = f_0 \,]].$$

For $i = 1, \ldots, n + 1$, we inductively define f_i and m_i as follows.

$$f_i \;=\; \lambda x. \begin{cases} f_{i-1}(x), & \text{if } x < m_{i-1}; \\ 1, & \text{if } x = m_{i-1}; \\ 0, & \text{if } x > m_{i-1}. \end{cases}$$

$$m_i \;=\; \mu m. [\, (\forall k \geq m)[\, M(f_i[m]) = M(f_i[k]) \text{ and } \varphi_{\mathbf{M}(f_i[m])} = f_i \,]].$$

It follows from a simple induction argument that each f_i is a member of $\mathcal{C}_n$, and thus that each m_i is well defined. It also follows that $\mathbf{M}$ on f_{n+1} has a mind change at each of the $n + 1$ many points $m_1, \ldots, m_{n+1}$, a contradiction. ∎

As an immediate corollary to the above, we have the following, which summarizes the advantages of allowing extra mind changes.

12.5 Corollary *Let $a \in (N \cup \{*\})$. Then,* $\mathbf{Ex}_0^a \subset \mathbf{Ex}_1^a \subset \mathbf{Ex}_2^a \subset \cdots \subset \mathbf{Ex}^a$.

§12.3 Number of examples required

Another freedom available to a scientist in the identification paradigm is that she can see as much data as she wishes before settling on a final conjecture. Practical systems for empirical inquiry seldom have such luxury. It is thus worth considering modifications on the identification paradigm in which a scientist is limited by the number of examples she can see before settling on a final conjecture. Here we discuss a proposal due to Wiehagen.

A simplistic approach to bounding the number of data elements would be to define a paradigm under which a scientist can see no more than a predetermined number of examples before converging. This approach is not satisfactory, however, since it does not allow the bound to vary among different functions in the collection to be identified (after all, the graphs of distinct functions might coincide on arbitrary long initial segments of N). In order to describe a paradigm in which the bound depends on the underlying reality being identified, we need a mechanism for naming these possible realities. One way to achieve this is to include in the paradigm's definition a parameter ψ, which is the programming system (numbering) in which a scientist's conjectures are interpreted. (**N.B.** In this section we allow the possibility that $\{\psi_i \mid i \in N\}$ is a strict subset of $\mathcal{P}$.) Until now such a parameterization was implicit and a scientist's hypotheses were interpreted in some fixed acceptable programming system for the partial recursive functions. The parameterized version of the **Ex** paradigm is as follows.

12.6 Definition Let ψ be a programming system.

(a) **M Ex**-*identifies $\mathcal{S}$ with respect to ψ* (written: $\mathcal{S} \subseteq \mathbf{Ex}_\psi(\mathbf{M})$) just in case for each $f \in \mathcal{S}$, $\mathbf{M}(f){\downarrow}$ and $\psi_{\mathbf{M}(f)} = f$.

(b) $\mathbf{Ex}_\psi = \{\, \mathcal{S} \mid \mathcal{S} \subseteq \mathbf{Ex}_\psi(\mathbf{M})$ for some $\mathbf{M}\,\}$.

It is easy to check that for any two acceptable programming systems, ψ and ψ', $\mathbf{Ex}_\psi = \mathbf{Ex}_{\psi'}$. Thus, if attention is restricted to acceptable programming systems, then choosing one over the other does not yield any extra learning ability. Most of the paradigms discussed in this book can straightforwardly be redefined with the underlying programming system as a parameter; we will denote the resulting classes simply by including the programming system in the subscript. For example, $\mathbf{Ex}_{n,\psi}$ denotes the collections of functions that can be identified with no more than n mind changes with respect to the acceptable programming system ψ.

Before formalizing paradigms with a bounded number of examples, we introduce a couple of technical tools. For each $\mathbf{M}$ and $\sigma \in \text{INIT}$, define

$$\text{conv}(\mathbf{M}, \sigma) = (\mu m \leq |\sigma|).[\,(\forall n \mid m \leq n \leq |\sigma|)[\,\mathbf{M}(\sigma[n]) = \mathbf{M}(\sigma)\,]\,].$$

Roughly, $\text{conv}(\mathbf{M}, \sigma)$ is the last mind change in the sequence $\mathbf{M}(\sigma[0]), \ldots, \mathbf{M}(\sigma[|\sigma|])$. Given a scientist $\mathbf{M}$ and $f \colon N \to N$, we also define

$$\begin{aligned}
\text{conv}(\mathbf{M}, f) &= \lim_{n \to \infty} \text{conv}(\mathbf{M}, f[n]) && (12.1)\\
&= \mu m.[\,(\forall n \mid m \leq n)[\,\mathbf{M}(f[m]) = \mathbf{M}(f[n])\,]\,].
\end{aligned}$$

Thus, $\text{conv}(\mathbf{M}, f)$ denotes the earliest convergence point, if any, for $\mathbf{M}$ on f.

We now introduce identification from a bounded number of examples in a given programming system. **N.B.** The paradigm described below is dependent on the order in which the function is fed to the scientist. For convenience of investigation, we assume that the function is presented to the scientist in canonical order. Such a requirement is a weakness of this model.

12.7 Definition (Wiehagen [199]) Let h be a partial recursive function and ψ a programming system.

(a) $\mathcal{S}$ is said to be h-**Bounded-Ex**-*identifiable with respect to* ψ (written: $\mathcal{S} \subseteq h$-**Bounded-Ex**$_\psi(\mathbf{M})$) just in case there exists a scientist $\mathbf{M}$ that **Ex**-identifies $\mathcal{S}$ with respect to ψ and, for all i with $\psi_i \in \mathcal{S}$, we have $\text{conv}(\mathbf{M}, \psi_i) \leq h(i)\!\downarrow$.

(b) h-**Bounded-Ex**$_\psi = \{\, \mathcal{S} \mid \mathcal{S} \subseteq h\text{-}\mathbf{Bounded\text{-}Ex}_\psi(\mathbf{M}) \text{ for some } \mathbf{M} \,\}$.

(c) **Bounded-Ex**$_\psi = \{\, \mathcal{S} \mid \mathcal{S} \in h\text{-}\mathbf{Bounded\text{-}Ex}_\psi \text{ for some } h \,\}$.

(d) **Bounded-Ex** $= \{\, \mathcal{S} \mid \mathcal{S} \in \mathbf{Bounded\text{-}Ex}_\psi \text{ for some } \psi \,\}$.

Surprisingly, **Bounded-Ex** is no less inclusive than **Ex**. Indeed:

12.8 Proposition (Wiehagen [199]) Bounded-Ex = Ex.

Proof: Fix an arbitrary $\mathbf{M}$. We construct a programming system ψ and a scientist $\mathbf{M}'$ such that $\mathbf{Ex}(\mathbf{M}) \subseteq \text{id-}\mathbf{BoundedEx}_\psi(\mathbf{M}')$, where $\text{id} = \lambda x.x$. This will establish the proposition. Recall that our standard pairing function $\langle \cdot, \cdot \rangle \colon N \times N \to N$ is one-one, onto, and monotone nondecreasing in both arguments.

For each i, n, and x, define

$$\psi_{\langle i,n \rangle}(x) \quad = \quad \begin{cases} \varphi_i(x), & \text{if, for all } y < x, \ \varphi_i(y)\!\downarrow \text{ and } n = \mathrm{conv}(\mathbf{M}, \varphi_i[x]); \\ \uparrow, & \text{otherwise.} \end{cases}$$

Since $\lambda \sigma.\mathrm{conv}(\mathbf{M}, \sigma)$ is recursive, we have that $\lambda p, x.\psi_p(x)$ is partial recursive. Observe that $\psi_{\langle i,n \rangle}$ is total if and only if φ_i is total and $\mathrm{conv}(\mathbf{M}, \varphi_i)\!\downarrow = n$. Moreover, if $\psi_{\langle i,n \rangle}$ is total, then $\psi_{\langle i,n \rangle} = \varphi_i$. For each $\sigma \in \mathrm{INIT}$, define

$$\mathbf{M}'(\sigma) \quad = \quad \langle \mathbf{M}(\sigma), \mathrm{conv}(\mathbf{M}, \sigma) \rangle.$$

It follows that, for each $g \in \mathbf{Ex}(\mathbf{M})$, $\mathbf{M}'(g)\!\downarrow = \langle \mathbf{M}(g), \mathrm{conv}(\mathbf{M}, g) \rangle$, $\psi_{\mathbf{M}'(g)} = g$, and $\mathrm{conv}(\mathbf{M}', g) = \mathrm{conv}(\mathbf{M}, g)$. Finally, since for all i and n, $n \leq \langle i, n \rangle$, it follows that for each $g \in \mathbf{Ex}(\mathbf{M})$, $\mathbf{M}'$ id-**BoundedEx**$_\psi$-identifies g. ∎

Note that the h witnessing the above is extremely simple. In contrast, we have the following which says that there exists a programming system ψ for which there are collections of functions that can be identified with no more than one mind change with respect to ψ, but that are not in h-**Bounded-Ex**$_\psi$ for *any* recursive function h.

12.9 Proposition (Wiehagen [199]) *There exists a programming system ψ for which there are collections of functions $\mathcal{S}$ such that $\mathcal{S} \in (\mathbf{Ex}_{1,\psi} - \bigcup_{h \in \mathcal{R}} h\text{-}\mathbf{Bounded\text{-}Ex}_\psi)$.*

Proof: Let X be any nonrecursive r.e. set and let f be a 1–1 recursive function such that $range(f) = X$. Without loss of generality, let $0 \notin X$. Let $g_* = \lambda x.0$ and, for each $i \in N$, let

$$g_i \quad = \quad \lambda x. \begin{cases} 0, & \text{if } x < i; \\ 1, & \text{otherwise.} \end{cases}$$

For each i, define

$$\psi_i \quad = \quad \lambda x. \begin{cases} 0, & \text{if } i \notin \{\, f(0), \ldots, f(x)\,\}; \\ 1, & \text{otherwise;} \end{cases} \qquad = \quad \begin{cases} g_n, & \text{if } f(n) = i; \\ g_*, & \text{otherwise.} \end{cases}$$

Clearly, $\lambda i, x.\psi_i(x)$ is partial recursive.

It is clear that $\{\,\psi_i \mid i \in N\,\} \in \mathbf{Ex}_{1,\psi}$. Suppose by way of contradiction that, for some recursive h, $\mathbf{M}$ h-**BoundedEx**-identifies each ψ_i. Let $k = h(0)$. Then it follows that $i \in X$ if and only if $(\exists j \leq max(k, h(i)))[f(j) = i]$. But this contradicts the nonrecursiveness of X. ∎

§12.4 An axiomatic approach to complexity of convergence

In this section we briefly discuss axiomatizations of various complexity measures for convergence. This discussion is based on work of Daley and Smith [54], which in turn was inspired by Blum's [19] axiomatic treatment of complexity measures for computable functions. As before, we assume in what follows that texts for functions are arranged in canonical order.

12.10 Definition Let $\mathcal{M}$ denote the class of all computable scientists. Suppose C is a partial function from $\mathcal{M} \times \mathcal{F} \rightharpoonup N$. We say that C is a complexity measure for convergence if and only if the following two axioms are satisfied.

(A1) $\mathbf{M}(f){\downarrow} \iff C(\mathbf{M}, f){\downarrow}$.

(A2) The relation $[\, C(\mathbf{M}, f) = n \,]$ is limiting-recursively decidable in $\mathbf{M}$, f, and n.[1]

These two axioms parallel Blum's axioms for the complexity of programs (see page 24). Note that the definition concerns complexity of convergence, not identification. In other words, there is no requirement that the final hypothesis be correct.

The following proposition shows that the mind change complexity measure described in Section 12.2 satisfies the above axioms. See Exercises 12-5 and 12-6 for other examples of measures.

12.11 Proposition (Daley and Smith [54]) *Let $\delta(\mathbf{M}, f)$ denote the number of mind changes made by $\mathbf{M}$ on f. Then δ satisfies the axioms given in Definition 12.10*

Proof: Clearly, $\delta(\mathbf{M}, f)$ is defined if and only if $\mathbf{M}(f){\downarrow}$. So, δ satisfies axiom (A1). For each $\mathbf{M}$ and $\sigma \in$ INIT, define

$$\delta(\mathbf{M}, \sigma) = \mathrm{card}\left(\left\{ x < |\sigma| \;\middle|\; ? \neq \mathbf{M}(\sigma[x]) \neq \mathbf{M}(\sigma[x+1]) \right\} \right).$$

Clearly, $\lambda \mathbf{M}, \sigma . \delta(\mathbf{M}, \sigma)$ is recursive. Note that, for each $\mathbf{M}$ and f,

$$\delta(\mathbf{M}, f) = \lim_{m \to \infty} \delta(\mathbf{M}, f[m]).$$

It is thus straightforward to show that δ satisfies axiom (A2).   ∎

Daley and Smith [54] have a number of further results on complexity measures based on this axiomatic approach.

---

[1] That is, there is a recursive functional Θ such that, for all $\mathbf{M}$, $f \colon N \to N$, and $n \in N$, we have that $\lim_{t \to \infty} \Theta(\mathbf{M}, f, n, t){\downarrow}$ and this limit is 1 if $C(\mathbf{M}, f) = n$ and 0 otherwise.

§12.5 Strictly minimal identification of languages

Identification places no constraint on the size of the final hypothesis, so long as it corresponds to the incoming function or language. More realism in this regard is easy to justify since conciseness is widely touted as a virtue of good theory. Similarly, there is reason to study small, final hypotheses in the acquisition of language by children. To the extent that developmental psycholinguists seek to characterize the form of the grammar in the child's mind, models of learning should recognize that final hypotheses cannot be arbitrarily large (assuming that the child cannot implement a Turing Machine whose states exceed the number n of synapses in the brain — or 2^n if we crudely attempt to model all possible brain configurations).

In this and the next section we consider two approaches to restricting the size of final hypotheses. We consider results only for language learning, leaving functions to the exercises. One of our main concerns is to study the dependence of size restrictions on the underlying programming system in which a scientist's conjectures are interpreted.

A natural restriction on hypothesis size is that it be minimal. Recall from Chapter 2 that the index of a program satisfies the requirements of a Blum program size measure. The next definition introduces a paradigm in which scientists are required to converge to minimal-size hypotheses in a given programming system

12.12 Definition

(a) **M TxtMin$_\psi$-identifies** L (written: $L \subseteq \mathbf{TxtMin}_\psi(\mathbf{M})$) just in case, for all texts T for L, $\mathbf{M}(T){\downarrow} = MinGram^\psi(L)$.

(b) $\mathbf{TxtMin}_\psi = \{\mathcal{L} \mid [\mathcal{L} \subseteq \mathbf{TxtMin}_\psi(\mathbf{M})$ for some $\mathbf{M}\}$.

12.13 Proposition *There is an acceptable programming system ψ such that $\mathbf{TxtMin}_\psi$ contains an infinite collection of infinite r.e. languages.*

Proof: For each y, let $L_y = \{\langle 0, y \rangle\} \cup \{\langle x + 1, 0 \rangle \mid x \in N\}$ and let $\mathcal{L} = \{L_0, L_1, L_2, \ldots\}$. Recall that φ is our standard acceptable programming system. We define a programming system ψ as follows. (The ψ_{2i+1} case in this definition guarantees that ψ is acceptable.) For all i, define:

$$\psi_{2i} = \lambda\langle x, y\rangle. \begin{cases} 0, & \text{if } x = 0 \text{ and } \varphi_i(\langle x, y\rangle){\downarrow} \text{ or } x > 0 \text{ and } y = 0; \\ \uparrow, & \text{otherwise.} \end{cases}$$

$$\psi_{2i+1} = \varphi_i.$$

For each σ, define

$$
\mathbf{M}(\sigma) \;=\;
\begin{cases}
2j, & \text{if there is a unique } y \text{ such that } \langle 0, y \rangle \in content(\sigma) \\
& \quad \text{and } j \text{ is the least number } \leq |\sigma|, \text{ if any, such that} \\
& \quad \{\, x \mid \Phi_j(\langle 0, x \rangle) \leq |\sigma| \,\} = \{\, y \,\}; \\
0, & \text{otherwise.}
\end{cases}
$$

We leave it as a straightforward exercise to check that $\mathbf{M}$ $\mathbf{TxtMin}_\psi$-identifies $\mathcal{L}$.   ∎

The $\mathbf{TxtMin}_\psi$ paradigm can be related in a striking fashion to $\mathbf{TxtEx}$. For this purpose, we introduce the following definition which is based on a related notion of Freivalds [61] (see Exercise 12-8).

12.14 Definition (Case and Chi [27])

(a) Suppose g and v are recursive functions. We say that $\mathcal{L}$ is *limiting standardizable via g with recursive estimate v* (written: $\mathcal{L} \subset \mathbf{TxtLsr}(g, v)$) if and only if, for each $L \in \mathcal{L}$, there is an i_L with $W_{i_L} = L$ such that, for every i with $W_i = L$ we have:

1. $\lim_{n \to \infty} g(i, n) = i_L$, and

2. $card(\{\, g(i, n) \mid n \in N \,\}) \leq v(i)$.

(b) We say that $\mathcal{L}$ is *text limiting standardizable with recursive estimate* (written: $\mathcal{L} \in \mathbf{TxtLsr}$) if and only if, for some recursive g and v we have $\mathcal{L} \subseteq \mathbf{TxtLsr}(g, v)$.

Intuitively, the role of g in the definition of $\mathbf{TxtLsr}$ is to provide indirectly a limiting recursive solution to a special case of the *grammar equivalence problem* ($\{\{\langle x, y \rangle \mid W_x = W_y\}\}$) where the grammars generate languages in $\mathcal{L}$; the v places some extra constraints on how g reaches its limit.[2] The notion of $\mathbf{TxtLsr}$ defined above is implicitly parameterized by the choice of acceptable programming system. Explicit parameterization is not called for, because it is easy to check that the class $\mathbf{TxtLsr}$ is independent of the choice of acceptable programming system. Here is the promised characterization of $\mathbf{TxtMin}_\psi$.

12.15 Proposition *For all $\mathcal{L}$, the following are equivalent.*

(a) *For some acceptable programming system ψ, $\mathcal{L} \in \mathbf{TxtMin}_\psi$.*

(b) $\mathcal{L} \in (\mathbf{TxtEx} \cap \mathbf{TxtLsr})$.

---

[2] This interpretation is due to John Case.

Proof: Let $\mathcal{L}$ be given.

(a) $\Longrightarrow$ *(b)*. Suppose that ψ is an acceptable programming system and that $\mathcal{L} \in$ **TxtMin**$_\psi$. Clearly, $\mathcal{L} \in$ **TxtEx**. It suffices to construct recursive functions g and v such that $\mathcal{L} \in$ **TxtLsr**(g, v). Since ψ and φ are acceptable, there are recursive functions, r_1 and r_2, such that, for all i,

$$\varphi_{r_1(i)} \;\; = \;\; \psi_i \quad \text{and} \quad \psi_{r_2(i)} \;\; = \;\; \varphi_i.$$

For each i, let T^i be the text such that, for each x and t,

$$T^i(\langle x, t \rangle) \;\; = \;\; \begin{cases} x, & \text{if } \Phi_i(x) = t; \\ \#, & \text{otherwise.} \end{cases}$$

Thus, T^i is a text for W_i. For each i and n, define $v(i) = r_2(i) + 1$ and

$$g(i, n) \;\; = \;\; \begin{cases} r_1(\mathbf{M}(T^i[n])), & \text{if } \mathbf{M}(T^i[n]) \leq r_2(i); \\ r_1(0), & \text{otherwise.} \end{cases}$$

It is immediate from the definition of g that, for each i, $card(\{\, g(i, n) \mid n \in N \,\}) \leq r_2(i) + 1 = v(i)$. Now suppose that $L \in \mathcal{L}$ and $W_i = L$. Then $\lim_{n \to \infty} \mathbf{M}(T^i[n]) = MinGram^\psi(L) \leq r_2(i)$. Hence, $\lim_{n \to \infty} g(i, n) = r_1(MinGram^\psi(L))$, which is a φ-grammar for L. Therefore, $\mathcal{L} \in$ **TxtLsr**(g, v) as required.

(b) $\Longrightarrow$ *(a)*. Let g and v be recursive functions such that $\mathcal{L} \in$ **TxtLsr**(g, v). For each $L \in \mathcal{L}$, let i_L be as in Definition 12.14(a). The following simple observation is crucial in our construction of ψ. The proof is obvious.

12.16 Claim *Suppose i is such that there are infinitely many n with $g(i, n) = i$. Then either (a) $W_i \notin \mathcal{L}$ or (b) $W_i \in \mathcal{L}$ and $i = i_{W_i}$.*

Let $A = \{\, (i, j) \mid i \in N \text{ and } j \leq v(i) + 1 \,\}$. For each $(i, j) \in A$, define

$$r(i, j) \;\; = \;\; \sum_{k=0}^{i} (v(k) + 2) \; - \; j - 1.$$

We note that r provides a recursive one-to-one correspondence between A and N. For each (i_0, j_0) and $(i_1, j_1) \in A$ we write $(i_0, j_0) < (i_1, j_1)$ if and only if $r(i_0, j_0) < r(i_1, j_1)$. Since r is a one-to-one correspondence between A and N, this is a total order on A. Moreover, by the definition of r we have

$$(i_0, j_0) < (i_1, j_1) \quad \Longleftrightarrow \quad [\, i_0 < i_1 \,] \text{ or } [\, i_0 = i_1 \text{ and } j_0 > j_1 \,].$$

We define a partial recursive $\eta \colon A \rightharpoonup N$ by the equation:

$$
\eta(i,j) \;=\; \begin{cases} i, & \text{if } j = 0; \\ g(i, k_j), & \text{if } 1 \le j \le v(i) + 1 \text{ and } k_j \text{ is the least number, if} \\ & \quad \text{any, such that } card(\{\, g(i,0), \ldots, g(i, k_j)\,\}) = j; \\ \uparrow, & \text{otherwise.} \end{cases}
$$

So if $\eta(i, j+1)\!\downarrow$, then $\eta(i, j+1)$ is the $(j+1)$-st distinct grammar in the list $g(i, 0)$, $g(i, 1)$, $g(i, 2), \ldots$; and if $\eta(i, j+1)\!\uparrow$, then this list contains fewer than $(j+1)$ distinct grammars. For each $(i, j) \in A$ and $x \in N$, define

$$
\psi_{r(i,j)}(x) \;=\; \begin{cases} \varphi_i(x), & \text{if (i) } j = 0; \\ 0, & \text{if (ii) } 1 \le j \le v(i)+1 \text{ and } \eta(i,j)\!\downarrow \;=\; p \text{ and} \\ & \quad max(x, \Phi_p(x)\!\downarrow) < card(\{\, n \mid g(p, n) = p \,\}); \\ \uparrow, & \text{otherwise.} \end{cases}
$$

Since r is a recursive one-to-one correspondence between A and N, it follows that $\lambda k, x\,.\,\psi_k(x)$ is well defined. It follows by clause (i) in the definition of ψ that ψ is acceptable. Recall that, for all i and s, $W_{i,s} = \{\, x \mid max(x, \Phi_i(x)\!\downarrow) < s \,\}$.

12.17 Claim *Suppose $(i, j) \in A$. Then:*

(a) *If $j = 0$, then $W^{\psi}_{r(i,0)} = W_i$.*

(b) *If $j > 0$ and $\eta(i,j)\!\uparrow$, then $W^{\psi}_{r(i,j)} = \emptyset$.*

(c) *If $j > 0$, $\eta(i,j)\!\downarrow \;=\; p$, and $card(\{\, n \mid g(p, n) = p \,\}) = m < \infty$, then $W^{\psi}_{r(i,j)} = W_{\eta(i,j),m}$.*

(d) *If $j > 0$, $\eta(i,j)\!\downarrow \;=\; p$, and $card(\{\, n \mid g(p, n) = p \,\}) = \infty$, then $W^{\psi}_{r(i,j)} = W_{\eta(i,j)}$.*

The above claim follows directly from the definition of ψ. We also have:

12.18 Claim *Suppose $L \in \mathcal{L}$ and (i, j) is the least element of A such that $\eta(i, j) = i_L$. Then:*

(a) *$W_{r(i,j)} = L$ (hence, $MinGram^{\psi}(L) \le r(i, j)$).*

(b) *$j > 0$.*

(c) *If L is infinite, then $MinGram^{\psi}(L) = r(i, j)$.*

Proof: *Part (a)*. If $j = 0$, then $\eta(i, 0) = i_L$ implies, by the definition of η, that $i = i_L$ and, by Claim 12.17(a), $W^{\psi}_{r(i,j)} = W^{\psi}_{r(i_L,0)} = W_{i_L} = L$. If $j > 0$, then by the definitions of ψ and η and the fact that $\lim_{n \to \infty} g(i_L, n) = i_L$, we also have that $W^{\psi}_{r(i,j)} = L$.

Part (b). Suppose $i_* = MinGram^\varphi(L)$. Then, by our choice of i_* and Claim 12.17(a), we have that, for all $(i, 0) < (i_*, 0)$, $W^\psi_{r(i,0)} \neq L$. Since $W_{i_*} = L \in \mathcal{L}$, we have that $\lim_{n \to \infty} g(i_*, n) = i_L$ and, hence, for some $j_* \in \{ 1, \ldots, v(i_*) + 1 \}$, we must have $\eta(i_*, j_*)\!\downarrow\, = i_L$. Thus, it follows that $j > 0$, although we may well have $(i, j) < (i_*, j_*)$.

Part (c). Suppose L is infinite. Suppose by way of contradiction that for some $(i', j') \neq (i, j)$ we have $r(i', j') = MinGram^\psi(L)$. By part (a) and the ordering on A, it follows that $(i', j') < (i, j)$. By the argument for part (b) it must be the case that $j' > 0$. Since $L = W_{r(i', j')}$ is infinite, it follows from Claim 12.17(b) that $\eta(i', j')\!\downarrow$. Let $p = \eta(i', j')$. By Claim 12.17(c) we have that, for infinitely many n, $g(p, n) = p$. Hence, by Claim 12.17(d), $W_p = W_{\eta(i', j')} = W_{r(i', j')}$, which by hypothesis is $= L \in \mathcal{L}$. So, by Claim 12.16, we must have $\eta(i', j') = p = i_L$. But since $(i', j') < (i, j)$, this contradicts our choice of (i, j) as the least element of A with $\eta(i, j) = i_L$. Hence, part (c) follows. $\square$

It is convenient to introduce a ψ-analog of $W_{i,s}$. Towards this end fix p_η, some φ-program for η. Then, for each $(i, j) \in A$ and $s \in N$, define

$$
W^{\psi,s}_{r(i,j)} \;=\; \begin{cases} W_{i,s}, & \text{if } j = 0; \\[4pt] W_{p,m}, & \text{if } j > 0 \text{ and } \Phi_{p_\eta}(i, j) \leq s, \text{ where } p = \eta(i, j) \\ & \text{and } m = card(\{\, n < s \mid g(p, n) = p \,\}); \\[4pt] \emptyset, & \text{otherwise.} \end{cases}
$$

By Claim 12.17 we have that, for all $(i, j) \in A$, $W^\psi_{r(i,j)} = \bigcup_s W^{\psi,s}_{r(i,j)}$, and, for all s, $max(W^{\psi,s}_{r(i,j)}) < s$. Moreover, deciding whether $x \in W^{\psi,s}_{r(i,j)}$ is recursive in i, j, s, and x.

Now let **M** be a scientist that **TxtEx**-identifies $\mathcal{L}$. We define a scientist **M$'$** as follows.

Program for M$'$ on σ.

Let $k = \mathbf{M}(\sigma)$, $n = |\sigma|$, and $p = g(k, n)$.

Find the least $(i, j) \in A$, if any, such that $r(i, j) \leq n$ and $\varphi_{p_\eta, n}(i, j)\!\downarrow\, = p$.

If no such (i, j) is found, then output 0 and halt.

If such an (i, j) is found, then:

Find the least $(i', j') \in A$, if any, such that $(i', j') \leq (i, j)$ and $W^{\psi,n}_{r(i', j')} = content(\sigma)$.
If no such an (i', j') was found, output $r(i, j)$.
If such an (i, j) was found, output $r(i', j')$.

End Program.

We claim that $\mathcal{L} \subseteq \mathbf{TxtMin}_\psi(\mathbf{M}')$. To see this, suppose T is a text for an $L \in \mathcal{L}$. Then $\mathbf{M}(T){\downarrow} = k$ and $W_k = L$. So, for all sufficiently large n, we have that $\mathbf{M}(T[n]){\downarrow} = k$ and $g(k,n) = i_L$. Therefore, in the program for $\mathbf{M}'$, for all sufficiently large n, the search for (i,j) finds the least (i,j) such that $\eta(i,j) = i_L$. We consider two cases.

Case 1: L is finite. In this case it follows from Claim 12.18(a) and our definition of $\mathbf{M}'$ that $\mathbf{M}'(T){\downarrow} = MinGram^\psi(L)$.

Case 2: L is infinite. Suppose $(i',j') \in A$ is such that $(i',j') \leq (i,j)$ and, for infinitely many n, $W_{r(i',j')}^{\psi,n} = content(T[n])$. Then it follows that $W_{r(i,j)} = L$. But by Claim 12.18, the only way that can happen is if $(i',j') = (i,j)$. Hence, by the program for $\mathbf{M}'$, for all but finitely many n, $\mathbf{M}'(T[n]) = r(i,j) = MinGram^\psi(L)$.

It thus follows that $\mathcal{L} \subseteq \mathbf{TxtMin}_\psi(\mathbf{M}')$. ∎

§12.6 Nearly minimal identification

We next consider paradigms in which scientists converge to hypotheses that are of minimal size, modulo a recursive fudge factor. (We say that the hypotheses are of "nearly minimal" size.) The next two definitions introduce this idea.

12.19 Definition Suppose ψ is a programming system and $h \colon N \to N$. We say that i is an *h-minimal ψ-grammar* for L just in case $W_i^\psi = L$ and $i \leq h(MinGram^\psi(L))$.

12.20 Definition (Case and Chi [27]) Suppose $h \in \mathcal{R}$.

(a) $\mathbf{M}$ *h-$\mathbf{TxtMex}_\psi$-identifies* $\mathcal{L}$ (written: $\mathcal{L} \subseteq h\text{-}\mathbf{TxtMex}_\psi(\mathbf{M})$) just in case, for each $L \in \mathcal{L}$ and each text T for L, we have that $\mathbf{M}(T){\downarrow}$ and $\mathbf{M}(T)$ is an h-minimal ψ-grammar for L.

(b) $h\text{-}\mathbf{TxtMex}_\psi = \{\, \mathcal{L} \mid \mathcal{L} \subseteq h\text{-}\mathbf{TxtMex}_\psi(\mathbf{M}) \text{ for some } \mathbf{M} \,\}$.

(c) $\mathbf{TxtMex}_\psi = \bigcup_{h \in \mathcal{R}} h\text{-}\mathbf{TxtMex}_\psi$.

The following proposition is immediate.

12.21 Proposition *For all acceptable programming systems ψ and ψ', $\mathbf{TxtMex}_\psi = \mathbf{TxtMex}_{\psi'}$.*

So, if the fudge factor is allowed to be any computable function, the notion of nearly minimal identification is independent of the underlying acceptable programming system.

We thus sometimes refer to **TxtMex**$_\psi$ (for acceptable programming system ψ) as simply **TxtMex**. If the fudge factor is required to be some fixed computable function, then drastic things can occur, as the next proposition demonstrates.

12.22 Proposition *For each computable h, there is an acceptable programming system ψ such that no infinite collection of infinite languages can be h-**TxtMex**$_\psi$-identified.*

As an immediate corollary of Proposition 12.22 and Proposition 12.13 we have:

12.23 Corollary *There are acceptable programming systems, ψ and ψ', for which we have **TxtMin**$_\psi \neq$ **TxtMin**$_{\psi'}$.*

Thus, **TxtMin**$_\psi$-identification is *dependent* on the choice of acceptable programming system ψ. If we take as a given that the notions of our theory must be recursively invariant, this corollary precludes the study of **TxtMin**$_\psi$-identification as an interesting criterion of language learning. On the other hand, it may be the case that the dependence of size-restricted paradigms on the underlying acceptable programming system is a fundamental fact about learnability rather than a mere mathematical inconvenience.

Proof (of Proposition 12.22): Fix an $h \in \mathcal{R}$ which we assume without loss of generality is strictly increasing. Let $\langle \sigma_j^s \rangle_{j,s \in N}$ denote a finite sequence uniformly formed from j and s such that: (i) $content(\sigma_j^s) = W_{j,s}$ and (ii) $\sigma_j^s \subset \sigma_j^{s+1}$. Let $\mathbf{M}_0, \mathbf{M}_1, \mathbf{M}_2, \ldots$ be a recursive enumeration of total computable scientists along the lines of Corollary 4.16. We define

$$
g = \lambda x. \begin{cases} 0, & \text{if } x = 0; \\ 1 + h(g(x-1) + x + 3), & \text{if } x > 0. \end{cases}
$$

Clearly, g is strictly increasing and recursive. For each i, define $\psi_i = \bigcup_s \psi_i^s$, where for each s and x,

$$
\psi_i^s(x) = \begin{cases} \varphi_{j,s}(x), & \text{if (i) } i = g(j) \text{ for some } j; \\ \varphi_{j+1,s'}(x), & \text{if (ii) } g(j) < i < g(j) + j + 3 \text{ for some } j \text{ and} \\ & \text{where } s' \text{ is the least number } \leq s \text{ such that for} \\ & \text{some } \ell < j \text{ we have } \mathbf{M}_\ell(\sigma_{j+1}^{s'}) = \mathbf{M}_\ell(\sigma_{j+1}^{s'+1}) = \\ & \cdots = \mathbf{M}_\ell(\sigma_{j+1}^s) = i \text{ (if no such } \ell \text{ exists, we} \\ & \text{take } s' = s); \\ \uparrow, & \text{(iii) otherwise.} \end{cases}
$$

12.24 Claim *For all i:*

(a) *If $i = g(j)$ for some j, then $W_i^\psi = W_j$.*

(b) *If $g(j) < i < g(j) + j + 3$ for some j and W_i^ψ is infinite, then $W_i^\psi = W_{j+1}$.*

(c) *If $g(j) + j + 3 \leq i < g(j+1)$ for some j, then $W_i^\psi = \emptyset$.*

The above claim follows immediately from the definition of ψ. We also have:

12.25 Claim *Suppose L is an infinite r.e. set with $MinGram^\varphi(L) > 0$. Let $j + 1 = MinGram^\varphi(L)$ and let A be the set of h-minimal ψ-grammars for L. Then:*

(a) *$A \subseteq \{ g(j) + 1, \ldots, g(j) + (j) + 2 \}$.*

(b) *For each $i \in A$ and each $\ell < j$, we have that $\lim_{s \to \infty} \mathbf{M}_\ell(\sigma_{j+1}^s) \neq i$.*

Proof: Let $S = \{ g(j) + 1, \ldots, g(j) + j + 2 \}$. Suppose $i \in S$ and there is no $\ell < j$ such that $\lim_{s \to \infty} \mathbf{M}_\ell(\sigma_{j+1}^s) = i$. Then it follows from the definition of ψ_i^s that as s goes to infinity, so does the s' of clause (ii). Hence, $W_i^\psi = W_{j+1} = L$. Since there are only $j + 1$ many $\ell \leq j$ and $j + 2$ many $i \in S$, there is at least one ψ-grammar for L in S. Let i_* be the least ψ-grammar for L in S. Since L is infinite, it follows from our choice of $j + 1$ and Claim 12.24 that $i_* = MinGram^\psi(L)$. Since h is strictly increasing, we have that $h(i_*) \leq h(g(j) + j + 3) < g(j+1)$. Hence, by Claim 12.24(c), all the h-minimal ψ-grammars must be $\leq g(j) + j + 2$. Part (a) of the claim thus follows. Part (b) follows using part (a) and the construction of $\psi_i^s(x)$. $\square$

We leave the rest of the proof to the reader. ∎

Jain and Sharma [89] discuss other properties of the h-**TxtMex** paradigm.

§12.7 Bibliographic notes

The subject of bounding the number of mind changes was first considered by Bārzdiņš and Freivalds [15].

Case and Smith [35] were the first to study the interaction of mind changes and anomalies in the final program. For other results relating to mind changes, see Case, Jain, and Ngo-Manguelle [28]. Case, Jain, and Sharma [31] investigate mind changes in the context of vacillatory identification of functions. Mind change complexity of indexed families of computable languages has been investigated by Mukouchi [135] and by Lange and Zeugmann [118]. Recently, Freivalds and Smith [66] proposed a generalized notion of mind changes based on the use of constructive ordinals to bound the number of mind changes. See Jain and Sharma [94] and Ambainis, Jain, and Sharma [4] for applications of this notion to the analysis of the complexity of learning natural classes of languages. More generalized notions of mind change complexity can be found in Ambainis, Freivalds, and Smith [3] and Sharma, Stephan, and Ventsov [174].

The approach of bounding the number of examples before a scientist converges as a measure of complexity is due to Wiehagen [199, 198, 197]. These references also present a number of variants on this theme.

The idea of total work performed by a scientist before the onset of convergence as a model of complexity is due to Daley and Smith [54]. Freivalds has [62] an alternative proposal in which the number of distinct hypotheses conjectured by a scientist is considered a measure for the complexity of identification.

Freivalds [62] made the first attempt at an axiomatization of the complexity of identification for functions. The approach presented in this chapter is due to Daley and Smith [54]. Schäfer-Richter [167] has an alternative axiomatization.

Restrictions on program size in the context of functions were first studied by Freivalds [61]. He also introduced the notions of nearly minimal identification and limiting standardizable with a recursive estimate. Chen [37] considered variants of nearly minimal identification for functions in the presence of anomalies in the final program. Kinber [107, 108] has a number of additional results on program-size restrictions for function identification.

Case and Chi [27] adapted Freivalds' definition of nearly minimal function identification to languages. Jain and Sharma [89] considered strictly minimal identification, nearly minimal identification, and analogs of some of Kinber's notions for languages. Case, Jain, and Sharma [30] investigated nearly minimal identification in the context of vacillatory identification of languages.

The subject of learning "fastest" hypotheses has not been as well investigated as that of learning succinct hypotheses. The interested reader is referred to Zeugmann [207].

Recently, the idea of reduction from recursion theory has been employed to compare the difficulty of learning classes of concepts. This notion, referred to as *intrinsic complexity*, was first investigated by Freivalds, Kinber, and Smith [65] in the context of functions. Jain and Sharma [93] studied the intrinsic complexity of languages. See Jain and Sharma [95] for the structure of these reductions and Jain and Sharma [94] for connections between intrinsic complexity and mind change bounds measured by constructive ordinals.

§12.8 Exercises

12-1 For each $f: N \to N$, let $\mathrm{cyl}(f) = \lambda\langle x, y\rangle.f(x)$. Intuitively, $\mathrm{cyl}(f)$ denotes the cylindrification of f.

(a) Show that $\{\,\mathrm{cyl}(f) \mid card(\{\,x \mid f(x) \neq 0\,\}) \leq n + 1\,\} \in (\mathbf{Ex}_{n+1}^0 - \mathbf{Ex}_n^*)$.

(b) Show that $\{\,\mathrm{cyl}(f) \mid (\overset{\infty}{\forall} x)[\,f(x) = 0\,]\,\} \in (\mathbf{Ex}^0 - \bigcup_{n \in N} \mathbf{Ex}_n^*)$.

12-2 Show $\{\,f \mid card(\{\,x \mid f(x+1) \neq f(x)\,\}) \leq n + 1\,\}$ is in $\mathbf{Ex}_{n+1}^0 - \mathbf{Ex}_n^*$.

12-3 Recall the convention that: $0 < 1 < 2 < \cdots < *$. Also recall that, for each $a \in (N \cup \{*\})$, $\mathbf{Ex}^a$ can be written as $\mathbf{Ex}_*^a$, that is, there is no bound on the number of mind changes. Suppose $a, b, c, d \in (N \cup \{*\})$. Show that $\mathbf{Ex}_b^a \subseteq \mathbf{Ex}_d^c \iff [\,a \leq c$ and $b \leq d\,]$.

12-4 (Sharma [173]) Adapt the notion of mind changes to the paradigm $\mathbf{InfTxtEx}$ (Definition 8.31) to define the paradigm $\mathbf{InfTxtEx}_n$. Show that $\mathbf{InfTxtEx}_0 \subset \mathbf{TxtEx}$. This somewhat surprising result says that the collections of languages that can be one shot learned from both positive and negative data can also be identified in the limit from only positive data. Additionally, show that $\mathbf{InfTxtEx}_1 - \mathbf{TxtEx} \neq \emptyset$.

12-5 Show that the function Conv defined in Equation (12.1) on page 265 satisfies the axioms given in Definition 12.10.

12-6 The following definition (due to Daley and Smith [54]) is intended to capture the total amount of work done by a scientist on a function before the onset of convergence.

12.26 Definition Let $\Phi_{\mathbf{M}}(f[n])$ denote the time (or any other suitable Blum complexity measure [19]) used by $\mathbf{M}$ on the evidential state $f[n]$. For each $\mathbf{M}$ and f, define

$$\mathbf{auc}(\mathbf{M}, f) = \begin{cases} \sum_{n \leq \mathrm{Conv}(\mathbf{M}, f)} (\Phi_{\mathbf{M}}(f[n])), & \text{if } \mathbf{M}(f)\!\downarrow; \\ \uparrow, & \text{if } \mathbf{M}(f)\!\uparrow. \end{cases}$$

The above is based on the integral $\int_{x_i}^{x_f} F(x)\,dx$ defining *work* in classical mechanics; **auc** stands for 'area under the curve.' Note that, as was the case with identification from a bounded number of examples, the above notion also assumes that the graph of the function is fed to the scientist in canonical order. Also observe that the **auc** measure is defined for a scientist on a function if the scientist converges on the function; it does not matter to what the scientist converges.

Show that **auc** satisfies the axioms given in in Definition 12.10.

This measure is developed in greater detail in Daley and Smith [54].

12-7 (Freivalds [61], Kinber [106]) The following provides the function analog of the **TxtMin** paradigm.

12.27 Definition

(a) We say that **M** **Min**$_\psi$-*identifies* f (written: $f \in$ **Min**$_\psi$(**M**)) just in case $\lim_{n \to \infty}$ **M**$(f[n])\downarrow = MinProg^\psi(f)$.

(b) **Min**$_\psi = \{\, \mathcal{S} \mid \mathcal{S} \subseteq$ **Min**$_\psi$(**M**) for some **M** $\}$.

Show that there is an acceptable programming system ψ for which **Min**$_\psi$ has an infinite r.e. class of functions as an element.

12-8 (Freivalds [61]) Freivalds introduced the notion of *limit standardizability with a recursive estimate* (abbreviated: **Lsr**) defined below:

12.28 Definition We say that $\mathcal{S}$ is *limiting standardizable via g with recursive estimate v* (written: $\mathcal{S} \subseteq$ **Lsr**(g, v)) if and only if, for each $f \in \mathcal{S}$, there is an i_f with $\varphi_{i_f} = f$ such that, for every i with $\varphi_i = f$ we have:

(a) $\lim_{n \to \infty} g(i, n) = i_f$, and

(b) $card(\{\, g(i, n) \mid n \in N \,\}) \leq v(i)$.

We say that $\mathcal{S}$ is *limiting standardizable with a recursive estimate* (written: $\mathcal{S} \in$ **Lsr**) if and only if, for some recursive g and v, $\mathcal{S} \subseteq$ **Lsr**(g, v).

(a) Prove that the notion of **Lsr** is independent of the choice of an acceptable programming system.

(b) Establish the following characterization of **Min**$_\psi$-identification. The following are equivalent for all $\mathcal{S}$.

(i) For some acceptable ψ, $\mathcal{S} \in$ **Min**$_\psi$.

(ii) $\mathcal{S} \in$ (**Ex** $\cap$ **Lsr**).

12-9 (Freivalds [61], Chen [37]) The following formalizes the notion of nearly minimal identification for functions.

12.29 Definition Let a be a member of $(N \cup \{*\})$ and let h be a recursive function.

(a) $\mathbf{M}$ h-**Mex**$^a_\psi$-*identifies* $\mathcal{S}$ (written: $\mathcal{S} \subseteq h$-**Mex**$^a_\psi(\mathbf{M})$) if and only if, for each $f \in \mathcal{S}$, we have that $\mathbf{M}(f){\downarrow}$, $\psi_{\mathbf{M}(f)} =^a f$, and $\mathbf{M}(f) \leq h(MinProg^\psi(f))$.

(b) h-**Mex**$^a_\psi = \{\, \mathcal{S} \mid \mathcal{S} \subseteq h$-**Mex**$^a_\psi(\mathbf{M})$ for some $\mathbf{M}\,\}$.

(c) **Mex**$^a_\psi = \{\, \mathcal{S} \mid \mathcal{S} \in h$-**Mex**$^a_\psi$ for some $h \in \mathcal{R}\,\}$.

Thus, a scientist $\mathbf{M}$ h-**Mex**$^a_\psi$-identifies $\mathcal{S}$ just in case for each $f \in \mathcal{S}$, $\mathbf{M}$ **Ex**^{a}-identifies f in the acceptable programming system ψ, and the final stabilized output of $\mathbf{M}$ on f is no bigger than $h(MinProg^\psi(f))$.

(a) Suppose that $a \in (N \cup \{*\})$ and that ψ and ψ' are acceptable programming systems. Show that **Mex**$^a_\psi = $ **Mex**$^a_{\psi'}$. (Thus, it makes sense to refer to **Mex**$^a_\psi$ as just **Mex**^{a}.)

(b) Suppose that h is a recursive function such that, for all x, $h(x) \geq x$. Show that there exists an acceptable ψ such that for all $\mathcal{S}$, $\mathcal{S} \in h$-**Mex**$_\psi \iff \mathcal{S}$ is finite.

(c) Use part (b) and Exercise 12-7 to show that there are two acceptable programming systems ψ and ψ' such that **Min**$_\psi \neq$ **Min**$_{\psi'}$.

12-10 (Chen [37]) Show the following:

(a) **Mex** $\subset$ **Mex**$^1 \subset$ **Mex**$^2 \subset \cdots \subset$ **Mex***.

(b) For each $n \in N$, **Mex**$^n \subset$ **Ex**^{n}.

(c) **Mex**$^* = $ **Ex***.

12-11 Using an argument similar to that for Proposition 12.15, prove: **Mex** $=$ **Ex**$\cap$**Lsr**.

12-12 For each $a \in (N \cup \{*\})$, define **TxtMex**^{a} to the obvious variation on **TxtMex** that permits a-many anomalies in the final grammar. Show the following:

(a) **TxtMex** $\subset$ **TxtMex**$^1 \subset$ **TxtMex**$^2 \subset \cdots \subset$ **TxtMex***.

(b) For each $n \in N$, **TxtMex**$^n \subset$ **TxtEx**^{n}.

(c) **TxtMex**$^* = $ **TxtEx***.

13 Beyond Identification by Enumeration

§13.1 Gold's and Bārzdiņš' conjectures

This chapter concerns the strategy of *identification by enumeration*. Under this strategy a scientist has a fixed list of possible hypotheses and, at any point in time, the current conjecture is always the first hypothesis on the list that is consistent with the current data. We consider only identification of functions. A similar study can be carried out for identification of languages from informants.[1] We formalize identification by enumeration as follows.

13.1 Definition

(a) A scientist **M** is an *enumerator* just in case there exists a recursive f such that $\{\varphi_{f(n)} \mid n \in N\} \subseteq \mathcal{R}$ and, for all $\sigma \in \text{SEG}$, $\mathbf{M}(\sigma) = f(i)$, where i is the least number such that $content(\sigma) \subseteq \varphi_{f(i)}$.

(b) $\mathcal{S} \subseteq \mathcal{R}$ is *identifiable by enumeration* just in case there exists an enumerator **M** such that $\mathcal{S} \subseteq \mathbf{Ex(M)}$.

Many collections of functions are identifiable by enumeration, as shown by the following, easy proposition.

13.2 Proposition (Gold [80]) *Each r.e. indexable class of computable functions (see Definition 5.10) is identifiable by enumeration.*

Since identification by enumeration can be viewed as a search for the correct hypothesis in a suitably generated space of hypotheses, this strategy captures an essential property of most practical systems of empirical inquiry. The naturalness of this strategy led Gold [80] to conjecture that:

> Identification by enumeration is the *only* method of identification in the sense that each identifiable collection of functions is also identifiable by enumeration.

---

[1] For identification of languages from texts, it can be shown that identification by enumeration is not a very powerful strategy, as even the class $\{\ \{n, n+1, n+2, \ldots\}\ \mid\ n \in N\ \}$ is not identifiable by enumeration.

This conjecture is appealing but false. The collection of self-describing functions, $\mathcal{SD} = \{\, f \in \mathcal{R} \mid \varphi_{f(0)} = f \,\}$, is identifiable, but it is easily shown that $\mathcal{SD}$ cannot be identified by any scientist that is an enumerator.

In defense of Gold's intuitions, refutation of his conjecture via $\mathcal{SD}$ seems like a trick. After all, to identify $\mathcal{SD}$ requires no more than fetching some coded value from the input function. In the 1970's, Bārzdiņš formulated a more sophisticated version of Gold's conjecture designed to transcend such counterexamples. He reasoned that if a class $\mathcal{S}$ of functions is identifiable only by way of a self-referential property, then there would be a total recursive operator Ψ that would transform the class into an unidentifiable one. The idea is that if a scientist is able to find the embedded self-referential information in the elements of a class, so can a total recursive operator which can then weed out this information. To see this in the context of $\mathcal{SD}$, consider the operator Ψ^L such that, if $g = \Psi^L(f)$, then $g(x) = f(x+1)$, for all $x \in N$. Ψ^L essentially "shifts the function f to the left." It is easy to see that $\Psi^L(\mathcal{SD}) =_{\text{def}} \{\, \Psi(f) \mid f \in \mathcal{SD} \,\} = \mathcal{R}$, and we know from prior work that $\mathcal{R} \notin \mathbf{Ex}$. Thus, Ψ^L transforms the identifiable class $\mathcal{SD}$ into an unidentifiable class $\mathcal{R}$ by removing the self-referential information from $\mathcal{SD}$ that made it identifiable.

Informally stated, Bārzdiņš' conjecture is:

> If the projection of a class of functions under all total recursive operators is identifiable, then the class is identifiable by enumeration.

More formally, we have:

13.3 Definition (Fulk [72]) $\mathcal{S} \subseteq \mathcal{R}$ is said to be *robustly* **Ex**-*identifiable* just in case for all total recursive operators Ψ, $\Psi(\mathcal{S}) \in \mathbf{Ex}$.

13.4 Conjecture (Bārzdiņš as formalized by Fulk [72]) *Every subclass of $\mathcal{R}$ that is robustly* **Ex**-*identifiable is contained in some r.e. indexable subclass of $\mathcal{R}$.*

This conjecture is also appealing, and also false. The next section presents a cunning refutation due to Fulk [72]. Beyond simply showing the conjecture to be false, the refutation demonstrates an identification strategy that is strictly more general than enumeration but in the same spirit.

§13.2 Fulk's refutation of Bārzdiņš' conjecture

Here is Fulk's result.

13.5 Proposition (Fulk [72]) *There exists a class $\mathcal{S}$ of recursive functions such that:*

(a) *For all total recursive operators Ψ, $\Psi(\mathcal{S}) \in \mathbf{Ex}$.*

(b) *$\mathcal{S}$ is not contained in an r.e. indexable class of computable functions.*

Proof: The argument is organized as a series of claims. We first introduce some definitions and notation.

For this proof, we let σ and τ (with or without decorations) range over INIT. Also, in this proof we shall identify each σ with $\hat{\sigma}$, the finite function with graph $content(\sigma)$. It will always be clear from context whether σ is taken as a partial function or a member of INIT.

Let η_0 and η_1 be partial functions. If there is an x such that $\eta_0(x)\downarrow \neq \eta_1(x)\downarrow$, we say that η_0 and η_1 are *inconsistent* (written: $\eta_0 \not\sim \eta_1$); otherwise, we say that η_0 and η_1 are *consistent* (written: $\eta_0 \sim \eta_1$). So, η_0 and η_1 are consistent if and only if $\eta_0 \cup \eta_1$ is a (single-valued) partial function.

Let Θ be an effective indexing of the class of recursive operators. That is, $\{\,\Theta_i \mid i \in N\,\}$ is exactly the class of recursive operators and $\lambda i, f.\Theta_i(f)$ is itself a recursive operator (of type $N \times (N \rightharpoonup N) \to (N \rightharpoonup N)$). See Section 9.8 of Rogers [158] for an example of such an indexing. Recall from Chapter 2 that each recursive operator Ψ has the following topological property.

> *Continuity:* For all α, $\Theta(\alpha) = \bigcup_{\sigma \subseteq \alpha} \Theta(\sigma)$.

We shall make strong use of this property in the following.

Our first claim introduces some technical machinery to help in the definition of $\mathcal{S}$. The proof of this claim is left to Exercise 13-1.

13.6 Claim *There are sequences of initial segments, $\langle \sigma_i \rangle_{i \in N}$ and $\langle \tau_i \rangle_{i \in N}$, that satisfy properties (A), (B), and (C) below.*

(A) *$\lambda i.\sigma_i$ and $\lambda i.\tau_i$ are limiting-recursive functions.*

(B) *For all i and all $j > i$, $\tau_i \subseteq \sigma_j$ and $\tau_i \subseteq \tau_j$.*

(C) *For each k and each $i \geq k$, either (C.1) or (C.2) is true.*

    (C.1) $\Theta_k(\sigma_i) \not\sim \Theta_k(\tau_i)$.

    (C.2) $(\forall \sigma_{ext} \supseteq \sigma_i)(\forall \tau_{ext} \supseteq \tau_i)[\Theta_k(\sigma_{ext}) \sim \Theta_k(\tau_{ext})]$.

Fix $\langle \sigma_i \rangle_{i \in N}$ and $\langle \tau_i \rangle_{i \in N}$ that witness Claim 13.6. Let $\mathbf{con}(\cdot, \cdot)$ denote the predicate such that, for all i and k,

$$\mathbf{con}(i,k) \quad \equiv \quad \Theta_k(\sigma_i) \sim \Theta_k(\tau_i).$$

13.7 Claim

(a) *Suppose that* $k \leq i$, Θ_k *is total recursive, and* $\mathbf{con}(i,k)$ *holds. Then, for all* $j \geq i$, $\mathbf{con}(j,k)$ *also holds.*

(b) *For each fixed* k, *the predicate* $\mathbf{con}(i,k)$ *is limiting-recursively (in* i) *decidable.*

Proof: Part (a) follows from Claim 13.6(C). Part (b) is an easy exercise. $\square$

Let f be a limiting-recursive function such that, for all i and x,

$$\varphi_{f(i)}(x) \quad = \quad \begin{cases} y, & (x,y) \in \mathit{content}(\sigma_i); \\ 1 + \varphi_{\varphi_i(x-|\sigma_i|)}(x), & \text{otherwise.} \end{cases}$$

Intuitively, $f(i)$ is a program for a function that extends σ_i by diagonalizing against the i-th possible r.e. indexable class of computable functions. Note that since $\lambda i.\sigma_i$ is limiting recursive, such a limiting-recursive f can be constructed using the s-m-n theorem (Theorem 2.1). Finally, we define

$$\mathcal{S} \quad = \quad \{\, \varphi_{f(i)} \mid i \in N \,\} \cap \mathcal{R}.$$

13.8 Claim $\mathcal{S}$ *is not contained in any r.e. indexable class of computable functions.*

Proof: Suppose by way of contradiction that there is a recursive function p such that $\mathcal{S} \subseteq \{\, \varphi_{p(i)} \mid i \in N \,\} \subset \mathcal{R}$. Choose i_0 such that $\varphi_{i_0} = p$. Since φ_{i_0} is total and its range consists of programs for total functions, it follows that $\varphi_{f(i_0)} \in \mathcal{S}$. Since $\varphi_{f(i_0)} \in \mathcal{S}$, there is a j such that $\varphi_{f(i_0)} = \varphi_{p(j)}$. Thus we have

$$\begin{aligned} \varphi_{p(j)}(j + |\sigma_{i_0}|) \quad &= \quad \varphi_{f(i_0)}(j + |\sigma_{i_0}|) \\ &= \quad 1 + \varphi_{\varphi_{i_0}(j)}(j + |\sigma_{i_0}|) \\ &= \quad 1 + \varphi_{p(j)}(j + |\sigma_{i_0}|), \end{aligned}$$

a contradiction. $\square$

Fix an arbitrary k such that Θ_k is total recursive. Our next goal is to show that $\Theta_k(\mathcal{S}) \in \mathbf{Ex}$. Since our choice of k is arbitrary, this will establish the proposition. To help show $\Theta_k(\mathcal{S}) \in \mathbf{Ex}$, we use the s-m-n theorem (Theorem 2.1) to define two limiting-recursive functions g and h as follows. For each i and x define:

$$\varphi_{g(i)}(x) = \begin{cases} \Theta_k(\tau_{ext})(x), & \text{if } (\exists \tau'_{ext} \supseteq \tau_i)[\Theta_k(\tau'_{ext})(x)\downarrow] \text{ and } \tau_{ext} \\ & \text{is the first such } \tau'_{ext} \text{ produced by} \\ & \text{some particular search;} \\ \uparrow, & \text{otherwise.} \end{cases}$$

Since $\lambda i.\tau_i$ is limiting recursive, it follows that one can construct a limiting-recursive g as above. For each $i \leq k$, define

$$\varphi_{h(i)} = \begin{cases} \Theta_k(\varphi_{f(i)}), & \text{if } \Theta_k(\varphi_{f(i)}) \text{ is total;} \\ \lambda x.0, & \text{otherwise;} \end{cases} \tag{13.1}$$

and, for each $i > k$, define

$$\varphi_{h(i)} = \begin{cases} \Theta_k(\varphi_{f(i)}) \cup \varphi_{g(i)}, & \text{if } \mathbf{con}(i,k); \\ \Theta_k(\varphi_{f(i)}), & \text{otherwise.} \end{cases} \tag{13.2}$$

Since $\lambda i.\mathbf{con}(i,k)$, f, and g are limiting-recursive, it follows that one can construct a limiting-recursive h as above. (Note: One *cannot*, in general, limiting-recursively decide whether $\Theta_k(\varphi_{f(i)})$ is total. But this is not a difficulty since (13.1) affects only finitely many values of h.)

13.9 Claim

(a) *For each i, if $\mathbf{con}(i,k)$, then $\varphi_{g(i)}$ is consistent with $\Theta_k(\varphi_{f(i)})$.*

(b) *For each $i \geq k$, $\Theta_k(\varphi_{f(i)}) \subseteq \varphi_{h(i)}$. Thus, $\Theta_k(\mathcal{S}) \subseteq \{ \varphi_{h(i)} \mid i \in N \}$.*

(c) *For each $j > i$, $[\varphi_{h(i)} \sim \varphi_{h(j)}] \Rightarrow [\varphi_{h(j)} \subseteq \varphi_{h(i)}]$.*

Proof: By Claim 13.6(C) for τ_i, we have that $\mathbf{con}(i,k)$ implies

$$(\forall \sigma_{ext} \supseteq \sigma_i)(\forall \tau_{ext} \supseteq \tau_i)[\Theta_k(\sigma_{ext}) \sim \Theta_k(\tau_{ext})].$$

Since $f(i) \supseteq \sigma_i$, part (a) follows from the definition of g.

Part (b) follows from part (a) and definition of h.

For part (c), first note that, for $i \leq k$, we have by (13.1) that $\varphi_{h(i)}$ is total, and hence, for such $i \leq k$, part (c) clearly holds. So assume $i > k$ and suppose $\varphi_{h(i)} \sim \varphi_{h(j)}$. By

(13.2), this implies that $\Theta_k(\varphi_{f(i)})$ is consistent with $\Theta_k(\varphi_{f(j)})$. By the definition of $\varphi_{f(j)}$ and Claim 13.6(B) we have $\varphi_{f(j)} \supseteq \sigma_j \supseteq \tau_i$. Hence, it follows that $\mathbf{con}(i, k)$ and

$$\varphi_{h(j)}$$

$$\subseteq \ \bigcup\nolimits_{\sigma_{ext} \supseteq \sigma_j} \Theta_k(\sigma_{ext}) \ \cup \ \bigcup\nolimits_{\tau_{ext} \supseteq \tau_j} \Theta_k(\tau_{ext}) \qquad \text{(by continuity and the definition of } h)$$

$$\subseteq \ \bigcup\nolimits_{\tau_{ext} \supseteq \tau_i} \Theta_k(\tau_{ext})) \qquad \text{(since } \dot\sigma_j \supseteq \tau_i \text{ and } \tau_j \supseteq \tau_i)$$

$$= \ \varphi_{g(i)} \qquad \text{(by } \mathbf{con}(i, k)\text{, the totality of } \Theta_k\text{, Claim 13.7(a), and the definition of } g).$$

So this case follows also. $\square$

We now proceed to prove that $\Theta_k(\mathcal{S})$ belongs to **Ex**. From Claim 13.9(b) we have $\Theta_k(\mathcal{S}) \subseteq \{\, \varphi_{h(i)} \mid i \in N \,\}$. Also as a corollary to Claim 13.9(c) we have:

13.10 Claim *For all j with $\varphi_{h(j)} \in \mathcal{R}$ and all $i < j$, either $\varphi_{h(i)} = \varphi_{h(j)}$ or $\varphi_{h(i)} \not\sim \varphi_{h(j)}$.*

We now construct a machine **M** **Ex**-identifying the class $\{\, \varphi_{h(i)} \mid i \in N \,\} \cap \mathcal{R}$. Let $H(i, t)$ be a recursive function such that $h(i) = \lim_{t \to \infty} H(i, t)$. For each $\sigma \in$ SEG, define

$$\mathbf{M}(\sigma) \ = \ H(i, |\sigma|), \text{ where } i \text{ is the least number } \leq |\sigma| \text{ such that } \varphi_{H(i,|\sigma|),|\sigma|} \sim \sigma.$$

Using Claim 13.10, it follows immediately that **M** **Ex**-identifies $\{\, \varphi_{h(i)} \mid i \in N \,\} \cap \mathcal{R}$. Thus the proposition follows. ∎

We note that **M** in the above proof can be seen as performing a more general sort of identification by enumeration. **M**'s search space is described by a limiting recursive function h, and not every $\varphi_{h(i)}$, $i \in N$, is total. This may be contrasted with the original notion of identification by enumeration in which the search space of an enumerator is described by a recursive function whose range consists exclusively of programs for total functions.

§13.3 Exercises

13-1 Show that $\langle \sigma_i \rangle_{i \in N}$ and $\langle \tau_i \rangle_{i \in N}$ as defined below are as required in Claim 13.6. For convenience, let $\sigma_{-1} = \tau_{-1} = \emptyset$. Now for each $i \geq 0$, inductively define σ_i and τ_i to be the lexicographically least pair from INIT that satisfies

(a) $\sigma_i \supseteq \tau_{i-1}$,

(b) $\tau_i \supseteq \tau_{i-1}$, and

(c) $(\forall k \leq i)[\Theta_k(\sigma_i) \not\sim \Theta_k(\tau_i) \lor (\forall \sigma_{ext} \supseteq \sigma_i)(\forall \tau_{ext} \supseteq \tau_i)[\Theta_k(\sigma_{ext}) \sim \Theta_k(\tau_{ext})]]$.

13-2 Before Fulk's work [72], Kurtz and Smith [116] gave the following, weaker formalization of Bārzdiņš's conjecture, which they refuted.

Conjecture: $\mathcal{C} \subseteq \mathcal{R}$ is r.e. indexable if and only if $(\forall \Theta \mid \Theta(\mathcal{C}) \subseteq \mathcal{R})[\Theta(\mathcal{S}) \in \mathbf{Ex}]$.

Proposition 13.5 implies that this conjecture is false, but we can give a direct refutation as follows.

13.11 Definition $\mathcal{S} \subseteq \mathcal{P}$ is said to be *stable* if and only if, for all recursive operators Θ such that $\Theta(\mathcal{S}) \subseteq \mathcal{R}$, $\Theta(\mathcal{S}) \in \mathbf{PEx}$.

(a) Suppose f is a limiting-recursive function and $\mathcal{S} = \{ \varphi_{f(i)} \mid i \in N \} \subseteq \mathcal{R}$. Show that $\mathcal{S}$ is stable.

(b) Construct a limiting recursive-function f such that $\{ \varphi_{f(i)} \mid i \in N \} \subseteq \mathcal{R}$ is not r.e. indexable.

(c) Conclude that the above conjecture is false.

Bibliography

[1] L. Adleman and M. Blum, *Inductive inference and unsolvability*, Journal of Symbolic Logic **56** (1991), 891–900.

[2] A. Ambainis, *Probabilistic and team PFIN-type learning: General properties*, Proceedings of the Ninth Annual Conference on Computational Learning Theory, ACM Press, 1996, pp. 157–168.

[3] A. Ambainis, R. Freivalds, and C. Smith, *General inductive inference types based on linearly-ordered sets*, Proceedings of Symposium on Theoretical Aspects of Computer Science, Lecture Notes in Computer Science, vol. 1046, Springer-Verlag, 1996, pp. 243–253.

[4] A. Ambainis, S. Jain, and A. Sharma, *Ordinal mind change complexity of language identification*, Third European Conference on Computational Learning Theory (S. Ben-David, ed.), Lecture Notes in Artificial Intelligence, vol. 1208, Springer-Verlag, 1997, pp. 301–315.

[5] D. Angluin, *Finding patterns common to a set of strings*, Journal of Computer and System Sciences **21** (1980), 46–62.

[6] ———, *Inductive inference of formal languages from positive data*, Information and Control **45** (1980), 117–135.

[7] K. Apsītis, *Asymmetric team learning*, Proceedings of the Tenth Annual Conference on Computational Learning Theory, ACM Press, 1997, pp. 90–95.

[8] S. Arikawa, S. Miyano, A. Shinohara, T. Shinohara, and A. Yamamoto, *Algorithmic learning theory with elementary formal systems*, IEICE Trans. Inf. and Syst. **E75–D No. 4** (1992), 405–414.

[9] S. Arikawa, T. Shinohara, and A. Yamamoto, *Learning elementary formal systems*, Theoretical Computer Science **95** (1992), 97–113.

[10] H. Arimura and T. Shinohara, *Inductive inference of Prolog programs with linear data dependency from positive data*, Proc. Information Modelling and Knowledge Bases V, IOS Press, 1994, pp. 365–375.

[11] G. Baliga and J. Case, *Learning with higher order additional information*, Algorithmic learning theory: Fourth International Workshop on Analogical and Inductive Inference (AII '94) and Fifth International Workshop on Algorithmic Learning Theory (ALT '94) (S. Arikawa and K. Jantke, eds.), Lecture Notes in Artificial Intelligence, vol. 872, Springer-Verlag, 1994, pp. 64–75.

[12] G. Baliga, S. Jain, and A. Sharma, *Learning from multiple sources of inaccurate data*, SIAM Journal of Computing **26** (1997), 961–990.

[13] J. Bārzdiņš, *Inductive inference of automata, functions and programs*, Int. Math. Congress, Vancouver, 1974, pp. 771–776.

[14] _____, *Two theorems on the limiting synthesis of functions*, Theory of Algorithms and Programs, vol. 1, Latvian State University, 1974, In Russian, pp. 82–88.

[15] J. Bārzdiņš and R. Freivalds, *On the prediction of general recursive functions*, Soviet Mathematics Doklady **13** (1972), 1224–1228.

[16] J. Bārzdiņš and K. Podnieks, *The theory of inductive inference*, Mathematical Foundations of Computer Science, Math. Inst. of the Slovak Academy of Sciences, 1973, pp. 9–15.

[17] D. Bickerton, *The roots of language*, Karoma, 1981.

[18] L. Blum and M. Blum, *Toward a mathematical theory of inductive inference*, Information and Control **28** (1975), 125–155.

[19] M. Blum, *A machine-independent theory of the complexity of recursive functions*, Journal of the ACM **14** (1967), 322–336.

[20] _____, *On the size of machines*, Information and Control **11** (1967), 257–265.

[21] G. Boolos and R. Jeffrey, *Computability and logic*, Cambridge University Press, 1980.

[22] R. Brown and C. Hanlon, *Derivational complexity and the order of acquisition in child speech*, Cognition and the Development of Language (J. R. Hayes, ed.), Wiley, 1970.

[23] J. Carbonell, *Machine learning: Paradigms and methods*, MIT Press, 1990.

[24] J. Case, *Periodicity in generations of automata*, Mathematical Systems Theory **8** (1974), 15–32.

[25] _____, *The power of vacillation*, Proceedings of the Workshop on Computational Learning Theory (D. Haussler and L. Pitt, eds.), Morgan Kaufmann, 1988, pp. 133–142.

[26] J. Case, *The power of vacillation in language learning*, SIAM Journal on Computing (1997), to appear.

[27] J. Case and H. Chi, *Machine learning of nearly minimal size grammars*, unpublished manuscript, 1986.

[28] J. Case, S. Jain, and S. Ngo Manguelle, *Refinements of inductive inference by Popperian and reliable machines*, Kybernetika **30** (1994), 23–52.

[29] J. Case, S. Jain, and A. Sharma, *On learning limiting programs*, International Journal of Foundations of Computer Science **3** (1992), no. 1, 93–115.

[30] _____, *Vacillatory learning of nearly minimal size grammers*, Journal of Computer and System Sciences **49** (1994), 189–207.

[31] _____, *Complexity issues for vacillatory function identification*, Information and Computation **116** (1995), 174–192.

[32] J. Case, S. Kaufmann, E. Kinber, and M. Kummer, *Learning recursive functions from approximations*, Second European Conference on Computational Learning Theory (Paul Vitányi, ed.), Lecture Notes in Artificial Intelligence, vol. 904, Springer-Verlag, 1995, pp. 140–153.

[33] J. Case and C. Lynes, *Machine inductive inference and language identification*, Proceedings of the 9th International Colloquium on Automata, Languages and Programming (M. Nielsen and E. M. Schmidt, eds.), Lecture Notes in Computer Science, vol. 140, Springer-Verlag, 1982, pp. 107–115.

[34] J. Case and S. Ngo Manguelle, *Refinements of inductive inference by Popperian machines*, Tech. Report 152, SUNY/Buffalo, 1979.

[35] J. Case and C. Smith, *Comparison of identification criteria for machine inductive inference*, Theoretical Computer Science **25** (1983), 193–220.

[36] K. J. Chen, *Tradeoffs in machine inductive inference*, Ph.D. thesis, SUNY/Buffalo, 1981.

[37] _____, *Tradeoffs in inductive inference of nearly minimal sized programs*, Information and Control **52** (1982), 68–86.

[38] N. Chomsky, *Syntactic structures*, Mouton & Co., 1957.

[39] _____, *Aspects of the theory of syntax*, MIT Press, 1965.

[40] _____, *Reflections on language*, Pantheon, 1975.

[41] _____, *Initial states and steady states*, Language and Learning (M. Piatelli-Palmarini, ed.), Harvard University Press, 1980.

[42] _____, *Rules and representations*, Columbia University Press, 1980.

[43] _____, *Knowledge of language*, Praeger, 1986.

[44] S. Cook, *Computability and complexity of higher type functions*, Logic from Computer Science (Y.N. Moschovakis, ed.), Springer-Verlag, 1991, pp. 51–72.

[45] N. Cutland, *Computability: An introduction to recursive function theory*, Cambridge University Press, 1980.

[46] R. Daley, *On the error correcting power of pluralism in BC-type inductive inference*, Theoretical Computer Science **24** (1983), 95–104.

[47] _____, *Transformation of probabilistic learning strategies into deterministic learning strategies*, Proceedings of the Workshop on Computational Learning Theory (D. Haussler and L. Pitt, eds.), Morgan Kaufmann, 1988, pp. 157–163.

[48] R. Daley and B. Kalyanasundaram, *Capabilities of probabilistic learners with bounded mind changes*, Proceedings of the Sixth Annual Conference on Computational Learning Theory, ACM Press, 1993, pp. 182–191.

[49] _____, *Use of reduction arguments in determining Popperian FIN-type learning capabilities*, Algorithmic Learning Theory: Fourth International Workshop (ALT '93) (K. Jantke, S. Kobayashi, E. Tomita, and T. Yokomori, eds.), Lecture Notes in Artificial Intelligence, vol. 744, Springer-Verlag, 1993, pp. 173–186.

[50] R. Daley, B. Kalyanasundaram, and M. Velauthapillai, *Breaking the probability 1/2 barrier in FIN-type learning*, Proceedings of the Fifth Annual Workshop on Computational Learning Theory, ACM Press, 1992, pp. 203–217.

[51] _____, *The power of probabilism in Popperian finite learning*, Analogical and Inductive Inference, Proceedings of the Third International Workshop, Lecture Notes in Artificial Intelligence, vol. 642, Springer-Verlag, 1992, pp. 151–169.

[52] _____, *Capabilities of fallible finite learning*, Proceedings of the Sixth Annual Conference on Computational Learning Theory, ACM Press, 1993, pp. 199–208.

[53] R. Daley, L. Pitt, M. Velauthapillai, and T. Will, *Relations between probabilistic and team one-shot learners*, Proceedings of the Fourth Annual Workshop on Computational Learning Theory (L. Valiant and M. Warmuth, eds.), Morgan Kaufmann, 1991, pp. 228–239.

[54] R. Daley and C. Smith, *On the complexity of inductive inference*, Information and Control **69** (1986), 12–40.

[55] M. Demetras, K. Post, and C. Snow, *Feedback to first language learners: The role of repetitions and clarification questions*, Journal of Child Language **13** (1986), 275–292.

[56] R. Dudley, *Real analysis*, Wadsworth & Brooks/Cole, 1989.

[57] H. Feldman, S. Goldin-Meadow, and L. Gleitman, *Beyond Herotodus: The creation of language by linguistically deprived deaf children*, Action, Symbol and Gesture: The Emergence of Language (A. Lock, ed.), Academic Press, 1978.

[58] J. Feldman, *Some decidability results on grammatical inference and complexity*, Information and Control **20** (1972), 244–262.

[59] L. Fortnow, W. Gasarch, S. Jain, E. Kinber, M. Kummer, S. Kurtz, M. Pleszkoch, T. Slaman, R. Solovay, and F. Stephan, *Extremes in the degrees of inferability*, Annals of Pure and Applied Logic **66** (1994), 231–276.

[60] R. Freivalds, *Functions computable in the limit by probabilistic machines*, Mathematical Foundations of Computer Science, Lecture Notes in Computer Science, vol. 28, Springer-Verlag, 1974, pp. 77–87.

[61] _____, *Minimal Gödel numbers and their identification in the limit*, Mathematical Foundations of Computer Science, Lecture Notes in Computer Science, vol. 32, Springer-Verlag, 1975, pp. 219–225.

[62] _____, *On the complexity and optimality of computation in the limit*, Theory of Algorithms and Programs, vol. 2, Latvian State University, 1975, pp. 155–173.

[63] _____, *Finite identification of general recursive functions by probabilistic strategies*, Proceedings of the Conference on Fundamentals of Computation Theory, Akademie-Verlag, Berlin, 1979, pp. 138–145.

[64] _____, *Recursiveness of the enumerating functions increases the inferrability of recursively enumerable sets*, Bulletin of the European Association for Theoretical Computer Science **27** (1985), 35–40.

[65] R. Freivalds, E. Kinber, and C. Smith, *On the intrinsic complexity of learning*, Second European Conference on Computational Learning Theory (Paul Vitányi, ed.), Lecture Notes in Artificial Intelligence, vol. 904, Springer-Verlag, 1995, pp. 154–169.

[66] R. Freivalds and C. Smith, *On the role of procrastination in machine learning*, Information and Computation (1993), 237–271.

[67] R. Freivalds and R. Wiehagen, *Inductive inference with additional information*, Electronische Informationverarbeitung und Kybernetik **15** (1979), 179–195.

[68] M. Fulk, *Inductive inference with additional information*, Journal of Computer and System Sciences, to appear.

[69] _____, *A study of inductive inference machines*, Ph.D. thesis, SUNY/Buffalo, 1985.

[70] _____, *Saving the phenomenon: Requirements that inductive machines not contradict known data*, Information and Computation **79** (1988), 193–209.

[71] _____, *Prudence and other conditions on formal language learning*, Information and Computation **85** (1990), 1–11.

[72] _____, *Robust separations in inductive inference*, 31st Annual IEEE Symposium on Foundations of Computer Science (1990), 405–410.

[73] M. Fulk and S. Jain, *Approximate inference and scientific method*, Information and Computation **114** (1994), 179–191.

[74] _____, *Learning in the presence of inaccurate information*, Theoretical Computer Science A **161** (1996), 235–261.

[75] M. Fulk, S. Jain, and D. Osherson, *Open problems in systems that learn*, Journal of Computer and System Sciences **49** (1994), no. 3, 589–604.

[76] W. Gasarch and M. Pleszkoch, *Learning via queries to an oracle*, Proceedings of the Second Annual Workshop on Computational Learning Theory (R. Rivest, D. Haussler, and M. Warmuth, eds.), Morgan Kaufmann, 1989, pp. 214–229.

[77] W. Gasarch and C. Smith, *Learning via queries*, Journal of the ACM (1992), 649–674.

[78] J. Gill, *Computational complexity of probabilistic Turing machines*, SIAM Journal of Computing (1977), 675–695.

[79] L. Gleitman and E. Newport, *The invention of language by children: Environmental and biological influences on the acquisition of language*, Invitation to Cognitive Science: Language, 2nd Edition (L. Gleitman and M. Liberman, eds.), MIT Press, 1995.

[80] E. M. Gold, *Language identification in the limit*, Information and Control **10** (1967), 447–474.

[81] K. Hirsh-Pasek, R. Treiman, and M. Schneiderman, *Brown and Hanlon revisited: Mothers' sensitivity to ungrammatical forms*, Journal of Child Language **11** (1984), 81–88.

[82] J. Hopcroft and J. Ullman, *Introduction to automata theory, languages, and computation*, Addison-Wesley, 1979.

[83] S. Jain, *Program synthesis in the presence of infinite number of inaccuracies*, Journal of Computer and System Sciences **53** (1996), no. 1, 583–591.

[84] _____, *Strong monotonic and set driven inductive inference*, Journal of Experimental and Theoretical Artificial Intelligence **9** (1997), 137–143.

[85] S. Jain and A. Sharma, *Learning in the presence of partial explanations*, Information and Computation **95** (1991), 162–191.

[86] _____, *Learning with the knowledge of an upper bound on program size*, Information and Computation **102** (1993), 118–166.

[87] _____, *On the non-existence of maximal inference degrees for language identification*, Information Processing Letters **47** (1993), 81–88.

[88] _____, *On monotonic strategies for learning r.e. languages*, Algorithmic learning theory: Fourth International Workshop on Analogical and Inductive Inference (AII '94) and Fifth International Workshop on Algorithmic Learning Theory (ALT '94) (S. Arikawa and K. Jantke, eds.), Lecture Notes in Artificial Intelligence, vol. 872, Springer-Verlag, 1994, pp. 349–364.

[89] _____, *Program size restrictions in computational learning*, Theoretical Computer Science **127** (1994), 351–386.

[90] _____, *On aggregating teams of learning machines*, Theoretical Computer Science **137** (1995), 85–108.

[91] _____, *Prudence in vacillatory language identification*, Mathematical Systems Theory **28** (1995), 267–279.

[92] _____, *Computational limits on team identification of languages*, Information and Computation **130** (1996), 19–60.

[93] _____, *The intrinsic complexity of language identification*, Journal of Computer and System Sciences **52** (1996), 393–402.

[94] _____, *Elementary formal systems, intrinsic complexity, and procrastination*, Information and Computation **132** (1997), 65–84.

[95] _____, *The structure of intrinsic complexity of learning*, Journal of Symbolic Logic **62** (1997), 1187–1201.

[96] _____, *Generalization and specialization strategies for learning r.e. languages*, Annals of Mathematics and Artificial Intelligence (1998), to appear.

[97] S. Jain, A. Sharma, and M. Velauthapillai, *Finite identification of function by teams with success ratio 1/2 and above*, Information and Computation **121** (1995), 201–213.

[98] K. Jantke, *Natural properties of strategies identifying recursive functions*, Electronische Informationverarbeitung und Kybernetik **15** (1979), 487–496.

[99] _____, *Monotonic and non-monotonic inductive inference*, New Generation Computing **8** (1991), 349–360.

[100] K. Jantke and H. Beick, *Combining postulates of naturalness in inductive inference*, Electronische Informationverarbeitung und Kybernetik **17** (1981), 465–484.

[101] C. Jockusch, *Degrees of generic sets*, Recursion Theory: Its generalizations and applications (F. Drake and S. Wainer, eds.), Cambridge University Press, 1980, pp. 110–139.

[102] B. Kapron and S. Cook, *A new characterization of type 2 feasibility*, SIAM Journal of Computing **25** (1996), 117–132.

[103] S. Kapur, *Monotonic language learning*, Algorithmic Learning Theory: Third International Workshop (ALT '92) (S. Doshita, K. Furukawa, K. Jantke, and T. Nishida, eds.), Lecture Notes in Artificial Intelligence, vol. 743, Springer-Verlag, 1992, pp. 147–158.

[104] S. Kaufmann and F. Stephan, *Robust learning with infinite additional information*, Third European Conference on Computational Learning Theory (S. Ben-David, ed.), Lecture Notes in Artificial Intelligence, vol. 1208, Springer-Verlag, 1997, pp. 316–330.

[105] M. Kearns and U. Vazirani, *An Introduction to Computational Learning Theory*, MIT Press, 1994.

[106] E. Kinber, *On a theory of inductive inference*, Proceedings of the 1977 International Fundamentals of Computation Theory, Lecture Notes in Computer Science, vol. 56, Springer-Verlag, 1977, pp. 435–440.

[107] _____, *On limit identification of minimal Gödel numbers for functions from enumerable classes*, Theory of Algorithms and Programs, vol. 3, Latvian State University, 1977, pp. 35–56.

[108] _____, *A note on limit identification of c-minimal indices*, Electronische Informationverarbeitung und Kybernetik **19** (1983), 459–463.

[109] E. Kinber and F. Stephan, *Language learning from texts: Mind changes, limited memory
and monotonicity*, Information and Computation **123** (1995), 224–241.

[110] E. Kinber and T. Zeugmann, *Inductive inference of almost everywhere correct programs
by reliably working strategies*, Electronische Informationverarbeitung und Kybernetik **21**
(1985), 91–100.

[111] _____, *One-sided error probabilistic inductive inference and reliable frequency identification*, Information and Computation **92** (1991), 253–284.

[112] M. Krishna Rao, *A class of Prolog programs inferable from positive data*, Algorithmic
Learning Theory: Seventh International Workshop (ALT '96) (A. Arikawa and A. Sharma,
eds.), Lecture Notes in Artificial Intelligence, vol. 1160, Springer-Verlag, 1996, pp. 272–
284.

[113] M. Kummer and M. Ott, *Learning branches and learning to win closed games*, Proceedings
of the Ninth Annual Conference on Computational Learning Theory, ACM Press, 1996,
pp. 280–291.

[114] M. Kummer and F. Stephan, *On the structure of degrees of inferability*, Journal of Computer and System Sciences **52** (1996), no. 2, 214–238.

[115] S. Kurtz and J. Royer, *Prudence in language learning*, Proceedings of the Workshop on
Computational Learning Theory (D. Haussler and L. Pitt, eds.), Morgan Kaufmann, 1988,
pp. 143–156.

[116] S. Kurtz and C. Smith, *On the role of search for learning*, Proceedings of the Second Annual Workshop on Computational Learning Theory (R. Rivest, D. Haussler, and M. Warmuth, eds.), Morgan Kaufmann, 1989, pp. 303–311.

[117] I. Lakatos, *Falsification and the methodology of scientific research programmes*, The
methodology of scientific research programmes, Philosophic Papers Volume 1 (J. Wor-
rall and G. Currie, eds.), Cambridge University Press, 1978, pp. 8–101.

[118] S. Lange and T. Zeugmann, *Learning recursive languages with a bounded number of mind
changes*, International Journal of Foundations of Computer Science 4 (1993), no. 2, 157–
178.

[119] _____, *Monotonic versus non-monotonic language learning*, Proceedings of the Second
International Workshop on Nonmonotonic and Inductive Logic, Lecture Notes in Artificial
Intelligence, vol. 659, Springer-Verlag, 1993, pp. 254–269.

[120] _____, *Characterization of language learning from informant under various monotonicity
constraints*, Journal of Experimental and Theoretical Artificial Intelligence **6** (1994), 73–
94.

[121] _____, *Set-driven and rearrangement-independent learning of recursive languages*, Mathematical Systems Theory **29** (1996), 599–634.

[122] S. Lange, T. Zeugmann, and S. Kapur, *Monotonic and dual monotonic language learning*, Theoretical Computer Science A **155** (1996), 365–410.

[123] P. Langley, H. Simon, G. Bradshaw, and Z. Zytkow, *Scientific discovery*, MIT Press, 1987.

[124] H. Lasnik, *The forms of sentences*, Invitation to Cognitive Science: Language, 2nd Edition (L. Gleitman and M. Liberman, eds.), MIT Press, 1995.

[125] E. Lenneberg, *Biological foundations of language*, Wiley, 1967.

[126] H. Lewis and C. Papadimitriou, *Elements of the theory of computation*, Prentice-Hall, 1981.

[127] E. Martin and D. Osherson, *Scientific discovery based on belief revision*, Journal of Symbolic Logic **62** (1997), 1352–1370.

[128] E. Martin and D. Osherson, *Elements of scientific inquiry*, M.I.T. Press, Cambridge MA, 1998.

[129] R. Matthews and W Demopoulos, *Learnability and linguistic theory*, Kluwer, 1989.

[130] L. Meyer, *Probabilistic language learning under monotonicity constraints*, Algorithmic Learning Theory: Sixth International Workshop (ALT '95), Lecture Notes in Artificial Intelligence, vol. 997, Springer-Verlag, 1995, pp. 169–184.

[131] _____, *Monotonic and dual-monotonic probabilistic language learning*, Third European Conference on Computational Learning Theory (S. Ben-David, ed.), Lecture Notes in Artificial Intelligence, vol. 1208, Springer-Verlag, 1997, pp. 66–78.

[132] E. Minicozzi, *Some natural properties of strong identification in inductive inference*, Theoretical Computer Science (1976), 345–360.

[133] T. Motoki, T. Shinohara, and K. Wright, *The correct definition of finite elasticity: Corrigendum to identification of unions*, Proceedings of the Fourth Annual Workshop on Computational Learning Theory (L. Valiant and M. Warmuth, eds.), Morgan Kaufmann, 1991, p. 375.

[134] S. Muggleton and C. Feng, *Efficient induction of logic programs*, Proceedings of the First Workshop on Algorithmic Learning Theory, Ohmsa Publishers, 1990, Reprinted by Ohmsa Springer-Verlag, pp. 368–381.

[135] Y. Mukouchi, *Inductive inference with bounded mind changes*, Algorithmic Learning Theory: Third International Workshop (ALT '92) (S. Doshita, K. Furukawa, K. Jantke, and T. Nishida, eds.), Lecture Notes in Artificial Intelligence, vol. 743, Springer-Verlag, 1992, pp. 125–134.

[136] E. Newport, L. Gleitman, and H. Gleitman, *Mother I'd rather do it myself: Some effects and noneffects of maternal speech style*, Talking to children: Language input and acquisition (C. Snow and C. Ferguson, eds.), Cambridge University Press, 1977.

[137] D. Osherson, *Computer output*, Cognition **20** (1985), 261–264.

[138] D. Osherson, M. Stob, and S. Weinstein, *Learning theory and natural language*, Cognition **17** (1984), 1–28.

[139] ———, *Aggregating inductive expertise*, Information and Control **70** (1986), 69–95.

[140] ———, *Systems that learn: An introduction to learning theory for cognitive and computer scientists*, MIT Press, 1986.

[141] ———, *Synthesising inductive expertise*, Information and Computation **77** (1988), 138–161.

[142] D. Osherson and T. Wasow, *Species specificity and task specificity in the study of language: a methodological note*, Cognition **4** (1976), no. 2, 203–214.

[143] D. Osherson and S. Weinstein, *Criteria of language learning*, Information and Control **52** (1982), 123–138.

[144] ———, *On the study of first language acquisition*, Journal of Mathematical Psychology **39** (1995), 129–145.

[145] D. Osherson, S. Weinstein, D. de Jongh, and E. Martin, *A first-order framework for learning*, Handbook of Logic and Language (J. van Bentham and A. ter Meulen, eds.), Elsevier Science Publishers, 1996.

[146] M. Ott and F. Stephan, *Structural measures for games and process control in the branch learning model*, Third European Conference on Computational Learning Theory (S. Ben-David, ed.), Lecture Notes in Artificial Intelligence, vol. 1208, Springer-Verlag, 1997, pp. 94–108.

[147] C. S. Peirce, *Collected papers*, Harvard University Press, Cambridge, Mass., 1958.

[148] S. Pinker, *Language acquisition*, Invitation to Cognitive Science: Language, 2nd Edition (L. Gleitman and M. Liberman, eds.), MIT Press, 1995.

[149] L. Pitt, *A characterization of probabilistic inference*, Ph.D. thesis, Yale University, 1984.

[150] ———, *Probabilistic inductive inference*, Journal of the ACM **36** (1989), 383–433.

[151] L. Pitt and C. Smith, *Probability and plurality for aggregations of learning machines*, Information and Computation **77** (1988), 77–92.

[152] K. Podnieks, *Probabilistic synthesis of enumerated classes of functions*, Soviet Mathematics Doklady **16** (1975), 1042–1045.

[153] K. Popper, *Objective knowledge: An evolutionary approach*, Clarendon Press, 1979.

[154] G. Pullum, *Learnability, hyperlearning, and the poverty of the stimulus*, Proceedings of the 22nd Annual Meeting of the Berkeley Linguistics Society (J. Johnson, M. Juge, and J. Moxley, eds.), Berkeley Linguistics Society, 1996.

[155] H. Putnam, *Probability and confirmation*, Mathematics, Matter, and Method, Cambridge University Press, 1975.

[156] ———, *What is innate and why: Comments on the debate*, Language and Learning (M. Piatelli-Palmarini, ed.), Harvard University Press, 1980.

[157] J. Quinlan, *Learning logical definitions from relations*, Machine Learning **5** (1990), 239–266.

[158] H. Rogers, *Theory of recursive functions and effective computability*, McGraw-Hill, 1967, Reprinted, MIT Press 1987.

[159] J. Royer, *Inductive inference of approximations*, Information and Control **70** (1986), 156–178.

[160] J. Royer, *Semantics versus syntax versus computations: Machine models for type-2 polynomial-time bounded functionals*, Journal of Computer and System Sciences **54** (1997), 424–436.

[161] J. Royer and J. Case, *Subrecursive programming systems: Complexity & succinctness*, Birkhäuser, 1994.

[162] W. Rudin, *Principles of mathematical analysis, 3rd edition*, McGraw-Hill, 1976.

[163] B. Russell, *A history of western philosophy*, Simon and Schuster, 1945.

[164] ———, *Human knowledge: Its scope and limits*, Simon and Schuster, 1948.

[165] Y. Sakakibara, *Grammatical inference: An old and new paradigm*, Algorithmic Learning Theory: Sixth International Workshop (ALT '95), Lecture Notes in Artificial Intelligence, vol. 997, Springer-Verlag, 1995, pp. 1–24.

[166] G. Sankoff and P. Brown, *The origins of syntax in discourse: A case study of Tok Pisin relatives*, Language **52** (1976), 631–666.

[167] G. Schäfer-Richter, *Uber eingabeabhangigkeit und komplexitat von inferenzstrategien.*, Ph.D. thesis, RWTH Aachen, 1984.

[168] B. Schieffelin and A. Eisenberg, *Cultural variation in children's conversations*, Early language: Acquisition and intervention (R. Schiefelbusch and D. Bricker, eds.), University Park Press, 1981.

[169] A. Seth, *There is no recursive axiomatization for feasible functionals of type 2*, Seventh Annual IEEE Symposium on Logic in Computer Science, IEEE Computer Society Press, 1992, pp. 286–295.

[170] ———, *Some desirable conditions for feasible functions of type 2*, Eighth Annual IEEE Symposium on Logic in Computer Science, IEEE Computer Society Press, 1993, pp. 320–331.

[171] E. Shapiro, *Inductive inference of theories from facts*, Tech. Report 192, Computer Science Department, Yale University, 1981.

[172] ———, *Algorithmic program debugging*, MIT Press, 1983.

[173] A. Sharma, *A note on batch and incremental learnability*, Journal of Computer and System Sciences (1998), to appear.

[174] A. Sharma, F. Stephan, and Y. Ventsov, *Generalized notions of mind change complexity*, Proceedings of the Tenth Annual Conference on Computational Learning Theory, ACM Press, 1997, pp. 96–108.

[175] T. Shinohara, *Rich classes inferable from positive data: Length–bounded elementary formal systems*, Information and Computation **108** (1994), 175–186.

[176] J. Shoenfield, *Mathematical logic*, Addison-Wesley, 1967.

[177] T. Slaman and R. Solovay, *When oracles do not help*, Proceedings of the Fourth Annual Workshop on Computational Learning Theory, Morgan Kaufmann, 1991, pp. 379–383.

[178] C. Smith, *The power of pluralism for automatic program synthesis*, Journal of the ACM **29** (1982), 1144–1165.

[179] C. Smith and M. Velauthapillai, *On the inference of programs approximately computing the desired function*, Analogical and Inductive Inference, Proceedings of the International Workshop (K. Jantke, ed.), Lecture Notes in Computer Science, vol. 265, Springer-Verlag, 1986, pp. 164–176.

[180] ———, *On the inference of approximate programs*, Theoretical Computer Science **77** (1990), 249–266.

[181] R. Smullyan, *Theory of formal systems, annals of mathematical studies, no. 47*, Princeton, NJ, 1961.

[182] C. E. Snow and C. A. Ferguson (eds.), *Talking to children: Language input and acquisition*, Cambridge University Press, Cambridge, 1977.

[183] R. Soare, *Recursively enumerable sets and degrees*, Springer-Verlag, 1987.

[184] R. J. Solomonoff, *A formal theory of inductive inference, Part I*, Information and Control **7** (1964), 1–22.

[185] ———, *A formal theory of inductive inference, Part II*, Information and Control **7** (1964), 224–254.

[186] F. Stephan, *Noisy inference and oracles*, Algorithmic Learning Theory: Sixth International Workshop (ALT '95), Lecture Notes in Artificial Intelligence, vol. 997, Springer-Verlag, 1995, pp. 185–200.

[187] P. Suppes, *Philosophy and the sciences*, Acting and reflecting (W. Sieg, ed.), Kluwer, 1990.

[188] B. Trakhtenbrot and J. Bārzdiņš, *Konetschnyje awtomaty (powedenie i sintez)*, Nauka, Moskwa, 1970, in Russian. English Translation: Finite Automata–Behavior and Synthesis, *Fundamental Studies in Computer Science 1*, North Holland, Amsterdam, 1975.

[189] H. van Riemskijk and E. Williams, *Introduction to the theory of grammar*, MIT Press, 1986.

[190] T. Wasow, *Grammatical theory*, Foundations of Cognitive Science (Michael Posner, ed.), MIT Press, 1989.

[191] J. Webb, *Mechanism, mentalism, and metamathematics*, D. Reidel, 1980.

[192] K. Weihrauch, *Computability*, Springer-Verlag, 1987.

[193] J. Werker, *Exploring developmental changes in cross-language speech perception*, Invitation to Cognitive Science: Language, 2nd Edition (L. Gleitman and M. Liberman, eds.), MIT Press, 1995.

[194] K. Wexler and P. Culicover, *Formal principles of language acquisition*, MIT Press, 1980.

[195] R. Wiehagen, *Identification of formal languages*, Mathematical Foundations of Computer Science, Lecture Notes in Computer Science, vol. 53, Springer-Verlag, 1977, pp. 571–579.

[196] _____, *Characterization problems in the theory of inductive inference*, Proceedings of the 5th International Colloquium on Automata, Languages and Programming, Lecture Notes in Computer Science, vol. 62, Springer-Verlag, 1978, pp. 494–508.

[197] _____, *How fast is program synthesis from examples*, Mathematical Methods of Specification and Synthesis of Software Systems (W. Bibel and K. Jantke, eds.), Lecture Notes in Computer Science, vol. 215, Springer-Verlag, 1985, pp. 231–239.

[198] _____, *On the complexity of effective program synthesis*, Analogical and Inductive Inference, Proceedings of the International Workshop (K. Jantke, ed.), Lecture Notes in Computer Science, vol. 265, Springer-Verlag, 1986, pp. 209–219.

[199] _____, *On the complexity of program synthesis from examples*, Electronische Informationverarbeitung und Kybernetik **22** (1986), 305–323.

[200] _____, *A thesis in inductive inference*, Nonmonotonic and Inductive Logic, 1st International Workshop (J. Dix, K. Jantke, and P. Schmitt, eds.), Lecture Notes in Artificial Intelligence, vol. 543, Springer-Verlag, 1990, pp. 184–207.

[201] R. Wiehagen, R. Freivalds, and E. Kinber, *On the power of probabilistic strategies in inductive inference*, Theoretical Computer Science **28** (1984), 111–133.

[202] R. Wiehagen and W. Liepe, *Charakteristische eigenschaften von erkennbaren klassen rekursiver funktionen*, Electronische Informationverarbeitung und Kybernetik **12** (1976), 421–438.

[203] R. Wiehagen and T. Zeugmann, *Ignoring data may be the only way to learn efficiently*, Journal of Experimental and Theoretical Artificial Intelligence **6** (1994), 131–144.

[204] K. Wright, *Identification of unions of languages drawn from an identifiable class*, Proceedings of the Second Annual Workshop on Computational Learning Theory (R. Rivest, D. Haussler, and M. Warmuth, eds.), Morgan Kaufmann, 1989, pp. 328–333.

[205] T. Yokomori, *On polynomial-time learning in the limit of strictly deterministic automata*, Machine Learning **19** (1996), 153–182.

[206] T. Zeugmann, *A-posteriori characterizations in inductive inference of recursive functions*, Electronische Informationverarbeitung und Kybernetik **19** (1983), 559–594.

[207] _____, *On the synthesis of fastest programs in inductive inference*, Electronische Informationverarbeitung und Kybernetik **19** (1983), 625–642.

[208] T. Zeugmann and S. Lange, *A guided tour across the boundaries of learning recursive languages*, Algorithmic Learning for Knowledge-Based Systems (K. Jantke and S. Lange, eds.), Lecture Notes in Artificial Intelligence, vol. 961, Springer-Verlag, 1995, pp. 190–258.

[209] T. Zeugmann, S. Lange, and S. Kapur, *Characterizations of monotonic and dual monotonic language learning*, Information and Computation **120** (1995), 155–173.

Notation Index

Author and Subject Index